T0247893

AMERICAN IMPERIALIST

AMERICAN IMPERIALIST

CRUELTY AND CONSEQUENCE IN
THE SCRAMBLE FOR AFRICA

Arwen P. Mohun

The University of Chicago Press   CHICAGO AND LONDON

The University of Chicago Press, Chicago 60637
The University of Chicago Press, Ltd., London
© 2023 by The University of Chicago
All rights reserved. No part of this book may be used or reproduced in any
manner whatsoever without written permission, except in the case of brief
quotations in critical articles and reviews. For more information, contact
the University of Chicago Press, 1427 E. 60th St., Chicago, IL 60637.
Published 2023
Printed in the United States of America

32 31 30 29 28 27 26 25 24 23   1 2 3 4 5

ISBN-13: 978-0-226-82819-0 (cloth)
ISBN-13: 978-0-226-82820-6 (e-book)
DOI: https://doi.org/10.7208/chicago/9780226828206.001.0001

Library of Congress Cataloging-in-Publication Data

Names: Mohun, Arwen, 1961– author.
Title: American imperialist : cruelty and consequence in
the scramble for Africa / Arwen P. Mohun.
Other titles: Cruelty and consequence in the scramble for Africa
Description: Chicago : The University of Chicago Press, 2023. |
Includes bibliographical references and index.
Identifiers: LCCN 2023004291 | ISBN 9780226828190 (cloth) |
ISBN 9780226828206 (ebook)
Subjects: LCSH: Mohun, Richard Dorsey, 1864–1915. |
Mohun, Richard Dorsey, 1864–1915—Travel—Africa. |
Commercial agents—United States—Biography. | Diplomats—United
States—Biography. | Explorers—Africa—Biography. |
Congo (Democratic Republic)—History—To 1908. | Belgium—
Colonies—Africa. | Belgium—Colonies—Race relations. |
LCGFT: Biographies.
Classification: LCC DT655.2.M65 M65 2023 |
DDC 967.51/022092 [B]—dc23/eng/20230202
LC record available at https://lccn.loc.gov/2023004291
♾ This paper meets the requirements of ANSI/NISO Z39.48-1992
(Permanence of Paper).

CONTENTS

ILLUSTRATIONS

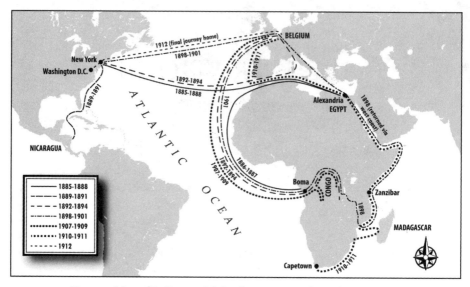

Figure 1. Map of R. Dorsey Mohun's international travels, 1886–1912

PROLOGUE

He'd never intended to work for the Belgian king. But intentions aren't actions. Still, a few years earlier, he had turned down Leopold II's first job offer. The accusatory voices of journalists, friends, and reformers reinforced his reluctance. He recognized the truths in their dark stories. The king's eloquent promises of free trade and an end to slavery amounted to a clever ploy, strategies designed to appease his European and American critics. Leopold's real goals were profit and control. The king's priorities mirrored those of many of the men who found their way into his private African colony, the Congo Free State.

During a stint as the US Trade Agent in Congo, he'd seen with his own eyes unfettered greed and cruelty as Europeans scrambled to enrich themselves. More than seen, really. He'd done things that he now preferred to keep quiet: burned villages, brutalized men in his employ, stood by while innocent people were killed for acts they had not committed.

Since then, he'd married, become a father, gained some prudence. He had not, however, mustered the courage to completely cut ties with Leopold. Now he was a breadwinner with what felt like limited options. The financial security of a multiyear contract would be a relief. Surely, family responsibilities mattered more than taking a vaguely humanitarian stand by avoiding any more involvement with the Congo Free State, as his friend Roger Casement had done. If he was honest with himself, he also itched for a challenge. Perhaps he thought he could do better than the other men in the king's employ. The decision was made: work for Leopold in Africa.

This is how I imagine my great-grandfather, Richard Dorsey Mohun, known as Dorsey, in the spring of 1897: a tall, narrow-shouldered man hunched over his desk, weighing his options. His sweat-soaked white shirt hangs limply beneath his stiff collar. The steady pounding of monsoon rains unleashes a torrent down the street outside. He doesn't notice. By now the discomforts of tropical places seem all too familiar. He has spent the past few years in this job, which he now disdains, sitting in the US consular office in Zanzibar's Stone Town, writing reports and dealing with the problems of stranded sailors and dwindling American trade. Rich lunches and rounds of drinks at the English Club have softened the boredom but widened his girth. Multiple bouts of malaria bloat his features. He is weary. In photographs from the time, he looks older than his thirty-three years.

He is not alone in the consular office. Noho bin Omari is there. Dorsey does not understand Swahili or Gujarati or most of the dozen or so languages that echo through Stone Town. He relies on Noho to translate, not just words but meanings. Like many of the Africans with whom Mohun worked, Noho's voice is elusive. Perhaps his descendants continue to tell Noho's story. Perhaps the American consul doesn't matter at all in how they remember their ancestor's life.[1] Ironically, Noho bin Omari's name survives in US records because Dorsey's successor initially suspected Noho was a fiction. He believed Dorsey pocketed the money provided by the State Department for translation and invented Noho to cover his tracks. That was before Noho presented himself to the new consul with two years of receipts in hand.[2]

If you dig into the past, you'd better be prepared for what you find there. Initially, I was ill prepared to contend with an ancestor who incontrovertibly and knowingly chose a path along the wrong side of history. I also did not imagine that poking around in family history would yield an extraordinary story of one man's involvement in one of the most notorious episodes in the European scramble for Africa: the short and brutal tenure of the Congo Free State, an enormous private colony in the center of the continent. Or that his story would reveal the remarkable influence of American money and expertise in the "new imperialism" of the late nineteenth and early twentieth centuries. But it did. As a result, this book is a history of how several generations of Americans shoved their way around Africa, sometimes meaning well but too often leaving a trail of destruction behind them.

My understanding of who Richard Dorsey Mohun was, and what he did in Africa, now differs significantly from what I'd gathered from family stories. Growing up I'd heard vague mentions of a relative who was an "African explorer." When questioned, my father offered a slim folder of newspaper clippings that seemingly confirmed that description. "African Explorer Dead" trumpeted a *New York Times* obituary that was almost certainly written by a close relative.[3] The idea of an explorer ancestor appealed to a family that eagerly consumed the contents of *National Geographic* and took the biographies of mountaineers and leaders of polar expeditions as exemplary. For us, the label *explorer* evoked heroic willingness to suffer physical hardship in pursuit of new knowledge. It was exciting—and self-flattering—to contemplate an explorer in the family.

Writing this book has forced me to confront the implications of that seemingly harmless descriptor: why it felt so appealing and what it disguised. So I've chosen to describe Dorsey not as an explorer but as an imperialist to call attention to the ways he and other US citizens participated in and profited from imperialism and late nineteenth-century global capitalism. Many white Americans have begun to face similar questions about how we describe our forebearers: enslaver or founding father? Heroic confederate soldier or traitor to the Republic? Such labels matter.

Another part of my family's mythmaking about Dorsey involved hazy stories about once-valuable stock in African mining companies. Looking back, I'm embarrassed about the subtext of entitlement underlying laments about a possible lost fortune. Dorsey did pursue his imperialist career in large part to help his family financially. And while he never grew appallingly rich, he made enough to set up his sons for very comfortable lives. He also helped some of the biggest names of the Gilded Age, including Guggenheim and Aldrich, become even richer. Creating this intergenerational wealth and the cultural capital that went with it cost hundreds if not thousands of African lives and contributed to the immiseration of many more people.

In the beginning, when all I had was Dorsey's obituary and family stories, I believed that his entire career had been spent working for the Congo Free State. As I researched, I learned that the Congo held just part of his story. Dorsey's decision to work for Leopold came midway through a nearly thirty-year career abroad. For most of that time, he worked either for the US government or for wealthy and ambitious American investors. His employment took him not only to Africa but also to Nicaragua and various parts of Europe. He was a particularly well-connected member of what historian Maya Jasanoff has called the "vanguard" of a "globally interrelated world." He both traveled through and helped create the emerging global systems of transportation, communication, trade, and imperialism.[4] Wherever Dorsey went, his commitment to family kept drawing him back to the United States. Thus his "globally interrelated" way of life had intimate, personal consequences as well as larger political and social ones.

Few if any of his American contemporaries could claim a résumé of equivalent variety and duration. But my great-grandfather was not unique. He belonged to the first large cohort of people born in the United States who sought employment and adventure abroad.[5]

The participation of Americans in late nineteenth-century globalization, particularly in relation to European imperialism, is one of the great undertold stories of United States history. Some of the same currents that carried unprecedented numbers of immigrants *into* the United States—economic opportunity, a sense of adventure, a desire to escape—also inspired men and women of every background, race, ethnicity, and social class to leave the US either temporarily or permanently. The pace of this expanding diaspora rapidly increased between the end of the Civil War and World War I, though we can't know exact numbers. Still, by 1910, nearly three hundred thousand returnees a year disembarked from commercial ocean liners in American ports. Many more, ignored by census takers, crossed over the Mexican and Canadian borders.[6]

These diasporic Americans were most visible in the places where the United States practiced a kind of formal empire—particularly Panama, Cuba, and the Philippines.[7] The artists and writers among them also float through popular culture, mingling with the European avant-garde.[8]

But Americans could also be found in the most remote corners of the globe, steaming in on the tides of imperialism, industrial capitalism, and the Christian missionary movement. Like Dorsey, more than a few chose Africa as a destination. Their ranks included Confederates-turned-mercenaries, zoologists, and prospectors.[9] Notable figures such as William Sheppard, the missionary descendant of enslaved Virginians, journeyed some of the same Congo waterways as the most famous American adventurer of all, Henry Morton Stanley.[10]

Dorsey belonged to a subcategory of these outgoers—people (most, if not all of them, white men) who facilitated the extraction of raw materials out of tropical places, provided the engineering and managerial expertise to build infrastructure, and opened up markets for European and North American products.[11] Many of these American imperialists were hired guns (sometimes literally) who took contracts with the highest bidder: sometimes private companies, sometimes foreign governments. Others worked for the US government or on government-sponsored projects.[12] Many clustered in places where they could profit from European imperialism without directly investing American dollars—and thus not seem like imperialists, or like figures worthy of historical study. Dorsey's story reveals just how important these midlevel bureaucrats and technical experts were to the business of empire. It also connects that work to domestic society, particularly the construction and maintenance of the white middle class.

While sailors and hired laborers often went out into the world with little more than the clothes on their backs, Dorsey and his fellow middle-class travelers carefully equipped themselves with the tools of empire: firearms, scientific equipment, ledger books and printed forms, quinine, and many, many tins of sardines. They also came laden with ideas: preconceptions about other cultures and ideological beliefs about their own special destiny as citizens of the United States. Characteristically, they often made sense of the unfamiliar through dichotomies and hierarchies, none more important than savage versus civilized.[13]

Nineteenth-century America was awash in information about the non-European world, some of it accurate but much of it misleading. Many literate Americans thought they knew a lot about the world and were eager to learn more. Schoolteachers drilled their charges in geography. Publishers churned out travel narratives. Missionaries and adventurers lectured to rapt audiences about their experiences and opinions.[14] The mass media celebrated the violence used by men like Henry Stanley against "natives" while also offering highbrow paeans on the importance of civilizing and Christianizing. Well-intentioned efforts to learn about other cultures, often in the form of collecting objects, mixed with sensationalizing forms of display, including now-notorious "human zoos."[15] In these encounters, a genuine desire to understand and learn mingled with one of the era's most destructive habits: justifying race-based cultural superiority.

Enduring beliefs about the United States' special place as the cradle of liberty also took up space in the crowded mental baggage of Dorsey and his fellow travelers. Raised on didactic tales about heroic founding fathers, many American imperialists imagined themselves as ambassadors of liberal democratic values more humane and committed to uplift than their European counterparts.[16] Like those founding fathers, they accepted and used the privileges their gender and race conferred, usually without a second thought. The post–Civil War emergence of the United States as a global power seemed to reify their status. These self-described white, Anglo-Saxon children of America's first Gilded Age believed they belonged on the right side of history by virtue of their ancestry and the time and place into which they had been born.[17] They also believed themselves capable of doing well while doing good.

For the thoughtful or reflective, those beliefs could be sorely tested by global realities. It took a great deal of moral courage to avoid being ensnared in the toxic amalgam of imperialism, colonialism, and capitalism. In time a few came to regret or repent of their former ideas and ways. Others broke apart from disappointment, hardship, and the impossibility of reconciling ideals and realities. In the course of his career, Dorsey knew people who reacted in all these ways. He represented yet another type—men who put one foot in front of the other, getting the job done, while trying to shake off a dawning awareness of the larger implications.

It is easy to vilify Dorsey and people like him. For more than one hundred years, the history of the Congo Free State has most often been told as a morality tale about heroes and villains. That approach helped end Leopold's reign and with it at least some of the cruelties that made the Congo particularly reprehensible among European colonies. But vilification without explanation courts what historian E. P. Thompson described as "the enormous condescension of posterity."[18] Just as often, professional historians have chosen to avoid biographical analysis of the motives and world views of these imperialist actors in favor of focusing on more admirable characters. The ironic result is that their stories continue to be told by hagiographic biographical dictionaries and anonymously authored Wikipedia entries.[19]

Historians' neglect of figures like Dorsey and the American imperialism he embodied also has present-day implications. The conviction that Americans are uniquely equipped to successfully help others while simultaneously serving their own self-interests continues to powerfully influence individual behavior, business decisions, and national policy. What historian Patricia Limerick called "the idea of innocence" has thrived as well: the belief that innocence of intention excuses injuries caused to Indigenous people, whether in the American West or around the globe.[20]

It is the historian's obligation to try to understand how people in the past understood themselves without condescension and without making excuses for their behavior—a fine line indeed, but one I have tried to walk in writing this book. How did this intelligent, well-intentioned man entangle himself with Leopold and the Congo Free State? How did he rationalize those decisions? His trajectory began with his own birth family's celebratory stories of ancestors they called abolitionists and humanitarians—people who thought they understood what was best for both formerly enslaved Africans and Indigenous peoples. He took jobs that tied him to the business of empire because his idea of being a good man prioritized loyalty to his employers and success as a breadwinner over any larger sense of humanitarianism.[21] Those decisions were reinforced by the expectations of the family members he loved best, intelligent people of good will who saw themselves as fully capable of making ethical and moral decisions—not only for themselves but also for others. His sense of himself as a man and a breadwinner ensured the financial well-being of his family. But it also drove the fateful decisions that eventually darkened his heart, led to his early demise, and caused great suffering to countless others.

Born in the nation's capital, then known as Washington City, Dorsey came into the world during the last throes of the Civil War. His world view took shape amid the contentious racial politics of emancipation and Reconstruction. But it was the Gilded Age that defined him. If family was his cause, the era's outward looking ambition, its worship of self-invention and entrepreneurial money making, was his compass.

This is his story. But it's also the story of many other men much like him, of the society that made them, and how they helped to irreparably change the world.

AFRICAN CONNECTIONS

Across the District of Columbia, the hopeful green of spring began to work its magic. New leaves unfurled from trees that had escaped the wood gatherers' axes. A fresh carpet of grass softened the edges of muddy roads cut to deep ruts by the Union Army's supply wagons, artillery caissons, and ambulances. Three years into the Civil War, the nation's capital had become a place of refuge, a place where life might start anew. No one felt this more than those seeking freedom from slavery. Even before Lincoln issued the Emancipation Proclamation, they'd been hurrying across the wooden bridge from Virginia into Union territory. Tucked amid their meager possessions were tiny pieces of blue sky: glass trade beads strung on thread, their special color offering protection against misfortune. So tiny, so taken for granted; these small objects whispered of a time before the Middle Passage. Or, depending on who was listening, the promise of global commerce and the ambitions of empire.[1]

Many of the new arrivals found shelter in the Swampdoodle neighborhood, competing with Irish immigrants for shanties and damp basements in a low-lying area north of the Capitol. Nearby, a family of white newcomers waited out the war in greater comfort.[2] It's unlikely any of them carried blue beads—they preferred the magic conferred by rosaries and crosses. But like their refugee neighbors, slavery and trade connected them to Africa. The address 392 L Street was the home of Anna Hanson Dorsey, a well-known author of popular Catholic literature. Recently widowed, she gathered remaining family together for the duration: her youngest, Ella, and her adult daughters, Angie and

Clare. Clare's husband, Richard, had recently joined the household. On April 12, 1864, he and Clare welcomed their first child, Richard Dorsey Mohun, into the world.

As the seat of government for a nation with global aspirations, Washington provided an unsurprising birthplace for an American who would become an imperialist with bureaucratic skills. But it was Richard Dorsey Mohun's upbringing and early work experiences that influenced *how* he would exercise those skills. Clare and Richard's son came of age in a place and time that filled his head with ideas about Africa and Africans long before he set foot on that continent.[3]

From his family and the white, middle-class culture that surrounded him, Mohun also constructed a theory of why Africa needed him and a set of precepts for how he might behave as a white American interacting with Africans. Those ideas found early roots in his grandmother's insistence that the family had already fully and heroically redressed its slaveholding past, ignoring both how recent it was and how thoroughly the family had embraced the status that had once come with slaveholding. The name Clare and Richard chose for their eldest son told part of the story. Richard, of course, was for his father, but in adulthood he chose to be known as Dorsey to his family and R. Dorsey Mohun professionally. For the family, Dorsey signaled ancestral connections to Maryland's history and its Catholic elite. Dorsey's namesake was Edward Dorsey (or Darcy), an early and very successful Catholic immigrant who, in 1650, received a patent for a large plantation known as Hockley-in-the Hole near Annapolis, Maryland.[4] Edward Dorsey and his descendants had been large-scale enslavers.[5] There is no evidence that the family ever talked about the systematic cruelty and exploitation that had earned this first Dorsey his fortune. Nor did they acknowledge the fact that, given the nature of American slaveholding practices, the many African Americans who had Dorsey as a surname were probably descendants of Edward Dorsey and his kin—and thus cousins, if not siblings, of the white Dorseys.

The family did talk and write about their efforts to protect the Republic from slaveholding's corrosive effects. Anna was exceedingly proud of her father, William McKenney, who, after a crisis of conscience, manumitted the people he owned.[6] But he did not simply free them; he urged them and everyone like them to leave the country. Inspired by conversations with many leading figures of the day, including James Madison and Henry Clay, he came to believe that people of different races could not successfully live together in a republic. The best solution for the United States was racial separation, preferably by an ocean. McKenney, like many white southerners who considered themselves progressive thinkers, strongly believed that free Black Americans should colonize the new West African state of Liberia.[7] Unlike most enthusiasts for colonization, who confined themselves to armchair philosophizing and the occasional financial contribution toward the cost of ships and supplies, McKenney became an active recruitment agent for the Maryland Colonization Society.

McKenney excelled at the job. His glowing descriptions of a new start in Africa convinced hundreds of Black men and women to abandon their lives in Maryland. Many of them subsequently died from the ocean voyage, endemic disease, and poor agricultural conditions.[8] McKenney became a controversial figure even in his own time, loathed by William Lloyd Garrison and other more egalitarian antislavery activists.[9] But in the family stories, Anna portrayed her father as an unambiguously heroic figure who helped forge a solution to white America's great dilemma: how to end slavery without creating a multiracial society. His ideas, predicated on the racialized theory that American Blacks were displaced Africans, threaded through family attitudes about the formerly enslaved people who made Washington their home.

McKenney's connections to Liberia—including his travels there—not only gave Dorsey and other descendants a sense of Africa as a real place, but also emboldened them to impose their values on the "dark continent."[10] Dorsey was not, in fact, the first Mohun sibling to consider going to the Congo. His sister, Lee, took steps to become a Dominican missionary before their grandmother Anna put a stop to Lee's plans. If she felt called to help Africans, Anna lectured, Lee could come home to Washington, DC. "We have Africa at our doors, seventy thousand negroes in and around this one city."[11]

In Dorsey's childhood, debates about colonization and Liberia remained heated. Some Black leaders and their allies decried "expatriation" of Americans of African heritage, asking why, for example, the

Irish had not also been asked to return to the homeland of their ancestors.[12] Clearly, the difference was the color of their skin. For Frederick
Douglass, Africa had no place in his future or the future of his people.[13]
Yet other newly free people considered emigration a plausible option.[14]
Rather than disband after the 14th Amendment extended citizenship
to formerly enslaved people, colonization societies focused their ener-
gies on Christianizing Africa.[15] Secretary of the Navy R. W. Thompson
neatly summarized the thinking of many advocates of colonization.
"Colored people" he opined, "can never reach social equality with their
white brethren" in the United States. But in Liberia, they would not only
help themselves but also help spread American-style democracy. "We
should do all we can to Americanize Africa" he trumpeted.[16] Liberian
colonization could be a win-win for everyone.

Much of the family history that Anna told her children and grandchildren, not to mention her continued enthusiasm for expatriation,
fit comfortably within the emerging racial logic of Jim Crow segregation and the practices of racial discrimination in white settler societies around the globe.[17] Like many of her contemporaries, she believed
unapologetically in white racial superiority but found slaveholders and
their Reconstruction-era successors loathsome. She was not unusual
among white, native-born Americans of her generation and social class
in believing that the future of the nation should lie first in the hands of
the descendants of colonial-era "heroes and statesmen"—as she like to
describe her ancestors—and second with northern European immigrants who could be assimilated into the dominant white, Anglo-Saxon
culture.[18] Everyone else needed to know their place.[19]

And then there was the Mohun side of the family. Dorsey's other
grandfather, Francis Mohun, was a scrappy Irish immigrant who'd grown
rich in the Washington building trade, first as a carpenter and later as a
contractor and lumber dealer.[20] Francis eventually cofounded a successful construction company that made him rich.[21] His wealth gave him
leverage in Washington. He used it not only to enrich himself further
but also to enter local politics, serving on the city council throughout
the 1850s before passing the seat to another family member.[22] Resent-
ment of the way native-born Protestants looked down on both Roman
Catholics and Irish immigrants fueled Francis's ambitions. His sense

of victimhood may also have shaped his attitudes toward slavery. He almost certainly used slave labor on construction projects before the Civil War. Even more tellingly, he was himself an enslaver, holding on to one domestic bondwoman, Mary Marlow, until 1862, when Congress bought the freedom of the District of Columbia's remaining slaves.[23] One wonders what the conversation between the in-laws on the subject of slavery might have sounded like. Or perhaps they avoided the topic, as polite people of their social standing often did.

CAPITAL LESSONS

A few days short of Dorsey's first birthday, pealing church bells and celebratory artillery fire from the district's ring of defensive forts stirred the city awake. Robert E. Lee had surrendered at Appomattox. It was the "end of the rebellion," as the family's favorite newspaper, the *Evening Star*, put it.[24] As staunch unionists who had lost relatives in the war, they joined the celebrations. Eight months later, the ratification of the 13th Amendment outlawing slavery provided additional welcome news— a potential step toward William McKenney's vision of America's future.

But like many residents of the District of Columbia, the Mohuns and the Dorseys were unprepared for what came next. Antebellum Washington had been a southern city where relations between Blacks and whites were governed not only by strict racial etiquette backed up by the threat of violence but also by "black codes"—legal statutes restricting Blacks from gathering in large groups, owning firearms, and being out after ten o'clock at night.[25] The war years shook up this status quo, as did the forty thousand or so formerly enslaved people who came to the city searching for refuge and opportunity.[26] There, they mingled with white newcomers, the small prewar Black community, and "old residents"—as Francis and his contemporaries sometimes styled themselves. By the end of the war, nearly half of white residents and two-thirds of Black residents of the district heralded from somewhere else. The population nearly doubled in this period, straining a city government that had struggled with basic matters such as sanitation and water supply even before the war.[27]

During the conflict, Black refugees had provided a much-needed workforce. As the war began to wind down, they found it more and more difficult to find work because of competition from white laborers and fewer war-related jobs.[28] Now tattered, hungry, desperate people huddled in tent camps or hastily constructed shacks at night and took to the streets by day. Unbound from slavery and from oppressive regulations, they gathered in large numbers to celebrate the benefits of freedom. On the anniversary of the Emancipation Proclamation in 1866, an estimated crowd of six thousand joined with Washington's Black elite for a day of speeches and parading through the streets.[29] For the "old timers" on L Street, the presence of these incomers would have been hard to miss. Public expressions of joy from these "sons of Africa" as they were sometimes referred to by the press, made many white residents uncomfortable.

Political efforts to aid newly freed people also competed with the Washington business community's big plans to turn this sleepy, dusty, southern town with a seasonal population of politicians into a modern commercial hub.[30] At war's end, Dorsey's grandfather Francis Mohun along with Francis's adult sons positioned themselves to take advantage of postwar rebuilding needs. They cannily switched their political affiliation from Democratic to Republican to better work the patronage system, and they joined a newly formed board of trade—effectively a chamber of commerce—to increase their political leverage.[31] Even Dorsey's father, whose primary business was a bookstore, joined in the excitement. He helped lobby Congress for a new railroad line connecting Washington and Richmond, Virginia—the former capital of the Confederacy.[32]

The businessmen's biggest plans would have to wait, for Congressional Radical Republicans glimpsed an opportunity for a very different kind of rebuilding. They would use their direct governing power to test, on a small scale, some of their ideas about how to implement Black suffrage and integration of the schools, both key to full citizenship. The Freedmen's Bureau and volunteers, Black and white, would help. Thus, the district became for a few short years what Radical Republican Charles Sumner described "an example for all the land" of how to implement new measures for racial equality.[33]

It's impossible to say whether the temporary triumph of the Radical Republican agenda contributed to the Dorsey-Mohun household's decision to move out of the city. On L Street, family members would have found it hard to ignore violent clashes between Irish-born and Black laborers over scarce jobs and housing.[34] They might also have shared their white neighbors' concerns about property values as African Americans moved into Swampdoodle.[35] Whatever the reasons, move they did—to rural Prince George's County in Maryland, on a small plantation estate called Woodreve.[36]

But within two years, the family moved back to a transformed capital.[37] Both the idealism and the chaos of the immediate postwar era began to give way to the mores of the Gilded Age. The influence of the Radicals had begun to fade and with it, the Freedmen's Bureau, which shut down its district activities for good in 1872. On Capitol Hill, Congress had also changed, as the nation's attention turned away from the plight of formerly enslaved people to other matters: industrialization, western expansion, and the United States' place in the world.

The family's wealth had reached a high point—although no one knew it.[38] Richard's bookstore prospered thanks to government stationery and publishing contracts. Financially comfortable, Anna, Clare, Richard, and a growing number of children moved to a townhouse in the fashionable Second Ward, only a few blocks from the White House and Lafayette Square, the most prestigious neighborhood in the city. Here they could surround themselves with the kind of neighbors they thought befitted their social status: a Superior Court Judge, an architect, two grocers, and numerous civil servants.[39] Every homeowner on the block was white. Most were native born. Washington had a significant population of middle-class Black intellectuals, but you would not know it around Lafayette Square.

The households in the Lafayette Square area reflected the aspirations and values of the post–Civil War white middle class. These were families with male breadwinners who had to work for a living but who earned enough to support their wives and extended families—and their domestic servants, who were often Black. For children growing up in such households, adults' interactions with household employees offered formative lessons in the exercise of white racial privilege. Because servants typically lived with families fulltime, often in tiny rooms high in a house, those lessons could be particularly intimate. They gave

white, middle-class people the feeling that they understood the men-
talities and behaviors of the people they often referred to as "colored."

This was certainly the case in the Dorsey-Mohun house. Thanks to
Richard's much-increased earnings, the family now employed at least
four servants, three of whom were Black. Together, they took care of
cooking, cleaning, childcare, and other requests. At sixty-eight, William Williams was by far the oldest person in the household, followed
by Emeline Clark. The family also employed Richardson Herbert, age 31.
None of the Black servants in this bookish household could read or
write. It is likely that at least some of them had been born into slavery.
All were old enough to have known people born in Africa and brought
to the United States against their will.[40]

What did this mean for Dorsey's later encounters with Africans in
Congo, Zanzibar, and Africa? Like many white Americans, he felt most
comfortable dealing with dark-skinned people as subordinates and servants. He took for granted that they should do his bidding and gave
little thought to what they might have sacrificed to work for him. From
his youthful experiences in Washington and in his own household, he
absorbed an informal code of conduct that he willfully violated in his
twenties and then tried to return to in later years: always pay for services
rendered and avoid corporal punishment. Failing to pay wages and resort-
ing to physical violence were the hallmarks of slaveholding. His family
was proudly not like southern slaveholders and their Reconstruction-
era successors. In the beginning, he thought he was too.

Dorsey and his family didn't get their ideas about Africa and Africans
just from family history and their interactions with people of African
descent. Plenty of other information and misinformation circulated
around Washington. A steady trickle of missionaries and reformers
"full of Africa," returning from Liberia and elsewhere, testified about
their experiences in newspaper articles and public lectures. They em-
phasized the day-to-day challenges of missionizing and the successes
of their missions.[41] By the 1880s the State Department had more than a
dozen consular posts in Africa staffed with agents tasked with collecting

information. Their reports analyzed commercial opportunities for American businesses. Navy ships cruised the African coastlines and made occasional upriver explorations that were eagerly reported on by the press and talked about in government receptions and parlor chats.[42] The Smithsonian Institution had also begun collecting and interpreting African cultural objects.[43]

Avid readers, especially ones with a bookshop-owning family member, could easily feed their curiosity with a growing list of titles by European and American writers. Travel, adventure, and geography books about Africa were very popular. Bayard Taylor, America's most famous travel writer, came out with *The Lake Regions of Central Africa* in 1873, when Dorsey was nine. Taylor unapologetically cribbed from the accounts of other travelers to describe a region Dorsey would come to know well.[44] A few years later, Anna sent a copy of the best-selling novel *King Solomon's Mines*, which described English explorers' search for a legendary African source of diamonds, to Lee as consolation for her thwarted plans to missionize the Congo.[45] Catering to a mass audience, these writers employed a series of tropes, some of which Dorsey would later recycle in his own accounts of Africa. They portrayed white explorers as civilizing, justice-dispensing heroes, admired by the "natives" who recognized their natural superiority. Africans, in contrast, were superstitious, exotic savages with strange customs and a propensity for irrationality and violence. Aware that stories about ritual cannibalism and seemingly unprovoked attacks on expeditions were particularly exciting to American and European readers, popular writers highlighted them—a habit that Dorsey would pick up.

In Dorsey's youth, no one had a bigger impact on Americans' perception of Africa than Henry Morton Stanley, the Anglo-American adventurer. Stanley was so famous that his encounter with the British missionary Dr. David Livingstone near Lake Tanganyika spawned a well-known catch phrase: "Dr. Livingstone, I presume." Beginning in the mid-1870s, the *Evening Star* published detailed accounts of Stanley's explorations of the Congo River basin.[46] According to his grandmother, Dorsey kept an album of newspaper clippings, though it has not survived. It is easy to imagine how those stories might have inflamed the imagination of a teenager just as they excited tens of thousands of adults.

Stanley's well-publicized travels also had a powerful effect on the geographical imagination of middle-class armchair travelers like the Mohuns and the Dorseys. "In the old school maps there was a blank space in the center of the African continent labeled 'unexplored regions,'" an article in the *Star* began. No longer. Thanks to Henry Stanley, the "'unexplored' region of the old maps of Africa had become the 'Congo basin' of the new."[47] In this era of progress and constant accumulation of knowledge, it seemed possible to truly know Africa.

In 1879 Dorsey's father died of congestive heart failure. The family was already having trouble making ends meet. Richard's business suffered during his prolonged illness. An economic depression contributed to their financial woes. Their social connections and proud family history did not ensure financial security. Washington offered plenty of examples of genteel poverty—a status the family was determined to avoid. All the women had taken on additional work writing for magazines and newspapers or processing information in government "bureaus," as they called them. Dorsey's mother Clare wrote a weekly gossip column for a Cincinnati, Ohio, newspaper and had taken on some secretarial duties for Lucy Hayes, the president's wife, whom she'd met while covering the White House.[48] With the death of the family's only male breadwinner, financial disaster seemed imminent. The women decided that fifteen-year-old Dorsey needed to get a job. As the eldest he would forgo further schooling to support his mother and siblings.

Like a growing number of middle-class American families, the Mohun-Dorsey clan concluded that their boys' best career opportunities lay in the United States' emerging status as a global economic and military power. Thus began Dorsey's apprenticeship as an American imperialist. His mother and grandmother initially fantasized that he could be a marine—fighting his country's battles "from the Halls of Montezuma to the shores of Tripoli" in the words of the service's hymn, which summarized its antebellum interventions in Mexico and North Africa. But he was far too young. Instead, Clare and Anna worked their connections to secure a civilian clerical position in the United States Department of the Navy. Thus Dorsey dutifully took on the role of male breadwinner. For the next six years, he donned a dark suit and starched white collar and walked a few blocks to the mansard-roofed edifice next to the White House, then known as the State, War, and Navy Building. Inside its sumptuous, overdecorated rooms, he did what was asked of him and waited for an opportunity.

ON THE EDGE OF AFRICA

The year was 1885. Dorsey was on his way to Egypt. Thanks to the intervention of a family friend, he'd been freed from his desk.[49] His new appointment as assistant paymaster did not sound glamorous. But it would allow him to spend the next three years cruising the Mediterranean and the west coast of Africa on the USS *Quinnebaug*. Later, he would let people believe he'd joined the Marine Corps. In truth he was never more than a civilian employee tasked with keeping the ship's books and doling out gold coin to sailors and suppliers.[50]

Traveling along the edges of Africa, the Middle East, and Europe, imagination and experience began to converge for the inexperienced twenty-one-year-old. Dorsey was making direct contact with people and places he'd only read about. He translated cultural attitudes he'd absorbed in Washington into the persona of an American in the world. In the company of the officers and crew of *Quinnebaug*, he also received a tutorial in the tricky dance of informal empire. The US Navy was charged with protecting American interests while maintaining good relations with European powers and the peoples they strove to subjugate. Ships like the *Quinnebaug* publicly asserted the potential for military engagement while carefully avoiding actual conflict (most of the time).[51]

On a Thursday morning early in June, Dorsey made his way to the crowded waterfront of Alexandria, Egypt, where he was to report for work. He'd been traveling for nearly a month, working his way down through Europe and making an obligatory stop in Jerusalem and Mt. Carmel to visit spots described in the Bible.[52] How to reach his ship in this huge, crowded harbor? Shoals of boats and boatmen eagerly offered to ferry travelers to and from the large ships, including the *Quinnebaug*.[53] These entrepreneurs would have had no trouble spotting this potential passenger on the quayside. Well over six feet tall, dressed in Western attire, he stood out among the sailors, stevedores, and hawkers. But neither his presence nor the sight of an American ship would have struck Alexandrians as unusual. Ships from the US Navy's European Squadron regularly dropped anchor there, and a growing number of American tourists and missionaries passed through Alexandria. After the Civil War, there had even been an influx of former confederate officers hired to reform the Egyptian military, sweating in their blue and gray wool uniforms, medals flashing in the bright Mediterranean sun.[54]

Thanks to the completion of the Suez Canal in 1869 and its importance as a cotton growing region, Egypt was a significant nexus in the emerging global network of transportation, trade, and empire. Alexandria was its crucial coastal gateway. Eager to promote trade in the East, the United States joined dozens of other nations in asserting a presence in the Alexandrian harbor.

The ship buzzed with activity. Officers from the British Navy had just paid a visit to request the Americans "dress" the *Quinnebaug* for a celebration of Queen Victoria's birthday. On the deck, the boatswain instructed apprentices to splice flags into decorative pennants. The carpenter carefully repaired caulking on the forecastle while the gunners and other crewmembers painted exposed surfaces. On Saturday, as the day of celebration dawned, the American crew hoisted an Egyptian flag in honor of the Khedive of Egypt, Tawfik, who arrived at his palace to the sound of a twenty-one-gun salute from Egyptian and French warships.[55]

Dorsey had arrived just in time to witness a complicated, if not convoluted, symbolic ritual constructed around the workings of European imperialism and the United States' relationship to it. Thanks to his family's connection with the Ottoman Empire, Tawfik was the hereditary ruler of Egypt. But in practice, he was a political puppet controlled by the British government, part of an evolving system of "indirect rule." So it came to be that an American ship flew the Egyptian flag at the request of the British government to honor an Egyptian ruler who, in turn, was celebrating the birthday of the British queen, who had the power to dictate how he governed.

Once aboard the ship, Dorsey could also see evidence of Egypt's place in global trade, in which the United States was still only an aspiring player. A forest of masts and the stump-like profiles of smokestacks from hundreds of ships interrupted the flat landscape. Some ships had come from as far away as China. Others flew the flags of Europe and the Americas. During the US Civil War, the harbor had been dredged and improved to better support the export of Egyptian cotton that replaced American supplies in the mills of Manchester, England. Under British control, that trade continued. However, some of that cotton returned to Egypt in the form of cloth and then, when worn out, was sent to the United States in the form of rags used to make paper in Philadelphia and Boston. The US government employed a rag inspector to check for signs of cholera and other diseases before the rags were loaded for export.[56] At the moment of Dorsey's arrival, the US Consul in Cairo was hoping for trade in more than dirty rags. A southerner, he regretted the high tariffs that made the import of US cotton-processing machinery uneconomical for Egyptians.[57] The presence of the British added another frustrating layer of complexity in his efforts to find more trade opportunities for US firms.

American commercial and political engagement with Egypt would continue. But both American capitalists and the Gilded Age politicians who served them increasingly believed that the most promising financial opportunities were in West Africa. Dorsey arrived in Alexandria at a pivotal moment in the European scramble to seize territory in Africa. A few months earlier, at the Berlin Conference, diplomats congratulated themselves on an agreement they believed would open the continent to free trade and European colonization while promising the right of self-determination for Indigenous people.[58] Leopold had secured personal control over a vast swath of the continent's center, which he named the État indépendant du Congo (or Congo Free State, in the anglophone world) as a gesture toward the ideals he'd expressed at the conference. His agents in Washington were busy working to obtain official recognition of his claims to sovereignty. They promised the United States unfettered access to new markets and raw materials. On September 11, 1885, President Grover Cleveland became the first head of state to officially recognize Leopold as the ruler of this vast African colony.

Five months later the *Quinnebaug* set sail for the Gates of Gibraltar and a cruise down the African coast. Other ships in the European Squadron had been visiting West Africa for a long time, typically stopping in Liberia, and venturing as far south as Angola.[59] The *Quinnebaug* made similar stops, but its ultimate destination was the mouth of the Congo.[60] Dorsey was curious enough to leave the ship, traveling upstream against the huge, muddy current of the Congo to Boma, where Leopold's agents had just begun to turn a former slave-trading entrepôt of crumbling eighteenth-century buildings and palm-roofed shacks into the headquarters of the newly established Congo Free State. The American visitor was not impressed.[61] The place seemed so inconsequential.

Twenty-three years old with his life in front of him, he could not have imagined his future would be so closely tied to this tiny town and the great river that flowed past it. Circumstance, not choice, had led him to this brief encounter in 1887. He hadn't signed on to the *Quinnebaug* because he imagined it as a first step toward a career in Africa. He'd simply gone where opportunity seemed to beckon. Like other budding American imperialists, he was confident in his own ability to rapidly master virtually any setting. Thus, he treated his time with the Navy as an apprenticeship in skills that he could use elsewhere: how to comport himself as a representative of the US government and where the boundaries were between self-interest and dutiful performance, and how to do practical things like keep accounts, discipline subordinates, and comport himself like a military man.

The African cruise was brief. Back in the Mediterranean, Dorsey's employment on the *Quinnebaug* was ending. As the United States' global ambitions ratcheted up, the Department of the Navy deemed the aging warship, with its vestigial sails, leaky wooden hull, and slow and unreliable engine, obsolete. The commander and crew received their orders: return the ship to the Brooklyn Naval Yard to be scrapped. Only the name would survive, passed on to a more modern vessel.[62]

Dorsey set his sights on one last task. He had not yet traveled up the Nile to see the Pyramids and other wonders of ancient Egypt. He needed to close the gap between the imaginative and experiential, not just for himself but because his family and friends at home expected it. He would have plenty of company from his fellow countrymen and women. As steamships and railroads made travel easier, Egypt attracted a growing number of American tourists eager to see the Pyramids and "Bible lands" for themselves.

Of all the places on the African continent Dorsey would come to know, Egypt was the most familiar and alluring to Americans. Over the course of the nineteenth century, waves of Egyptomania swept the country. The half-completed Washington Monument, modeled after Egyptian obelisks, loomed over the national mall of Dorsey's childhood, drawing a parallel in stone between the founders and the ancient Pharaohs. Enslaved people compared their bondage to the Biblical captivity of the Israelites in Egypt, while their enslavers held up Egypt as the first great civilization built on slaveholding. A wide range of people followed the discoveries of archaeologists and flocked to displays of mummies and other artifacts. They followed debates among ethnologists over the racial identity of ancient Egyptians.[63] Among the things the archaeologists uncovered were ancient blue beads buried with the dead for luck.[64] For a few piastres, replicas could be had from sellers outside the tourist hotels.

Most Americans didn't think of Egypt as part of Africa at all. Ancient Egypt figured in schoolbooks and popular literature most prominently as one of the wellsprings of Western civilization—an exotic part of the classical world and the dramatic historical setting for scenes from the Old Testament. If pressed, American travelers might have assigned contemporary Egypt to the "Orient" or Near East—in the sphere of the Ottoman Empire and therefore host to titillating cultural practices such as the maintenance of harems.[65]

Some of the biggest celebrities of the era visited Egypt. Lincoln's secretary of state, William Seward, toured the Pyramids on his seventieth birthday. Ulysses S. Grant and William Tecumseh Sherman also made pilgrimages to Giza.[66] So did Mark Twain. Frederick Douglass's visit in 1887 fulfilled a longtime dream. Unlike many of his fellow travelers, he concluded that the ancient Egyptians were Africans and that their accomplishments should be a source of pride for Black Americans.[67]

Extensive newspaper coverage, fueled by telegraphic communication, made heavily filtered versions of contemporary Egypt visible even to those who stayed at home. Contrasts between the poverty of present-day Egypt and the imagined glories of the Pharaonic age was a common theme. But readers also gobbled up coverage of the efforts of the Khedive, Ismaï'īl Pasha, to modernize his country. They produced gushing reports, such as "Egypt's Khedive: How Modern Pharaoh Acts and Looks," published in the *Boston Globe*.[68] "I know more about Thotmes [*sic*] III than Ismail Pasha, Viceroy of Egypt," one atypically honest reporter admitted, before providing detailed analysis anyway.[69] Largely ignorant of the enormous human cost of khedival rule, others looked for parallels and connections with the United States' struggle for liberty.[70]

"We had a long delightful letter from Dorsey last evening," his grandmother wrote Lee, now an initiate in an Ohio nunnery. "He has been in Egypt again and this time went to the Pyramids, explored them inside, and scrambled by the help of a Bedouin to the top." He also visited the ruins of Memphis, "once the seat of so much splendor and power." For an extra thrill, his guide directed him to slide head-first into what he described as funeral or burial caves. The adventure plunged him "into Egyptian darkness," dramatically playing on the double meaning of race and the unknown. Anna, who had never traveled farther than a few hundred miles from Washington, was thrilled that her grandson had made contact with a world she knew only from books.[71]

Dorsey's reference to the Bedouin is the only hint that he had not conducted this journey on his own. It is likely that the man who helped him to the top of a pyramid as well as whoever urged him to slide into a cave were subcontractors of a professional guide or dragoman. Most American tourists who could afford it hired a dragoman to translate, interpret and describe, and generally smooth the way. But, like the many guides and interpreters who would help Dorsey and people like him, very few are named and even fewer speak for themselves through surviving sources.[72]

After this brief adventure, Dorsey returned to Washington, hoping to parlay his résumé into a diplomatic posting. He applied to become the US consul to Belfast, Ireland—perhaps reasoning that his father's Irish roots would give him an advantage. His mother and grandmother set about lobbying on his behalf.[73]

The plan failed. Dorsey's glancing encounter with Africa and ink-stained accounting for the Navy best qualified him for a different kind of work. He would become part of a vanguard working on American infrastructural projects abroad—a sector that would boom a decade later when the United States found itself with a de facto empire in the aftermath of the Spanish-American War.[74] A family connection to Admiral Daniel Ammen, a central figure in a plan to build an American-controlled interocean canal across Nicaragua, gave him the political connections he needed. Ammen had already helped Dorsey's brother, Louis, get a job with the canal company. Ammen encouraged Dorsey to apply to become captain of one of the Nicaragua Mail and Transport Company's steamships.[75] But the former paymaster's assistant received only an offer to work as an auditor, a closer match to his skills.

In Nicaragua, Dorsey encountered a different group of diasporic Africans: Caribbean islanders who worked as contract laborers for the canal company. Because Nicaragua was part of both an earlier period of globalization and the new one of resource extraction and global trade, the country was home to a group of people who felt the power of blue beads: the Indigenous Moskit people who had traded with Europeans for centuries, accepting beads as one form of currency.[76]

Nicaragua was a revelation. For the first time, Dorsey worked as a de facto colonial administrator—the agent for a national project of exploiting another country's resources. The experience taught him about the practical business of executing a plan created far away. Along the canal worksite, he also witnessed (and probably participated in) the casual cruelty of overseers and managers (including his brother, Louis), who abused contract laborers—more survivors of the African diaspora—men who, far from home, had little recourse. He tasted greed inspired by the possibility of sudden wealth from deals made on the side. He felt the fear of dying in a strange place, his vigorous young body debilitated by both named and nameless tropical diseases. The whole setup was corrosive of idealism or even good intentions. It was also an education he would not soon forget.

THE NICARAGUA CANAL

In 1889 it wasn't at all obvious that the United States would construct a canal in Panama. In fact, many prominent politicians and business leaders argued that the United States should not be in the business of building canals or other large transportation projects in foreign countries. Americans should instead let Europeans shoulder the risks of building and operating these ventures. Critics could point out that the French had not being able to replicate their Egyptian success in Panama. They'd recently sunk $87 million into a Panamanian canal project with little to show for it. Still, those in government who subscribed to the ideology of manifest destiny increasingly looked to the Caribbean as they dreamed of expansion. Beginning with Ulysses Grant, a series of presidents had stated and restated the necessity for an American canal under American control in Central America as a key element of their hemispheric vision.[77]

Perhaps more importantly, practical-minded individuals saw huge profits to be made with the creation of a faster water route for transporting people and goods between the Atlantic and the Pacific Oceans—completing a global circuit that already included the Suez Canal. Businessmen and politicians in the southern United States were particularly keen on this idea; they understood the effect a canal would have on port cities such as New Orleans and Mobile. This was the kind of informal imperialism the United States could get behind.

Many Americans looked not to Panama, but to Nicaragua, which was significantly closer to the United States and had a relatively stable and friendly government.[78] And American technical experts had declared that a Nicaraguan route would be cheaper and easier to build than a Panamanian canal or the third alternative: a ship railroad across the narrowest part of Mexico.

As with the later Panama Canal Project, the American-controlled Nicaraguan Canal Construction Company faced the problem of transporting their middle-class American employees to a location that by definition had little infrastructure and was poorly connected to commercial transportation networks. They solved the problem by chartering ships. Thus, Dorsey sailed on a company freighter from New York to Greytown, the planned eastern terminus for the canal and operational headquarters for the company. A reporter from the *New York Times* described the scene Dorsey would have viewed as his ship steamed into Greytown harbor. From the deck he could see a "long breakwater extending straight out into the sea." A "wide clearing cut like a grand avenue further than the eye can see through the dense forest that covers the lowland skirting the sea." The beginning of the canal itself was also apparent in the form of a "broad excavation."[79] The town appeared as a low expanse of humble buildings, including palm-thatched survivors from an earlier era and new timber and corrugated iron barracks. Storage buildings and machine shops also dotted the landscape, all under construction by the company.[80]

Nicaragua provided a taste of the environmental conditions Dorsey would encounter in equatorial Africa. He arrived during the rainy season, when torrential downpours turned the dirt streets of Greytown to mud and the San Juan River overflowed its banks, depositing sand and silt into the harbor nearly as fast as the dredges could remove it. The atmosphere was steamy, even fetid. Everything grew moldy and riddled with rot. The same kinds of disease conditions that doomed the French effort in Panama also overshadowed the Americans in Nicaragua. Clare worried on her son's behalf about the prevalence of yellow fever, a terrible infectious disease that racked its victims with fever and chills, bodily pain, and worst of all, *vómito negro*, or black vomit. She was right to be concerned. Dorsey fell ill near the end of his time in the country, descending into periods of delirium.[81] In the early days, however, there was work to be done, lessons to be learned, and opportunities to capitalize on.

As it turned out, Dorsey's official job of auditing took up very little of his time. At $100 a month, it also paid less than his sister Laura was earning in the bureaus in Washington. He began looking around for other income sources. He'd learned early to be anxious about never earning enough money. And side hustles were common among expatriate American and European bureaucrats and consuls, especially in the tropics. The spirit of the times—particularly the emphasis on unbridled entrepreneurship—encouraged activities that would later be seen as corrupt. Distant, indulgent, or nonexistent oversight made them possible.

Dorsey began organizing what he described as "trading expeditions." The governments of Nicaragua and neighboring Honduras had granted what were called "concessions" to collect and export natural resources, a practice he would encounter in a different form in the Congo Free State just a few years later. On behalf of the Emery family of Boston (known to their contemporaries as the "mahogany kings"), Dorsey supervised the transportation of logs out of Honduras. A Kansas City company separately engaged him to buy hides, coffee, and gold dust and move them to the coast for export.[82] Dorsey acquired such a range of knowledge during this time that his employer later noted that he had "special knowledge of the rubber trade" in a letter of reference.[83]

Dorsey well understood that working for other people was not the ultimate pathway to wealth. He had bigger dreams: owning shares of a concession or even the land that concessions exploited. Less than a year after arriving in Greytown, he bought eight acres of land and "put it in coffee." He had been living like a "miser" to do so, he told his mother.[84]

Meanwhile, brother Louis accidentally fell into a position that included far too much power for a person of his age and temperament. Sometime in the winter of 1891, the company named him postmaster and chief of police at Greytown. Louis was twenty-one years old and had absolutely no training for either job. He wrote his grandmother that he had trouble "keeping on a straight face when he'd meet the cops or have cases brought before." "Oh how I sighed," he wrote. "I nearly strangled in the effort to be dignified."[85] What became of the people brought before him was not communicated.

Dorsey did convey his admiration for his brother's casual bravado in a different situation. Louis had been put in charge of a large company of contract laborers—nearly six hundred men, by Dorsey's count—who were engaged in earthmoving in the jungle. One morning the workers refused to pick up their tools. As Anna repeated the story, Louis "straightened himself up, drew out his six shooter and took aim and after a strong emphatic swear in Spanish . . . informed them that if they did not go to work, he'd shoot every one of them." At the end of the day, Louis marched the troublemakers to the train to Greytown. There they were handed over to the "authorities" for dismissal.[86]

This arbitrary and callous decision spelled financial disaster for the workmen. Most were from Jamaica or Malaysia. As in the better-known story of contract laborers who built the Panama Canal, these men had left their homes and families to risk malaria and yellow fever in the

Nicaraguan jungles while working for about half as much as similar laborers in the United States.[87] They formed part of a global labor market for civil engineering projects such as railroads and canals that moved vast numbers of workers from agrarian societies to places like Nicaragua, where local workers were unwilling to engage in backbreaking construction work for low wages.

In early 1891 "the bottom fell out of the Nicaragua tub," as Anna put it. The company ran out of funds and was unable to secure additional investment to cover costs. White-collar workers like Dorsey and his brother were furloughed. In November Dorsey arrived in New York aboard the *Hondo*, a company-owned ship.[88] He was traveling in the company of dozens of others whose contracts had been terminated. Together these Americans and Europeans passed through customs on their way to rejoining the global circulation of imperialists for hire.[89]

Dorsey already knew where his next job would be. His family had tapped yet another personal connection to secure him a position. James G. Blaine was one of the most powerful men in Washington, a sometime-presidential candidate, and secretary of state to multiple presidents. He was also one of Anna's friends. With Blaine's help, Dorsey obtained the position of US commercial agent to the Congo Free State. After a three-year detour through American efforts to build infrastructure for US global capitalism, he was headed back to Africa.

It was not his dream job, but it paid well: $5,000 a year.[90] He could start immediately. Louis was to come along as his assistant. Since King Leopold required a personal interview with any such appointees, he planned to visit Brussels first.

AFRICA IN MIND

A cold rain was falling all along the Eastern Seaboard on February 27, 1892, as Dorsey boarded the steamship *Merra*, which would take him across the Atlantic. His ultimate destination was the settlement of Boma, at the mouth of the Congo River, but his route would be indirect. The *Merra* was bound for Genoa, Italy. From there, Dorsey planned to follow a leisurely path northward to Brussels—and an audience with Leopold II, who claimed the right to personally approve the US commercial representative to the Congo Free State.[1]

Although months away from setting foot on the continent, Dorsey must have had Africa on his mind almost constantly. What would he encounter? What dangers might he face? Winding his way through Europe, he determined to enjoy himself as much as possible. He was acutely aware that many white men, including his predecessor, did not survive their time in the tropics. He would capitalize on the time he had in Europe, making new social and professional connections and learning as much as possible about how to not only stay alive but also prosper in this dangerous and unfamiliar environment.

Many people he encountered along the way also had Africa in mind. For some, the Congo and its people constituted an exotic fantasy experienced solely through books and newspapers. Henry Morton Stanley, who had explored the Congo basin beginning in the 1870s, was a huge celebrity for these readers. Many literate Americans and English-speaking Europeans would have been familiar with his publications, including *How I Found Livingstone* and the multivolume work *In Darkest*

Africa.[2] For others, including the Belgian king, this vast swath of land nurtured a dream of wealth and power. They imagined a place where those with daring and foresight could grow rich. For the experienced few who had actually lived and worked there, however, Africa proved infinitely more complicated, entangling greed, professionalism, curiosity, and ruthless exploitation of Indigenous inhabitants in the name of discovery and development.[3]

Dorsey originally intended to travel with his brother, Louis, a companion he could trust. But sometime close to departure, Louis found love in Washington and then secured a better professional opportunity in Mexico. Working for an American mining company put him on a well-known path for American imperialists. A decade later, Louis would die of acute dysentery on board a ship in the Philippines. He'd taken on an engineering position aiding US forces during the Spanish-American War.[4]

The family reconsidered how to make the most of this opportunity and decided that Dorsey would travel with his eldest sister, Laura, for at least the first part of his journey.[5] Although no one said it directly, the trip offered a reward and a respite for the oldest Mohun daughter who had gone to work in "the bureaus" at fifteen to help support the family. Laura would finally see the landmarks of Western civilization she had heard and read about most of her life. She brought with her a list of social contacts—friends of friends in Paris and Rome. Perhaps she would even meet an eligible young man. She intended to secure a blessing directly from the pope himself. As the granddaughter of Anna Hanson Dorsey, America's most popular Catholic writer, she felt confident in asking for an audience. After all, Pope Benedict had already twice sent his benediction to her grandmother in thanks for her service to the church.[6]

As the light began to ebb on that gray, late-winter afternoon, tugboats nudged the *Merra* into the Hudson River. Once under its own power, the steamer threaded through the crowded harbor. As in the ports Dorsey had visited on the *Quinnebaug*, a forest of masts still dominated the docks and the waterways punctuated by the funnels of steam ships. Cargo ships from around the world vied for space with naval vessels and local schooners. Although neither of the siblings made note of it, they would have passed by the Statue of Liberty. Did Dorsey know it originally had been designed to tower over the entrance to the Suez Canal—not as a symbol of liberty but as an evocation of empire?[7]

Dorsey lost no time in assessing the ship's amenities. The *Merra* was not one of the grand ocean palaces, such as *The City of Paris*, beginning to compete for the North Atlantic passenger trade. She was principally a mail ship, carrying only twenty first-class ("cabin") passengers. In this intimate setting, all the passengers took their meals together. The men shared what Dorsey described as a "stuffy" smoking lounge. The cabin stewards did double duty, entertaining the passengers by singing and playing musical instruments during dinner. Dorsey had experienced far worse in the Navy and the canal company's steamers, and he found the present service to his liking, pronouncing the food "good" and the drinks "very good."[8] From his time in Washington, he'd developed a taste for champagne, and during the long hours at sea, he happily indulged.

Was anyone worth knowing aboard? "I have met some charming people," Dorsey recorded in one of the several sturdy canvas-covered diaries he'd brought along. Already, he had posterity and publication in mind, so he was careful about what he wrote. But he could not resist occasionally using the diary as a silent confidant. It would have been different if fun-loving Louis had come, but Laura could be quite judgmental. "The Flaggs of New York, Mr. Scribner of Scribner's [publishing house], and Mrs. Sarah Orne Jewett," a well-known writer, were among the passengers worth getting to know.[9] There were also "some rather pretty girls on board." But "the passengers as a whole do not amount to much." For the first few days out, he barely saw any of them. "Weather cold, snappy seas," he noted. "The weather is going to be bad." Laura stayed in her cabin, overcome by seasickness. Dorsey contented himself with two male dinner companions. He particularly enjoyed the company of "a jolly Catholic priest" whom the other men jokingly elected "president of the smoking-room club."[10] That moment of naughtiness must have had extra resonance for the son of a pious Catholic family. Now in his late twenties, he was determinedly his own man.

The other passengers eventually began to emerge from their cabins. Dorsey spotted his sister chatting with "a pretty girl" on deck, who nevertheless looked "rather miserable and sick." She introduced herself to him as "Miss Barry of New York" and briefly expressed an interest in learning more about Africa—perhaps taking a cue from information she had gleaned from Laura. Dorsey wasn't the only one sizing up the possibilities. Miss Barry had her eye on the tall, handsome, coolly confident traveler.

Initially, however, he wasn't sure he wanted anything to do with the young woman. "I don't like seasick so unless she gets better will give her a wide berth," he callously decided.[11] Within a few days, he had changed his mind and was actively seeking her out. "Talked on many subjects and read extracts from the lives of the 'Artistic Masters of the Old World.'" She would fit right into Dorsey's bookish family. "Wonderfully attractive girl," he wrote. By the time the ship passed the Azores, he had decided that he was in love and had begun to wonder whether his "wandering life" and "bachelor habits" had unfitted him for being a "fit husband for any woman"—perhaps a veiled reference to the prostitutes and heavy drinking available in Greytown, the Navy's ports of call, and, only slightly more discreetly, in Washington.[12] Nevertheless, now that love had at last found Dorsey, or at least tiptoed in his direction, most of his waking hours passed in the stimulating company of Miss Barry.

Ten days into the voyage, the ship passed the Rock of Gibraltar. Dorsey recognized the stunning sights from his time on the *Quinnebaug*. "Passing Marseille, Cannes, Nice, all the other beautiful towns on the Riviera," he recorded. "The scenery is magnificent. All the mountains are covered with snow and at their feet the towns lie looking like emeralds set in large diamonds." He felt growing certainty that Miss Barry might reciprocate his affections. As the ship finally entered the harbor at Genoa, he confessed his love to her. "She was surprised, but did not refuse me," he wrote in his tidy script. "She confessed she cares for me but did not wish to bind one to her as I was going to the Kongo for so long. I could not get more than that from her." Shortly afterward, he concluded with uncharacteristic melodrama, "Thus is all my happiness to come to an end?"[13]

He decided to take a bold step. He booked his sister, Miss Barry, and the Flaggs (a mother-daughter pair) into a hotel with the plan that the Flaggs would keep his sister company while he spent one last day sightseeing with the object of his affections. Within a few hours, on a hillside, contemplating the view of the city, he proposed marriage to Miss Barry, who "confessed her love for me but would not bind me in any engagement." No fool, she likely recognized the folly of committing to someone who might soon die in Africa or just disappear without explanation. They agreed to write each other, however; and in the Cathedral San Lorenzo, she offered up a prayer for Dorsey's safe return. Then she gave him permission to kiss her and to call her by her first name, Harriet.[14] In the future, he would call her Harry (as in Miss Harry Barry!).

The next day, the four women agreed to travel onward together to Rome. Laura had indeed succeeded in securing a brief audience with the pope—to the eternal pride of her mother and grandmother.[15] Dorsey headed in the opposite direction, stopping to see some old friends in Monte Carlo, where he won 3,000 francs in the Casino, followed by a few days in Paris, where he won another 1,000 francs at billiards and pronounced the show at the Moulin Rouge "rather disgusting" (which didn't stop him later from sketching one of the cancan girls inside the cover of his diary).[16] Moral arbiter and enjoyer of male pleasures—the mores of the era gave him permission to have it both ways.

Ten days after docking in Genoa, Dorsey arrived for the first time in Brussels. He had booked a room at the Hotel Bellevue, where foreigners doing business with the king often stayed because it was located just around the corner from the Royal Palace. But he couldn't go to the palace directly. He had to wait to be summoned. In the meantime, he planned to call on various officials of the Congo Free State as well as on George Roosevelt, the US consul at Brussels.[17] Then it would be time for savoring more cosmopolitan pleasures. "Have bath and dine at 8. Afterwards to the opera," he recorded on his first night.[18]

The next day, he set out across the city. The Brussels he encountered—and would return to periodically over the next fifteen years—was a city in transition. Its most powerful resident focused some of his considerable will on creating a suitable capital for a vast empire: a place that would impress visitors and encourage the Belgian people to think of themselves as at the center of a much larger world than the one they daily inhabited and negotiated—something far greater than a small, lowland country uncomfortably wedged between powerful Germany and France.[19] A Belgian guidebook of the time warned its readers that the city was "destined to become one of the most beautiful capitols of Europe," but at the moment it existed somewhere between "destructions and constructions."[20]

In the name of progress, portions of a largely premodern city of narrow, crooked streets and ancient churches had been leveled. Streets had been widened, old buildings pulled down, and vast public structures erected. The new Palais de Justice, the guidebook said, was "the most grandiose and vast in Europe. As with the Acropolis in Athens, it is situated on an elevated plateau where it dominates the capital."[21] Brussels had witnessed other gilded ages, as evidenced by the grand merchants' houses in the Grand Place, facades decorated with liberal amounts of gold leaf. But this ambition must have seemed familiar to someone who'd grown up in Washington, DC, in the boom years after the Civil War. There are only so many ways to establish a country or city as prosperous and wealthy. Belgium had become an independent country only in 1830, and Leopold was in a hurry to establish its place among nations. Both the remaking of Brussels and the establishment of colonial possessions were central to his plans.[22]

But while Washington aspired visually to emulate ancient Rome and Second Empire Paris while denying any connection to Africa or the people of African descent who constructed and maintained it, Brussels explicitly connected itself to Africa without apology. Decorations of banana leaves and the sculpted faces of Africans adorned numerous city monuments. Four years after Dorsey's initial visit, Leopold even ordered the construction of a tiny, idealized version of the Congo just outside the city. Three hundred Africans living and working in grass-thatched huts and paddling dugouts around an artificial waterway provided the centerpiece for an international exposition at Tervuren. Over the course of Leopold's reign, it became harder and harder not to have Africa in mind.[23]

Dorsey made friends with two hotel guests who also had business related to the Congo Free State.[24] One was William George Parminter, a former British Army major who had worked for Leopold since 1883, playing a leading role in the creation of the system of roads and transfer stations between the upper Congo and the coast. Parminter typified the kind of expatriate whom Leopold liked to hire to build and manage his colony. He was a man whose ambition outstripped what the British Army offered. Parminter had been appointed director of the Société Anonyme Belge pour le Commerce du Haut Congo—an elaborate title for a trading company that collected ivory at various trading stations in the Congo for shipping to Europe, where it would be fashioned into toothbrush handles and piano keys for bourgeois consumers.[25] Given the tiny number of Europeans and Americans who had visited the Congo in the 1880s—by one estimate, only 430 whites were working in the whole of the Congo in 1889, and the number of English speakers was even smaller—it was not surprising that Parminter knew both of Dorsey's predecessors: Willard Parker Tisdel and Emory Taunt. He had, in fact, helped Taunt prepare for a journey past the Stanley Falls to the upper part of the Congo.[26] Dorsey did not record Parminter's assessment of Taunt, but the State Department had already made him aware that excessive consumption of alcohol and poor management of money had undermined Taunt's effectiveness before several bouts of a tropical fever finished him off.[27] Dorsey would learn many more unsavory details when he reached the Congo.

In his interactions with Belgian officials and others associated with the Congo Free State, Dorsey cultivated the impression that he was a seasoned and sophisticated hand in the business of building the infrastructures of empires. Perhaps he even believed it himself. He made a convincing enough case to Albert Thys, a very high-ranking official in the shadowy network of shell companies set up by Leopold to exploit the Congo while maintaining the appearance of benevolently presiding over an international free trade zone. Thys authorized Dorsey to invite an old friend from his Nicaragua days to come to the Congo. Dorsey also assured Thys that he would be able to recruit five hundred West Indian laborers for the railroad Thys was building.[28] His own small contribution to reversing the diaspora.

He wasn't socializing merely to have a good time or to promote himself, however. Dorsey was feverishly trying to gather as much information as possible about how to manage his new situation. Parminter was thus a very useful person to befriend, for he knew as much as anyone about the day-to-day workings of the Congo and could address some of Dorsey's ignorance. Parminter quickly introduced Dorsey to his former second-in-command and close friend, Roger Casement. Dorsey was eager to learn what this experienced Africa hand could teach him. Casement had arrived in Africa in 1884 and had worked with Parminter for four years, organizing the movement of goods and supplies within the Congo before helping to survey the path of a railway through the Congolese jungle. His particular skill seems to have been the recruitment of ever-scarce local labor. His most recent job had been to organize a "transport system" of porters who would carry goods along a new route around the Congo River cataracts.[29]

Like many others, including novelist Joseph Conrad, who had shared a room with Casement during part of the ill-fated sojourn that resulted in *Heart of Darkness*, Dorsey was immediately smitten.[30] Casement had what many people described as "Irish charm." He was gregarious, whimsical, and sentimental. He was also striking, with black, curly hair and bright blue eyes. Like Dorsey, he was well over six feet tall.

Thus began the other great romance of Dorsey's youth: one that vied with the charms of Miss Barry for his attention. The two young men, only a year apart, quickly discovered they shared much. Part of their bond was professional: they'd both leaped into the unknown to pursue the opportunities of empire. Both were taking up diplomatic posts to further their countries' trade ambitions. More personally, they had both lost beloved parents (Dorsey felt a sense of kinship with people he thought of as orphans). Both had literary leanings and harbored a strong romantic streak. And there was the common bond of Irishness—more distant for Dorsey than for his new friend, but nevertheless important.

Casement would eventually be put to death for his Irish nationalist activities and his sexual relationships with other men, but that was a long time in the future, as was his decision to aid E. D. Morel in exposing the horrors of what came to be known as "red rubber." At this moment, Casement still believed in the grand project of European imperialism, even if he had grown squeamish about Leopold's approach. By 1892 he had informed Albert Thys and Parminter that he no longer wanted to work for the State.[31] He told at least one person that he had seen what would later be called "atrocities" during the Congo reform movement. He had also participated in them. Charm alone was not enough to convince hundreds, if not thousands, of African men to leave their villages to work as porters. The Irishman had been at least marginally involved in the so-called punitive raids in which Europeans raided native settlements, capturing men who were then pressed into service. He certainly knew the human cost of Belgian efforts to build an infrastructure for trading in the Congo. Unfortunately, no record survives of how much Casement revealed to Dorsey about the dark side of his experiences.[32]

Business and colonial activities aside, Casement made excellent company. The two young men took meals together, went to the theater and the opera, and frequented the swimming baths. This kind of male friendship, with its erotic undertones, was not unusual at the time.[33] Dorsey's behavior suggests that he saw no tension between his hope of convincing Harriet to marry him and his warm feelings toward Casement. He eagerly collected letters from Harry and even introduced the charming Irishman to his sister, who had arrived in Brussels on her tour of Europe.[34] He wanted two people he cared about to meet. For a brief moment, he imagined bringing his two worlds together.

The formality of having a king personally interview and approve the appointment of a particular individual as a commercial representative was unusual in the context of nineteenth-century diplomacy. Trade consuls and trade representatives were relatively low-level appointees charged with looking for opportunities for American businesses in foreign countries. They did not even have official diplomatic immunity. Most were political appointees with personal reasons for wanting to live abroad. Many did little or no actual work for the government once on site.[35] Others used their position to run various illicit businesses.[36]

But nothing was normal about the Congo appointment. Since 1885 Leopold had functioned as sovereign ruler of the Congo not on behalf of the Belgian people, as was the case with other imperial possessions of constitutional monarchies, but for his own personal benefit. In one sense, this arrangement was reminiscent of an older age of European absolutism. At the same time, the Congo Free State was very much a product of the times: an extreme manifestation of nineteenth-century globalization, capitalism, and imperialism, cunningly legitimized by two utterly modern and seemingly progressive ideologies: free trade and antislavery. Leopold sometimes described himself the "proprietor" of this vast entity, which was perhaps particularly apt.[37] He also liked to characterize himself, less accurately, as a "philanthropist," which re-inforced the attractive idea that it was possible to do well while doing good in Leopold's African realm.

If the conditions surrounding Dorsey's appointment were unusual, the United States' role in establishing and supporting the office of the trade representative itself appeared even more peculiar. As Mark Twain later wrote, the United States, as "self-appointed Champion and Pro-moter of Liberties of the World," had found itself in the position in the Congo Free State of being "the only democracy in history that has lent its power and influence to the establishment of an *absolute monarchy*."[38] How had this inversion of principles happened? Having come of age at the epicenter of American politics, Dorsey grasped, better than most, the big picture events that had led to the United States' involvement with Leopold and the Congo. At the center of the story were several old family friends, including Rutherford B. Hayes and George G. Blaine.

The story went something like this. The bargain that brought Ruth-erford B. Hayes into the White House mandated the withdrawal of federal troops from the South, putting an official end to Reconstruction and signaling a definitive shift in national priorities. After his inaugura-tion, Hayes declared, "The importance of enlarging our foreign trade cannot be overestimated."[39] How, exactly, this expansion was supposed to happen remained unclear. Nor was it obvious how to reconcile this goal with isolationism, attachment to protective tariffs, and resistance to a standing military in peacetime, all deeply rooted American political values. Many Americans, including people in power and prominent in public life, adamantly argued that the United States should not participate in the scramble for imperial possession that preoccupied the major (and minor) European powers of this period. On the other hand, imperialism was an unavoidable fact of global commerce. To make matters even more complicated and frustrating, many European nations heavily taxed or restricted imports from other nations into their colonies so that their own manufacturers could enjoy the benefits of protected markets.

Enter explorer Henry Morton Stanley and American businessman Henry Shelton Sanford, who was a lobbyist for Leopold II. In 1884 the two men appeared in Washington to garner support for the creation of the État indépendant du Congo, or Congo Free State. They visited in anticipation of the Berlin Conference, which would explore the division of European control over the African continent. Much of Africa had not yet been explored or claimed by Europeans, so the stakes could not have been much higher. Stanley and Stanford told Congress (and anyone else who would listen) that the new colony would be based on a distinctive economic model. Most importantly, individuals and companies would have the opportunity to engage in trade with the Congo and the Congolese without the usual restrictions (those based on national origin of the traders or source or destination of the goods). Sanford even promised that Americans would be able to buy land in the Congo.[40]

Sanford and Stanley furthered their case by dangling the enticing claim that tens of millions of native people inhabiting the proposed territory eagerly awaited American manufactured goods. In particular, the Congo represented an enormous potential market for the rough cotton textiles beginning to be turned out by southern mills. This claim was plausible, even to those who knew something about Africa, because cloth already served as an important medium of exchange in Central Africa. But it wasn't just about the economy. Sanford and Stanley also had moral arguments ready for the kind of Republican politicians with whom Dorsey's family tended to hobnob: they suggested that Leopold was committed to ending the slave trade practiced by Arab traders from Zanzibar and East Africa, who sold Congolese people into bondage in the Indian Ocean region. Eventually, creation of a Congo Free State might even lead to a self-governing nation along the lines of the US's former commonwealth Liberia. The two men even offered a religious argument, citing the prospect of saving pagan souls for Christ by opening previously unexplored territory to missionaries.

Republican senators, eager not only to develop new markets but also to make a gesture of reconciliation toward their southern colleagues, helped ensure that the measure recognizing the Congo Free State passed.[41] The State Department then dispatched an American representative to the Berlin Conference. There, Leopold deftly manipulated the participants into signing a treaty granting him personal control over almost a million square miles of territory in the center of Africa, which included the Congo River and the ports of Boma and Banana on the Atlantic.

More than a little suspicion and ambivalence followed from many knowledgeable Americans, including new president Grover Cleveland.[42] Willard Tisdel, the newly appointed commercial agent for the Congo Free State, went on a fact-finding tour of the Congo at the request of Cleveland's secretary of state. Tisdel was the wrong person to be entrusted with providing a clear-eyed analysis as he traveled up-country to the Belgian station at Stanley Pool—a wide spot in the Congo River named by Belgians in honor of the famous explorer. Tisdel felt ill for much of the trip, which reinforced his suspicion of the region and his hatred not only for the local tribes but also for his own porters. He later reported that "there is nothing about the natives of the Congo region to convince me that they have ever lived in a better condition than they do today. They are the lowest of the low. They have no intelligence." His method of asking for shelter from local chiefs involved a combination of threats and plying them with gin. In contrast he was deeply respectful and grateful for the courtesies shown to him by the Belgians at Stanley Pool, who even made a point of hoisting an American flag over his hut.[43]

Perhaps it wouldn't have mattered whether the United States had sent a more astute and sympathetic observer. George Washington Williams, a prominent Black politician and minister, traveled through the Congo during Tisdel's tenure. Williams was so shocked by the abusive policies of Leopold's agents that he published a widely read "Open Letter" to

Leopold.[44] His fact-finding and condemnation had no impact on people like Dorsey or on American policy toward Leopold's exploitation of the Congo. Consumers at home wanted their ivory billiard balls and rubber galoshes at good prices; and plenty of people, including several US senators and other politicians, dreamed of making their own fortunes out of ivory trading, rubber plantations, or fantastic mineral discoveries.[45] Many white Americans also tolerated or even applauded efforts to control nonwhites closer to home, including lynchings and the mass eradication of Native Americans.

Dorsey was about to be sold on Leopold's public vision of the Congo Free State by the master himself. As others learned before and after, Leopold's was a form of seduction that even ambitious and otherwise worldly men found hard to resist.[46] On March 25, Dorsey received notice to present himself at the palace the next day for an audience with the king. The palace gates stood scarcely more than a five-minute walk from the Hotel Bellevue. Dorsey did not record whether he arrived on foot or whether, emulating his parents, who had taken a carriage the three blocks to the White House for appearance's sake, he arrived in grander style.

The palace's bland, block-long exterior gave little hint of what he might find inside. A contemporary guidebook warned its readers "not to judge it by the façade." Like Leopold's transformation of Brussels, the palace interior had been designed to give the impression that Belgium indeed equaled other European nations. The main entrance featured an enormous grand staircase, "l'escalier d'honneur." Paintings by old masters adorned the walls, including works by Van Dyck, Rembrandt, and Rubens. The whole effect was one of "taste and richness."[47]

In his diary Dorsey did his best to convey professional nonchalance. "Had a long conversation with the King who expresses himself being much gratified by the Government sending a special agent to the Kongo."[48] While he remained surprisingly coy about what was said, it is clear from his later writings—and behavior—that he received some version of Leopold's compelling free trade/antislavery pitch. The new trade consul left as an enthusiastic believer in Leopold's antislavery argument, which resonated with his self-image as the descendant of "abolitionists." He also harbored the dream of making a personal fortune by trading in rubber and ivory and of returning home as a rich man.

Dorsey booked passage from Antwerp on the steamer *Congo*.[49] Roger Casement, who was traveling to Sierra Leone to take up the position of British consul, had agreed to be his cabinmate. "Am glad as he is an awful decent chap," Dorsey told his diary.[50] Dorsey also outfitted himself with gear, beginning with firearms. "The gun is the sultan of Africa" was an African adage familiar to Congo veterans.[51] Being well armed was necessary not only for self-protection but also for hunting, the most important recreation of white men in the Congo and a meaningful totem for both Africans and Europeans. At Jansen's, a local gun merchant, Dorsey ordered a Winchester rifle, Colt .45 revolver, and a .577-caliber express rifle suitable for killing big game. He also bought plenty of ammunition: four hundred cartridges for the elephant gun and one thousand cartridges for the other weapons. In the next few days, he also purchased a steamer chair and books, arranged for someone to act as his financial representative, and "indulged in cocktails at the English Club."[52]

Then it was time to embark. Antwerp was the second-largest port in Europe at the end of the nineteenth century. Travelers would have been struck by the miles of iron sheds that stretched along the south bank of a deep tidal river, sheltering commodities flowing into northern Europe: ivory and rubber from Africa, but also grain from the United States and Canada. Prominent along the waterfront were the ships of the Red Star Line, an American-owned company that carried millions of immigrants to the New World during its half century of operation. The city was indisputably an important node in the global circulation of goods and people.

In the custom of the day, Dorsey and Casement invited friends and family to join them onboard their ship for final goodbyes. Major Parminter and Dorsey's sister Laura were among the guests who decided to stay onboard the *Congo* partway down the river. Death and the fear of dying in a strange land were also onboard. At least one passenger could not endure the uncertainty that lay ahead. "Left the dock at 10 amidst much cheering etc." Dorsey wrote. "At 10:30 the 3rd officer shoots and kills himself. None of the passengers excepting C. T. and I know of it." They hastily rolled the body up in a tarpaulin and loaded it onboard a tugboat. "None of them knew of the corpse," Dorsey noted, savoring being in on the grisly secret. One of the other temporary passengers, a Mrs. Heyn, pulled Dorsey aside. She "looked at me with tears in her eyes and said 'Mr. Mohun, if you meet my son Reggy in the Kongo and he is ill, you will look after him won't you?' Poor Mother. I certainly will look out for him." And then he made a final note. "Goodbye to civilization. I wonder how many of the passengers now going out will live to reach Antwerp again."[53]

At the last minute, the steward handed Dorsey a letter from Harry. He dashed off a response and handed it to the channel pilot to take ashore. "Dear little sweetheart," he told his diary, "She always does the right thing."[54]

Within days, a longing to be somewhere else set in. "Our long passage of 23 days had begun," Dorsey wrote. "What a difference this voyage and the one from New York." There were no celebrities or pretty girls onboard, no one to talk to except Casement. The rest of the passengers were Belgians who could not speak English. Dorsey's French was "limited to the most conversational phrases." Aware of his own shortcomings, he took a certain pleasure in the captain's "frightful efforts" at English. "He manages to carry on a conversation but makes very heavy weather in the attempt."[55] April 10 was Palm Sunday. "I can't help thinking I would like to be home today. What crowds of people are in the churches," he wrote. Two days later, he made a poignant note: "my birthday."[56]

Midway through the journey, the ship stopped at La Palma in the Canary Islands. Casement and Dorsey went ashore for dinner at the Quincy Hotel. Casement ran into a cousin staying there. The cabinmates played billiards and drank champagne. Dorsey sent letters to Harry and his family, cabled Parminter, and then his last taste of the comradery and comforts of Europe were over.[57] Four days later, Casement left the ship in Sierra Leone; Dorsey gave him his shotgun as a going-away present. He was very sorry to see Casement go, "as he is one of the best fellows I have ever met." They promised to stay in touch. The heat and humidity were increasingly oppressive. The Belgians did not bother to bathe, Dorsey noted with revulsion. He consoled himself by taking potshots at passing whales with his elephant gun.[58]

A few days later, a change in the color of the water indicated that the ship was approaching the mouth of a great river. Forty miles from the coast, tannins leached from distant inland jungles and yellow sediments from equally distant floods clouded the water.[59] Even the air contained a different odor—not unpleasant, but utterly distinctive. Then the coast came in sight, deceptively flat, giving no hint of the rugged inland terrain just beyond the horizon. The ship anchored at Banana, a tiny settlement perched on a flat finger of land along the north bank of the mouth of the Congo River.

The palm trees and makeshift buildings likely reminded Dorsey of Greytown, Nicaragua. But Banana did not even have a proper wharf—a small clue to informed observers that the state did not really welcome outside traders despite Leopold's promises and pronouncements.[60] The ship stopped only long enough to pick up a pilot before proceeding up the river. Seven hours later, the vessel docked at Boma, headquarters for the Belgians on the lower Congo. Reginald Heyn was first to welcome Dorsey, boarding the ship soon after anchoring. Despite Mrs. Heyn's worried words in Antwerp, her son seemed none the worse for wear.[61]

Dorsey commented on the changes to the town since the *Quinnebaug* had dropped anchor in the Congo five years previously. He admired the addition of "a hotel, two fine large stores, and five or six factories" (by which he meant warehouses for gathering and packing ivory and rubber).[62] The town also included a Catholic church famed for its iron walls, which protected against termites. Other "improvements" he noted included a hospital for Europeans and a trolley that carried the town's white officials to meals at the hotel dining room.[63] For a traveler experienced in the colonial outposts of the late nineteenth-century world, the place would have seemed both legible and familiar—churches, government offices, and the bureaucratic apparatus for facilitating the extraction of resources. Prostitutes, haggard Europeans, clouds of biting insects, and nearly unbearable heat were ubiquitous features too. The architecture would have also been recognizable—rough stone vestiges of the older Portuguese slave-trading port that Boma had once been now crumbling within view of whitewashed offices with wide verandas and the walls of the church, also painted white. "A great deal of taste" has been deployed in the construction of the state-owned buildings, Dorsey reported to his superiors in Washington. The place seemed clean and orderly.[64]

Dorsey made no mention of the Africans he encountered. That doesn't mean they weren't present. He must not only have seen groups of Black men on the docks and throughout the town but also interacted with them, beginning with the unloading of the *Congo*. In a place like Boma, white visitors did not do any manual labor, including carrying luggage for themselves. Most new arrivals lacked even the most basic linguistic skills to describe their needs and desires. Before their feet touched the ground in Africa, they were already dependent on the help of interpreters and other mediators. Other travelers, however, remarked on the presence of Africans, from troops of porters gathered in the shade of trees to chain gangs of prisoners being marched through town.[65] Boma was also a garrison town for the state's African mercenaries, the soldiers of the Force Publique. Beginning at six in the morning, the bugler's calls instilled a European sense of time and discipline in new recruits.[66] Like Washington, the town itself was spatially divided along racial lines. Much smaller Boma consisted of a "lower" town where Africans congregated and an "upper town" commanded by Europeans. These social arrangements carried more than a whiff of familiarity for someone who had grown up in the post–Civil War South.

Heyn and his colleagues invited Dorsey a few miles upriver for dinner. Two days later, he presented his credentials to the Belgian governor. "Does not speak English so our conversation was not extensive or brilliant," he reported in his diary. Soon after, he fell ill with an unnamed malady that left him too weak to write for nearly a month and depleted for many weeks beyond. It was the first time he'd ever been seriously sick without a family member to take care of him. In Nicaragua, when yellow fever had struck, he and Louis had consoled each other. In Matadi, he suffered alone—like the fictional Kurtz in *Heart of Darkness*—dependent on the good will of State officials who could compel African "servants" to care for Dorsey's bodily needs. The possibility of dying far from everyone he loved must have seemed frighteningly real.

Africa was no longer just an idea but rather a reality to be contended with.

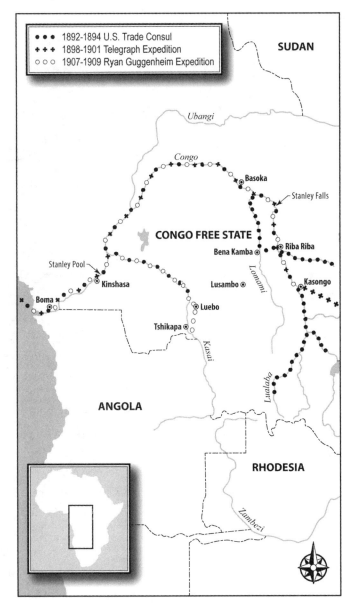

Figure 2. Map of R. Dorsey Mohun's travels in the
western Congo, 1882–1909

* 3 *

THE JOURNEY
UP-COUNTRY

Dorsey had no intention of remaining on the coast. He could muster little patience for the boring alcohol-soaked dinners with the same people
each night and the long, listless days of mosquitos and relentless heat.
Just beyond the bend in the river and over the first set of barren, red-
dirt hills lay nearly a million square miles of possibility and adventure.
Although not yet fully recovered from his illness, Dorsey began moving
"up-country." Over the next few months, he would travel more than a
thousand miles by steamer, canoe, and foot.

Mindful of the failings of his predecessor, Emory Taunt, and of the
expectations held by State Department officials in Washington, Dorsey
stayed focused on the task at hand: surveying the country for its economic possibilities.[1] What crops and commodities could be produced
or acquired here? What American goods could be sold to Africans? Although he dutifully crafted reports detailing the possibilities, he already
understood that Leopold and his minions had no intention of actually
allowing free trade.[2] He also planned to gather scientific and ethnographic information as well as objects for the Smithsonian Institution's
collections. And while not officially part of his job description, Dorsey
aspired to take on the mantle of explorer—to go where no Europeans
had gone before, to fill in some of the blank spaces on the map.

Like novelist Joseph Conrad, who had set out along the same path
to the African interior two years earlier, Dorsey had only a vague idea
of what awaited him. Little given to self-reflection, he understood that
the weak, unprepared, or unlucky might be broken by such a journey.

But he had less insight into what dark choices might confront a strong, resourceful, and ambitious man like himself. Unlike Conrad, who detested most of the Europeans he met (except Roger Casement) and could not look past the human suffering in his path or muster the will to overcome sickness and disappointment, Dorsey adapted.[3]

What did adaptation mean? In the simplest sense, it meant coping with harsh physical conditions and hardships—lack of food and clean water, heat, insects, and disease. With characteristic pragmatism, Dorsey recalibrated psychologically and physiologically to fit the circumstances. He also gradually adapted to the complex cultural dynamics of the Congo Free State, which brought together disparate tribal groups, Swahili-speaking Arabs, and white men who had drifted there from across the globe, but especially from northern Europe. The success of his journey ultimately depended on gaining the cooperation of all these people. But the immediate challenge lay in learning how to interact with Africans. Getting anything done, including travel, required their help, whether purchased, coerced, or given willingly.[4] In this particular task, Dorsey succeeded. But he did so at a high cost for many of the Africans who aided him.

One of the startling facts about the Congo Free State is how few Europeans were there—a mere four hundred when Dorsey arrived, compared with perhaps a million Africans. Leopold was acutely aware of this population imbalance. Characteristically, he used it to his own propagandistic advantage, publicizing African participation in what he claimed was a project of civilizing them and encouraging their self-governance—most notably in the form of the Force Publique, a paramilitary force comprising Africans, some from the Congo, and some mercenaries and conscripts from Zanzibar, Soudan, and other parts of the continent.[5]

At the beginning of his journey, Dorsey seems to have been relatively unconcerned about venturing into an unfamiliar place where he might be the sole European or American. A naive sense of superiority, the backing of the State, and an arsenal of guns bolstered his confidence that the Africans he depended on would do his bidding. But his lack of African language skills and his rudimentary French meant that he would have trouble communicating his needs and desires. The solution? Hire someone to act as his interpreter, personal servant, and general fixer—a "boy," in the parlance of English-speaking imperialists.[6]

Back in Boma, Dorsey had sent Harriet a picture of himself and "Philip."[7] The photo reveals that Philip was not a boy at all in the literal sense of a child; rather, he was a young man close in age to his employer.[8] Dressed in a dirty, checkered shirt, a length of cloth knotted at his waist and falling to the ground, he glances sternly to one side of the camera. Dorsey's rifle rests in Philip's right hand—a photographic convention that signified both trust and servitude. "It's the fashion here," another traveler wrote about the practice of having a servant carry one's gun.[9] Philip was short, barely reaching Dorsey's shoulder. He had come from Sierra Leone seeking work. One of Dorsey's later traveling companions described Philip as a member of the Hausa tribe.[10] He had probably learned his language skills from missionaries. Perhaps he was also an orphan. Dorsey never tells us.

It is striking that Dorsey made the effort to have this photograph taken. While members his family had the habit of sending studio images of one another, the surviving photos do not include servants, other kinds of employees, or even friends and colleagues. The gesture suggests he saw hiring Philip as a kind of accomplishment, evidence that he had joined the company of other explorers, chief among them Henry Morton Stanley, who also had his picture taken with his "boy" more than a decade earlier, an image Dorsey may have been familiar with.[11]

Dorsey sent this picture to Harriet. "To my dear Harry with love, R. D. L. Mohun," he wrote on the back, trying to pull his worlds back together and perhaps courting her with a show of imperialist status. He expected Harriet to show the photograph to her friends and relations, hence the use of his full name. For her—and for us—the photograph gives a face to Dorsey's one constant travel companion, a silent witness to the long journey ahead. His proud countenance suggests that whatever Dorsey thought, Philip saw himself as a full partner in the enterprise. In terms of expertise, Philip was the one who knew what he was doing. Did he view Dorsey as a supernatural being, a person returned from the underwater land of the dead? In this era, many Africans explained the pallor of white men, their taste for canned sardines,

Figure 3. "Philip" and R. Dorsey Mohun pose for a professional
photographer in Boma (author's collection).

and their technological knowledge in this way.[12] Or had he already seen
through Dorsey's differentness to recognize an ordinary man, out of
place in Africa? Such was the nature of globalization and European imperialism: bound together in a profoundly unequal relationship, two
men of similar age and utterly different cultures and life experiences
embarked on a dangerous journey together.

THE CARAVAN

About sixty miles from the Atlantic, the broad, relatively slow-moving river began to change character. Mangrove swamps and grassy banks gave way to steeper cliffs over a narrower channel.[13] Steamers traveling upriver struggled against a stretch of water the Belgians called the Chaudron Infernale and English speakers referred to as Hell's Kitchen.[14] The churning water and the sound of the steamers' struggling engines gave travelers a hint of what was to come. During the time he waited in Matadi, the last major European settlement on the lower river, Dorsey received a particularly frightening taste of the river's power. A boat ferrying him to an appointment capsized in a whirlpool. He had to tell his supervisor in Washington that he was sending in an expense report without receipts because it was "as much as I could do to save myself."[15]

Just upstream from Matadi, travelers confronted a far more formidable barrier. For nearly two hundred miles, hard rock walls channeled tens of millions of gallons of water per minute into a narrow torrent rushing through a gap in the Crystal Mountains. This series of waterfalls and rapids, known collectively as the Cataracts, rendered this stretch of the river unnavigable.[16] This geographical impediment proved particularly frustrating to State officials because steamboats were essential to trade and military control of the interior.[17] Above the last set of falls, the river broadened out again into what was called Stanley Pool, which had two large port settlements, Kinshasa and Brazzaville. From either, it became relatively easy to communicate with the interior. Steamboats and canoes could travel through the center of Africa along the six thousand miles of the long bow-shaped curve of the Congo and its many tributaries.[18] First, however, they had to get around the cataracts.

Everything had to be dragged or carried on the backs, shoulders, and heads of hired porters: for starters, food, supplies, and mail, bagged in waterproof cloth or soldered into zinc boxes to withstand tropical downpours and river crossings. But the porters also had to carry all the parts of the steamboats that plied the smooth, upper reaches of the river. Components of steamboats and artillery guns, too large for a single man to carry, were rigged on poles that multiple men could balance on their shoulders.[19]

Huge caravans of porters, soldiers, and civilian travelers regularly left Matadi, heading uphill over the Cataract Caravan Road. This route wasn't a road at all. In many places, it was little more than a lacy skein of narrow paths worn smooth by the continual passage of human feet. Dorsey's predecessor estimated that more than five thousand porters traveled the route each month.[20] Dorsey thought the number might be higher: perhaps eighty thousand loads a year—a staggering five million plus pounds of goods going in and out of the central Congo using only the human power and skill of porters.[21] This labor-intensive form of transportation was not only very expensive but also socially disruptive. Employers provided porters with a minimal daily ration of grain that they also carried. Porters were expected to supplement these calories by gathering, buying, or stealing from villages along their route. As the scale of the enterprise grew, this form of procurement became unsustainable. Villagers moved up into valleys to get away from the road. Water supplies also became polluted with human waste, leading to devastating epidemics of dysentery and other waterborne diseases.[22]

State officials, therefore, were eager to build a railroad around the cataracts. When Dorsey arrived in 1892, the state was already engaged in the brutal business of constructing one. In the manner of the era's imperialist engineering projects, white overseers and experts directed huge crews of coerced and contract laborers who sculpted the earth and rock and laid the tracks, often using little more than hand tools. For Dorsey and colonial officials, the deaths of a thousand Africans and perhaps fifty Europeans, cut down by accidents and disease, constituted a reasonable price to pay for easier access to the riches of the interior.[23] But as eager as state officials were to complete the railroad, it wasn't ready by the time Dorsey set out on his journey.

Over the next fifteen years, Dorsey would gradually gain knowledge about the porterage business in Africa. But in late August 1892, he had little to go on beyond the advice of Casement and state officials in Boma and Matadi. His prior experiences in Nicaragua and elsewhere had not prepared him for tasks such as securing porters or negotiating prices. He also seems to have picked up some misconceptions about how to interact with the porters. His approach would cause problems on the road.

Figure 4. Caravan route from Matadi to Leopoldville. The paths carved by the passage of tens of thousands of human feet remained on the land long after the railroad replaced the caravans (*Panorama du Congo* [Brussels: Imprimerie scientifique Charles Bulens, 1912]).

Suffering the heat, mosquitos, and boredom, Dorsey waited almost a week in a Matadi hotel while an agent, who went unnamed in Dorsey's accounts, secured the necessary porters. He spent his time dining and shopping, including buying a case of champagne for the road. The cost of porterage was enormous. He ended up paying 4,965 Belgian francs, or about $1,000—20 percent of his yearly salary. But then he was bringing a huge volume of goods—ninety-seven "loads," which would require at least one hundred porters.[24] The bales and boxes contained everything from canned food and liquor to clothing, scientific instruments, guns, and ammunition. Of necessity, he had also brought trade goods—mostly lengths of cloth known as "handkerchief." That year, a checkered pattern was preferred, perhaps explaining Philip's choice of shirt in the photo.[25]

On Monday morning, August 29, Dorsey finally began the journey to the interior. Besides Philip, his traveling companions were three Belgian priests, Dominican "white fathers" bound for a mission station.[26] The day before, Dorsey had set his affairs in order, writing letters and paying bills before hearing mass at the Belgian church in an uncharacteristic show of religiosity. A Belgian official set off fireworks in his honor. He planned to be gone for three years, but there was a very real possibility that he might never return.[27] Dorsey and his companions took the train to the end of the line at the Mpozo River, eight miles from Matadi.[28] From there, they set off on foot or perhaps riding in a hammock-like contraption slung between two porters, as was the European custom. Dorsey does not say whether he chose to be carried.

In other parts of Africa, members of caravans traveled in close contact with each other for protection. European travelers, in particular, depended on Africans to buffer them from animals, thieves, and other risks.[29] Perhaps because the route around the cataracts was so highly trafficked, Dorsey's porters did not stay in one group. Twenty porters had left a few days earlier. He expected to meet up with the rest at the end of each day. These rendezvous were crucial because the porters were carrying most of his food.

The Caravan Road itself was daunting: a thin thread across a rocky landscape, often taking the most direct route between two points even if it meant going straight up or down hills. Impeding their forward progress was the Palaballa Range. Day after day, Dorsey tersely noted the steep vertical climbs in intense tropical heat. "Very hilly country. No vegetation of any sort. Red clay and sandstone formations, very little water, large boulders heaped upon fantastic shapes here and there."[30] Where the travelers did find water, they also found mosquitos—vast clouds of them. The path itself had been created by the aggregation of choices made by previous travelers. Numerous Europeans, accustomed to paths and roads shaped by the passage of draft animals and wheeled vehicles, remarked on how narrow most of the trail was, often not more than ten inches wide.[31] Sometimes on a flat plain, multiple trails ran side by side, shaped by the footsteps of porters who took the opportunity to walk abreast of each other for a spell, talking or singing to pass the time.[32]

Dorsey marveled at the strength and endurance of the men carrying his loads. "How they manage to get into their awful hills barefooted, bareheaded, and almost naked" was beyond him, he wrote. Dorsey observed that "when camp is made, they run into the bush to get the rats and snakes" to cook over the fire. They also supplemented their diet with grubs and "white ants" (termites). Dorsey was particularly struck by their nonchalance in the face of routine physical hardship. In the evening, he observed, the men used their short knives to dig the larvae of the sand fly called "jiggers" out of the soles of their feet.[33]

The caravan was Dorsey's introduction to the complicated, morally fraught dynamics of wage labor in the Congo. The porterage system was an African invention, but like other practices that originated endemically, it was changed, made harsher, and ultimately destroyed by the European presence in the Congo. Many of the men had entered the trade by choice, whether for adventure or to earn enough money for a bride or property or out of desperation over poverty. Others were deceived or dragooned.[34]

Earning a living in this way was fraught with peril. Injury and death were commonplace.[35] Porters who fell behind might be relieved of their loads and abandoned. Sometimes devastating diseases swept through whole caravans. Hunger and dehydration also took their toll, as did the depredations of robbers and hostile locals. In the diary he kept while traveling the Cataract Caravan Road, Joseph Conrad tersely noted the evidence of casualties: "Saw another dead body lying by the path in an attitude of peaceful repose." A few days later: "passed a skeleton tied-up to a post." Europeans also succumbed. Conrad briefly memorialized "a white man's grave—no name. Heap of stones in the form of a cross."[36] The same sights may very well have still been there when Dorsey passed through. But he chose not to describe them in his diary.

Much of the Caravan Road passed through uninhabited or sparsely populated country. As traffic increased with the state's incursions into the interior, conflicts between porters and locals increased in proximity to villages. Porters' raids on fields and harassment of women motivated villagers to relocate away from the main route.[37] Thereafter, the caravan system became more dependent on larger market towns for supplies and trading opportunities. Dorsey's first experience of provisioning took place about two-thirds of the way through the first leg of the journey, at Manyanga. Moving down out of the arid high country into a fertile valley, he and his companions came to an enormous market of "1,200 or 1,500 people." Victorian that he was, Dorsey was initially bothered by their "stages of nakedness," but he entered the crowd anyway.[38] He sent Philip to purchase fresh food—"cabbage palm kernels and a few fowls"—presumably for himself and the priests.[39]

At Manyanga, Dorsey found himself back in familiar, Europeanized surroundings. His host was A. C. Parminter, nephew of Major Parminter, the useful friend he'd made at the Hotel Bellevue in Brussels. That oasis of comfort lay thousands of miles to the north, but Dorsey could evoke a hint of it. Out came one of the bottles of champagne the porters had hauled from Matadi, which Dorsey gladly shared with the younger Parminter. The latter had bad news, however: while Manyanga was typically where one relay of porters would give way to the next, no fresh porters were available. Itching to move on, Dorsey was forced once again to wait.

Over the next week, he repeated the same routine each day: writing long letters to Harry and reports to the State Department, cleaning guns, and reorganizing the loads. He also played tennis with Parminter and smoked a few pipes of tobacco. He was growing increasing callous about the Africans surrounding him, his worst impulses condoned by the attitude of Parminter and other Europeans. "Had a swim," he told his diary. "Made all the factory hands go in and Parminter and I enjoyed a comfortable dip in their center. If an alligator comes, he can make a meal of one of the natives."[40] His growing sense of frustration and impotence had found an outlet in bullying people who couldn't say no to him.

What had caused the shortage of porters who should have been coming down several times a week carrying ivory from the trading posts in Kinshasa? Dorsey had been hearing rumors of a coming war between the state and the competing Arab traders who had settled in the central Congo.[41] Now, Parminter explained, growing tensions had made travel on the state side of the Congo River "unfriendly." If porters could be secured, they would have to travel on the northern, French-controlled side of the river.[42]

So be it. Nine days later, everything was packed up and a new group of porters headed north. At first everything went fine. But on the second day, the caravan began a hard climb through difficult country. The heat became nearly unbearable. "Water bad and food scarce for carriers," Dorsey reported. The next day, most of the porters lagged. By day's end, only a few men had arrived at the campsite, none of them carrying the Europeans' food supply. Dorsey and the priests split a single can of sardines. Philip went to look for the other men. He returned at midnight having found no signs of them. Two days later, Philip ventured out on another scouting expedition, locating the porters eight miles away from a designated rendezvous point. On the return, he purchased food for Dorsey and the priests at a market, though not enough. "Hungry is no word for how we feel," Dorsey wrote. After seven days of travel, Dorsey, the priests, and Philip staggered into Kinshasa with no sign of either the porters or Dorsey's possessions.

Situated on the southern side of a widening of the Stanley Pool, Kinshasa was an important trading center for the Société Anonyme Belge pour le Commerce du Haut Congo, or SAB, one of Leopold's concession holders. In 1892 it consisted of a handful of houses and the usual warehouses for storing ivory. Dorsey remembered it as well for its giant bottle-shaped baobab trees, some two feet in diameter and eighty feet high. He also noted that the surrounding country stretched out into loamy black fields fertilized by the river's annual floods. "A great deal of cotton is growing wild," he later dutifully reported, but the United States was not looking to import cotton from the Congo.[43] Kinshasa was important for a more interesting set of economic activities involving the trade in ivory.

Dorsey quickly set his sights on cultivating the most important person in town. Camille Delcommune was the local director for the SAB. He also controlled the passenger lists of the SAB's boats going upriver.[44] Dorsey could not travel any farther without Delcommune's help. Still dusty from the road, he headed straight for Delcommune's house and did some namedropping, principally of Major Parminter, who, as director of the SAB, also happened to be Delcommune's boss. Delcommune responded by inviting Dorsey to join him for dinner and stay overnight. A few days later, Dorsey borrowed Delcommune's horse to ride down to Leopoldville. This imposition on Delcommune's hospitality was particularly presumptuous because horses were very rare, high-status objects in Central Africa: the lack of suitable fodder, combined with the risk of infection from animal trypanosomiasis vectored by the tsetse fly, killed most imported horses and donkeys very quickly. It also proved pointless. The astute horse balked at crossing a bridge and would go no farther. Dorsey went on by foot.[45]

Delcommune proved less amenable to Dorsey's request to join one of the SAB's ivory-gathering expeditions. Dorsey speculated that Delcommune thought he was a scout for a competitor. Meanwhile, Kinshasa provided a startling lesson in the scope of the SAB's ivory concession. After viewing the loading of one of the state's steamers, Dorsey did a little math. The boat was carrying 3,200 tusks (about forty tons). At 25,000 Belgian francs per ton, the cargo had a market value in Europe of a million Belgian francs, or $200,000.[46] While the Treaty of Berlin opened the Congo to ivory gathering by non-Belgian companies, import and export duties ensured the state held a near monopoly. "Out of decency, it should be stopped," Dorsey complained to his diary. He thought the state should be abolished and turned into a traditional European trading company.

He continued to pressure Delcommune to let him ride along on an ivory-gathering expedition. The station head eventually gave in, but he required Dorsey to pay 1,000 Belgian francs for the privilege. Dorsey wrote to Parminter asking that he direct Delcommune to charge less. He felt the SAB owed him something because of his efforts to secure West Indian workers for the cataracts railroad project.[47]

The problem of Dorsey's missing baggage remained. He could not realistically go on without his equipment and supplies, and, while he might have found a way to purchase food and basic goods (at exorbitant cost), he could not replace the scientific equipment or the books and papers. As the wait stretched out, he grew furious. Finally, after nearly a month, the porters began trickling into the compound of a Brazzaville factory across the river from Kinshasa. Dorsey was more angry than relieved. It did not occur to him to be grateful for the effort the porters had made on his behalf. "I vent my feelings on the Cafila of caravan" (meaning the headman or supervisor), he wrote, "by giving him a sound thrashing which he will not soon forget."[48]

This "thrashing" was likely delivered in public in full view of the other porters as well as Europeans. It signaled that Dorsey was becoming part of a culture in which white men expressed their anxiety and frustration with an illegible culture and hostile environment through violence and then justified their actions by saying that violence was the only thing the locals understood. Such fits of temper were often rationalized as "teaching a lesson" to Africans who were deemed incapable of understanding subtler forms of communication. Over the next few months, Dorsey would be drawn deeper into this way of coping. In the Congo there was little or no social pressure to behave differently and plenty of company and encouragement from other men who joined in a variety of violent activities, from killing animals to waging "war" on the locals.[49]

In *Heart of Darkness*, Conrad famously fictionalized the way that men described as "the gentlest, quietest, creature to walk on two legs," or, in the case of his antihero, Kurtz, "an emissary of pity, and science and progress," could be drawn into this spiral of violence.[50] But he missed the essentially social quality of both the madness and the violence. His narrator ultimately blames the "wilderness" for Kurtz's mental breakdown. But the plant and animal world didn't cause this behavior. Europeans learned the habit of callous violence from one another. Europeans like Kurtz might have put heads on fence posts in isolation as the wilderness slowly stole their sanity, but they inherited their ideas from others. Moreover, much of the violence characteristic of the Congo Free State was practiced by groups of men, not individuals, and it was condoned, ignored, or actively participated in by the men who held authority over these groups. The ability to countenance violence in others and to participate in it without stepping over an invisible boundary was a common characteristic of many of the most "successful" white men of the Congo, including those such as Casement, who later turned against the State. Dorsey was still figuring out where that line lay, but he was learning rapidly.

IN SEARCH OF IVORY

Since dining with Casement and Parminter in the gilded breakfast room of the Bellevue Hotel ten months earlier, Dorsey had heard more and more about the profits that could be had from trading in ivory. In the factories of Kinshasa, he had fully grasped the amount of potential wealth it entailed. Now he had a chance to see how the SAB acquired the ivory and perhaps grab a small portion of the profits for himself.

"The word 'ivory' rang in the air, was whispered, was sighed," Conrad's narrator, Marlowe, explains in *Heart of Darkness*, recounting the atmosphere at the fictional trading station modeled after those operated by the SAB. "You would think they were praying to it. A taint of imbecile rapacity blew through it all, like a whiff from a corpse."[51] Over the next few months, Dorsey would undergo a crash course in the practicalities of ivory trading. He would also deepen his understanding of what drove Europeans to risk their lives and abandon their professed values in pursuit of elephant tusks or, more precisely, in pursuit of prosperity.

The siren song of ivory trading had drifted upriver long before the SAB arrived and before the Congo Free State had taken shape in Leopold's fertile and pecuniary imagination. A small amount of African ivory had been making its way into Europe for a very long time— shaped by artisans into religious art and fancy trinkets for the wealthy. In the early nineteenth century, demand exploded as industrial methods that had been developed made it possible to turn ivory into an extraordinarily wide range of products. Between 1823 and 1873, the price paid by wholesalers in Europe shot up by 400 percent. The ivory boom coincided with European efforts to ban the Atlantic slave trade, a central part of trading wealth in the Congo basin since the sixteenth century.[52]

Equatorial Africans who made their homes along the river were the first to deploy existing trade networks to transport tusks to the coast. The Bobangi people, who had long traded in slaves, fish, and manioc, dominated the early ivory trade. By the mid-nineteenth century, about one hundred Bobangi traders had grown quite powerful by securing tusks from Pygmy hunters and then moving them downriver in huge canoes.[53]

Meanwhile, on the east coast of Africa, another group of traders increased their efforts to profit from the growing demand for ivory in Europe. These were the vilified and so-called Arab slave traders Dorsey had heard so much about. The descendants of Omani Arabs who had intermarried with Africans in Zanzibar and on the east coast of Africa, these traders had begun moving inland. By the time Dorsey arrived in Africa, the Arabs had created extensive settlements in the upper Congo, living and working in uncomfortably close proximity to the Belgians, securing ivory supplies (and also slaves) and transporting them to the coast, where they would be sold to Indian Ocean trade networks.[54]

Until railroads were built and steamboats were introduced above the cascades, both the Arabs and the Bobangi were essential to European ivory markets. The Europeans lacked the means to procure large amounts of ivory directly by elephant hunting, and they also lacked the transportation networks to move ivory from the forests and fields, where elephants lived, to the coast. Leopold hoped to change this situation by wresting managerial control over the middlemen and suppressing the competition—techniques quite familiar to more conventional businessmen of the era. Beginning in 1889 the State issued a series of decrees asserting that only those with official concessions could exploit resources in areas designated by the Belgians. Both the Bobangi and the Arabs resisted these declarations, sometimes violently.[55] Dorsey arrived in the Congo just as Leopold had finally abandoned any real commitment to free trade, pushing these tensions to a boiling point.

Dorsey had heard shreds of news and rumors about these violent clashes. Now he was about to be drawn in. He would also have a chance to witness the disappearance of a way of life for the Bobangi and other peoples in the Congo. Whether or not he was aware, the whole process eerily echoed the gradual destruction of Native Americans in his home country, including the role of trading posts and the Bureau of Indian Affairs created by his great-uncle Thomas L. McKenney.[56]

At seven on a late October morning, Dorsey boarded a launch to begin the journey up several tributaries of the Congo River—the Kasai and a recently mapped waterway known variously as the Loukényé or Loukenia (it is now known as the Loukenie River).[57] Setting off across the vast, slow-moving expanse of Stanley Pool provided his introduction to a way of traveling and a stretch of the Congo River that would become increasingly familiar to him over the next two years. Philip was along, as well two other "servants" whom he didn't identify.[58] Sometime in the next twenty-four hours, they transferred to a small river steamer, the *Baron Labermont*, which would be their home for the next two months. The boat probably resembled the *Roi de Belges* captained by Conrad: flat on the bottom to pass over sandbars and snags unhindered, most Congo steamers also had a low profile above the water. A one- or two-story superstructure of iron supports allowed the stacking of a maximum amount of cargo but not much comfort for passengers.[59] Wire netting suspended from the roof could be let down as protection against arrows. There was not enough room on board for the Europeans' baggage, which had to be towed behind in a whaleboat. To complete this ramshackle flotilla, a canoe lashed to the side of the steamer carried forty African workers, many of them Zanzibaris far from home. Their job was to cut wood each night to fire the boiler—and to "fight if necessary."[60] Fernand Demeuse (known to Dorsey as Stephen) also came onboard. Later known as a scientist and explorer, a collector of rare plants, and one of the best-known photographers of the Congo in this era, on this trip Demeuse was tasked with the grubbier business of gathering ivory as an agent of the SAB.[61] He was another exact contemporary of Dorsey, born in the same year—another young man looking for adventure.

A leisurely affair, travel by steamer bordered on tedious (unless the boat ran aground or caught fire). It took Dorsey's boat all day to travel up the length of the Pool from Kinshasa. The next morning, the river began to narrow between high hills. Looking downstream, Dorsey was awed by the enormity of the river, which expanded to several miles wide at this point. It seemed, he thought, as "if one were looking out at the sea." Small, sandy islands, each dotted with a single palm, looked to him "very much like ships at a distance."[62] Much of the Congo basin was covered by thick jungle punctuated by marshy ground and occasional savannas of coarse grass that towered over the heads of travelers. That leafy abundance came right up to the river as the boat went slowly by.

Forward movement ended each day around half past two when the woodcutters went inland to secure fuel for the next day. Hunting provided the principal form of amusement onshore for European passengers. Philip's responsibilities included locating game and carrying Dorsey's guns, including a hugely heavy "express" rifle for elephant hunting.[63] Dorsey eagerly shot and killed what he could, which mostly meant ducks and guinea fowl as well as the occasional hippo, which the Zanzibaris eagerly consumed. But struck by ivory fever and a more general bloodlust, what he really wanted to do was kill elephants.

Over the next two months, the party saw endless signs of the huge mammals: broken bushes, huge tracks, piles of manure, elephant ticks on the sides of trees, even elephants themselves on the edge of the river, one so close they could almost touch it from the deck. But Dorsey proved inept or unlucky at taking one down. A month into the trip, he noted with chagrin, "I shot a guinea fowl. So ridiculous going after elephants and coming back with a bird."[64]

For all the ivory traders, the mass slaughter of elephants lay in the future. Demeuse mostly bought "fossil" or "antique" ivory, gathered from the remains of elephants that had died from natural causes.[65] The Batwa tribes, from whom the Bobangi[66] traders secured most of their ivory, did kill elephants. But without adequate firearms, the task was extraordinarily difficult and dangerous. It involved building traps consisting of deep pits with stakes at the bottom or sneaking up on grazing elephants and cutting a nerve in one of their legs with a knife (which seems virtually impossible).[67] Sawing the tusks off the carcass was much easier.

A few days into the trip, Dorsey began encountering signs that the local trading culture was still very much alive along the river and its tributaries. "Passing many canoes," he wrote, "going to Kinshasa to sell their ivory." He counted nearly forty vessels.[68] Soon thereafter, the steamer left the Congo, entering the Kassai River. Demeuse and the captain, experienced in trading for ivory, began looking for opportunities. Eager to learn this skill, Dorsey paid close attention to the Africans with whom Demeuse hoped to trade. Demeuse had brought along the standard currencies of Central Africa: cowries for small purchases, and printed cotton textiles and standard lengths of brass rods for larger ones.[69] Large and small bells, tin plates, and looking glasses rounded out the list of trade goods. Dorsey later told his superiors that a kind of American-made cotton sheeting known as Merikani was very popular.[70] The boat was also equipped with a significant arsenal of European weapons in case something went awry (or not the way the Europeans hoped it would go).

Not surprisingly, some people from the riverside villages made it abundantly clear they did not want the steamer to land. "At nearly every one," Dorsey observed, "a fetish woman or man would appear and go into the most beautiful contortions to prevent the steamer from landing."[71] Others were friendlier. A week out from Kinshasa, the travelers stopped at Msuata's village, where Stanley had established one of the first trading posts in the upper Congo. "Old Papa Gobila is still in charge," Dorsey reported. "The State has given him a large gold medal, which he wears around his neck suspended by a silver chain." The ship's company paid a substantial amount in brass rods for a goat; Dorsey estimated the cost at $7. Dorsey also bought a piece of fine grass cloth, "soft to the touch as silk." Papa Gobila knew his customers. Dorsey later donated the cloth, along with other artifacts, to the Smithsonian.[72]

In another large village, housing what Dorsey estimated to be at least five hundred people, the ship's party bartered for eggs, fowls, fish, and vegetables. The chief also offered ivory "but wanted too much for it."[73] A day later, another transaction went badly awry. Several tribesmen approached the boat offering to sell wood. Two armed Zanzibaris mercenaries accompanied members of the crew to obtain it from the village. One of the crewmen did not come back. According to Dorsey, the villagers refused to return him and "declared war." "We have made all preparations for an assault tomorrow," Dorsey wrote in eager anticipation. The ship's arsenal, which included not only hunting weapons but also nine flintlocks and thirteen chassepots, was distributed to a war party, which ambushed the village. Dorsey proudly estimated that they engaged "fully five hundred natives." No one was killed, for the tribesmen quickly realized they were outgunned and disappeared into the bush. On the way back to the boat, the party found the missing crewman with a broken leg stranded in the long grass.[74]

Small "wars" were commonplace among tribal villages that didn't have established relationships through trade or marriage. Such conflict long predated the European presence. But intertribal warfare didn't involve the kind of lethal weaponry deployed by Europeans. There was an incentive not to destroy too much property, which could otherwise be appropriated, or create too many casualties, who might otherwise become wives or slaves.[75] In contrast Europeans tended to follow a scorched earth policy—shooting to kill and burning villages to the ground, the better to "teach a lesson" to the locals. As with other forms of violence, such skirmishes contained an element of sport. Dorsey called it "fun."[76]

In this case, it is also striking that both the initial hostile interactions and the coordination of the attack were mediated by translators: Philip and perhaps other people on the boat. That small space was, in and of itself, a virtual Tower of Babel. None of the Europeans on board were native speakers of the same language. English-speaking Dorsey spoke only a rudimentary French; Demeuse was a native French speaker who may or may not have spoken English; the engineer was Swedish.[77] The Zanzibaris probably spoke Swahili, which was in itself a creole language. Philip spoke French, English, and bits and pieces of local languages—how well remains an open question. Without doubt, linguistic and cultural misunderstandings contributed to this and other, often tragic, encounters between Europeans and Africans.

Other encounters with locals piqued Dorsey's curiosity and sharpened his observations. His diary entries reveal that he was, in some ways, his mother's son: equipped with an eye for the human story, at least when he chose to be. "This morning the chief of Inogo came in for a palaver with a following of some five hundred warriors and 30 women. He is blind," he noted. "Sat on a lead box, wives around him and one woman standing in front holding a 5′ spear." Where words failed him, he made a sketch of the chief's elaborate hairstyle and head ornaments. He took pleasure in the chief's delight in the gift of a knife, pieces of cloth, and beads. "Rather decent people and seem more likely to make trade than war," he opined.[78]

A week later, he had a more startling encounter. "Natives came this morning accompanied by their chief who is an ugly old hag with breasts hanging halfway down to her waist and a grass cloth around her loins and a large brass ring encircling her neck," he recorded. "She seems to have complete control of her people." Raised by forceful women, he knew strong female power was entirely possible. But the entry conveys his acute discomfort with the idea of bargaining with a nearly naked older woman casually surrounded by a group of male warriors. Other meetings further complicated his understanding of his trading partners. Another chief offered "much ivory" if they would help him wage war against a neighboring tribe. "We declined with thanks," Dorsey wrote.[79]

By early December, the steamer had made its way up a series of increasingly narrow tributaries beyond the markings on the map. If no European had mapped these streams, Atlantic trade had made an impact. "Meet corn for the first time," Dorsey wrote. "It [was] delicious and as good as we get at home." Their progress had slowed to a crawl, hindered by a strong current and rocky bottom. Finally, they could go no farther in the steamer. The canoe that had been home to the Zanzibaris was detached, and twenty-three men paddled Dorsey and Demeuse upstream until a strong current checked their forward progress too. Dorsey calculated they had traveled four days farther east in this watershed "than any white men" had before. Reluctantly, they turned around.[80]

The trip home was faster. On the twentieth of December, they were back in Kinshasa. In their absence, Delcommune had fallen ill with what Dorsey called "hemateuric," probably hematuric bilious fever—the symptoms of which included bloody urine, kidney infection, nausea, and fever all caused by acute malaria. "Seems no hope for him. Poor chap," he wrote. Christmas was dreary. Nothing felt as he thought it should. Even the weather refused to cooperate; it was "hot as blazes." He could not push his longing for the company of Harry and his family out of his mind. He found it particularly hard to be alone with his hopes and memories on birthdays and holidays. The next day, Delcommune died. Dorsey was shaken. His great adventure, influenced by romantic stories and taken on with a young man's sense of immortality, felt increasingly like a slow, grinding struggle against unseen forces. His ambition to enrich himself by participating in the ivory trade had come to naught. It was hard to imagine what would make the stress and physical discomfort worthwhile. On the last day of the year, he wrote, "Wonder where I shall be this time next year. Maybe home. I hope so."[81]

✳ 4 ✳

ARAB ENCOUNTERS

Dorsey had heard rumors of war ever since he arrived in the Congo. Stories of clashes between the State and the powerful Arab[1] traders who controlled the central Congo swirled around mess halls and steamer decks along with grisly accounts of Arab atrocities and betrayals.[2] But, at least for the moment, Dorsey continued to focus on carrying out his consular mission as he chose to understand it. War's consequences—frightened porters, long detours, local people unwilling to trade—were mostly minor impediments to his assessment of the Congo and its resources.

As a new year dawned amid the baobab trees and steamy heat of Kinshasa, Dorsey sublimated his holiday loneliness into a flurry of planning. He intended to head to Kwango and Kwilu, two minor tributaries of the Congo. Upriver at Bolombo, he contracted with a Congolese man named Dumbele to help hire forty men as soldiers and workers. They would replace the Zanzibaris provided by the State on his last voyage. Dumbele, whom Dorsey had likely met on one of the State's steamers, had worked his way into the position of quartermaster. He was also the son of a local chief. His combined tribal status and trusted position with the State gave him an advantage as a fixer and intermediary for clients such as Dorsey. Dumbele convinced the American commercial agent to pay each of the recruits an advance of six feet of red cloth and twenty brass rods. Dorsey thought it a good investment. He believed Dumbele to be "thoroughly reliable" and was confident that all the men would be ready and available when the time came.[3]

Late in January, he returned to Bolombo. Dumbele and his men were waiting, ready to board the steamer. "Each man had his mat and ditty box, and many have their wives," Dorsey observed. He took pleasure in an invitation from Dumbele's father to return for a hippo hunting party in the bush. Then they were off, heading downriver to Kinshasa to change to the *Baron Labermont*, which of course Dorsey knew well. "We get under way amidst the howls, yells, and clapping of hand of the crowd on the bank" he recorded, as they left Dumbele's village.[4]

Less than a week later, the American consul impulsively decided to abandon the whole enterprise in favor of going to war. The arrival of the late Camille Delcommune's brother prompted the decision. Given up for dead after his Katanga expedition failed to return when planned, Alexandre Delcommune reappeared in Kinshasa bearing news that the State's efforts to drive the Arabs from the central Congo had begun in earnest. The State's military commanders, Francis Dhanis and Louis-Napoléon Chaltin, together with Inspector General Gaspard Fivé, were beginning to sweep through the Arab settlements of the upper Congo. They were converging on Stanley Falls, which had come under the control of an Arab leader named Rachid, who had worked with the Belgians up until that point.

Dorsey would soon become intimately familiar with these men and places. At that moment, however, they were just names linked to rumors, gossip, fragments of information, and points on a map. Naively, he thought he understood the implications of the latest news. If the State succeeded, Leopold could say he had accomplished one of his humanitarian goals: the elimination of Arab-sponsored slave trading in the Congo. For an American raised on stories about the Civil War and his family's own "abolitionism," the opportunity to witness history being made was irresistible. Who knows what glory might follow? He telegraphed a press release announcing his plans to the *New York Herald*.[5] It would be worth the effort if Harry and his family read about his adventures in the same newspaper that had carried Stanley's account of finding Livingstone.

The view as he departed Stanley Pool no longer seemed exotic: same river, a different riverboat, the *Archiduchesse Stéphanie*, named after one of Leopold's daughters. Flood season had peaked, swelling the vast river to a muddy lake. The passenger list included his friend Steven Demeuse, along with another official of the SAB. The steamer's minimal interior space was given over to three "ladies of the C.B.M."—missionaries headed for an uncertain fate in the interior. "No room for me" in the enclosed part of the boat, Dorsey wrote. "Put my tent on the aft part which forms a most comfortable cabin."[6]

A few days' upstream, the steamer stopped at Basoko, a trading center that also housed a large garrison of African Force Publique soldiers commanded by Louis-Napoléon Chaltin.[7] As usual, Dorsey wasted no time engaging the local authorities. In his report home, he told his supervisor that Chaltin had invited him to join his upcoming military expedition up the Lomami River to the Arab strongholds of Bena Kamba and Riba Riba. Observing the military adventures of a foreign power (even a peculiar political entity such as the State) was not normally part of the job description for United States commercial agents, but Dorsey rationalized that it fell under his mandate to survey the Congo's resources. The Kasanga, as the area was called, was considered the "richest and most populous" region of the Congo basin, he wrote to his supervisor. But it was currently too dangerous to visit without protection from a "strong expedition" such as Chaltin's.[8] And, after all, he was only going along to map the area's resources.

Invitation extended and accepted; Dorsey reboarded the steamer now bound for Stanley Falls, where he would join Chaltin a few weeks hence. In the meantime, he wanted to see the Falls and its surroundings while it still was under Arab control. But he wasn't feeling his best. The familiar sensation of fever haunted the voyage: "not well, too much blood in my head," he wrote. It took four long days of struggling upstream to reach the falls.[9]

The *Archiduchesse Stéphanie* docked at a settlement Europeans called Stanleyville (now Kisangani), the most important trading center of the upper Congo. Beyond this point, the river tumbled over a series of rapids and cascades for more than sixty miles. Only local fishermen with their enormous basketwork fish traps braved the white water, clambering out above the falls on a rickety structure of tied wooden poles. Everything else had to be portaged around. Above the falls, the river bore a new name: the Lualaba.

Dorsey had reached the heart of the Arab-controlled territories. Although diplomats and mapmakers in Europe had designated the Eastern Congo from Basoko to Lake Tanganyika as belonging to the State, the reality was more complicated. Over the past few decades, a remarkable leader known as Tippu Tip had gained control over a vast region—about half of the State's holdings. Tip, whose given name was Hamed bin Muhammed, was the most powerful of the traders. Gradually moving inland from the east coast of Africa, he and his fellow traders had settled along the upper reaches of the Congo and its eastern tributaries, intermarrying and trading with the various Bantu tribes.[10] Their towns and villages were extensive and intended to be permanent. Nyangwe, described by Europeans as the Arab capital, was home to thousands of people fed by extensive rice fields. European travelers nicknamed the town "Little Bengal" for its resemblance to settlements in India's Ganges River delta.[11]

Tip and those who worked with and for him had developed a complex relationship with the Africans who made their homes in these areas. To begin with, though their ancestors were Omani Arabs, Tip and many of his fellow "Arabs" were the offspring of Zanzibari Arabs and Africans. They spoke a creole language, Swahili, which was becoming the dominant tongue on the east coast.[12] Tip himself was the product of a union between an Arab trader and an African woman. To most Europeans, the trader's face marked him as a mixed-race African or "mulatto."

For other Africans, the Arab traders were both feared oppressors and the source of wealth and power. They did not hesitate to terrorize local populations, and they sold human captives into the Indian Ocean slave trade. This, along with their procurement of vast amounts of ivory, made a few African tribal leaders immensely wealthy. The traders obtained power with firearms, but they maintained it partly through collaborators, including tribal chiefs and some men who were enslaved or formerly enslaved.[13]

Dorsey was about to witness firsthand the equally complicated relationship that the Arabs, particularly Tip and his family, maintained with Leopold and the Congo Free State. In 1887 Leopold appointed Tip as governor or "Vali" of the Arab-held area. Tip received a salary and a uniform, was obliged to fly the State's flag, and was supposed to curtail the internal trading of slaves, both between African tribes and between Africans and Arabs. In exchange he could continue to carry on "legitimate commerce" in the region—meaning trade in ivory and rubber but not slaves. Seemingly in direct contradiction, however, Leopold also asked Tip to help the State procure local laborers for the railroad and for the Force Publique. Arab traders had as much trouble as Europeans convincing men to leave their villages to work for wages. So State agents resorted to "liberating" enslaved people from villages and indenturing them to recoup their purchase price. Forced into hard labor far from friends and family, many of these individuals did not live long enough to claim their freedom.[14]

These arrangements initially suited both men. Tip recognized that he could not hold out against the State's superior firepower, and Leopold knew he did not yet possess the resources to drive the Arabs, his economic competitors, out of the Congo. But by 1890 the balance of power had decidedly tipped in favor of the State. Seeing the handwriting on the wall, Tip departed for Zanzibar, leaving his nephew Rachid to govern from Stanley Falls.[15] To make matters even more complicated, parts of the so-called Arab Zone remained controlled by other Arab and Arab-allied leaders who did not share Tip's philosophy of cooperation with the State.[16] They resented the State's embargo on the importation and sale of arms as well as the recently imposed export tax on ivory sold to the SAB. Upstream, these tensions had already sparked violence against station agents. Towns and villages had also been attacked. In the east, Dhanis had been using State forces to retaliate since the previous spring, eventually defeating one of Tippu Tip's ex-slaves, an African known to Europeans as Ngongo Lutete, who consequently became Dhanis's ally. In Stanley Falls, however, the peace still held as Arabs, Africans, and Europeans went on trading as if nothing had changed—at least for the time being.

Dorsey reported, "8 March arrive at Stanley Falls. State Station very well situated on right bank. SAB diagonally opposite on [the] left."[17] The Arab town stretched across the plain, behind the headquarters of the State, with Rachid's house occupying a prominent rise close by. In the days that followed, Dorsey witnessed Arabs and Europeans living and working side by side, extracting the riches of the Congo. For example, at the SAB's factory he observed the State's agent, a Russian named Langheld, buy ivory from hundreds of Arab traders who had come from smaller trading stations. That same afternoon, Rachid put in an appearance, accompanied by numerous retainers. Dorsey was impressed and charmed. "Rather a good-looking Mulatto," he wrote, "exquisitely clean and has very good manners. Quite the gentleman."[18] Rachid did not fit the racial stereotypes Dorsey had first internalized in Washington. Like others of the trader elite, Rachid habitually dressed in white from his headdress to his robes—stressing a cleanliness that Europeans in the Congo found difficult to maintain in their own dress. In contrast, Dorsey's attire was probably dirty khaki reeking of sweat and tobacco.

Two days later, Dorsey accompanied Nicolas Tobback, the State's "Resident" at the Falls, to Rachid's compound. Officially, Tobback was a liaison between the Arabs and Brussels. Informally, he also spied on the movements of Arab forces in the east and kept an eye on Rachid.[19]

Dorsey witnessed several interactions between Tobback and Rachid. He admired Tobback's diplomacy and courtesy toward the Arabs and the people he described as "half Arabs." He was also impressed by Tobback's ability to manage Rachid's expectations. The Arab trader still positioned himself as the State's ally in the growing conflict with other Arabs and their allies. For his loyalty, he demanded one thousand additional rifles as well as ammunition. Dorsey watched attentively as Tobback told Rachid he would make the order and carefully wrote notes in a book. Later, the Resident confided in Dorsey that the guns would not be forthcoming. Demeuse, too, was dodging Rachid's demands, which included selling him a small steam launch. Demeuse countered that he could not do so until Rachid settled a considerable debt to the SAB amounting to twelve tons of ivory, worth an estimated $60,000.[20]

Rachid welcomed Dorsey to his home with courtesy. Dorsey and Tobback politely sat and sipped what Dorsey described as "bad coffee"—probably a thick, Turkish-style brew. The house fascinated the American visitor. Like other Arab dwellings in Congo, East Africa, and Zanzibar, it combined luxury with fortresslike architecture. He observed that the walls were decorated with mirrors and clocks "keeping any sort of time." Later, he sketched the exterior: windowless except for a dozen holes that served as gun ports.[21]

At some point, Dorsey made the mistake of telling Rachid that he planned to witness Chaltin's assault on one of the Arab settlements upstream. Rachid grew enraged, saying something that Dorsey viewed as "exceedingly discourteous."[22] Soon thereafter, news arrived of Dhanis's successful attack on another Arab settlement. "Arabs rather chalky," Dorsey gloated.[23] Rachid was no fool. He must have already realized that the days of his cozy arrangement with the State were numbered.

Back in Basoko, Dorsey waited for Chaltin's men to prepare the *Ville de Bruxelles*. Planks were nailed around the ship's entire exterior as protection against the Africans' lances and the poisoned arrows and muskets of their Arab allies. "She looks more like a dry goods box than ever," Dorsey joked.[24] When everything was ready, 150 African soldiers and two Belgian officers came on board. They pulled away from the bank in a hard rain and a few days later turned southward into the mouth of the Lomami River.

The area boasted a dense population, with villages on both banks and extensive banana and palm oil plantations. The Europeans struggled to interpret what they were seeing and experiencing. At some villages, the locals were friendly, providing wood and even welcoming the expedition with tales of Arab atrocities. At other places, people on the shore waved away or even shot at the steamer. Then Dorsey and his companions began to see bodies in the water—mostly headless. "No cause for this apparent murder could be found," Dorsey reported, "until that evening [when] the steamer stopped at a large village which was in flames."[25] Dead and dismembered bodies lay everywhere. There were no apparent survivors. Dorsey found the sight of a dead toddler with his hands bound behind his back particularly distressing.[26]

A few hours later, the expedition group found an old woman and two children hiding in a banana orchard. After much coaxing, they stated that their village had been attacked by Arab "slave hunters" (Dorsey's terminology) who had fled when the steamer came in sight. They had taken nearly one hundred people with them, presumably to be traded for ivory. Twenty were later found killed in the bush. Dorsey hypothesized that the slave hunters deemed these twenty too slow to keep up.[27]

For Dorsey, the whole episode vividly demonstrated the necessity and humanitarianism of the State's military efforts against the Arabs. "What brutes they are," he exclaimed in his diary. "If only people in Europe and America could but realize the awful part of this business. Many would be forthcoming to stop it."[28] The experience removed whatever doubts he might have had about the righteousness of the State's challenge to the Arab presence in the Congo. He was beginning to fantasize about heroically finishing his McKenney grandfather's abolitionist work by rooting out slavery in one of its last strongholds.

Day after day the steamer chugged up the river toward Chaltin's forces at Bena Kamba, a major Arab trading center. Dorsey went back to his routine of the previous winter: taking potshots at elephants and poking around in the bush for signs of the Arabs while the soldiers cut firewood each evening. His thirtieth birthday on April 12 merited a note in his diary. "My birthday. Came down to an old Arab camp and cut wood. . . . 3 natives came in a canoe. The chief gave us 2 bunches of plantains. They are glad we are going to fight the Arabs."[29]

Their destination, Bena Kamba, held great symbolic significance for officers of the State. The previous year, station agent Arthur Hodister and his two assistants had been killed there and, it was rumored, ritually cannibalized on the orders of Nserera, the Arab leader in control of the area. Hodister was not just another expendable servant of the State. Now largely forgotten (except by a few literary scholars who think he served as Conrad's model for Kurtz in *Heart of Darkness*),[30] Hodister was something of a legend among those knowledgeable about the early history of Leopold's involvement with the Congo. He knew everybody and had participated in several major expeditions.

In his last years, Hodister found a way to negotiate the complex mix of European, Arab, and African people and cultures in the area. Unlike Dorsey, Casement, Demeuse, or Tobback, all of whom worked hard to define distinctly European identities through their clothing, dietary choices, and behavior, Hodister adopted many of the markers and affectations of an Arab trader. He dressed in white robes and a head wrap or "kilemba," collected a retinue later described as "slaves and concubines," and even acknowledged the children he'd fathered with a native woman. He also created his own trading company, the Syndicat Commercial du Katanga.[31] His fluency in Swahili, the language of the traders, made much of this appropriation possible, as did his deep knowledge of the Congo.[32] Until his demise, this approach seemed to be working—though his death may have been the ironic result of a commercial misunderstanding. The Belgians, however, read it as stark evidence of why the Arabs could neither be trusted nor tolerated, even when they appeared as suave and civilized as Rachid.

Dorsey knew at least some of Hodister's story by the time the steamer came within view of Bena Kamba, which stood on a high bluff surrounded by an orchard of ragged-leafed plantain trees.[33] The passengers on the *Ville de Bruxelles* had been expecting and perhaps hoping for a fight, but the trading station—recently stocked with $250,000 in beads, cloth, brass rods, and other trade goods—had been ransacked and seemed abandoned. Chaltin was nowhere to be seen. Revenge for Hodister would have to wait.

Then shots were fired and Chaltin's advance guard came into sight. The Belgian commander was bursting with news. He had "completely demolished" the Arab town of Talgri, seizing prisoners, equipment, and twenty tons of food. Less positively for him, disease now coursed through his forces. A number of soldiers and one Belgian officer, Mr. Coppée, had smallpox. The expedition's doctor, Mr. Dupont, had a bad case of dysentery. Another officer had contracted a hematuric fever.[34] Chaltin planned to send the sick Europeans back to Basoko immediately for medical care.

Clearly, he was shorthanded. Would Dorsey do him the honor of commanding the company's two Krupp field cannons as well as the seventy men needed to transport and operate them? Dorsey said yes. He later reassured Washington that it was all above board, since he had asked Chaltin to draft a document explaining that he would receive no payment for joining the army of a foreign government while a representative of the United States.[35] For his part, Chaltin believed that Dorsey had been a US Navy officer and knew what he was doing.[36] All that time watching drills aboard the *Quinnebaug* was about to pay off for Dorsey—or so he hoped.

Warfare held a powerful allure for Dorsey, as it did for many of his generation of American men. While born too late to participate in the tumult of the Civil War, his generation came of age in a society obsessed with its meanings and memorialization. For them, participating in battle represented a peak, life-changing experience—not to mention an indisputable proof of manhood fulfilled. Most of Dorsey's contemporaries had to satisfy themselves vicariously.[37] But Dorsey had stumbled across an opportunity to prove himself in the crucible of war—and to right some of the wrongs he had witnessed.

Because admirals and generals credited with saving the Republic and vanquishing slavery had frequented the Mohun-Dorsey household and figured in the family's dinnertime gossip, Dorsey had internalized a relatively pragmatic view of the qualities needed to lead in war. In his observation, war made heroes of men who were, upon close inspection, still human. This more practical view of military leadership didn't mean he wasn't itching to try his hand at it.

Although eager to proceed, the members of the Chaltin Expedition, as it came to be known, had to wait. Reinforcements were due to arrive from upstream. Dorsey took the time to practice aiming the guns. "Fire the Krupp cannon this morning 300 meters range at a tree and place the shot exactly. Fired again across the river but shell went about a foot high." Meanwhile, Chaltin inspected his personnel and equipment. Smallpox was taking a harsh toll. Out of a force of nearly five hundred, three men died of the disease in one day. Two more followed the next day. Another succumbed to eating "poisoned toadstools," according to Dorsey.[38]

The body count also included three Basoko prisoners. A fellow prisoner had told the Europeans that his compatriots had murdered a State-employed officer named Bokarri, which seemed to explain why he had failed to appear at the rendezvous. Chaltin shot the three accused men. The next day, lookouts spotted Bokarri in a canoe heading downriver. Once Bokarri landed, Chaltin ordered the accuser brought to face Bokarri and explain himself. Yet the prisoner insisted that he had told the truth. "We are dumbfounded," Dorsey wrote in his diary, but "there is nothing to be done."[39] What had happened? A crucial piece of information had been lost in translation with lethal consequences.

With the entire company finally assembled in one place, they took to the road, heading overland for Riba Riba, unfamiliar territory for the Europeans, the Force Publique soldiers, and other Africans in the company. (Dorsey doesn't say so, but Philip must still have been by his side.) The landscape was rugged, Chaltin wrote, "a place of vast solitude where luxuriant vegetation spread out in a jumble of beautiful but encumbering finery." The commander had only his compass to guide the expedition, and the company struggled to find its way through towering grasses. He was grateful to run into a group of friendly locals, two of whom offered to come along as guides.[40]

Even in dry weather, the route was too rough for wheeled vehicles, so in groups of four, the men took turns carrying the cannons, each of which weighed 240 pounds. Another group carried the gun carriages, while dozens of others shouldered the shells.[41] As torrential rain transformed empty ravines into rivers and lakes, a difficult march turned into a near impossibility. Faced with the flooded landscape, the entire expedition came to a complete halt. Chaltin ordered the men to build a bridge across the water, an enterprise that consumed an entire day. They gingerly moved the baggage and artillery across the makeshift bridge, being "very careful," Chaltin said, "to avoid accidents." Without the guns, an important advantage the company held over the Arabs would have disappeared.[42] Sometime in this onerous process, the local guides abandoned the expedition. Dorsey concluded that they had decided that "we were too weak" to have a chance against the Arab fighters and their allies, even with the guns.[43]

Signs of the former Arab presence confronted them along the way, but so far, they had met no actual Arab fighters. They had, however, come across a horrifying line of sixteen severed heads, reportedly placed across the road as a warning by a local chief allied with the traders. Dorsey was taken by this chief's "extraordinary" name, Equansala-montea.[44] Finally, on the 29th of March, they reached an enormous swamp that halted their forward progress. Forward scouts reported that a large force of Arabs had camped on the other side of a river and were beginning to move their equipment by boat. Chaltin ordered Dorsey to move the cannons to a point where a shot could be fired into the camp. Other commanders positioned their troops to fire on the boats as they crossed the river.

Dorsey ordered the gunners to shoot one shell into the center of the camp. A cacophony erupted—drums, horns, men yelling orders, women screaming, and children crying—as the Arabs spotted the Belgian troops. The residents of the camp fled while the Arab soldiers tried to buy them time by firing their muskets as well as shrapnel composed of trade goods: beads and pieces of brass rods. Chaltin's troops continued firing until no one fired back. Dorsey and a few men swam across to take stock. They found the bushes covered in blood, but "we could not find an Arab, dead or alive," Dorsey reported. He thought the bodies must have been removed, "which is the custom of these people, if circumstances permit."[45]

Descriptions of the Battle of Riba Riba, as this skirmish came to be known, appeared in official reports, newspaper accounts, and eventually the history books. The company had not yet reached the actual town of Riba Riba, which had already been abandoned, but they had nothing else to call this fight. There was no name on European maps for the river crossing where an employee of the US government supervised the lobbing of shells into a camp of refugees while mercenary African soldiers fired their Italian rifles into a defensive fuselage of musket balls and trade goods, including the ubiquitous beads, turning a stash of Congolese wealth into ammunition. For Belgian readers of the newspaper *L'Étoile*, Chaltin described the battle as a "grand success for the State." He declared, "We have proved ourselves *the masters* [italics in original] and that the Arabs, like the natives, must submit themselves to our laws when we want them to." Chaltin also offered a special "homage" to Monsieur Mohun, "who I put in charge of the artillery." The American consul "was for me a very special auxiliary. His conduct under fire was irreproachable."[46] For the first time, but not the last, Dorsey's name appeared in the Belgian newspapers in service to the State. The calm bravery captured by "irreproachable" must have given Dorsey a sense of satisfaction when he saw it in print.

❋

The return trip to Bena Kamba became a death march for Chaltin's forces. The number of smallpox cases had exploded into a full-blown epidemic. When only a few men had been sick, the healthy could carry them. Now, men had to be left where they fell. Marching through the long grass, Dorsey stumbled over corpses abandoned a few days previously on the way to Riba Riba. They had bloated and decayed in the intense heat. "The stench from the dead," he reported, "was overpowering." It must have taken enormous self-discipline to stumble onward through nausea and disappointment as the miasmas of the charnel house overwhelmed the momentary thrill of victory. When they finally arrived in Bena Kamba, 104 soldiers had died in three weeks out of a total of 505. The casualties of enemy fire could be counted on one hand. The rest had succumbed to disease.[47]

Chaltin decided the expedition should return to Basoko to unload the sick, disinfect the steamer, and take on 250 fresh soldiers as well as sixty thousand rounds of ammunition and seventy rounds for the artillery. A few days later, early in the morning, the *Ville de Bruxelles* chugged through a gray dawn mist toward the landing at Stanley Falls. More bad news awaited there. Rachid had seized the moment to trap Tobback and others allied with the State inside a fortified compound. The Arab forces fired heavily on the steamer but seemed unable to hit anything consequential. As soon as the vessel was made fast, Dorsey ordered the gunners to begin dropping shells on the factory where he had first met Rachid two months earlier. As State troops swarmed the fleeing Arabs, Dorsey turned his guns on Rachid's house. Rachid and several men Dorsey described as "Arab chiefs" fled out the back, escaping in a large canoe. Soon large numbers of Arab-allied soldiers began surrendering.[48]

Rachid had been so confident of his success, he had made no provisions for removing the contents of the house. Everything was as before—the carpets on the floor, the clocks and mirrors on the walls, and a huge stash of ivory, guns and ammunition, and cloth goods, including "blankets, burnooses, and long white shirts without number." Chaltin kept the guns and ivory for the State but let his soldiers have most of the textiles as a reward.[49] He and Tobback helped themselves to some elegant Arab knives and scimitars as well as one of Rachid's robes. They became a tiny part of the vast colonial booty flowing out of Africa and into European and American collections.[50]

The following afternoon, Tobback received a message that "many slaves, soldiers, women etc. belonging to the Arabs, desired to give themselves up." Over the next two days, nearly two thousand people identified themselves to the State and handed over their weapons. In his report to Washington, Dorsey offered a businesslike assessment that these surrenders amounted to a significant loss in resources for the Arabs. But the scenes also must have given him a shiver of recognition, echoing stories about formerly enslaved Americans tearfully reunited with friends and family in the aftermath of the Civil War. "I witnessed many extraordinary scenes," he wrote. "A great many of the soldiers found fathers, mothers, brothers or sisters amongst the slaves.... Some of the meetings and recognitions were really affecting." Many of the freed men offered to join the fight against the Arabs, the Belgian officers told him.[51]

Dorsey's true thoughts on the events he witnessed—and participated in—remain difficult to ascertain. How much of his interpretation of these reunions reflected what he *expected* to see or even what he thought his supervisor wanted to know? Like many travelers, he drew analogies to his own culture and experience. Much of what he learned came filtered through interpreters and the explanations of the Belgians. On the other hand, he was never a truly naive observer. Most probably, the joy of reunion was real for many of the people he witnessed. Moreover, no one—not even the officers of State—could know the larger implication of these victories. For Dorsey, some larger meaning had to exist—if only to compensate for the hardship of months of hard travel and the horror of stumbling through a field of rotting soldiers' bodies. He needed the sense of an injustice righted to accept the larger story.

One more battle awaited in a large Arab town called Romi, downstream from Stanley Falls. This battle received no notice in his diary, but when he wrote about it later he included a claim common to explorers' accounts but disputed by historians: that Africans practiced ritual cannibalism.[52] As he told it, the Arabs sustained such heavy losses that they were unable to retrieve the fallen as they had at Riba Riba. In the aftermath, "the natives who swarmed like vultures over the whole place, began cutting up bodies to eat." Chaltin gave orders that anyone with human flesh in his possession would be shot. "I saw several natives carrying arms and legs down to the beach, but a bullet soon put an end to these proceedings." Dorsey asked why the African troops would carry on such a practice. "They do not eat flesh on account of a liking for it, but as the Arabs were their enemies, they gain all the strength possessed by them when they eat the meat," he was told.[53]

Once more, the State's forces piled onto two steamers and headed back to Stanley Falls, where the Europeans congratulated themselves on routing the Arab forces. Inspector General Fivé issued an Ordre du Jour to be published. Dorsey translated his purple prose:

> To the officers and soldiers at the Falls. The Victories which you have gained bring to a glorious end a long and hard-working period, during which our efforts have been unable to suppress the crimes and acts of brigandage of our enemies the Arabs. Tired of being called upon to obey the laws of humanity they revolted and attacked us. Everywhere they have been vanquished.

Dorsey was among the seven Europeans singled out for recognition for "exceptional bravery and devotion."[54] Everyone at home would have reason to be proud. For the first time in his life, he had a plausible claim to be part of the family's tradition of abolitionists, heroes, and statesmen.

Dorsey made plans to continue his survey of the Congo's resources. He also planned to visit an old acquaintance from Nicaragua, an American named W. C. Unckles, who was managing four rubber-collection stations in the southernmost area of the State. The ninety-day journey upriver involved a seemingly relentless series of mechanical failures and accidents. Part of the trip involved the *Florida*—the same steam launch that had carried Stanley on his last trip to the Congo and had helped make Joseph Conrad miserable in his brief sojourn as a riverboat captain.[55] Dorsey now had enough experience to take over for the captain when he fell ill with dysentery for several days. "Navigation difficult. Many sand banks and an incredible number of snags," he grumbled.[56] Two days later he lost control of the boat, slamming into the bank, and causing the boat to spin around completely. At that point, the captain roused himself from his sick bed and took over.[57]

Even more difficult to manage than the *Florida* was the steam launch *Rhone*, which picked up Dorsey and his party after the *Florida* turned back. The *Rhone* was woefully underpowered for battling the swift current. In a moment of frustration, the boat's engineer declared, "She is a sewing machine and not a steamer." Soon after, the engine gave out, requiring a day of repairs.[58] Dorsey took the opportunity to shoot a few more animals. The pattern of progress and delay continued, day after day, until they finally struggled into the entrance of the Sankuru River and soon thereafter tied up near the SAB factory run by Unckles.[59]

Dorsey's observations suggest that in 1893, it was already apparent that rubber operations sanctioned by the State were unsustainable. Before he even landed in Matadi, Dorsey knew that the State was struggling to recruit labor to collect rubber. "At my suggestion," Dorsey claimed, Unckles had brought ten Nicaraguan rubber cutters to the heart of the Congo. There he aimed to introduce what Dorsey described as the "American way" of rubber tapping—bleeding the vines without killing them. Unfortunately, he did not describe the cultural interactions between these Central American men, so far from home, and the Africans they were supposed to tutor.[60]

Dorsey liked what he saw. Unckles's operation had proved very successful in increasing the production of rubber.[61] Dorsey also thought rubber production offered a real economic opportunity for local people, unconnected with the complications of the ivory trade, among them slaving and domination by Bangela middlemen and Omani Arabs. Unckles, he reported, offered a "fair price" for the raw rubber. Consequently, tribal leaders were eager to trade and had set their wives and slaves to the task of "filling calabashes with milk [rubber sap]."[62] Unckles had also made a "friend for life" and an ally of a chieftain by showering him with gifts of cowries, cloth, trade beads, and brass wire. In return, the chief had promised that no one would harm "a hair on the head" of Unckles or of his Nicaraguan employees.[63]

The trip up the Sankuru also introduced Dorsey to another American who was taking advantage of the Congo's economic opportunities. Near a place he called Ikango, an "American negro," originally an immigrant to Nigeria, had created a successful coffee plantation—confirmation of his McKenney grandfather's vision of American Blacks successfully returning to Africa.[64] Dorsey did not bother to record his name, however.

In mid-November, Dorsey had reached the larger town of Lusambo. Another steamer arrived with the startling news that the Arabs were not defeated. Yet another leader, Rumaliza, had amassed a force of twenty thousand men "fully armed" and determined to recapture the former Arab territories of the Eastern Congo, known as the Maniema. Francis Dhanis, the State's military commander in charge of the area, had issued a desperate call for reinforcements. "The case being an extreme one I did not hesitate one moment what course I should pursue," Dorsey wrote. He committed himself and a small group of soldiers to the service of the State. They would head east, overland to the Lomami River and onward.[65] He dutifully wrote out a description of the situation and his own actions on the form provided by the US State Department for consular dispatches and sent it out with the mail on one of the Congo Free State steamers. No mail from the United States had reached him for months. The lack of communication with Harry and his mother must have distressed him, but the lack of directives from the State Department freed him to decide his own course of action. No one told him he couldn't join Dhanis, so that was what he decided to do.

THE MESSY BUSINESS
OF HERO MAKING

An impulse to help the State's cause and a taste for battle weren't the only or even the most important reasons why Dorsey abandoned his consular duties and headed for Lomami. He wanted to meet Francis Dhanis. Although Gaspard Fivé officially governed the Congo on behalf of Leopold, Dorsey grasped that in the fall of 1893, history lay in the hands of the impulsive and utterly confident officer who had issued the call for reinforcements.

Dhanis was crucial to the State's campaign against Arab control of the central Congo. Indeed, his decision to cross the Lomami River into Arab territory in the fall of 1892 set the conflict in motion. He had done so in defiance of his superiors, who believed that State troops could not win. Having interacted with Arab leaders and seen their troops at close quarters, Dhanis knew the Arab forces were poorly equipped with outmoded weapons—no match for Krupp field guns and Albini rifles. Son of a Belgian father and an Irish mother and raised between two cultures, Dhanis also exemplified the kind of liminal person who could be extremely effective in the mixed cultural space of the Congo. He repeatedly deployed his personal charm and formidable linguistic skills to make alliances with local chiefs and some Arab leaders.[1]

For Dhanis, his fellow Belgian officers, and other Europeans and Americans (including Dorsey) who had traveled to Central Africa to seek their fortunes, the Congo was a place where bold, unconventional decisions might reap enormous rewards. The opportunity to become wealthy drew many of these seekers forward. But Africa also offered—at least in theory—the opportunity for anonymous men from middling social backgrounds to elevate themselves in ways they never could have done back home. It gave them the chance to become heroes or celebrities—in part because European and American cultures found the idea of Africa exotic and fascinating and worshipped soldiers and explorers as quintessential heroic figures.[2]

But this celebrity making also took place by deliberate design. Leopold excelled at recruiting and motivating the kind of men he needed. He and they understood what might today be called public relations; specifically, they understood, as one historian put it, that "the courageous man becomes a hero only when he is declared to be one."[3] The extraordinary publicity around Stanley and his expeditions served as recruiting literature for the State. Leopold also liberally bestowed public rewards and honors on those who successfully served his ends. He made Dhanis a baron even before what became known as the "Arab Campaign" ended.[4]

Men with experience in the Congo could also make themselves and their compatriots into heroes by writing articles and memoirs for the popular press or becoming a subject for professional reporters.[5] A significant market existed for such publications. In the style of the day, these literary efforts often involved a complicated amalgamation of genuine admiration, promotion, and moral instruction that lifted up military leaders, missionaries, and explorers as exemplars.[6] Dorsey already knew how some of this worked. Before leaving for Africa, he had already made a deal with the *New York Herald*, the leading newspaper for heroic journalism, to do some reporting. He'd already sent one press release about his adventures. He may also have been aware that Chaltin was planning to write about the Riba Riba expedition for the Belgian press. Now he was drawn toward Dhanis and the opportunity to learn about heroism firsthand from the personification of the imperial soldier-hero. Perhaps he also hoped to find heroic opportunities for himself. Not surprisingly, the entire effort would turn out to be a messy business.

Dorsey was not the kind of person to express regret either privately or publicly, but there's no question that the march east from Lusambo was both miserable and regrettable. Some of that misery lay out of his control. Swarms of small yellow bees plagued the caravan, crawling over everyone and everything for nearly seven days.[7] But other problems were of his own making. He had hastily rounded up a group of porters who quickly proved to be unwilling participants—either that or they hadn't understood what they were getting themselves into. Early on, these porters began abandoning the caravan, taking some of the chop boxes, which stored the food, with them. Some of Dorsey's own supplies disappeared, including a bottle of arsenic. "I sincerely hope these two thieves ate it along with the rest," he fumed.[8]

Then rumor reached Dorsey that some of the Force Publique soldiers intended to desert when they neared their home villages. Dorsey grew irate. He gathered the Africans together and gave them a speech about how they should be grateful for the opportunity to join Dhanis's efforts to throw off the yoke of their Arab oppressors. He reminded them that they were also being paid for their services, and he delivered an ultimatum: disappearing with chop boxes constituted theft. And theft was punishable by death.

He let the company know that he had empowered a group of soldiers to shoot deserters. Two hours later, rifle shots rang out. A sentry had shot dead two porters who had decided to make a run for it.[9] "I regretted this very much," Dorsey wrote, "but I felt I must teach these people a lesson."

What happened next showed how much he had internalized the peculiar logic of the State. Even more remarkably, he felt no compunction to hide or apologize for his actions. Dorsey cut off the right hands of the two dead porters and ordered a Sergeant Pirotte to "mount these hands on a spear in the center where every man could see them."[10] And he didn't stop there. Two days later, he learned that three men had been discovered stealing rifle cartridges. This time, the offenders were held flat on the ground while a corporal administered one hundred lashes with a "chicotte," a long whip made from sun-dried hippo hide that could inflict significant injury, thanks to its intricately braided, razor-sharp edges. Dorsey followed the whipping with another speech about how the State's rules permitted punishment by death for any soldier who sold his arms or ammunition.[11]

Finally, his destination came in sight. Dorsey sent the porters ahead into the town of Kasongo, happy to be rid of them. The ruined city spread out across a flat, treeless plain, filled with impressive brick and adobe buildings, luxurious gardens of palms and fruit trees, and white-washed walls bright in the tropical sun. Kasongo was a testament to Arab aspirations to permanence in Central Africa and had once served as the stronghold of Tippu Tip and the largest ivory depot in Africa. At its peak, Dorsey was told, the population numbered forty thousand.[12] But the Belgian artillery and tropical climate had taken their toll. Most of the houses now stood in a "dilapidated condition, but what remain show how splendidly they were constructed," Dorsey observed. He found his way to Dhanis's headquarters, where Dr. Sidney Hinde, an English doctor working for the State, greeted him.[13] Hinde was prob-ably the first native speaker of English Dorsey had interacted with in months. More than one hundred years later, his sense of relief in receiv-ing Hinde's "hearty welcome" is still palpable in his account.[14]

The American consul's first encounter with Dhanis did not last long, as Hinde had diagnosed the commander with "fever and rheumatism." Even so, he made a marked impression on Dorsey. Dhanis was almost his same age but had spent nearly a full decade in the Congo, bootstrap-ping himself from junior officer to the State's most influential military leader.[15] Unlike Dorsey, who had ended up in the Congo as a result of accident, patronage, and expedience, Dhanis had dreamed since childhood of being an African explorer in the mold of Henry Morton Stanley. Dhanis had immersed himself in books about European adven-turers, real and fictional, during an unhappy stint in a Catholic boarding school.[16]

Like the ill-fated Hodister, Dhanis had a gift for languages. In ad-dition to complete fluency in French and English, he had mastered Swahili well enough to form strong alliances with regional Arab and African leaders. Emile Leméry, who served under Dhanis, declared his ability to speak various tongues "as if they were his own" a key part of his successes.[17] Dhanis had a reputation among Europeans in the Congo for effectively earning the loyalty and respect of tribal leaders through his linguistic skills, his nuanced understanding of cultural differences among tribal groups, and his practical innovations, such as allowing

wives on long marches, a change that seemed to prevent mutiny, desertion, and intertribal conflict.[18] Unfortunately, surviving written records
don't record what *Africans* made of the Belgian Irish commander, but he
was clearly more nimble and adept than most Belgian officers.

Dorsey was surprised to discover that this towering figure was, at
five foot eight, nearly a head shorter than he was. In all other ways,
however, Dhanis measured up to expectations; he was charming, intelligent, competent, and very, very determined. Dorsey felt a strong
sense of kinship with Dhanis. The commandant, he wrote, favored his
Irish mother. He also liked the fact that Dhanis spoke English without a
French accent, slipping easily into the clubby slang of their generation's
British adventurers.[19] At the end of their first meeting, Dhanis thanked
Dorsey in the "warmest manner" for responding to his call for reinforcements. Dorsey felt thoroughly gratified. This was the place to be.[20]

With Dhanis gathering reinforcements and supplies in preparation
for engaging Rumaliza, Dorsey found himself with no responsibilities
and time to spare. Dhanis's troops would not be leaving for the "front"
for a few days. For the first time in many months, Dorsey shook off
the tension and anxiety.[21] The looming specter of violence and death
seemed to recede, and physical and psychological discomfort gave
way to a sense of being at home. Watching the sun set over the rolling
countryside, he fell into a rare reverie. "The scene is one of surpassing
loveliness," he wrote. "How wrong an idea of Africa we have gotten
from recent books of travel, which only go into the desert side of life
out here, and never seem able to break away from the fallacy that the
sun never shines, or that scenes of homely peaceful farm life can never
be met with."[22]

It didn't hurt that he was in the lap of luxury. The Arabs had abandoned the city in haste, leaving behind all their household goods. Hinde
later remembered that "even the common soldiers slept on silk and
satin mattresses, in carved beds with silk mosquito curtain." European
goods, "the use of which we had almost forgotten," abounded: candles,
sugar, matches, silver and glass goblets. The former residents had also
left behind ample food stocks, including rice, coffee, and corn as well
as "European luxuries" such as raisins and sardines. The orchards and
gardens yielded oranges, pineapples, and bananas, among other fruits.[23]

For men like Dorsey and Hinde who had been sleeping on camp beds and eating out of cans, their temporary residence must have seemed extraordinary.

Dhanis had taken over the house of a man named Moussanghela, who had been the architect for the monumental buildings in Kasongo and another nearby town, Nyangwe. Dorsey described the building as "enormous"—one hundred feet long, twenty-five feet high, encompassing fourteen rooms and a central courtyard lush with trees and flowers. He admired the mahogany doors and window frames lavishly carved with inscriptions from the Koran.[24] Best of all, the house had two earth closets (toilets) and a bathroom. "The tank containing water for the bath is a large canoe, swung on a turnstile," he recorded. To take a bath, he only needed to pull the plug and stand under the gushing water. He set "the boys," including Philip, to filling the reservoir so that he could bathe to his heart's content, washing away the grime and the sweat of the march and the stench of the sick and fallen.[25]

Once again, the evidence all around him pointed to Arab rule as both a benefit and a curse for the local population. He admired the extensive farms and bustling marketplace; he also decried the coerced labor that enabled Arab merchants to live in such luxury. He seemed oblivious, however, to the way he and many representatives of the State had adopted some of the worst aspects of Arab rule—including forced labor and the draconian punishments of whipping and cutting off hands—without preserving any of its benefits. There is a deep, historical irony in the fact that in his most elegiac moments, Dorsey compared the African countryside to the area around Warrenton, Virginia. Virginia was, after all, built on the backs of enslaved peoples. In Dorsey's time, the state's white inhabitants seemed intent on returning African American residents to a condition as near as possible to slavery, using the law as well as social and economic coercion.[26]

The company Dorsey was keeping only reinforced these attitudes. Now back among English speakers, he could absorb a more nuanced set of rationalizations for the Belgian intervention in Africa than those starker views expressed by Delcommune or Chaltin. Sidney Hinde served as an articulate apologist for the State. Hinde had dedicated his services to Leopold after being recruited by a physician friend, Thomas

Heazle Parke, who had rightly grasped that Hinde had tired of working in European hospitals and longed for a life of adventure.[27] Commissioned as a medical officer, he ended up doing a great deal more than caring for the sick and wounded. Three years after the end of the Arab Campaign, he would publish a book titled *The Fall of the Congo Arabs*, which portrayed Dhanis not only as a military hero but also as a social reformer seeking to civilize the Congolese and eradicate distasteful cultural practices. Hinde was particularly obsessed with ritual cannibalism, which he thought he detected everywhere.[28] It is more difficult to figure out what Dorsey absorbed from Dhanis, other than that he began to pay more attention to tribal differences among the men under his command.[29]

Three days before Christmas, Dorsey joined Dhanis, Hinde, and two hundred fresh soldiers for the short march to Bena Mussa, where the State's forces were being marshaled. The enthusiasm and discipline of the Force Publique soldiers particularly impressed the American. Someone told him that many of the men had been "Arab slaves" and had "voluntarily offered their services to Dhanis."[30] Their destination was spectacular: a camp positioned partway up a dramatic mountain range, with peaks and spires of rock stained dark with iron ore. Blacksmiths traveled to the mountain from hundreds of miles away to gather material they could shape into metal tools and implements, including perhaps the iron nails that studded the fetish figures Dorsey had seen brandished up and down the Congo and its tributary rivers.[31]

And what of the enemy? Rumaliza, he learned, had entrenched his forces at Kalambare, inside a series of enormous "bomas"—fortified enclosures, made of tree trunks and thorny branches nearly ten feet high, equipped with trenches and additional fortifications in anticipation of artillery fire. He had established supply lines to the rear that the State's forces could not easily disrupt. It was going to be a hard fight. Dhanis declared that they would set out on Christmas Eve.[32]

As he waited, Dorsey continued to revel in the creature comforts of the way Dhanis ran things. "My tent is up, a grass covered house at the bank to snooze in during the heat of the day," he wrote. He ordered his servants to prepare a tub "into which I am bundled by my boys." After a long soak, he donned a comfortable linen gown confiscated from the Arabs and settled into a canvas chair to enjoy a pack of cigarettes provided by one of Dhanis's subcommanders. "How I did enjoy that smoke, after two months deprivation of tobacco," he remembered.[33]

On Christmas Eve, the States' forces set up camp very close to Rumaliza's forts.[34] Both sides sent spies to gather information about the other's battle preparations. The Belgians had already begun firing artillery shells into the boma, to no apparent effect. Dorsey estimated that his camp was only six hundred feet from the largest enclosure. On Christmas night, the Europeans decided to sing in celebration of a holiday that otherwise seemed part of a world very far away. Rumaliza was not entertained. He sent a message to Dhanis presenting his "compliments" and requesting quiet because he wanted to get a good night's sleep before recommencing the fight. "Our answer to this was a shell from the cannon and a continuation of the hilarity," Dorsey wrote. Christmas dinner consisted of goat, manioc, and sweet potatoes.[35]

Fighting over the next few days did not go well for Dhanis's troops. Rumaliza more than held his own. Worse yet, Chaltin, still at Stanley Falls, had flatly refused to share either troops or supplies with Dhanis.[36] As Dorsey told it, Dhanis lamented that he had no one to send as his envoy to the garrison at Basoko and plead for assistance. The American consul saw his chance to display a bit of heroism. He volunteered to go, prompting a compliment in Dhanis's best British slang: Dorsey was "a brick."[37] "When can you go?" he asked. "Immediately," Dorsey replied. Or almost immediately.

On New Year's Day, Dorsey headed downriver once again. This time, he had brought some extra reading: the journals of a deceased German adventurer known as Emin Pasha. He had borrowed the journals from Dhanis, who had discovered them, along with some of the Pasha's other belongings, mysteriously abandoned in Kasongo.[38]

Why was Dorsey interested? He wanted to write an article about the Pasha that would appeal to publishers back home. In 1894 the name Emin Pasha would have rung a bell among Europeans and Americans who followed news about Central Africa.[39] Emin had become an unlikely hero of

European colonialism in Africa. Born in Silesia (now part of Poland) in 1840, he was named Isaak Eduard Schnitzer by his Jewish parents—the first of many names he would carry, each connecting him with different religions, cultures, and political regimes as well as the British, Ottoman, and Austro-Hungarian empires. At age six he was baptized Eduard Carl Oscar Theodor Schnitzer at the request of his Protestant stepfather. Like Hinde, he had trained as a physician, but he skipped his state licensing exam in favor of a peripatetic life of adventure, leveraging a gift for languages, a polymath's ability to absorb information, and reputedly a great deal of sophistication and charm. A winding path took him into the Ottoman Empire, where he adopted yet another name, Hairoullah Effendi. Dodging a burdensome relationship with his Turkish employer's widow, he resurfaced in Egypt in 1875, now bearing the moniker Mehemet Emin. In 1879 the British general Charles Gordon recruited this Jewish man who had renamed himself after the Prophet of Islam to govern part of the southern Sudan, then called Equatoria, on behalf of the Khedive of Egypt, bestowing on him the Ottoman title of Pasha.[40]

Gordon played a key role in Britain's shadow governance of Egypt. Unfortunately for him and Emin, British and Egyptian policies in the Sudan fueled a religious and political uprising led by a group known as the Mahdists. Gordon famously succumbed while trying to hold the city of Khartoum, becoming a martyr to British imperialism.[41] Emin Pasha fled south to the edge of the Congo watershed. European newspapers publicized the fact that Emin was stranded between the Mahdists and a vast tropical forest unexplored by Europeans. In response, and with the help of Tippu Tip, Henry Morton Stanley organized what became called the Emin Pasha Relief Expedition, a largely disastrous effort of which Hinde had been a part. Thanks to poor planning, bad luck, and even worse decision-making, hundreds of recruits died of disease or starvation. Stanley did eventually reach Emin, but the Pasha proved unwilling to abandon his position. Stanley struggled back to Europe, leaving him behind. Soon thereafter, Emin was murdered under mysterious circumstances. As far as the newspapers were concerned, this story was all about European heroism and Arab treachery.[42] Stanley blamed Tippu Tip for his failure, going so far as eventually to sue him. He also declared himself to be a hero.[43]

The Pasha's story quickly became entangled not only with two of the most mythic and powerful figures in the Congo, Stanley and Tip, but also with individuals in Dorsey's more immediate orbit. In particular the American had either recruited or been assigned the services of Omari bo Amisi, a Zanzibari soldier. Omari was a survivor of the Emin Pasha Expedition, a testament to his toughness and his good luck.[44] He and Dorsey formed a strong working relationship. Omari had stories to tell about the expedition, ones that potentially gave Dorsey an original angle that newspaper or magazine editors might be interested in publishing.

Even with these firsthand accounts, however, Dorsey did not immediately find the story for which he was looking. Omari seems to have waited to tell Dorsey what he knew, and the Pasha's journals had yielded nothing of value to the frustrated American. Written in tiny, spidery script that required a magnifying glass to decipher, the diary included German and English entries as well as a few passages in Italian, French, Arabic, and Turkish. Dorsey declared them "most uninteresting reading," perhaps because he couldn't understand most of them.[45] He temporarily abandoned the idea of writing an article.

Eighteen days after bidding Dhanis adieu, the American consul arrived at Basoko. He had begun expressing his dual loyalties to the United States and the Congo Free State in a particularly conspicuous way: flying the American stars and stripes on one side of the launch and the State's flag with its single star on the other.[46] He viewed this dual display as a kind of personal emblem and was surprised when no one knew who he was when he stepped ashore.[47] No matter. They would soon enough.

The commandant, a man named Freytag, was suitably welcoming once his visitor's connections to Dhanis had been established, inviting Dorsey to discuss what needed to be done over a milky glass of absinthe in his private quarters. As Dorsey told it, supplies and men were provided without further questions. Apparently the Belgian commanders at Basoko imagined the Arab threat upstream as far more pervasive and dangerous than Dorsey had actually found it. He was happy to have

Figure 5. R. Dorsey Mohun with "color bearers" holding Congo Free State and United States flags. The seated man on the right is Omari bo Amisi (R. Dorsey Mohun, "The Death of Emin Pasha," *Century* 49, no. 4 [February 1895]: 593).

them think of him as astonishingly brave for having traveled from Kasongo with only a small number of troops.[48]

The return trip took 221 hours and thirty-five minutes, almost double the time needed to go downstream.[49] "There is no use reciting the events of this tedious voyage upriver," Dorsey wrote to the State Department.

Disappointingly, while he had been away, Rumaliza had recognized he could not triumph in the face of Dhanis's overwhelming firepower. The Arab leader fled his fortified boma in the middle of the night. There would be no dramatic victory for Dhanis or Dorsey.

Dhanis revealed that he had big plans for opening the Maniema to business, specifically giving the State a monopoly on the ivory trade. Dorsey found his lack of high-mindedness disturbing, especially in the aftermath of a war that supposedly had been fought to eradicate slavery and open the central Congo to free trade. "I hear nothing but talk of ivory," Dorsey wrote, "nothing about exploring and opening the country, nothing but the amount of ivory they can get out of the people."[50] Dorsey also witnessed a disturbingly paranoid and megalomaniac side to Dhanis's personality. "For a young man his head has grown too suddenly. Flushed with success he must be entirely above the ordinary men of mortals," the American confided to his diary. "Is he King here or is it in contemplation to make him Emperor of Manyema?" he wrote, conjuring up a familiar image of an imperial soldier, far from home, gone mad with power.[51] The two men had exchanged harsh words: Dhanis had accused Dorsey of being a liar and a spy because Dorsey asked to make a copy of an Emin Pasha letter in Dhanis's possession. Later in the day, they "buried the hatchet," but through the rest of their long acquaintance, Dorsey treated the mercurial Irish Belgian commander with caution.[52]

Still, he was reluctant to part ways with Dhanis altogether. He was an important man to know and had offered Dorsey a new opportunity: accompany Sidney Hinde on an expedition to find a water route from Kasongo eastward to Lake Tanganyika, a potential alternative to the tedious, overland porterage route that the Arabs had carved out to bring ivory to the east coast of Africa. Here was a genuine opportunity to map territory that was virtually unknown to Europeans. Dorsey couldn't turn the offer down. He and Hinde, accompanied by Philip, Omari, and a group of African soldiers, would follow the Lualaba River by canoe, hiring paddlers and porters as they went. If all went well, they would cross the continent completely, descending from Lake Tanganyika to the east coast. From there, Dorsey could return to Europe by boat. His three-year term of service to the United States was due to expire at the end of the year.

Dorsey prepared. He had learned at least a few important lessons from his experiences. He put in an order for smallpox vaccine to inoculate the soldiers. There was no way he was going to repeat the horrific death march after Riba Riba. The vaccine came in a hermetically sealed tube, soldered into a tin. Although Dorsey worried that it still might not be viable, he vaccinated a few of the men anyway.[53] Two weeks later, one of them showed the cowpox pustules that would give him immunity to the more dangerous infection. "That makes it all right as all the rest can be inoculated from his scabs," he noted, referencing a once-common practice.[54]

Hinde, the nominal head of the expedition, distributed rifles, cartridges, and uniforms to the African soldiers, though he had nothing good to say about them. As far as he was concerned, they were all lazy and untrustworthy.[55] Dhanis, back in his charming mode, wrote Hinde a letter in French charging him with the mission. The letter was clearly written for posterity, and Hinde took it as such, later reproducing it in his memoir.[56] A week later Dhanis sent Dorsey a much more intimate message in English thanking him for the first of many hand-drawn maps. He took care to include a few flattering lines. "You have discovered the only unknown part of the Congo and it is a very important event which must be given to the public." Miraculously, the letter found its way to Dorsey, who by then was already far upstream. He carefully kept it as a souvenir.[57]

On the morning of March 18, 1894, the expedition marched out of Kasongo. The rolling countryside on either side of the road was dense with small villages nestled in rice fields. Dorsey estimated that perhaps one hundred twenty-five thousand people made their homes within a twenty-mile radius. Struck by the region's beauty and apparent prosperity, he declared it "magnificent."[58]

Early in the afternoon, they arrived in Senga, a village on the riverbank where they planned to pick up their canoes and the Waquenia paddlers who would take them through the first set of rapids.[59] Working in a heavy downpour, they assembled a dozen canoes. Dorsey somehow ended up with the largest one. A typical example of what the Belgians called a "grande pirogue," its hull consisted of an enormous, hollowed-out tree trunk. The vessel was large enough to carry sixty paddlers, twelve soldiers, and their equipment. Dorsey stored his bed and luggage in a "house" built on the canoe (probably a tent-shaped shelter covered with thatch or leaves).[60] Philip was also part of the company. In his capacity as cook, he'd brought along several milk goats and a container of coals for making fires.[61]

The river quickly challenged the expedition's progress. Although the main tributary of the Congo River, the Lualaba presented a very different personality than the wide, placid waterway between Stanley Falls and Kinshasa. Above Kasongo, the river transformed into a series of rapids, requiring some crew members to pole the canoes while others clambered along shore using long vines to pull the vessels against the fast current. Further upstream, the expedition encountered a sea of grass, obliging the crews to walk waist-deep while towing the heavily laden canoes, whose rough hulls dragged against the waterweeds. The Lualaba was going to make the crew earn every mile they traveled.[62]

Ten days into the journey, things fell apart. The disasters started with Philip, who had developed a persistent high fever and the jaundiced eyes symptomatic of liver failure. Dorsey blamed Philip's drinking, which had begun with a binge in Kasongo. But clearly something more serious than a hangover had overcome the usually unstoppable Philip. Most likely, he was suffering from an acute attack of malaria. "I am afraid he will die," Dorsey confided to his diary. "Hinde and I are doing everything for his comfort but have no hope he will pull through."[63] A few days later, Dorsey tersely recorded, "Philip, my Sierra Leone boy, who has been with me since July 1892 died today at 2:30 while he was being carried from the boat."[64]

Dorsey couldn't figure out an appropriate way to mourn Philip either publicly or privately. His journey would not have been possible without the help of his constant and loyal traveling companion across thousands of miles. But nothing in Dorsey's worldview afforded him a way to talk about their relationship in terms of friendship let alone allowing him to call Philip a hero in the archetypal sense of courage, duty, and attending the needs to others. Nor did Dorsey possess the ability to express grief. Instead, in his diary he tallied up the back pay he owed his servant, reducing their relationship to a wage labor transaction.[65] Such was the heartlessness and emotional disassociation of white men in the heart of Congo.

Hinde was also sick. "Seedy" was how Dorsey described his symptoms.[66] Suffering from fever and diarrhea, the British doctor could not keep food down and was becoming increasingly weak. He diagnosed himself as suffering from an internal abscess. Finally, Dorsey initiated an uncomfortable conversation about returning to Basoko, where expert medical care was available.[67] Hinde was the official head of the expedition, but he acquiesced to Dorsey's suggestion. In his memoir, Hinde described himself as "delirious," declaring that he remembered little of the return trip.[68]

But in his diary, Dorsey told a remarkable and shocking story about his efforts to care for his European companion. Hinde was thirsty for milk. "Not being able to find a milk goat," Dorsey recorded, "I determined to take the milk from some of the healthy-looking young mothers in the village." He brought a bag of trade beads with him into a riverside settlement and offered a bargain. He had long since abandoned whatever Victorian anxiety he'd once harbored about bare-breasted African women. Now, he insisted on inspecting potential milk donors for infections. "It was a curious sight to see them line up in the afternoon to be milked just like a cow," he noted nonchalantly.[69] Whether he told Hinde where the milk came from remains a mystery.

A week later, the expedition reached a State military post on the Lualaba with land access to Kasongo. The crew carried Hinde off the canoe in a hammock. He declared that he was already feeling better. Dorsey followed on a donkey, taking command of the soldiers and the "loads."[70] His grand expedition was over, with little to show for it. But he had survived—unlike poor Philip, buried in an anonymous, shoreside grave thousands of miles from home.

Back at Dhanis's headquarters in Kasongo, a flurry of activity was underway. One by one, the major Arab leaders arrived with their caravans to surrender. Apparently, Dhanis had offered at least some of them a kind of amnesty. Local State officials and perhaps Leopold and his advisors in Belgium had realized that eradicating the Arab presence in the central Congo was a pipe dream. Tens of thousands of Arabs as well as the descendants of relationships between Arabs and Africans lived in the region (as they do today). Practicalities aside, Dhanis and others also viewed at least some of the Arab leaders as worthy adversaries, courageous and honorable in their own way. Nearly every European Dorsey encountered seemed to believe that the Arabs had had a civilizing effect on the Indigenous population. It would not be too much to say that a kind of mutual admiration and respect colored the interactions between the Arab leaders and their captors.

A few days after Dorsey's arrival, Commander Lothaire arrived, accompanied by Rachid and a large group of other Arabs. Dorsey gloated a little. "Rachid had on a dirty tweed coat, a miserable waist cinch and filthy fez . . . not like his magnificent appearance at Stanley Falls, when he wore beautiful silks and linens, and took pride in the large diamond on his little finger." The Arab recognized Dorsey immediately and extended his hand. Dorsey ignored it. Later, Rachid sent an interpreter to ask why Dorsey had treated him "coldly." Dorsey was still stinging from the dressing down Rachid had given him in Stanley Falls about joining Chaltin's campaign. Eventually, Rachid appeared to apologize; in return, Dorsey gave him some trade goods. There was nothing to gain by holding a grudge.[71] The Congo had long been a place of complicated alliances. The State's war to end Arab control proved no different in this respect. Many Arab leaders who had come to Kasongo seemed to be treated more as guests than prisoners. Dhanis also planned to take some of his Arab friends and allies back to Belgium with him.[72]

A coda to the story of hero making in the Arab Campaign remained. Conversations had swirled in Dhanis's camp about identifying the murderers of several prominent Europeans, including Hodister and Emin Pasha, who had come to be seen as martyrs. Now, the victors savored the possibility of revenge—if they could identify the perpetrators. Dorsey went so far as to declare "we will catch them all" in his diary, with "we" testifying to his identification with the Belgians.[73]

Did they find the alleged killers? Early in May, an Arab named Said ben Abedi surrendered and was delivered to Kasongo. For months,

Dorsey had heard Abedi's name mentioned in connection with Emin Pasha's death.[74] Was Abedi Emin's murderer? Dorsey hoped not. He liked the look of the man whom he described as "young" and "inoffensive looking." Abedi claimed innocence but fingered two men from his company. In the meantime, Dorsey's sergeant, Omari, stepped forward with intelligence of his own: two more participants had been lurking under the Europeans' noses, working as soldiers in the State's forces at Nyangwe. Even though Omari had not participated in Abedi and Emin Pasha's caravan, his connection to the Emin Pasha Relief Expedition seems to have given him authority on the subject. The suspects, Mamba and Ismailia, were brought to Kasongo. Suddenly, Dorsey had an original angle on the Emin Pasha story that he could sell as an article to the popular press. He also had the opportunity to write himself into the story. He lobbied Commander Lothaire, who oversaw the prisoners, for permission to interrogate them with the Omari's help. Lothaire said yes.

The next morning, Dorsey and Omari sat down with the prisoners in the guardhouse attached to the mansion occupied by Dhanis. Through Omari, Dorsey spent most of the day questioning the men. He learned that after Emin Pasha refused to return to Europe with Stanley, Abedi offered to include Emin in his caravan, which aimed to transport ivory and slaves south into the Congo watershed. Mamba and Ismailia had indeed been part of that caravan, for Abedi had enslaved them both. But in a manner typical of Omani Arab slaveholding, the two men retained the power to act independently and to control other Arabs and Africans. Ismailia, in particular, held a great deal of authority. He told Dorsey that he had led multiple slave-gathering expeditions at Abedi's behest and had supervised Emin's porters.[75] Abedi left Emin in a small town named Kinema while he went to seek permission to pass through the territory. In his absence, a group of men, including the suspects, slit Emin's throat. They claimed to be acting under threat from a local Arab leader named Kibonge. To prove they'd done the deed, they sent Kibonge a trophy: Emin's head in a box.[76]

Now here was a story Dorsey could sell to the press. He put these accounts together with information he had gathered from other sources, including Emin's own possessions, into an article he titled "The Death of Emin Pasha." The prestigious American magazine the *Century* published it in February 1895.[77] The facts that Dorsey shared with his readers were largely accurate, as far as he knew, but he crafted the story to cater to his readers' expectations. He framed the interrogation as a detective story in which he played lead investigator, identifying suspects, discerning a motive, and eliciting a confession. In addition he described the killing as racially motivated. He remarked on the Arab leaders' "hate towards all whites," an attitude engendered, in part, by the killing of Arabs and forcible seizure of ivory during earlier expeditions. And although he declared his belief that Abedi was not involved in the Pasha's death, he did not share the crucial information provided by his informants that Abedi and Emin had been very good friends (although he wrote this tidbit down in his diary).[78] To heighten the drama and carve out a footnote for himself in history, he wrote an extended description of the questioning process, which reads like an interrogation from a mystery novel. Dorsey asked the two men:

> "Did you not see Emin Pasha killed?"
> "We did not."
> I said "You lie! We have two men here at Kasongo who say you and Mamba were two of the murderers."

He then separated the suspects, telling Omari to take Mamba away. Dorsey explained his strategy to his readers. "I followed Omari and told him to come to me in half an hour and say that Mamba had confessed that he and Ismailia had a hand in the killing." This ruse resulted in a full confession from both men. The story ends with both men learning that Dorsey had no power to dispense justice himself. Instead, the two men would be turned back over to Lothaire to await a decision about whether they would be executed.[79]

Dorsey's report to the State Department suggests a different and less sensational sequence of events. He spoke with several Arabs in Kasongo about the motive. They told him that the killing was probably a "stupid error" on the part of Kibonge, who was trying to compete for status with Muni-Mohare, the Arab leader who had been credited with ordering the killing of Hodister.[80] In this interpretation, Emin Pasha's death amounted to a minor incident of collateral damage resulting from the broader struggles between various Arab leaders.

Because the deaths of Emin Pasha and Hodister had received extensive publicity in European and American newspapers—which portrayed the two men as martyrs to the cause of civilization, empire, and the State's antislavery campaign—the State went to a great deal of trouble rounding up the perpetrators and dispensing what superficially resembled European-style justice. Mamba and Ismailia were put on a boat and taken down to the State's temporary headquarters at Kibongo. There they stood trial along with two minor chiefs who had been identified as responsible for Hodister's death. All received the penalty of death by hanging.[81]

Dorsey's official report sits alongside yet another version of the story—this one focused on the State's methods—that appeared in his diary. On the same morning that Dorsey and Omari questioned the suspects, another drama played out in Commander Lothaire's camp. Lothaire was trying to solicit volunteers from the Force Publique soldiers for a march to Lake Tanganyika. The soldiers he approached showed little inclination to join him. In response Lothaire summoned four sentries, who grabbed one of the men and shot him dead for refusing orders. The other reluctant soldiers quickly said they were ready to leave immediately. "It is in this fashion a handful of white men are enabled to keep up discipline and govern this huge country," Dorsey concluded.[82] He had taken another step in internalizing the logic of violence and coercion that governed the activities of the State's representatives in the Congo.

Dorsey's time in the Congo was coming to a close. His three-year term as commercial agent was almost up. He was hopeful that Harriet would now accept his proposal of marriage, since he had not only survived the Congo but had covered himself in glory. But before he returned to the United States, he had a happy bit of business to which he attended. Leopold had invited him to Brussels to be made a Chevalier of the Ordre Royal du Lion in recognition of his service to the Congo Free State.

The other heroes of the Arab Campaign were also heading home. For the return voyage to Brussels, Dhanis had commandeered the entire second-class section of the *Köningin Wilhelmina* for a party that included the retinues of Saïd Ben Abedi, now cleared of any responsibility for Emin Pasha's death, and Piana Senga, another regional leader and State ally.[83] Onboard, as well, were several children whom Dhanis had chosen to be educated at State expense and returned to the Congo to help manage the colony.[84]

By the time the veterans of the Arab Campaign stepped onto the docks in Antwerp, Leopold's publicity machine was ready and waiting. The press wanted to hear their stories. In a bit of vanity, both Dhanis and Chaltin were growing long, extravagant mustaches in anticipation of being photographed.[85] Champagne was chilled and receptions planned. Dorsey happily joined his Belgian compatriots as together they prepared to receive a hero's welcome.

✳ 6 ✳

A HERO'S WELCOME

Many people eagerly awaited Dorsey's return from Africa. But perhaps no one wanted to see the returning traveler more than Harriet. After taking care of business in Brussels, Dorsey hurried to Paris. Harriet had been living there with her older sister, Anna Rebecca, who was married to an expatriate American businessman.[1] The reunion must have been a happy one. Their brief shipboard romance sealed with moonlight promises in Italy had survived more than two years of separation. Letters and photographs miraculously delivered after long journeys in porters' packs, river boats, and ocean liners had kept the relationship alive.[2] It didn't hurt that Harriet's bet on a relative stranger's chances for making a success of himself in Africa had now been publicly validated by one of the crowned heads of Europe and confirmed by a raft of celebratory newspaper articles.

It is impossible to know much about what he said to Harriet in that Paris visit (or what she said in return), but one fact is clear: they agreed to join their lives together. A date was set, November 22, only a few months hence. The wedding would be at St. George's Episcopal Church in New York. The lovers parted after their Paris sojourn, with Dorsey heading back to Brussels while Harriet set about booking a steamer ticket for New York.

At the height of the age of imperialism, Harriet was certainly not alone in taking on the role of the imperial wife. Many women tied their fortunes to men whose ambitions took them to Africa, India, and other corners of globe. Some followed their partners, but many others waited in places like Paris, passing their days scanning the newspapers or waiting for the mail or perhaps happily living their own lives.[3] In the final pages of *Heart of Darkness*, Conrad portrays the narrator Marlowe's visit to Kurtz's grief-stricken fiancée. Deep in the Congo, Marlowe had promised the dying man that he would deliver a packet of letters. Still haunted by Kurtz's final words, "the horror, the horror," he found himself confronted by a pale young woman in mourning clothes. It was clear to him that she wanted to believe that her beloved had been a kind and heroic man to the end. She demanded that Marlowe repeat Kurtz's last words. Marlowe made a quick decision to save her feelings. "The last word he pronounced was—your name," he declared, blatantly lying.[4]

Dorsey had no need of a surrogate to tell the world his story. He fully planned to do it himself. Like Conrad's narrator, he had the advantage of being the sole white witness to some events. He and his fellow crusaders in the Arab War had already more or less agreed on what they would tell the world about what happened and why. His mother and grandmother and other family members would take what he told them and add their own spin. He also owed the State Department a final report, which could also be deployed for other purposes. With a little luck and persistence, he hoped to attract the attention of the press and an American public eager to buy stories about African exploration and adventure. Finally, he planned to deliver more than four hundred objects he'd collected to the Smithsonian's collections, where they not only could be used to further the institution's mission of research and public education but also would provide a material testament to Dorsey's status as an explorer.[5]

There was one more stop to be made before heading back to the United States. At the Royal Palace in Brussels, Leopold waited, like a spider in a gilded web. He had his eye on the brash American as a recruit for the coterie of international adventurers employed by the State and its various extractive enterprises. Dorsey had all the characteristics the Belgian monarch valued in freelance imperialists: bravery, a certain kind of ruthless determination, American political connections, and just a touch of gullibility. He also seemed to have an iron constitution. However, multiple conversations at the palace and the glittering prize of being appointed to the Ordre du Lion failed to secure a commitment from the American.[6] No matter. Leopold was a patient and wily man.

On October 20, 1894, Dorsey set sail for home on the ocean liner *New York*. The medal awarded him by Leopold was in his luggage. He intended, he told his superiors, to deposit it in the State Department until Congress decided whether he could accept the honor.[7] For added drama, he'd brought along a live, half-grown leopard, which he showed off to the press. He told reporters he'd raised the cub on condensed milk after it was orphaned and that it was destined for an American "jardin zoologique."[8]

Finally back in Washington, Dorsey was reunited with his family. "We have been quite happy having Mohun Africanus and Mohun Mexicano with us," Anna Hanson Dorsey wrote to Dorsey's sister Lee on November 8. "Mohun Mexicano" was Dorsey's brother, Louis, returned from working as civil engineer in Mexico. As usual, Dorsey's grandmother was eager to brag about her grandchildren, especially the oldest. Dorsey, she told Lee, is "covered in glory by his exploits in Africa."[9] In a letter to her friend and editor, Father Hudson at Notre Dame, she proclaimed that her grandson had taken part in the "death blow to slavery for which the Belgian King decorated him in person."[10]

Anna was slowly dying of heart failure, shrunken by age and illness. But her literary instincts and opinionated pen remained lively as ever. She evoked her grandson's appearance with a Shakespearean reference. "Like Othello" she told Lee, Dorsey "tells us 'of the dangers he has passed' and looks a black, he has been so blackened by African suns." For Father Hudson, she provided assurances that Dorsey intended to "light down on the Protestant Missionaries in the Congo Free State" as soon as Congress approved his acceptance of the Order of the Lion. He had told his grandmother that they were the worst "mercenary trafficking money grubbers he ever saw," using "all their time, energy and resources to trade with the natives and scoop in all they can."[11] Her eldest grandson knew exactly what she wanted to hear.

It was good to be home. A lot had happened in the family during Dorsey's absence. The Georgetown house had been sold and a new residence acquired on California Street, a fashionable address near Washington's embassy district.[12] There were new nieces and nephews, new publications, and the usual income-seeking plans to catch up on. The most shocking news came from Ohio, where Lee, now a Dominican

Figure 6. Anna Hansen Dorsey, ca. 1889 (author's collection)

nun, had suffered a terrible accident. During a school pageant, a spark
had fallen into a pan of flash powder, igniting it. With characteristic bravado, "Sister Stephanie" as she was known in the Church, grabbed the
flaming pan and carried it outside. She had burned her hand so badly
that it was later amputated.[13]

Washington had also changed. In the aftermath of the 1892 election,
the family's Republican "friends" in high places had been replaced
by the second administration of Grover Cleveland, a Democrat who
styled himself a reformer. He was intent on overhauling the spoils systems, in part because he loathed dealing with office seekers. He also

opposed American expansionism and tried, as his biographer put it, to maintain "a policy of unyielding opposition to imperialist tendencies, Latin-American or Pacific adventures, and overseas entanglements in general."[14] He was not overly successful at this, but Anna's powerful friend and proponent of American imperialism, James G. Blaine, had been banished from the State Department and from policy-making circles. Rutherford B. Hayes had passed away. The family's longer list of influential friends increasingly consisted of decrepit, irrelevant, and out-of-favor old men.

The nation was also reeling from the effects of the worst economic depression of the nineteenth century. Industrial unemployment had skyrocketed. Huge numbers of farmers lost their land as agricultural prices plummeted. Banks and other financial institutions failed. Six months before Dorsey's return, a ragtag collection of unemployed workers, known as Coxey's Army, poured into Washington demanding that the federal government create infrastructure jobs and other relief measures. As in the previous downturn of the 1870s, federal employment and therefore the family's fortunes were somewhat buffered from the harshest consequences of the economic crisis. But with a decline of federal revenues, Congress was under pressure to cut costs. For the Committee on Foreign Affairs, reducing the salaries and expense accounts of commercial agents and consuls posted in seemingly inconsequential corners of the globe seemed like a way to save thousands of dollars with few or no political consequences.

This was the era of a much smaller federal government and direct management by Congress in ways that are unimaginable now. The congressional committee not only considered the larger problem of consular salaries but Dorsey's salary specifically. They proposed it be reduced $5,000 to $2,000 for the rest of his term, which ran until April 1895. Representing the Foreign Affairs Committee, Mr. McCreary of Kentucky, who had introduced the measure, argued that the "obscure man" employed as the US commercial agent in Boma was not deserving of the full salary because his primary accomplishment was establishing the fact that there were few trade opportunities open to Americans in the Congo Free State. Therefore, "from a commercial point of view absolutely no benefit has accrued to the United States from the expenditures."[15] Without political recourse or friends in high places, Dorsey had become an easy target. Patronage was a harsh mistress.

None of these changes boded well for Dorsey's future prospects in the diplomatic service.[16] Nonetheless, the Dorsey-Mohun clan were determined optimists. They also remained resolutely confident in their own abilities to stay afloat in the partisan tides of Washington, DC.

RECKONING WITH THE STATE DEPARTMENT

On the first of November, Dorsey walked up the steps of the same mansard-roofed office building where he had begun his working life more than a decade before. This time, he was headed to the offices of the State Department to report in. After the excitement and celebrity of his homecoming, he had once again become an anonymous civil servant—a name on a series of reports addressed to Edwin Uhl, the assistant secretary of state appointed by the Cleveland administration. He was equally unknown to Walter Gresham, Cleveland's secretary of state. Gresham, like his boss, had taken up his post as a reformer and professional—in some sense, the antithesis of the showy, political Blaine. He had been brought in to clean up some of the Gilded Age corruption and overreach of the diplomatic service. He was also an outsider to the Catholic and Republican circles in which Dorsey and his family traveled.

Nevertheless, Dorsey probably felt little trepidation. The representative from Kentucky's claims notwithstanding, Dorsey's reports showed that he had accomplished a great deal during his three years in the Congo—certainly more than his ineffectual, ill-fated predecessor, Emory Taunt. Although the State Department had provided frustratingly little guidance or instruction, he'd managed to carry out efficiently the specific tasks he'd been assigned: namely, recovering Taunt's body and effects. He'd also done his best in trying to accurately assess the commercial potential of the Congo, particularly in agricultural and commodities production.[17] And, to top it all off, he'd been recognized by Leopold for his contributions to the fight against slavery. What little written feedback he'd gotten from his supervisors had praised his zeal and energy. No evidence survives about what was said during that meeting, but Dorsey's actions afterward suggest nothing dampened his expectations.

About to take a bride, he looked forward to a diplomatic career in more comfortable places. He harbored absolutely no intention of returning to the Congo, having rejected Leopold's offer of employment, and he had gone so far as to advise the State Department to eliminate the Boma commercial agency completely. Behind him: the bachelor adventures of his twenties. Ahead: the comforts of marriage and domesticity.

THE WEDDING

It was mid-November. Half a world away from Washington, equatorial Africa sweated under a blazing sun. But in the northeastern parts of the United States, leaves had begun to fall and there was a chill in the air as Dorsey boarded a train for New York to get married. That journey was a different experience than the one familiar to millions of travelers today. Washington's Union Station had not yet been built. Instead, he probably caught the Pennsylvania Railroad's Congressional Limited Express from the 6th and B station, which stood where the National Gallery of Art is now. Thanks to the cool weather, conductors could close the train's windows, allowing first-class passengers to settle into velvet-upholstered luxury without the pervasive smell of coal smoke and the risk of cinders that was a part of travel behind steam-powered engines. A smoking car beckoned a gentleman like Dorsey, who was a white man and could afford the right kind of ticket.

Outside, the distinctive landscape of the metropolitan corridor flashed by. On this Monday morning, much of the population was hard at work: the factories of Baltimore, Wilmington, Philadelphia, and Trenton belching smoke; men leaning into their shovels along the railroad sidings; women hanging laundry between the lines of narrow brick row houses, hoping it wouldn't rain; kids on railroad platforms hawking newspapers; and somewhere inside those brick-faced tenements and workshops, people turning ivory and rubber from distant places into the things of everyday life.[18]

Dorsey's immediate destination was the Everett House on Union Square, one of the city's most fashionable hotels.[19] Harriet was staying a few blocks away in a townhouse owned by her family.[20] Four days later, the couple made their oaths in the chancel of St. George's Church, surrounded by neo-Gothic splendor. The ceremony was modest by the standards of Gilded Age society. Harriet wore a light gray traveling dress and carried a prayer book covered in white velvet. Her uncle, Horace Barry, gave her away. Still, her family had enough social pull to ensure that Dr. William Rainsford, a minister well known to New York society, performed the rites in a church that enjoyed the patronage of J. P. Morgan. The ceremony attracted a few lines of gushing coverage in the papers.[21] The church and the ceremony were Episcopalian. Dorsey's family did not attend. There were limits to ecumenicalism. According to the rules they understood, any children from the union would not be raised as Catholics.[22] In every other way, they welcomed Harriet into the family.

Afterward, the newlyweds headed directly to the docks to catch a ferry across the Hudson. In Jersey City, they boarded a train for Washington, temporarily disappearing out of the papers and the Dorsey-Mohun clan's correspondence.[23]

THE PROBLEM OF INCOME

By January, Dorsey had emerged from his honeymoon idyll and begun planning. He applied to Secretary of State Gresham for a position as secretary to the American legation in Tokyo.[24] This position was a step up from commercial agent and a desirable change for a family man. He had many reasons to believe the position could be his—despite the lack of a high-ranking patron—among them positive attention in both the press and Washington circles. He had placed his account of interrogating Emin Pasha's purported killers in the February issue of *The Century Illustrated Magazine*—a prominent publication with a wide readership. It immediately garnered widespread notice and praise.[25] While his request for permission to accept the Ordre du Lion appointment seems to have been ignored, news of the honor helped make him appointment seem like a person of consequence.

His rising status was confirmed in late January by an invitation to attend a series of receptions at the White House. Dorsey and Harriet, now "Mrs. R. Dorsey Mohun," were invited for an evening event for the diplomatic corps as well as daytime receptions for military officers and members of Congress. Following in the footsteps of his parents, he and Harriet could step out of their carriage on the West Portico to be announced. He must have truly felt he'd arrived. He kept the invitation for the rest of his life.[26]

Meanwhile, a testy conversation had been going at the State Department about some of Dorsey's activities in the Congo, which he had quite openly and unapologetically described in his reports. "Did Mr. Mohun render these voluntary military services while holding a commission from the United States?" asked Mr. A. A. Adee, the undersecretary delegated with investigating Dorsey's request about the Order of the Lion. "If so, is such service compatible with his office and should we intervene to sanction his reward therefore?"[27] The bureaucrat designated to dig up the facts responded that Dorsey had repeatedly told the State Department that he was taking up arms against the slave trade. His supervisors had not expressly sanctioned these activities but neither had anyone raised any objections. In fact, on at least one occasion, his supervisor had "commended his zeal and energy."[28]

For good measure, the consular bureau digested the relevant parts of Dorsey's report. This only opened up more questions for Adee. This time he sent an irate handwritten note to Assistant Secretary Uhl, Dorsey's supervisor. "Shelling hostile encampments and burning native villages may be a good way for a consular officer to acquire a knowledge of the country to which he is sent, but it hardly seems compatible with our ideas of consular functions" he fumed. "I do not feel like recommending this application to Congress."[29] Adee seems to have been one of the many Americans who did not approve of the methods or goals of European imperialists in Africa.

The real damage from Adee's moral outrage wasn't to Dorsey's ability to accept the honor—he had, in fact, already done so, and he certainly didn't give it back.[30] The damage was to his ability to obtain another diplomatic position. None of this was apparent to him in February when he learned someone else had been given the Tokyo secretaryship. Undaunted, he promptly applied to be the second secretary to the legation, tapping the secretary of agriculture, whom he had met on the *New York*, to write an additional letter of recommendation.[31]

Never one to just sit and wait, and characteristically anxious about money, especially now that he was supporting a wife in addition to helping his mother financially, Dorsey turned his attention to another enterprise. It nicely coupled enhancing his reputation as an explorer with the opportunity to acquire some additional funds. He set about completing arrangements to sell the objects he'd collected on his travels in Africa to the Smithsonian Institution.[32]

It seems strange now that a civil servant would sell objects collected while earning a federal salary while on assignment to another government entity. But expectations were different then and, more importantly, Smithsonian curators depended on people like Dorsey to build collections. "Much valuable assistance has also been rendered by officials of the Departments' who have found it practicable to perform certain work in the interest of the Museum," wrote Mr. G. Brown Goode, assistant secretary, in his annual report. "Mr. R. D. L. Mohun of the Consular Bureau has presented a large and valuable collection of ethnological objects from the Kongo region." In the same year, other consular agents had sent in items from Thailand, South Africa, Venezuela, Iceland, and other distant lands.[33]

Having grown up amid the Capitol's intellectual and political elite, Dorsey was undoubtedly familiar with the Smithsonian Institution. Over his lifetime, a serious of ambitious directors transformed the Englishman Smithson's quixotic bequest into a significant cultural and physical presence. In 1881 the institution opened the United States Museum in what is now known as the Arts and Industry Building on the National Mall just adjacent to the iconic 1855 "castle."[34] Curators then set off on an intensive effort to build collections, increasing the number of objects "seventeen-fold" between 1881 and 1895.[35] They intended to make the National Museum a "museum of record" worthy of the nation's post–Civil War ambitions and sense of its own importance.[36] That "record" included the arts and natural sciences but also what the museum called "ethnology."

Appropriate to a society in the throes of being transformed by industrialization, a key area of collecting was what the curator of ethnology, Otis T. Mason, called "aboriginal industries."[37] The bulk of Dorsey's collection fell into this category. It included hundreds of examples of textile making: a lavish length of palm fiber cloth in shades of purple and gold made by the Teke people for one of their chiefs; dozens of foot-square pieces of a different type of palm fiber cloth, which Dorsey said were used by the Ngala "as money"; greasy plant leaves wrapped around a more unusual example of local industry: bars of soap.[38]

Dorsey's mandate also included collecting "examples of native life"—what we'd now call "material culture." He bypassed (or could not obtain) the kind of dramatic objects that some of his contemporaries deposited in the collection, such as ritual masks and human-size fetishes. Instead, he gathered up mostly small things: twinned male and female figures carved of warthog teeth and strung on a cord to be worn around the neck; small fetishes made of wood and skin and filled with medicine; cups, spoons, bottles, and other objects of everyday life. Typical of the European adventurers of his time, he also could not resist acquiring dozens of bladed weapons: knives, spears, and axes that told the story of European technological superiority while appealing to the era's fascination with war and violence as masculine pursuits.[39]

Finally, a small proportion of what he brought to the Smithsonian can only be described as booty and souvenirs of war. Inside the cover of a leather-bound Koran, he penciled "captured at Kasongo" and his own name.[40] Kasongo was the abandoned Arab town occupied by Dhanis, where Dorsey had enjoyed soft beds and canned food after months on the road. He had also helped himself to a wooden Koran stand and panels from doors carved in the Zanzibari style. A length of hand-forged iron chain, he told the registrar, was an "Arab slave chain." In his imagination, it bore physical testimony to the rightness of the Belgian cause and his decision to join it. He also couldn't resist donating a Congo Free State flag, perhaps the one that flew behind his launch going down river.

Other than the book in which the list of objects was recorded and the objects themselves, now stored in a facility on the outskirts of Washington, no record survives of what Dorsey told the Smithsonian ethnology staff about the objects. His diary gives some evidence of what he purchased and where he purchased it. Whether he helped himself to more than the Koran and the doors cannot be known. It didn't really matter to Otis T. Mason, who authorized the purchase of the collection. He had his own plans for the story the objects could be used to tell. He had

Figure 7. Ivory figures fashioned by the Luba people from warthog tusks and collected by Mohun (Smithsonian National Museum of Natural History)

already assigned an assistant curator named H. Walthers to prepare the collection for display at the Cotton States and International Exposition in Atlanta, Georgia.[41] The objects were used there and subsequently as part of ethnographic exhibits that documented the evolution of culture as it was then understood, justifying both imperialism and, in Atlanta, southern white supremacy. Like exhibits at the Brussels Exposition a few years earlier, it was meant to provide a "scientific" counterpart to the more sensational exhibit of Africans living on public display in a specially constructed village.[42]

THE ZANZIBAR OPTION

By April of 1895, Dorsey's employment situation was beginning to feel desperate. He finished up his report for the State Department and did what he could to sell more articles about his experiences. He had failed twice to secure a diplomatic post. Perhaps he should not have declined Leopold's offer of employment. At that point, Dorsey's mother Clare stepped in again. Using black-edged mourning stationary to signal her status as a widow (albeit one whose husband had been gone for more than a decade), she penned a pleading letter to Henry T. Thurber, President Cleveland's private secretary and an attorney from Detroit. Their connection may have come through the Catholic Cardinal Bishop Foley of Detroit, who was a longtime fan of Dorsey's grandmother's writings and friend of the family.

"Dear Mr. Thurber, Do you think I could see the President and do you believe it would at all help Dorsey's case to do so?" Clare asked, before going on to argue that Dorsey "did his duty, did it well." "I can but feel he deserves the promotion asked for as he has been a good man, Mr. Thurber." For good measure, Clare added the names of some of Dorsey's recommenders and offered Thurber her "mother's gratitude."[43]

Miraculously, Clare's end run around the normal channels worked. Perhaps less surprisingly, Dorsey's new appointment was not to Japan, a place for which he had no linguistic or cultural preparation. Rather, the White House nominated him for appointment as the United States Consul for Zanzibar. Dorsey's appointment solved a small problem for the State Department and the Cleveland administration. The Zanzibar consulate had long been manned by New Englanders who worked for two large trading houses selling American-made goods, including textiles and kerosene, to both passing ships and to East Africa. Because the consul also had the power to act as a judge in trade disputes, this created a conflict of interest. In 1894 the problem had gotten to the point that a lawyer for the State Department advised closing the consulate. This action, however, angered the Sultan of Zanzibar and left Americans in the region without consular services. As an experienced civil servant and a non–New Englander with no financial ties to East African commerce, Dorsey embodied a solution.

By some twist of late nineteenth-century American imperialist thinking, this man who had made a name for himself fighting Omani Arabs was about to become the principal US representative to the capital of their trading empire. Zanzibar was home to the Sultan of Zanzibar as well as Tippu Tip and other wealthy traders who had made their fortunes from the slaves and ivory of the Congo. It was also a British protectorate, partially controlled through the sultan. In short, it was a complicated place very different from the Congo Free State.

✳ 7 ✳

THE CONSULAR LIFE

From the deck they could see sapphire blue waters, white coral sands, and lush green foliage. Outlines of buildings appeared and disappeared along the shoreline providing architectural evidence of the vast wealth of the Omani Arabs who had made Zanzibar the center of their trading empire. Tropical breezes wafted the scent of cloves and other spices. And, for a final touch of the exotic, dhows, the triangular-sailed vessels of the Indian Ocean, were sailing low across the channel. This tiny archipelago, within sight of the East African coastline, was no blank spot on a map. By the time Dorsey and Harriet gazed out over the ship's railing at their new home, descriptions of Zanzibar's beauty were already travelers' clichés. More importantly, the islands held far greater political significance than their size would suggest.[1]

It had been a long journey. The State Department's generous allowance of sixty paid days in transit facilitated Dorsey's habit of taking the long route to a new job.[2] The couple had stopped in London to order furnishings and supplies for the consulate. While there, why not sip champagne and go to the theater? From London, they made their way south, probably to Marseille. This sunny Mediterranean city was the northern terminus for European shipping lines traveling to and from East Africa via the Suez Canal.[3]

For the last stage of their journey, the American consul and his wife boarded the *Kanzler*, the nearly new flagship of the German East Africa Line (Deutsche Ost-Africa Linie [DOAL]). The *Kanzler* had been built to carry mail—as well as German colonists, officials, and soldiers—between Europe and Germany's recently acquired African territories. It offered comfort and speed at a price subsidized by German colonial ambitions. Harriet was probably not the only female passenger. While Leopold couldn't imagine a role for European women in his private empire of rubber, ivory, and prestige; the Germans hoped the promise of a new life in East Africa would provide a safety valve for the country's restless citizenry. Imperialism was increasingly a family affair in the German colonies.

The Mohuns' choice of vessel put them in direct contact with the political complexities of European imperialism in the region. Here, in the two thousand miles between Sudan and northern Mozambique, the scramble for Africa was playing out among more than a half dozen sovereign entities, including Germany, Great Britain, France, Italy, Portugal, the Sultanate of Zanzibar, and regional tribal kingdoms on the mainland.[4] Zanzibar formed the calm eye of this political cyclone.

A well-known figure in the story of German incursions into Africa was also onboard the *Kanzler*. Dorsey and Harriet shared the first-class dining room with Hermann von Wissmann, who was on his way to take up a post as governor of German East Africa.[5] There's no record of Dorsey's interactions with Wissmann, but they certainly would have had a lot to talk about, especially after the ladies retired and the men shared stories over brandy and cigars. The dapper German officer was a celebrated and, in some quarters, notorious explorer, soldier of fortune, and colonial official—cut from the same mold and with some of the same experiences as Dhanis, Parminter, and other career soldier-explorers whom Dorsey had met.[6] Wissmann had, in fact, worked for Leopold. A decade earlier, he'd explored the Kasai region of the Congo basin as one of the Belgian king's foreign mercenaries.[7] Observation of the Belgian use of African soldiers and police in the Congo may have been one inspiration for his later creation of paramilitary units of African soldiers, known in German imperialist circles as *Wissmanntruppe* and across East Africa as *askiris*.[8]

This was not Wissmann's first visit to Zanzibar. He was well known to both the Omani Arabs and the British. Six years previously, as a regional commander he successfully led an effort to crush an Arab-led uprising on the East African coast. The particularly brutal and culturally insensitive behavior of the Germans in the aftermath had led the then-sultan of Zanzibar, Ali bin Said, to reluctantly accept the status of a British protectorate for his territories rather than risk the violence and humiliating consequences of a German takeover. Now Wissmann was back, ready to make his presence felt in a prestigious and powerful new role.[9] His first stop was a visit to the Sultan's palace.[10] There was a new ruler on the throne, Hamid bin Thuwaini Al-Busaid, whose cooperation the Germans needed to fully exploit their mainland holdings. The Sultan, dissatisfied with the deal made by his predecessor, welcomed Wissmann with a lavish party. The British suspected he was testing the possibility that German hegemony might be preferable to working with a British government that had stripped him of most of his revenue sources and now threatened to prohibit slaveholding.[11] In contrast to the bare-knuckle tactics Dorsey was familiar with from the Congo, imperialism in Zanzibar more closely resembled the British occupation of Egypt: a complicated dance between unequal partners involving seduction, deceit, and a constant search for more advantageous arrangements. The Sultan was the nominal sovereign, but the British put significant limits on his power and had installed one of their own, Lloyd Mathews, as "First Minister" to give the Sultan advice and keep an eye on the machinations of his followers.[12]

As the newly appointed representative of the United States government, the American consul was destined to be mostly a bystander to the political machinations of Europeans and Arabs. In fact, the policies of the Cleveland administration required it. The United States also had little to gain or lose in East Africa or the Indian Ocean. The consulate hung on as a vestige of an earlier era when American whaling and trade had played an important role in the region.[13] Because the United States had been the first Western power to recognize the sultanate with a consulate in 1833, it held a sentimental place in the minds of the Omani rulers—a reminder of an era in which they had been the dominant power in the region.[14] Now Merikani textiles largely bypassed the Sultan's customs houses and American traders' warehouses on their way to the African interior, and fewer and fewer American ships dropped anchor in the harbor to reprovision and load or unload cargo.

Being on the margins may have been good for family life, but it did not suit Dorsey's temperament or view of himself. The ambitious new

American consul had discovered he liked to be at the center of the frame. He disembarked in Zanzibar equipped with a growing set of tools to make that happen. The political dynamics of the region and the nature of his position mitigated against another round of self-invention. But that didn't mean he wasn't going to try. This time, he believed he'd found in Harriet a partner who shared his goals and would help him realize his ambitions. Even better—he would not have to face a new place alone.

LEARNING THE PLACE

A small group of Americans waited on the quay as the *Kanzler* dropped anchor in the Zanzibar City harbor. They stood ready to offer a warm welcome to their newly arrived compatriots. The delegation was led by Mr. Howden Smith, who worked for Arnold Cheney Company, one of the two American trading companies on the island. Smith offered the couple a place to stay until they could find a house to rent.[15]

Smith was Dorsey and Harriet's first guide to Zanzibar. Twenty-eight years old and a native New Yorker, he had been working on the island long enough to claim some expertise about the place.[16] Consequently, Dorsey and Harriet initially relied on him to reestablish the consulate and set up a household. Smith also offered an entrée into the social world of European and American merchants and diplomats, though as a clerk in a trading firm he could not claim much standing.

The short trek to Smith's residence provided a powerful visual introduction to their surroundings. In the 1890s Zanzibar City was neither a grim, colonial entrepôt like Matadi or Greytown nor a capital in the mold of London or Washington, DC. Rather, it was another kind of place—the island center of a prosperous commercial empire. Most of the impressive buildings along the waterfront were of recent construction, built to last out of blocks of white coral.[17] The houses and the tall white walls of the Sultan's palace and harem dominated the waterfront. Here, in long sheds, representatives of trading firms from around the world bid for cloves, ivory, and other commodities.[18] It was the Sultan's distinctive red flag, not the British flag, fluttering in the sea breeze. Subtle signs of the Sultan's Ibathi Muslim faith could also be glimpsed in the architecture and, five times a day, heard in the muezzin's call to prayer. Beyond these prominent symbols of Arab wealth flowed a warren of narrow streets. Here, Hindu merchants, French Comorians, Portuguese Goans, and Swahili traders engaged in smaller-scale commerce, living with family members above their shops and warehouses.

Along the waterfront and in the streets, Africans—some from the archipelago, some from the mainland—worked, often in the most physically difficult jobs, or waited in the patient way of people who must toil each day or go hungry. Labor was one of the major sources of Arab wealth. In 1895 buying and selling human beings, mostly Africans from inland areas, was still legal on the island itself. The vast clove plantations relied on bound labor. Pressured by antislavery politics in London, British administrators frowned on the practice but were wary of upsetting their relationship with local elites by forcing its prohibition outright. At the moment of Dorsey's arrival, they had succeeded only in prohibiting the transport of enslaved people in and out of Zanzibar. Hence, at least some of these people toiling in the city would still have been enslaved. Others, including those who sometimes had made portaging or providing quasi-military protection for caravans a profession, sometimes belonged to or were bound into a condition that looked worryingly like slavery to the British.[19]

If this mix of peoples were not complicated enough, gangs of sailors from across the world walked arm in arm, temporarily released from the ships in the harbor. Like sailors on shore leave everywhere, they were looking for prostitutes and for grog shops, well disguised in a place where alcohol was not openly consumed. Teetotalers and other straightlaced souls also had the option of the Sailor's Rest, which offered more wholesome distractions.[20]

The European diplomatic enclave occupied a prime piece of real estate on a point of land known as Shangani, less than a quarter mile from the Sultan's palace as the Indian house crow flies.[21] In the white, fossilized coral houses of the old city, representatives of the most powerful winners and losers in the game of empire lived side by side. In case anyone doubted who was really in charge, the British consulate, with its prominently displayed flags and pride of place on the waterfront, made an unequivocal statement. So did the name on the large walled park on the landside of the consulate. Once the pleasure gardens of a former sultan, it had been renamed Victoria Garden.[22]

And, because nothing about the cultural landscape of Zanzibar was simple, it probably surprised no one that the man Europeans knew as Tippu Tip, notorious Arab trader in ivory and slaves, not to mention uncle to Dorsey's former nemesis Rachid, lived only a few blocks away, behind a set of elaborately carved doors, behind which he sometimes entertained European and American visitors.[23]

The evening of Dorsey and Harriet's arrival, Howden Smith threw a dinner party. The editor of the English-language newspaper, the *Gazette for Zanzibar and East Africa*, was among the invitees. The next morning, he reported on the résumé of the male half of the couple, decorating his brief article with a few flattering adjectives. "Mr. Dorsey Mohun previously held the distinguished post of US agent to the Congo," the editor told his readers, though he seems to have gathered the false impression that Dorsey had been "in command of the U.S. Government expedition to the Manyuema [*sic*]."[24] Perhaps he had misunderstood what the American had said in the course of a wine-soaked evening. Or perhaps Dorsey felt the need to inflate his credentials. He knew very well there had been no US government expedition, only his own decision to sign on as an artillery officer with Chaltin. This small misrepresentation would be followed by others as Dorsey strove to establish himself as a person of consequence in Zanzibar.

A month later, the *Gazette*'s editor found himself in desperate need of material. Normally, international news items selected from the Reuters news agency's wire service filled the front page. Zanzibar was one of the most important telegraph stations in East Africa—another node in the network of nineteenth-century globalization. Underwater cables crisscrossing the Indian Ocean came ashore in the harbor, offering easy access to information from across the world.[25] But the main cable had broken, leaving the city cut off. Dorsey offered a partial solution. The editor could reprint his article on interrogating the purported killers of Emin Pasha. Apparently, he'd brought along his *Century Illustrated Magazine* clippings just in case.

For good measure, he also offered an unpublished story: "Sport on the Kongo: Dumbele and the Rogue Elephant." This artful construction was aimed directly at a very particular audience: the male members of the British delegation. He was looking to convince them that he was, in the language of the time, "clubbable."[26] The core of the story was based in fact: Dorsey had indeed gone hunting with the father of Dumbele, the young man who had helped him recruit porters for the expedition to Kwango and Kwilu, which he abandoned to go to war with Chaltin.[27] The game they'd sought were hippo, which could provide large amounts of meat for Dumbele's tribe. But Dorsey changed and embroidered crucial details to fit British understandings of sport hunting as, as one historian has put it, "a symbolic activity of global dominance."[28] He identified Dumbele as a "cannibal." He changed the animal to the more prestigious elephant. At the center of the story, he spun a tale about saving Dumbele from being killed by an old "tusker" through quick action with an elephant gun.[29] The lie was particularly bold (or perhaps a form of wish fulfillment) since he'd never managed to shoot an elephant in Congo despite months of trying.

Was anyone impressed? Did they believe him? Perhaps not. But the point was made that he understood certain conventions. It worked. Dorsey was accepted into the English Club, where he and Harriet could socialize with people whom they considered their equals and where Dorsey could collect information to send back to the State Department.

To make things more complicated, Harriet had begun to feel the effects of being pregnant with a child conceived soon after their arrival. A photo made to send home to friends and family depicts them staring out of a setting of imperial domestication. The scene includes a Zanzibari servant in fez and tunic sitting on the floor, potted palms, bamboo furniture, and, in the background, sentimental lithographs of religious figures and romantic tableaux. It is a portrait of two people who had finally arrived in their era's version of middle-class adulthood and are either exhausted or disappointed by what they have found there. Included in the portrait is one of many local people they employed to maintain their comfortable ennui.

Figure 8. Dorsey and Harriet with an unidentified domestic servant in the parlor of their Zanzibar house (author's collection)

THE JOB

The late nineteenth century ushered in a golden age for written instructions. Like other US government offices, the consulate contained a small library.[30] Among the volumes, one tome stood out for its sheer size and heft. In more than eight hundred densely packed pages, *Regulations Prescribed for the Use of the Consular Service of the United States* explained the responsibilities and proper protocols for consular appointees.[31]

Until the civil service was reformed in 1906 (and to a certain extent even afterward), many consuls ignored the government's efforts to prescribe their efforts, instead treating the job as a sinecure, doing the bare minimum or improvising, as Dorsey had done.[32] But the former burner of villages and artillery officer in service to a foreign power seems to have taken the *Regulations* as his bible, scrupulously following its instructions.

That process began with getting appropriate credentials. An "exequa-tur" from a representative of the local sovereign power gave Dorsey permission to transact certain kinds of consular business.[33] It is telling that Dorsey sought out the British consul, rather than a representative of the Sultan's court, to sign the paperwork, even though the United States' consular treaty was with the Sultan. The need for an exequa-tur should have afforded him the opportunity to pay an official visit to the British consul general, Sir Arthur Hardinge. Unfortunately for him, Hardinge was not on the island. Hardinge's second-in-command, the delightfully named Basil Cave, must have been reluctant to sign, because Dorsey found himself having to temporarily proceed without the necessary documents.[34]

He did have an audience with the Sultan, Hamad bin Thuwaini, at the palace. The experience included reminders of his visit to Rachid's house in Stanley Falls two years earlier—the tiny cups of coffee, the walls decorated with clocks, the elaborate gestures of courtesy. But Thuwaini had used some of the vast wealth and trading connections of his kingdom to create an air of both Eastern luxury and borrowed European modernity. The coffee was accompanied by glasses of delicately perfumed sherbet. The clocks were from London and Switzerland, not mass-produced timepieces from the factories of Waterbury, Connecti-cut, purchased by more ordinary Zanzibaris. Liveried servants and uni-formed guards added an element of ceremony. Dorsey reported that the Sultan "expressed himself as being greatly pleased at the consulate being reopened as it was the eldest in date of formation in his dominions."[35]

Having made the most important contacts, Dorsey next set about establishing an office. He rented a suite of rooms from a landlord, Harmise bin Said.[36] The State Department regulations specified that "the arms of the United States should be placed over the entrance to the consulate." Under normal circumstances, this small signifier was the only external indication the building was an outpost of the United States, although regulations also allowed the display of the American flag on special occasions such as July 4th or "for protection."[37]

In theory US consuls had substantial powers and responsibilities. They could hold trials and, in specific circumstances, even condemn American citizens to death. They could marry people. They were responsible for ensuring the safety of American sailors, including those who had fled cruel masters and dangerous ships. They could call in American gunships if American lives and property were in imminent danger, although consuls were warned that this power should be used "only when public exigencies absolutely require it."[38] They could also handle large amounts of money and property.[39] Dorsey was required to obtain a $2,000 bond from a New York bonding agent before taking the job lest he succumb to the temptation to supplement his wages.

However, in practice, the job mostly consisted of boring paperwork— filling out customs declarations, registering American ships as they came and went, collecting information about imports, exports, and markets, which in Zanzibar did not require an adventurous trip inland. Consuls were also supposed to courteously respond to inquiries from American citizens. The surviving examples in Dorsey's files suggest Americans had a limited understanding of the business opportunities the sultanate might offer and an entitled sense of the services an American civil servant might offer them. Correspondents included the Cleveland Twist Drill Company, the *Street Railway Journal*, and the Savage Repeating Arms Company, which requested Dorsey distribute their brochures to local gun dealers (of which there were none, at least legitimately).[40]

Within a month, the State Department's rule that consuls "keep open daily during the usual business hours of the place" and that consuls should also be "ready and willing to perform the duties at any time" was beginning to chafe.[41] It quickly became apparent that the day-to-day nature of the job was reactive. It required stifling initiative in favor of being available to perform the services specified in the consular manual. Traffic through the consulate ebbed and flowed with the arrival and departure of ships. Even if the harbor was empty, Dorsey was still obliged to put on a starched collar, coat, and tie in preparation for sitting in his office, waiting.

Dorsey hatched a plan to ease the situation. He requested permission to hire Howden Smith as an assistant. Howden needed extra income and Dorsey needed both Howden's local knowledge and a partial reprieve from boredom. Taking a lesson from his time with Dhanis about the value of being able to access local languages, he also made use of a special provision in the consular treaty to hire a translator. Noho bin Omari would remain in his service during his entire posting in Zanzibar.[42]

With Smith and Omari in place, Dorsey and Harriet could turn more of their attention to "making friends" and establishing a place for themselves in the small society of European and American expatriates. The pursuit of useful social connections bordered on habitual for Dorsey, but this time his goals were more complicated. As always, he had an eye out for professional opportunities, but it wasn't at all obvious who might open those doors for him. He was also operating as part of a couple. However, he was much less inclined than his father had been to let his wife take center stage. His actions suggest he wanted to be recognized as a person who mattered. It was Harriet's job to help him achieve that goal.

It was to Dorsey and Harriet's advantage that many if not most of the people they hoped to cultivate had plenty of time on their hands. Zanzibar's elite expatriates filled that time by socializing in an endless round of dinners, outings, sporting events, and other organized activities. Eager to maintain through charm and hospitality what he could not retain through military superiority, the Sultan also contributed by hosting *barazzas*,[43] or receptions for various groups, and by lending his brass band, fancy dress guards, and other accoutrements of his court for bigger events.

Although members of the European enclave were too polite to say so publicly, socializing with the same small group of people month after month could be something of a bore. Zanzibar was marginally better than some other postings because many Europeans, some of them famous, stopped there on their way to somewhere else. A decade after his last visit, the expat community was still gossiping about Henry Stanley's bad manners. During Dorsey's time, the community waited in vain for a rumored stop by Mark Twain.[44] New arrivals offered the possibility of fresh stories and at least slightly novel opinions.

By early November Dorsey was looking to liven things up by putting his own sensational visitor on display. He had either started or taken over something called the Zanzibar New Society, which offered provocative talks and conversation in the style of a salon. Its meetings got off to an exciting start with a talk on cannibalism by Dorsey's former traveling companion, Sydney Hinde. Hinde had joined the British Foreign Service and was on his way to a posting in East Africa.[45] He had been making a name for himself in England, presenting his "shocking" expose of the purported practice of consuming human flesh in equatorial Africa. His lecture, given at Dorsey and Harriet's house, was reprinted on the front page of the *Gazette* under the title "Cannibals and Their Customs."[46]

Hinde's visit brought Dorsey's two worlds together. It can't have been entirely comfortable. To begin with, the two men didn't really like each other all that much. But more importantly, they were eyewitnesses to each other's actions; keepers of each other's secrets with the power to expose the complicated realities underlying oft-told tales.

And what of Harriet, about whom Dorsey had undoubtedly spoken as the two men made their way up the waterways of the upper Congo? She must also have been measuring the man across the dining room table against the stories she'd heard. Perhaps, she also wondered what she could ask Hinde about the man she'd married. Hinde's physician's eye may also have detected that Harriet's pregnancy was now about four months along. Sweating uncomfortably in the tropical heat under the ruffled bodice of her white cotton dress—Harriet provided visible proof of Dorsey's ongoing domestication.

Another Christmas in the tropics—this one perhaps less lonely for Dorsey. But some sense of dislocation remained. The temperature hovered in the eighties around the clock. Although the Shangani district was surrounded by water, the sea breeze was a mixed blessing, carrying with it a touch of coolness but also the odor of rotting detritus that continually washed up on the shore—kelp mixed with unspeakable things.[47] The persistent buzz of mosquitos, particularly around water, prompted not only annoyance but also dread for those familiar with new theories about the causes of malaria. At night, everyone sought relief from the sweltering streets and buildings on the flat rooftops.

In the European community, missionaries and diplomats did their best to shake off the torpor and generate a festive holiday spirit. At the English Club, garlands festooned the public rooms. On the other side of the "creek" in the poorer part of the city, missionaries instructed their flocks in the miracle of the nativity. The Cathedral of Christ Church Zanzibar offered both high and low services as well as evensong with procession and carols.[48] Lloyd Mathews, the British "First Minister," longtime advisor to the Sultan, took it on himself to play Santa Claus—personally distributing gifts to each European child.[49]

Meanwhile, behind the elaborately carved doors of a few wealthy Arab merchants' houses and in the inner chambers of the palace, a sense of discontent with the British government's influence grew stronger. That discontent had many sources. Most recently the British Parliament elected to appropriate the Sultan's share of customs duties—an enormous sum of £200,000—for their own purposes.[50] The merchants and traders also feared that intense political pressure in England would soon result in the manumission of men, women, and children who toiled in the clove plantations and otherwise created wealth, comfort, and status for their owners. The discontent was not entirely unknown to Hardinge, Cave, and Mathews, but they felt confident they could maintain control in Zanzibar without the overt use of force. Both Hardinge and Mathews prided themselves on their understanding of Arab culture and their ability subtly to manage the Sultan. They were monitoring the influence of the Sultan's advisors and the actions of the Sultan himself.

The nature of the protectorate model required give and take. One compromise involved allowing the Sultan to build up a private military force as a palace guard. By December there were nearly one thousand men-at-arms. Many of these soldiers were discretely housed on the other side of the island in a palace close to the terminus of a new road being built under British direction. The Chwaka area also hosted a force of *askiris*. These soldiers kept order among the road-building laborers and protected the small contingent of Europeans in charge.[51]

A few days before Christmas, tensions briefly broke out into the open as members of these two forces took matters into their own hands to defend the honor of their employers. Forty-one men were killed or injured. By the twenty-ninth conflict had spread to Dunga, the site of the palace itself—putting a damper on holiday festivities that included a mock battle as a Boxing Day entertainment. Hardinge considered bringing in additional troops from India to reinforce the *askiris*. Instead, under threat, the Sultan agreed to reduce the size of his guard.[52]

Still, the British were worried. The Sultan's troops at Dunga had wielded what one observed described as "imaginary" guns.[53] But angry men armed with real weapons posed a much greater potential threat. January 1, 1896, brought a public announcement of a new gun-control policy aimed at keeping wealthy traders, members of the court, and even the Sultan himself from importing weapons and arming allies and hired fighters with them. Travelers bringing weapons and ammunition onto the island would be required to deposit them in a warehouse controlled by a subcommissioner of the protectorate. They would have to prove they had a legitimate use for the weapons. The government could seize weapons already on the island unless the holders could prove they had acquired them legitimately. And, in case there was any confusion about the purpose of the regulations, Clause VIII firmly stated "Firearms and ammunition imported by the Protectorate administration for the use of its Regular troops or Police force are exempted from the Provisions of this Regulation."[54]

Meanwhile, the dance of diplomacy continued. Ever eager to be at the center of things, Dorsey joined British vice-consul Basil Cave on a visit to the mainland city of Dar es Salaam to "offer congratulations" to Wissmann on the occasion of the German Kaiser's birthday.[55] A week later, a delegation of three "high ranking" Germans returned the favor by joining the celebrations held to mark the third anniversary of Thuwaini's ascension to the sultanate.[56] Even the ladies were invited to join in. The Sultan's first wife, referred to by the Europeans as the Sultana, held a reception for the European women. "Mrs. Cave and Mrs. Dorsey Mohun were both too unwell to attend and their presence was missed" reported the *Zanzibar Gazette*.[57] Those in the know read "unwell" as now very far along in Harriet's pregnancy.

As spring approached, Zanzibar's residents looked forward to cooler weather. January and February were the hottest months. Monsoon season would bring with it cooling rains. In 1896, the rains did not, however, calm political tensions. Dorsey reported to Washington that the diplomatic community feared that an ongoing open rebellion in British-controlled East Africa would ignite an uprising in Zanzibar. The British had imposed a curfew and had begun trying to arrest the wealthy Arab merchants they believed had supplied weapons to the rebels. Other European powers had stationed gunboats in the harbor, where they floated menacingly among the dhows. What had he gotten Harriet and his unborn child into? And why wasn't the American flag flying on any of those ships of war? Forbidden from incurring the expense of a telegram except in absolute emergencies, Dorsey wrote his superior requesting that the US Navy protect the American trading firms in the city. He did not mention his personal situation.[58] He dutifully folded the dispatch in three and sent it out on the mail boat.

His request was not stamped as "read" in Washington until a month later. By then, much had happened. The rebels on the coast had moved into German territory, where they were outgunned and forced to surrender. Their leader, Mubarak bin Rashid, a member of a prominent Zanzibari trading family, proposed to von Wissmann that they join forces against the British. The German governor thought better of it. Instead, he and the British consul general, Arthur Hardinge, joined in common cause. They offered an amnesty to the Mazrui tribesmen who laid down their arms. Mubarak was hanged. Hardinge cooked up a pretense for the execution he thought would keep the peace with the Sultan. Mubarak, he explained, "had committed high treason against the Sultan of Zanzibar by assuming the title of Emir ul Mumenin (Commander of the Faithful), which in his Majesty's domain implied sovereign authority." Problem solved—for the time being. Hardinge and Wissmann met in Zanzibar to congratulate themselves. Hardinge later claimed he found Wissmann "exceedingly friendly and even cordial." Their encounter "laid the foundation of friendship between us."[59] So went the dance of empire in East Africa.

Then, finally, the baby arrived. Reginald Dorsey Mohun was born at the University Mission Hospital on April 18. His proud parents nicknamed him Rex. "The American community has received an addition," trumpeted the *Zanzibar Gazette*.[60] Dorsey's beloved friend, Roger Casement, now stationed as a British consul in Lorenço Marques in the Portuguese colony of Mozambique, agreed to be Rex's godfather. A few months later, he sent a charming gift: a small, handwritten "fable" about a foolish chicken's encounters with a fox, illustrated with his own watercolors.[61] A photographer came to the Mohuns' house to take pictures of the baby. The couple ordered multiple copies of an image of Harriet gazing adoringly at her newborn, which they sent to family members. One went to a now very frail Anna and the Washington members of the family, another to Sister Stephanie, still in St. Mary's in Ohio.[62]

What was it like for Harriet so far from home and family? As the couple had calculated, Zanzibar offered a measure of safety and comfort that other postings might not. The ladies of the diplomatic community had little else to do besides offer advice and company. Servants who could take care of small children were easy to come by. At least two young Zanzibari women seem to have looked after Rex. Zanzibar was the headquarters of the University Mission, which deployed graduates of Oxford and Cambridge into the African interior. The Mission's hospital was well staffed with doctors and nurses from Europe. But childbirth and its immediate aftermath was a fearful time for even the most elite and protected nineteenth-century women. Suffocating heat, malaria, and waterborne diseases added to the risk mother or child might not survive.[63]

Dorsey, meanwhile, had his hands full with his consular duties—and even a large-scale emergency. On July 16, news of a shipwreck reached him. An American barque, the *John D. Brewer*, had sailed onto a reef south of the island.[64] The ship was carrying six thousand cases of kerosene that had been consigned to Arnold Cheney and Company. It was the American consul's job to oversee salvage operations and to make sure the surviving sailors were given safe passage home. By the beginning of August, he'd arranged for twelve "distressed seamen" to travel to Marseille and from there to New York. Dorsey also needed to depose the captain about the events that had led to the wreck—information that would be eventually communicated to an insurance company in New York.[65]

He was also keeping tabs on the political situation in Zanzibar. Gossip at the English Club suggested that protectorate officials continued to worry about the Sultan's loyalty to Britain. Inside the court, Lloyd Mathews kept a close eye on the comings and goings of Thuwaini's friends, advisors, and kinsmen. Hardinge decided to authorize the arrest of Hilal bin Amr, whom Dorsey described as "a rich and influential Arab, who has great influence over the Sultan." Hilal had made himself "so obnoxious to the British," Dorsey reported, that they decided to pull him out of his house, march him to the harbor, and put him on the first boat to exile in Aden.[66] No wonder Thuwaini described himself as like "a little bird in the claws of a powerful eagle." The eagle, he supposedly said, "can either drop the bird and let it die, or he can carry it to a place of safety."[67] By the spring of 1896, the former fate seemed more likely.

And then a shocking thing happened. Dorsey had spent the morning in the bazar behind the Sultan's palace. A committee of British and American ladies had given him a list of prizes to buy for a gymkhana. This set of athletic contests was to be part of festivities held in honor of the arrival of the British fleet, which was steaming down the channel toward the city. Thirsty, he decided to reward himself by stopping by the English Club for drinks and conversation. The usual rituals were being observed when a club servant rushed in breathlessly announcing that the Sultan was dead and his nephew, Khalid, had seized the throne.[68]

This turn of events was not acceptable to the British government or its representatives. As Hardinge put it, Khalid was not "a suitable candidate for the office of British 'protected Sovereign,' obliged to defer in many matters to the advice of the Protecting Power." This was Khalid's second try at taking over the Zanzibar Sultanate, which he considered rightly his by descent from Sultan Barghash bin Said, the most powerful and effective of Zanzibar's nineteenth-century rulers. Khalid, in Hardinge's estimation, "deeply resented the dismemberment of his father's dominions by Germany and England and would never have willingly submitted to the dictation of European Agents."[69] Hardinge was also under intense political pressure from Parliament to bring an end to slavery in Zanzibar—an act that Khalid was sure to oppose. Khalid would have to go.

The next day, Dorsey received two messages delivered to his office on the assumption that the United States would remain neutral during the crisis. The first was written in elaborate Arabic calligraphy. Dorsey's translator, Noho bin Omari, rendered the message as:

This is to inform you that my brother Hasid bin Thwaini has died and I have inherited the Sultanate. As Zanzibar contains many subjects of foreign kingdoms who might be injured by the guns of my troops and that of my enemies, if they might attempt to interfere, I am not to be blamed in such a case.[70]

The second message came from Hardinge's second-in-command, Basil Cave. It explained that Khalid and his followers had taken possession of the palace and were refusing to leave it. Cave declared this "an act of open rebellion against the Government of Her Britannic Majesty." Khalid had been warned the palace would be destroyed if he didn't vacate it. Cave advised Dorsey to "place all the protégés of the American Consulate in a place of safety before eight o'clock tomorrow morning."[71] The same afternoon, Dorsey took Harriet and infant Rex down to the harbor and watched them board the *Philomel*, a British naval ship anchored in the harbor. "My mind was relieved of any fears on their account" he later wrote.[72] Women and children out of the way, it was time to strap on his revolver and confer with the men about next steps.

In Dorsey's account, again putting himself at the center of the story, he was talking with Mathews when he received word that a representative of Khalid wished to speak with him. He followed the messenger to a private house. The emissary handed him a telegram addressed to Queen Victoria announcing Khalid's ascension and expressing the hope that "friendly relations will continue as before." The telegraph office had refused to send the message. Dorsey also declined and quickly returned to the British "lines" clutching his revolver in case he ran into any hostile supporters of Khalid.[73]

It's possible that this really happened. Zanzibar was a small place. The Sultan and members of his court made a habit of cultivating as many allies among the European powers as possible to provide themselves options. But, as Dorsey ascertained, the United States had nothing to gain by aiding Khalid.

That evening he joined Harriet onboard the *Philomel* for dinner. From the deck, they could see British warships, which had arrived that day, lying at anchor. The intermezzo from an Italian opera wafted over the dark waters from the flagship where the captain entertained a few dignitaries. Rumors had circulated that the Sultan's death had not been from natural causes. If so, Khalid had timed his coup poorly. Instead of a gymkhana, the officers were anticipating an entirely different kind of competition. Power and perhaps the end of slavery on the island would be the prizes.

At dawn, Dorsey joined a crowd on the roof of the English Club to take stock of the situation. Through his binoculars, he could see the Sultan's red flag hanging limply in the still air. Khalid was still in the palace. Dorsey went back to his house, hoisted the largest American flag in his possession, and went up to the roof with his male employees, whom he had armed with rifles. All around him, his neighbors were also on their roofs, hoping to see something exciting. Precisely at nine, the shelling started. The British ships aimed all their firepower at the waterfront palace and the harem complex next door. Forty-five minutes later, the shelling stopped. Dorsey was excited: "The clouds of smoke rising from the guns of the gunboats and the burning palace made a fine picture."[74] Inspired, he grabbed his camera and headed out—his mother's son in pursuit of a good story.

He was not far from home when he found one: Khalid and his surviving followers covered in dust and blood were converging on the gates of the German consulate. "It was none of my affairs so I said nothing, until Khalid was inside the consulate and safe." Then he informed the hapless sergeant leading the British patrols of the streets who had gotten past them. "I felt sorry for the poor fellow, as he showed his feelings in his face, and I could see plainly that he knew he had lost the chance of a lifetime."[75] Inside the compound, the Germans stripped Khalid's men of their weapons, many of them elaborately decorated prized possessions, and spirited Khalid through the garden that bordered the shore. On the horizon, a German man-of-war was waiting to transport the now-deposed Sultan off to Dar es Salaam.[76]

The involvement of the German consulate in Khalid's escape didn't ruin the friendly relationship between Hardinge and Wissmann. Exile in German territory relieved the British of figuring out how to prevent Khalid from being a further threat while preserving the ideology of the protectorate as a partnership with the British government.[77] As the new Sultan, the British chose Hamid bin Mohammed, an elderly man who was willing to play a ceremonial role without questioning British orders. He offered them a bargain: he would acquiesce to the legal end of slavery in Zanzibar. In return the British guaranteed his thirteen-year-old son would inherit the throne. Wary about having to manage another independent-minded sultan, the British government sent the teenager to Britain to be educated at Harrow, the elite boarding school. This strategy, in the opinion of later British observers, ruined the young man as a convincing and effective token sovereign.[78]

Life returned to normal, more or less, for Dorsey, Harriet, and little Rex. The Sultan held a party for the wives of foreigners to reward them for their bravery. Harriet and the other ladies each received a piece of jewelry described as a "rich gold necklace and pendant bearing His Majesty's name."[79] Another photographer came to the house to take pictures of a rapidly growing Rex. His lens caught the baby reaching out from the arms of his elaborately dressed and coiffed Zanzibari caretaker. Another woman, also garbed in a boldly printed tunic and white leggings, holds his toys toward the camera.[80] Like so many of the Africans important in this story, their names have been lost to time.

Life at the office also went on as before, with Dorsey competently dealing with tasks while periodically sending reports to Washington. It took another year to settle affairs related to the salvage of the *Brewer*. The abolition of slavery on January 1, 1897, initially proved anticlimactic because the law required slaves to step forward to request their freedom and contained other measures, resembling American Reconstruction-era "black codes," which ensured enslaved people working in the clove plantations could not easily claim their freedom.[81]

The endless rounds of parties and afternoons at the club did not feel the same, however. A sense of ennui had overcome the little expat colony. Dorsey was also suffering from malaria, and a surge of smallpox cases had left both parents fearful for little Rex. The couple gradually reached a decision. Dorsey would finally take Leopold up on his offer of employment. Harriet and Rex would live in Brussels cosseted in the safety and relatively familiar comfort of a European capital. Their adventure was over. They had not been able to find a way to bring Dorsey's two worlds together.

Figure 9. Reginald "Rex" Mohun and his unidentified
Zanzibari caretakers (author's collection)

The family of three left Zanzibar in early November of 1897.[82] By the
time they reached New York in early December, Dorsey was so sick he
could not leave his bed.[83] When he finally arrived home to introduce
his son, the family reunion was incomplete. Anna had passed away the
previous Christmas. Dorsey had written to her about the family's experience in the Bombardment. His efforts at vivid description lodged in

her mind. In her last days she had obsessed over the fear that little Rex must have felt, periodically "bursting into tears," according to Dorsey's sister Laura.[84]

In Washington, the increasingly unfamiliar political landscape and the chilly welcome Dorsey received at the State Department seemed to confirm that Harriet and Dorsey had made the right decision. The Gilded Age, as Dorsey had known it, was under assault from many quarters. A new more muscular, bureaucratic, modern United States was taking shape under the twin banners of progressivism and empire. Before the couple set sail, the United States would be at war with a declining European power—Spain—and on its way to becoming a global power. Dorsey's brother Louis was on his way to Manila on a US Navy ship. But the opportunities of the Spanish-American War and the American empire it expanded came a few months too late for Dorsey, whose résumé would have qualified him for service in Cuba or the Philippines. He had already decided to throw his lot in with Leopold and the Congo Free State.

* 8 *

INFRASTRUCTURES
OF EMPIRE

Dorsey and Harriet's sojourn in the United States lasted only a few months. Fearful of what might befall him, Dorsey made a will. To Harriet he bequeathed everything except the medal Leopold had awarded him; he wanted Rex to have it. If he died serving the Congo Free State, his son would have tangible evidence of Dorsey's heroism.[1] Harriet had different ideas about remembrance. She and Rex visited a Washington photography studio. One photo survives. Mother and son observe an object outside the camera's range, absorbed in silent conversation. The mood is intimate. Mothers, sons, and soon-to-be-absent fathers—the pattern establishing itself in another generation.

On the photo's cardboard backing, written in confident cursive script, are their full names, the place, and the date. Harriet had begun to sign her name in the French fashion: Harriette—perhaps in preparation for fitting in among the francophone Brussels elite. It was time for the couple to reinvent themselves again. Dorsey would join the ranks of American contractors hired to build the infrastructure for globalization. Harriet planned to make a home in Belgium in the company of other expatriate wives.

In the spring of 1898, they packed their trunks and bundled up Rex for another ocean voyage. This time, the trip involved no happy detours. They went directly to Antwerp. From there, a train carried them the short distance to Brussels. More layers of grandiosity had accreted around Brussels in Dorsey's absence. Leopold had busied himself pouring profits from rubber and ivory into enhancing the city's international

Figure 10. Rex and Harriet, 1898 (author's collection)

prestige and propagandizing about his African colony. The recent Brussels International Exposition had thus far proven to be the most conspicuous and popular of these efforts. An idealized version of the Congo Free State featured prominently in the host country's self-portrayal. Near the medieval village of Tervuren, where a private hunting reserve had once hosted kings and archdukes, exhibits on Africa and Belgium's colonial ventures were presented for the masses and potential investors alike. The State had forcibly recruited two hundred and seventy

Africans to do some of its promotional work. Displayed in fenced "villages nègres" and "villages civilisés," they drew an estimated 1.2 million fairgoers who unashamedly ogled the captives in this human zoo.[2]

By the time the Mohuns disembarked in Antwerp, the exposition had closed. But Leopold was so enthusiastic about the African exhibits that he decided to make at least part of them permanent. Accordingly, the temporary Palace of the Colonies was turned into the Royal Museum for Central Africa, which still exists.[3] The model Congolese villages were dismantled and most of the inhabitants sent home. Seven remained, their bodies buried underneath simple headstones along the external wall of a nearby medieval church, their ghosts shivering in the dim light of a European winter.[4]

The exposition was as close as Leopold and many of his top advisors would ever come to visiting the Congo (Leopold had been to Egypt on his honeymoon). His advisors confidently carried out the work of managing Leopold's holdings on the basis of information gleaned from reports, newspapers, and their own imaginings.[5] Day-to-day administrative planning for the Congo Free State rested in the bony hands of Edmond van Eetvelde, who had cleared some time in his busy schedule to meet with Leopold's newest American recruit.[6] Van Eetvelde was a dour, chilly figure who affected the mannerisms of a "gentleman Anglais" learned during his own youthful turn as imperialist for hire in Bombay and Calcutta.[7]

In his French-accented British English, Van Eetvelde informed Dorsey that he would be assigned to manage a district in the far northeast corner of the State near the source of the Nile and Lake Albert Nyaza. The job involved helping Leopold maintain hold of a recently claimed territory, known as the Lado Enclave, as British and French expeditions raced to gain control over the Sudan.[8] Dorsey and Van Eetvelde had already corresponded about the necessary preparations, and the assignment seemed set. But Leopold liked to personally bless his appointments, particularly when they involved Americans. By now, Dorsey knew the protocol. He waited for a summons to the palace. It came ten days after his arrival.

A few years later, Dorsey reconstructed the scene. Ushered into Leopold's office, he found that the king, "in the uniform of a General, was standing by his desk"—a towering figure with a lush white beard. He resembled the robber barons and Civil War generals of Dorsey's youth. This was not entirely coincidental. The king was, in fact, a Gilded Age capitalist endowed with the powers of a constitutional monarch. He was also an admirer of his self-made counterparts across the Atlantic.

A moment of confusion ensued as the American decided to bow to his new employer and Leopold responded by offering his hand in an expression of republican equality. "Sit down, Mr. Mohun. I must have a long talk with you," Dorsey remembered him saying. Overriding Van Eetvelde, Leopold decided he had a better use for Dorsey: he would lead an expedition to build a telegraph line from a Belgian fort on the western shore of Lake Tanganyika northward through Stanley Falls. Leopold aimed to connect the easternmost parts of the Congo Free State with the coast. With the cooperation of the British and international telegraph companies, nearly instantaneous communication from the heart of Africa to the rest of the world would become possible.[9] A recent, tense meeting with Cecil Rhodes, who was building his own "Cape to Cairo" telegraph line, had given the project fresh urgency.[10]

The word *expedition* had a nice taste to it, savoring of traveling into the unknown. So, too, did Dorsey's new titles: District Commissioner 1st Class and "chef" of the telegraph expedition. Flattered and with little idea what he'd agreed to, Dorsey said yes. Nineteen years had passed since he'd walked into the Navy Department and into his first job. At age thirty-five, Clare and Richard's eldest son had finally secured a position he felt was appropriate to his experience and ambitions. No matter that he knew nothing of telegraph construction. Lack of technical expertise had never stopped him before. Besides, at least as Dorsey remembered it, Leopold told him that he was the right man for the position not because he knew anything about telegraph technology but because leadership of the expedition required "tact in dealing with the natives" and the ability to act "on your own judgement."[11] Telegraph experts could be hired. Dorsey knew how to organize expeditions, how to hire and manage African workers, and, from his time in Nicaragua and as a trade consul, how to do the accounting and reporting required in a big bureaucracy. He had faith in his own abilities and the confidence of his employer.

Bound by the prejudices of their age and, in Leopold's case, by the lack of any real understanding of Africa, both men failed to foresee the most difficult challenges confronting the expedition. They believed Africa and Africans were the problem. European technical and organizational expertise would provide the answers. Perhaps not surprisingly, the reality turned out to be much more complicated.

Dorsey hit the ground running, leaving Harriet to furnish a house, hire servants, and begin to create a life for herself and Rex. Within forty-eight hours of meeting with the king, the newly appointed "chef" boarded the night boat to England—with permission to hire a team—the responsible eldest child earnestly trying to do his very best, happy to be in charge of something and someone.

Telegraphy was key information technology in the coordination of both global commerce and empire. London was the epicenter of both the largest empire the world had ever known and the financial capital of the Western world. It was also literally a hub for the global system of telegraph lines. So it made sense that London was also the undisputed center of the telegraph industry. The firm of Siemens Brothers, prominently located at the Marble Arch in Westminster, dominated both the manufacture of telegraphic equipment and the operation of the submarine cable networks into which landlines, such as the ones being built by Leopold and Rhodes, connected.[12] London was also the gathering place for an international coterie of telegraphic experts for hire. Based on recommendations from Siemens staff, Dorsey quickly hired five men who, between them, had experience spanning the British empire. The chief engineer, Frederick Thornton, was hard-bitten Australian who had built telegraph lines in South Africa and Australia. The four "linemen," tasked with overseeing African construction workers, included A. J. Carey, who had been a sergeant in the Royal Engineers, and H. J. Clipperton, who had worked for the Eastern Telegraph Company.[13]

Everyone understood mortality rates among Europeans in equatorial Africa were among the highest on the continent. Dorsey also knew from his own experience the frightening and debilitating consequences of illness for men far from home. Thus, he carefully selected an expedition physician with extensive tropical medicine experience in Niger and Bombay, R. H. Castellote.[14] Two familiar names from Dorsey's adventures during the Arab War also appeared on the roster. Nicholas Verhellen, who'd served under Chaltin with Dorsey, agreed to return to the Congo. He'd lead a group of African mercenaries charged with protecting and keeping order in the expedition. Antoine Dhanis, younger brother of the famous hero of the Arab War, joined as the expedition's "secretary."[15] This tiny handful of Europeans would be vastly outnumbered by the thousands of Africans Dorsey planned to hire along the way.

Dorsey purchased camping equipment from the outfitter Edging and Sons and a chest stocked with medical supplies from Burroughs, Wellcome (it survives in the Smithsonian's collections, minus the opiates removed in the 1970s).[16] All else was left to employees of the State, who pulled together construction tools and three hundred miles of wire for the telegraph lines, six months of canned food for the Europeans, trade goods and bales of cloth to pay workers and acquire goods in Africa, plus much else.[17] Dorsey also invested in his beloved cases of champagne as well as other liquor for the Europeans. Putting extraordinary faith in the State's mail service, he contracted with a news agency in Brussels to send him a dozen different newspapers and magazines to fill his off-hours in the construction camp.

Never one to neglect appropriate costuming, he visited a tailor. Among his purchases: a light-colored "explorer's suit" in the style made fashionable by Henry Morton Stanley. He also purchased an indispensable symbol of European imperialism: the hat known in the English-speaking world as a sun or pith helmet and, perhaps more tellingly, in French as a *casque colonial*.[18] He hoped the right clothes would signal his authority, especially to those with whom he did not share a language. Experts advised the correct choice of clothing would also protect white Europeans from the tropical climate. The light color of the suit was intended to reflect the sun's damaging rays just as the extended brow of the sun helmet protected the wearer's nose, ears, and neck as well as the top of the head.[19]

While Dorsey had the opportunity to pick his own people, supplies, and equipment, he had much less say in choosing the expedition's route.

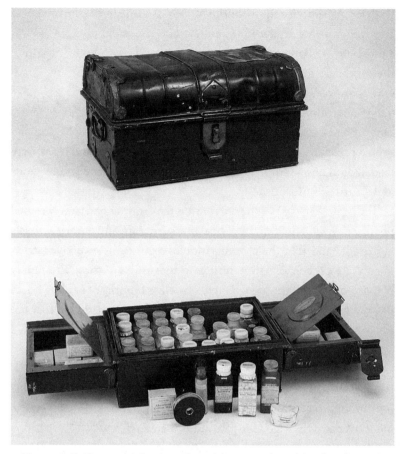

Figure 11. R. Dorsey Mohun's medicine chest, purchased for the telegraph
expedition (Smithsonian National Museum of American History)

Three days before he was due to leave on the chartered German East Africa Line ship *General*, a set of orders arrived. Somewhere in the musty
Brussels offices of the State, as bureaucrats pored over maps, a consequential decision had been made. The expedition would enter Africa on
the east coast. Supplies and personnel would be put on riverboats at the
mouth of the Zambezi River and would move north and east to Lake
Tanganyika. There, the easternmost terminus of the telegraph would
be established at the State's military outpost at M'Toa. The expedition
members would construct the line east to west, roughly following a
former Arab caravan route.[20]

Bringing supplies up from the mouth of the Zambezi involved an enormous V-shaped detour of almost two thousand miles. M'Toa is almost directly west of Zanzibar as the crow flies, while the mouth of the Zambezi is a thousand miles to the south. Generations of Arab traders had moved goods and people from the east coast of Africa to Lake Tanganyika along a well-established east–west caravan route. Before Dhanis had driven the Arabs out of the Eastern Congo, M'Toa had been a prosperous town from which caravans of slaves and ivory were loaded onto dhows for the trip across the lake and whence trade goods and Zanzibaris moved west.[21]

The Arab War was not the only reason the caravans had largely ceased plying the route, however. Political pressure from antislavery activists in Britain had led to the promulgation of regulations severely restricting private expeditions from hiring porters in East Africa. The supply of free workers willing to sign on for grueling months of hauling boxes did not come close to meeting demand.[22] Dorsey estimated that the 160 tons of materials on the Antwerp docks would have to be divided into four thousand "loads."[23] He didn't dare antagonize British officials by using coercion or hiring potentially enslaved workers directly from labor contractors. Thus, antislaving rules made it virtually impossible for him to directly hire enough men to carry the supplies and equipment overland through German and British territory.[24]

The solution was to leverage the British government's inconsistency in enforcing its own policies. By detouring south, the Congo Free State could subcontract the problem of transportation to the African Lakes Company (ALC).[25] Established to facilitate British Christian missionizing in Central Africa, the ALC operated steamboats on the string of waterways slicing up through the center of equatorial Africa. They also promised porters to caravan goods through stretches of the route not navigable by water, the longest of which was the 275-mile Stevenson Road linking Lake Nyassa and Lake Tanganyika.[26] The company had the blessing and cooperation of the British government in recruiting porters and other African workers, which allowed agents to skirt official policies about forced labor—an option not available to Dorsey.[27]

The remoteness of M'Toa in one of the farthest corners of Leopold's colony and a supply line that depended on the goodwill of a foreign

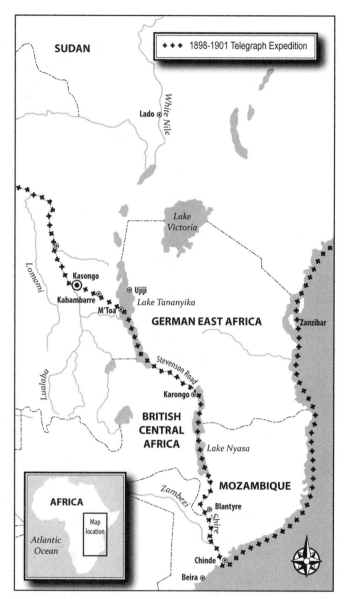

Figure 12. Map of the telegraph expedition route

power offered many potential impediments. That's something of an understatement. Why do it this way? Most probably some combination of strategy and Leopold's impulsiveness directed the decision to begin building at Lake Tanganyika rather than at Stanley Falls. Leopold and his advisors may have hoped that the expedition could help pacify the State's eastern borders. Antoine Dhanis's eldest brother Francis was already in Congo, tasked with tamping down a guerrilla war ("revolt" in the parlance of the day) that was threatening the State's control over the region. A regional communication system offered a means of better military coordination than runners and bugle calls. The 160 tons of baggage included telephone equipment that could be installed in the local telegraph stations, obviating the need to locate a telegraph operator who knew enough Morse code to send an emergency message to a nearby military encampment. Telegraph and telephone lines could also provide rapid intelligence about the activities of Rhodes.

On August 20, Dorsey bade Harriet and Rex goodbye. He had committed to a three-year contract. At best, it would be a long time until he saw them again. But there was also a very real chance that someone would lay his bones under a big tree and scratch his name into the bark to be gradually erased by time. He chose not to share such thoughts with posterity.

The trip was a slow misery. "Very hot and not at all amusing," Dorsey recounted.[28] Late-summer heat intensified as the *General* entered the Mediterranean. Cabins and common rooms captured and held the thick air. No amount of scrubbing eradicated the odor of hallway toilets, cooking odors, the acrid smell of marine paint, and body odors of the passengers. Deck spaces offered only a partial respite for weary passengers. Deep in the bowels of the ship, a small army of stokers suffered more. For thousands of miles, they took brief turns shoveling coal to the ship's giant reciprocating engines before fleeing for fresh air to avoid succumbing to heat prostration. Miserable indeed.

Verhellen, Thornton, Castellote, Dhanis, and the four foremen were also on board.[29] Knowing they had signed on to spend three years working together, these veterans of prior expeditions passed the long weeks finding ways to bond: comparing experiences, salty stories, card games, and other forms of competition. They also schemed about how to please the boss and better ensure the expedition's success. Perhaps they'd begun to realize the American's relative lack of experience. Dorsey continued to fret about recruiting even a small core group of African workers, especially the soldiers needed to provide security. Castellote and Verhellen offered to make a detour to Bombay to hire Sikhs, who were employed as mercenaries throughout British East Africa. While waiting to go through the Suez Canal, Dorsey and some of the others disembarked in Port Said to send telegrams to people who might facilitate the recruitment process. A plan formed. Dorsey and Thornton would go on to Aden and Zanzibar. Castellote and Verhellen would head to India. Everyone would reconvene in Chinde, where the trip upriver was scheduled to begin.[30]

In Aden, Dorsey's worst fears were confirmed. He'd hoped to recruit four hundred Somalis there as "permanent men" for the expedition. Over drinks at the Union Club, General O'Moore Creagh, acting representative of the British government there, offered what Dorsey described as a "charming" refusal. In an Irish accent, O'Moore explained, "I am not allowed by H.M. Government to allow recruiting so I am forced, to my regret, to say No."[31]

In theory the same ban applied in Zanzibar. Unauthorized recruiting for service outside the archipelago had been forbidden since 1891.[32] But, in Dorsey's experience and worldview, personal relationships could often be used to override policy. He sent word ahead about his impending visit. The results included an invitation to stay at the British consulate and a small item in the *Zanzibar Gazette* describing the telegraph expedition and Dorsey's search for workers. Only partially tongue in cheek, the editor warned his readers that "all cooks and skilled natives had better be put under lock and key in Zanzibar until Mr. Mohun has left."[33]

Dorsey departed Zanzibar with far fewer men than he'd hoped for—less than one hundred. He'd had to offer generous compensation and also promise British authorities that he would personally return the men to the island after three years. For good measure, he was issued a set of rules and policies printed by the British East African government.

Worried about ruining his cordial (and useful) relationship with Arthur Hardinge, Dorsey carefully studied the document, marking it up in pencil. He began diligently working to comply with the terms even before leaving Zanzibar. Thus, he purchased a suit of clothes, a blanket, and a water bottle for each man as well as seventeen cooking pots—one for every six men.[34] He also advanced six months' salary, which he claimed the men immediately used to "purchase jewelry for their women."[35] The men wanted their wives, mothers, and sisters to have some financial security if they did not return.

Ali bin Juma, Hamed bin Imana, and Barata bin Juma were among the new hires who crowded onto the deck of the *General*. While the others joked, sang, and socialized, Hamisi bin Imana was caring for thirty muskat donkeys. Dorsey had purchased the animals in Zanzibar so that he and the other white expedition members would have an alternative to walking or riding in a hammock-like device slung between porters, called a *machilla*. Donkeys could also be used to move supplies quickly if needed.[36]

Racial and imperial conventions dictated that the Zanzibaris would sleep and otherwise spend the voyage on the deck while the Europeans occupied the cabins. Young men, excited to be going on an adventure and adept at passing the time, the new hires turned their space on the deck into a site of competition and pleasure by staging games and contests as well as engaging in what Dorsey described as a "wild dance" each night, the exoticism of which amused and entertained European passengers.[37]

German East Africa Line ocean liners were far too large to push over the sandbar protecting Chinde's harbor. Therefore, the *General* made port farther south in Beira in what is now Mozambique. There, passengers and cargo were transferred to smaller coastal vessels. The Zanzibaris were not welcome to disembark in the Portuguese-controlled town, but Dorsey could do as he pleased. Aware that the comforts of Europe were about to become increasingly unavailable, he went ashore. Beira thus became another addition to the growing list (Matadi, Greytown, Port Said) of sunbaked, tin-roofed points of departure in which he'd spent the evening drinking and telling half-truths and tall tales. Beira was a town where white men shed their inhibitions and acted in ways that would have been unacceptable in the places they'd come from.

During a rowdy evening at the newly opened Beira Club, Dorsey met yet another handsome Anglo-Irish adventurer.[38] Ewalt Grogan's connection to Africa came courtesy of his relationship with Cecil Rhodes. Grogan could (and probably did) boast of having volunteered to serve in one of Cecil Rhodes's military adventures in southern Africa. There, next to a campfire, he'd listened intently as Rhodes evangelized about the great things that would result from British colonization. These experiences firmly tied Grogan's imagination and future to the continent.[39]

One of Grogan's contemporaries described him as having "the easy charm of a man supremely confident of his own abilities."[40] Some of that confidence seems to have been innate, but it was bolstered by wealth, social connections, and a pair of pale blue eyes set in a ruggedly handsome face. Both men and women found him compelling. Grogan was about to test that confidence by embarking on the second leg of a journey that, if successful, would make him the first European (and likely the first person) to travel from the Cape of Good Hope to Cairo over land. His motivation, he later claimed, was to win the hand of a lady by earning the approval of her stepfather—a romantic claim for a notorious rogue and philanderer. The possibility of global fame offered a tantalizing secondary consequence.[41] Keeping him company and perhaps out of certain kinds of trouble (Grogan had "accidentally" shot a Portuguese officer when last in Beira) was his fiancée's uncle, Arthur Henry Sharp.[42] Somewhere amid the chatter and boasting, Dorsey discovered that he would be traveling to Chinde with Grogan and Sharp.[43]

The next morning, everyone reconvened onboard a smaller ship, the *Peters*. This leg of the journey would take twenty-four hours. The two Englishmen may have been worse for wear after their night of drinking because it wasn't until dinnertime that they discovered their baggage had not followed them. Tents, "chop boxes," and most of their hunting equipment (they planned to disguise their real mission by shooting lots of animals) had been put on another boat heading south to Delagoa Bay. According to Dorsey, each blamed the other, leading to "language that was not usually heard in polite society."[44]

In due time, the *Peters* dropped anchor just off the coast. Their destination emerged from the horizon as a long finger of low-lying ground pounded on one side by Indian Ocean breakers and scoured on the other by an outflow of the Zambezi known as the Chinde River. Seven years earlier the British concession of Chinde had been nothing but sand, swamp, and mosquitos. The sand and mosquitos remained, but Harry Johnston, the energetic first governor of Britain's new Central African protectorate, oversaw the rapid construction of a makeshift naval base and transshipment port to service his landlocked territory. Technically, the town and naval base sat on land that was part of Portugal's spoils from the Berlin Treaty—a tiny bit of Mozambique's coastal edge. But the Berlin Treaty guaranteed free navigation of the Zambezi. Thus, the Portuguese government found it hard to say no to Britain's request for a ninety-nine-year lease on this tiny speck of land.[45] Enticed by the offer of British naval protection, the ALC moved its commercial steamboat operations from the Portuguese river port of Quelimane.[46]

A sturdy fence separated the Portuguese territory from the base. Brightly painted British gunboats made a show of racing up and down the river. And union jacks floated above some of the buildings. But Chinde otherwise functioned as a testament to the internationalist goals of the Berlin Treaty. The mail for the eastern part of the Congo Free State went upriver from Chinde. So, too, did Bibles and medical supplies for both Catholic and Protestant missions, not to mention liquor, cloth, and trade beads. Adventurers and preachers, storekeepers, and government officials from various European powers waited in Chinde to go upstream or to return home. They shared some of that space with an equally diverse group of Africans and Asians drawn there as mercenaries, porters, and merchant traders.[47]

The "port," if it could be called that, consisted of 420 feet of embankment along the river. Hastily constructed wooden warehouses with corrugated iron roofs filled the waterfront. Since most seagoing vessels drew too much water to tie up, smaller boats towing flat-bottomed steel barges ferried everyone and everything to shore. Dorsey, like most other European visitors, did not think it worthwhile to remark on the African stevedores who shifted his expedition's 160 tons of supplies and equipment into the shallower boats, cajoled donkeys and cattle into the same lighters, or helped Europeans in and out of the oversize baskets used to transfer more privileged passengers. The Zanzibaris presumably used the ship's ladders.

A former British vice-consul did leave a partial picture colored in the language of his time and social class. "Numbers of half-naked natives, singing, shouting, and gesticulating, were engaged in loading and unloading two or three steel cargo-lighters, their toil supervised by several khaki-clad Europeans of somewhat neglected appearance, whose pallor and emaciation bespoke considerable ill-health."[48] All the way up the river system and through the lakes, the same backbreaking and dangerous process was routinely repeated without anyone seeming to take much notice.

The ALC's operations were unreliable at best. The company was undercapitalized and haphazardly staffed. Although cartographers rendered the Zambezi and its main tributary, the Shire, as broad blue lines on their maps, both were shallow and became virtually impassible in dry years.[49] Boats broke down, got stuck on sandbars, and were otherwise delayed. Consequently, there was no set schedule. An agent of the ALC informed Dorsey that only one boat was immediately available. It did not have enough capacity to carry the expedition's loads as well as personnel and livestock. Dorsey grabbed the opportunity to at least send most of the loads upriver to Chiromo, the first point of transfer. He then wrangled a deal with the British vice-consul to set up a military-style camp where he, Dhanis, Thornton, the Zanzibaris, and a corral full of donkeys and cattle, could stay until another boat or boats became available.[50] Grogan and Sharp invited themselves to make use of the mess tent since they remained without their baggage. After a week, the two English adventurers borrowed a tent from the expedition and went off to hunt to kill time (and some wild animals).[51]

Someone broke out the expedition's camera to make photographs. Thirty white tents crowd one of the images, tightly staked against the sea breeze blowing sand and salt across the flat, nearly treeless ground. The same stiff wind whips an enormous Congo Free State flag held firmly vertical above tidy ranks of uniformed Zanzibaris.[52] Drilling soldiers helped pass the time in a way that must have seemed constructive to the Europeans. Like many of their contemporaries, Dorsey and his European traveling companions believed that the breakdown of discipline, system, and order was a principal cause of failure for African expeditions.

Once a day the Zanzibaris gathered to receive their rice ration. The photographer framed his shot carefully to emphasize the authority of an unidentified European in the foreground keeping an account of how much was being dispensed and making sure no one received too much or too little.

Dorsey entertained guests, focused as usual on building a useful network of contacts. He retreated to his tent to draft letters—reporting to Brussels and writing to the ALC agent with a request to arrange passage for the "Indian Soldiers" he hoped would arrive with Verhellen and Castellote.[53] Later events suggest that he also corresponded with his old friend Casement. To his mother and Harriet perhaps he sent notes to say the first step of the expedition was a success. A kiss for Rex! What else did he say? None of the letters survive.

After a week of waiting, the auspiciously named *Sir Harry Johnston* tied up on the riverfront. The steamer had been stuck on a sandbar

Figure 13. Soldiers distributing the rice ration
(Royal Museum for Central Africa)

and required maintenance. African Lakes Corporation employees reinforced the interior of the hull with cement and strapped the steam engine with wire to retard its gradual disintegration from vibration and inevitable collisions with sandbars, logs, and other objects.[54] Livestock were loaded into two smaller boats secured to either side. Everyone climbed on board. Two weeks after arriving in Chinde, the expedition's eight Europeans and one hundred Africans finally headed upstream, chugging slowly through the mangrove swamps of the Zambezi delta and out into the vast, slow-moving reaches of the lower river.[55] The goal was to follow the Zambezi into one of its tributaries, the Shire, before reaching the first of the rift lakes, Nyassa. It was already mid-November, almost three months since the *General* had departed Antwerp, and the expedition had a long way to go before building could commence.

While it is true that river-going steamboats played an essential role in European penetration of Africa's interior, only from the perspective of another century or the chilly offices of European imperial bureaucracies could the operational history of this essential technology be seen as easy or uncomplicated.[56] Having spent several years dealing with the Congo Free State's water transportation system, Dorsey had some sense of what he was getting into. But the effort and frustration of trying to get from Chinde to M'Toa starkly revealed both the ALC's makeshift operational methods and its dependence on African labor.

"We must have touched every sand bank from Chinde to Chiromo," Dorsey complained. "Every time we struck hard the Zanzibaris would jump out and push." The captain had promised extra food rations for the work, which involved not only extra effort but also contending with the risk of crocodiles. Dorsey claimed to have counted "hundreds—I was going to say thousands—sunning themselves on the sand banks," offering a bit of self-correcting hyperbole.[57]

Because the boats carrying the livestock had no rudders and the steamer itself had a very shallow draft, the whole lashed-together ensemble periodically pivoted in a circle, understandably disconcerting the passengers (and probably the livestock). Nevertheless, the *Johnston* made good enough time to catch up with the boat carrying the expedition's loads, which had been stuck on a sandbar for five days.[58] Between tugging and pushing, the *Johnston*'s captain and crew and the Zanzibaris dislodged it. Together, the tiny armada chugged upriver. In its wake, the smell of wood smoke and a dusting of ashes provided the only evidence of the stokers and woodcutters whose exertions enabled the boats' progress.

Two familiar faces peered out from the crowd on Chiromo's landing. Sharp and Grogan had taken a break from hunting to check whether the newly arrived boat was carrying their lost luggage. No luck. But Chiromo was a good place to wait only because nothing was likely to get past them. All the cargo that arrived from Chinde had to be transferred to smaller boats to negotiate the even shallower Shire River. While the dockworkers shifted their loads, Dorsey and the other white men headed off to what passed for a club to share a drink or two and plan the next leg of the journey. It was decided that Thornton, the Australian chief engineer, and the "poseurs" would hike overland to the next stop at Katunga.[59] Dorsey and Dhanis would go by boat as far as possible and then would supervise the Zanzibaris and porters going overland to Blantyre on the upper Shire. Weary of his young traveling companion, Sharp decided to tag along with Dorsey and Dhanis, leaving Grogan to wait for their still missing belongings.[60]

This leg of the journey provided a vivid introduction to the labor practices of the ALC. As Dorsey already knew, piloting a riverboat was considered a white man's job. But recruiting competent Europeans willing to do the job in Central Africa, where the British government's own statistics put the mortality rate at between 9 and 20 percent per annum, proved exceedingly difficult.[61] The ALC thus resorted to hiring working-class British men from various metalworking trades on the theory that they could learn to pilot on the job and might also be able to maintain and repair engines.

The captain on the Chiromo-to-Katunga run was a blacksmith by trade. He also exemplified another pattern that Dorsey observed up and down the rift valley: Europeans who survived tropical diseases and stayed any amount of time tended to succumb to despair, alcoholism, and mental illness. Around noon on the second day, the captain appeared on the

upper deck "roaring drunk" and brandishing a rifle into which he was trying to load a cartridge. Dorsey and Sharp wrestled him down to the lower
deck and locked him "under the hatches" to sober up. To save money (or
perhaps because of a shortage of acceptable employees), the corporation
had also paid the blacksmith-captain to function as the boat's engineer.
"Not having the 'Captain' to annoy them," Dorsey reported, "the pilots
took us up the river splendidly, never touching a bank."[62] Although, he
didn't explicitly say so, the pilots were Africans who had made this run
many times under the nominal guidance of various captains.

After several slow days of travel, the boat finally arrived at Katunga.
This tiny port marked the southernmost tip of the British protectorate.[63]
Shaped like a long, thin lozenge, five hundred miles long and between
fifty and one hundred miles wide, it ran up the west side of Lake Nyasa
for part of its length. Exemplifying the political complexity of the region, its neighbors included Northern Rhodesia, Portuguese Mozambique, and German East Africa.

The protectorate owed its existence to the vision, influence, and determination of two men: David Livingstone, the nineteenth century's
most famous African missionary-explorer and a beloved figure in the
English-speaking world; and the ubiquitous Cecil Rhodes, less beloved
but much admired. Livingstone's influence went back further and more
profoundly marked the region. A trained physician steeped in both humanitarian Christianity and the Scottish Enlightenment's belief in the
possibility of human progress, Livingstone was horrified by Arab and
African slaving practices and eager to atone for Britain's earlier complic-
ity in the slave trade. He imagined a form of missionizing that would
combine catechizing Africans with economic development in the form
of "industrial missions," which taught a variety of skills that might be
marketable as European colonies took hold in Africa. "Legitimate trade"
would thus render slaving economically unnecessary.[64]

Livingstone died in 1873 at Ujiji on Lake Tanganyika, then an Arab
trading center. His African followers disinterred his body, cured it with
salt, disguised it as a bale of cloth, and caravanned it to the coast, where it
was loaded on a ship bound for London. There, the Scotsman was buried
with great pomp in Westminster Abbey. Livingstone's memory proved
a great inspiration to successive waves of missionaries pushing up the

Zambezi from Chinde. It was also an effective political tool for compelling the British government to incorporate the missionary strongholds of Blantyre and Albercorn into its empire. However, the region lacked obvious strategic or economic value. Consequently, a series of British prime ministers, beginning with Lord Salisbury, struggled to find a way to satisfy pressures from antislaving and missionary groups without further burdening a budget that was already strained by the costs of a global empire.[65]

The initial solution for administering on the cheap was to let the ALC, which already ran stores and trading posts as well as the transportation system, do the work of governing. It rapidly became clear that the company lacked the necessary working capital, let alone expertise, to run an entire colony. Into the breach stepped the ubiquitous Cecil Rhodes. He pledged £9,000 a year to be used for governance. Overall authority would rest with a British governor, who would be in the awkward position of reporting to both London and South Africa. Not surprisingly, Rhodes's motivations were complicated. Key elements included his aspiration to "paint the map red" by creating a corridor of British territories from the tip of Africa to the Mediterranean. He also viewed the protectorate as a bulwark against the aspirations of other European powers, especially the Portuguese, whose territories butted up against Rhodesia.[66]

By the time Dorsey arrived, Rhodes's subvention had ceased, and the protectorate's first governor and Rhodes's agent, Harry Johnston, retired after spending half a decade waging a brutal war of pacification carried out by Indian mercenaries.[67] Dorsey's experiences while passing through the protectorate illustrate the distinctive way British imperialism worked in Central Africa, particularly concerning the problem of labor recruitment. But because the only surviving account of this part of the telegraph expedition was written in 1904, after Belgian practices in the Congo came under intense attack in Britain, the picture Dorsey paints is intended to defend his Belgian employer and point out that the British, especially missionaries, were hypocritical in criticizing the humanitarian failings of the Congo Free State.

Things got off to a bad start in Katunga. The contract Dorsey negotiated with the ALC promised enough porters to carry one thousand loads around the rapids to the next big town, Blantyre. Dorsey also expected the agent would provide two mule carts in which the Europeans could ride over the steep pass. The agent overpromised on both counts. Few porters waited around in Katunga for employment and so had to be recruited from nearby villages every time loads arrived.[68] Porters also could not count on being paid in cloth or other trade goods. Instead, they might be compensated in chits that could only be used to pay a British government instituted "hut tax." Labor recruiters accompanied by armed soldiers routinely dragooned local men who could not show tax receipts.[69] So, understandably, people hid from the recruiters, and the loads that Europeans needed someone to carry sat, sometimes for months or even years, in warehouses and on docks.

Eventually, the agent borrowed a cart from the Katunga factory, and Dorsey rode out of the steamy, tropical river valley over a mountain pass and into the cooler highlands, leaving young Dhanis behind to make sure their remaining equipment and supplies followed.[70] Along the road, coffee trees bloomed—their snowy clusters of flowers marking the edges of European-owned farms. Like porterage, coffee cultivation required intensive labor from people who had their own fields and lives and might not be available just because Europeans needed them to work. One of the other uses of the hut tax was to compel agricultural labor.[71] The telegraph expedition passed through the highlands during the peak years of a coffee boom. It would not last, pushed into decline by drought and the difficulties of shipping agricultural commodities out of the landlocked protectorate that lacked a functioning rail system.[72]

Finally, though, Blantyre was in sight. Wary of losing contact with his loads, Dorsey decided to have the Zanzibaris set up the expedition's tents between the Blantyre mission church and the ALC headquarters, where an allée of Australian eucalyptus trees planted by the missionaries provided shade.[73] There they would wait until everything had gone ahead and was ready to be placed on a steamer at the southern end of Lake Nyassa.

Blantyre sat at the epicenter of efforts to realize Livingstone's vision for Africa and Africans. In the late 1890s an estimated two thousand Africans found permanent employment constructing the enormous brick church, which provided a focal point for the town. The workforce included skilled carpenters and masons trained in the nearby industrial mission, which also offered instruction in telegraphy and, for the women, laundry work—all skills the mission boards imagined would be marketable in Central Africa's Europeanized future.[74] Blantyre also featured a hotel and a high street lined by sturdy buildings also made of the bricks produced by African workers in a mission-run factory—perhaps not surprising since bricks were the best-known product of the town's namesake in Scotland, which was Livingstone's hometown.

Although he enjoyed the town's hospitality and even went to church services on Sunday morning, Dorsey could not resist probing the realities beneath the idealism, which he snidely described as "a bale of cloth in one hand and a bible in the other."[75] He suspected that the missionary's efforts intentionally or unintentionally turned Africans into consumers of the products turned out by the mills of Manchester and New Lanark, for which they paid dearly. He also accused the ALC of increasing the profitability of its stores by selling alcohol, which would have been anathema to the staunchly Presbyterian board of directors in Glasgow. Both accusations were not without merit, because Cecil Rhodes had injected a significant amount of capital into the trading part of the company, for which he expected a return.[76] "What struck me most about these well-kept establishments" Dorsey wrote "was the vast amount and varieties of spirits, wine, and beer exposed for sale."[77] The storekeeper swore that this was only because the European settlers were a thirsty lot, not because the alcohol was traded with Africans—something that, along with selling guns and ammunition, was generally seen as crossing an invisible line.[78]

Ten days later the expedition moved on. If Dorsey is to be believed, the missionaries breathed a sigh of relief as the Zanzibaris marched down the road, since these young men had passed the time by trying to seduce young women from the mission. Dorsey found the whole thing amusing. He recounted a heated exchange with a missionary who swore that his parishioners would never allow their virtue to be compromised. Whether or not the exchange ever happened, later events confirmed Dorsey's description of the Zanzibaris as "great mashers." With pay in their pockets, they unapologetically paid or seduced local women to act as temporary "wives."

Still in the heart of ALC territory, unexpected delays and unfulfilled promises became less of a feature of the journey. The most memorable moment of drama and uncertainty came when someone threw a match into the shallow southern end of Lake Nyassa, igniting the marsh gas.

Figure 14. Telegraph expedition members camped somewhere
along the road to M'Toa in 1898. The Zanzibaris are unidentified.
From the left, white members are Thornton, Verhellen,
and Dorsey (Royal Museum for Central Africa).

A sheet of flame spread across the water, scorching two mule saddles
in a barge behind the steamer. Disaster averted, the steamboat moved
steadily on, stopping only to drop the mail at Kota Kota.[79]

Karonga, at the north end of the lake, marked the starting point for
the Stevenson Road over which everything would have to be portaged.
Here, Dorsey's well-laid plans ran afoul of the ALC's operational methods. Forward progress ground to a halt. Responsibility for finding porters
fell to the company's agent, a former missionary named Wright, who told
Dorsey he'd taken the job because he thought it might be a better way to
"reach" the "natives." This explanation made little sense in religious terms
because "reaching" mostly involved pressing locals into service as porters.
Wright's partner in labor recruitment was the tax collector, whom Dorsey
identified with a single initial. Mr. Y's official position provided cover for
impressment in the name of collecting the hut tax. Despite their nominal
authority, neither the missionary nor the government official seemed capable of securing the thousand men needed. Wright offered that he might
be able to hire one hundred men a month. Dorsey estimated it would take
more than two years to move everything in that case.[80]

All the expedition members looked for ways to pass the time while the problem was being resolved. The Zanzibaris went back to seeking temporary wives, much to the disgust of Wright. Disdainful of most of the missionaries, Dorsey defended the Zanzibaris. Eventually, he offered to make sure that the women were compensated out of the Zanzibaris' pay, carefully accounting disbursements in his ledger to comply with British employment rules.[81] Not surprisingly, none of the Europeans admitted that they might also have availed themselves of temporary African "wives." Instead, they turned their attention to the most acceptable pastime of European explorers: hunting.

Dorsey and Thornton also focused on technical matters. In 1898 a brand-new brick building in Karonga marked the northernmost terminus of Cecil Rhodes's Cape-to-Cairo telegraph line.[82] Dorsey and Thornton made themselves known to a Mr. Fox, who was in charge. Here, on the edge of empire, Europeans with competing interests often set them aside in the name of mutual aid and hospitality. Fox allowed Thornton to supervise the construction of a three-mile-long telegraph line between the expedition's camp and the African Transcontinental Telegraph (ATT) office to test the expedition's equipment. It worked beautifully. Pushing the limits of hospitality, Dorsey also obtained permission to send a telegram through ATT's system all the way to Pensacola, Florida, via Cape Town, London, and back. This little experiment would have cost a great deal of money if he'd paid market rates.[83]

As Christmas neared, Grogan reappeared. He'd been hunting along the Songwe River when Africans brought word that his missing traveling companion, Sharp, might be in Kasongo along with their baggage. As it turned out, Grogan just missed rendezvousing with Sharp, who'd finally parted ways with Dorsey to go on to Ujiji. No matter, he was in time for the expedition's holiday festivities and was also in need of a doctor. "Christmas and New Year's we had sports for the men," Dorsey remembered, "and Christmas night we entertained the collector, Mr. Stack, members of the Rhodes Expedition and the ALC agents to dinner."[84] Grogan was too sick to attend the party but availed himself of Dr. Castellote's medical services and spent the holiday in bed with a cup of tea.[85]

Once on the mend, Grogan manage to recruit twelve local men as soldiers to provide security as he recommenced his journey toward

Cairo. The Englishman armed the fresh recruits with Snider rifles. Dorsey, unwilling to appear inhospitable, agreed to let Munie Ngomma drill them in the skills and behaviors expected of native troops. The men abandoned Grogan's expedition a few weeks later just as he rejoined Sharp at Ujiji. Later, this episode would be a source of disagreement between Dorsey and Grogan. Dorsey said Grogan was abusive even beyond the usual European standard of punishment. Grogan said the men were ungrateful.[86] One thing was certain: during their five-month acquaintance, Grogan violated nearly all of Dorsey's standards for appropriate behavior. The personification of a wealthy recreational adventurer, he disregarded the European code of up-country hospitality through freeloading and ingratitude. Seemingly unguided by any sense of loyalty or responsibility, he'd served only himself. Disorganized, intemperate, foul mouthed—the list went on and on. Now this: failing to get along with "the natives" by ignoring the written and unwritten rules of European hegemony. Good riddance.

And so the weeks turned into two months of waiting. In mid-February, Dorsey finally felt satisfied that enough porters had been found to confidently move onward. A new collector ("Irish," Dorsey noted approvingly) had proved a more energetic recruiter than his predecessor, although his sources and methods blatantly violated the intent of the British labor rules. "The carriers employed mostly came from Awemba country and were slaves sent down to earn money for their masters," Dorsey wrote. He claimed many showed signs of mutilation, including severed limbs. That detail was a rebuke against British claims of Belgian atrocities after the fact and may or may not have had any basis. It is probably true, however, that they appeared a "weedy, half-starved lot."[87] The collector also helped Dorsey recruit as many as one hundred "Karonga men" to supplement the Zanzibaris who made up his "permanent" workforce. Like most of the Zanzibaris, they seem to have been promised the high-status work of being soldiers, and they had labor contracts to comply with British law.[88]

At the beginning of March, the expedition's "chef" mounted his donkey and followed one of the last group of porters out of Karongo. He stopped partway up the steep mountain pass to take in the scene. "At our feet lay the fertile Karongo plain. Beyond was the Nyassa, its shores dotted with villages and the iron-roofed houses of the Europeans gleaming in the early morning sun." In the distance, the blue shadows of the Livingstone Range were wreathed in clouds. By the end of the day, they had climbed to four thousand feet in altitude.[89] The Awemba porters had almost no clothing—another violation of British policy that Dorsey made no effort to remedy. Paralyzed with cold, the men piled around the campfires. Dorsey found it impossible to get them moving until midmorning.[90]

After five days of struggling up and down the narrow track, the caravan reached Fife, a halfway point where loads were transferred to a new group of porters. It was one of four stations operated by the London Missionary Society. At each, Dorsey was "cordially received," and "everything was done to make me comfortable."[91] No need to huddle around a fire.

Finally, the porters made the descent onto the plain surrounding Lake Tanganyika. Dorsey was reunited with a group of "his" Zanzibaris, who gleefully ambushed him on the trail. He was less glad to see Grogan yet again. The Englishman had been trophy hunting while he waited for the boat that would take him across the lake. He was full of bitterness about a revenue collector who'd given him "an awful slating" for not paying £25 for a hunting license before he shot an enormous rhinoceros.[92]

The next day, both Dorsey and Grogan crammed their cargo and traveling companions onto the somewhat ironically named *Good News*. Commissioned in the early 1880s by the London Missionary Society, the *Good News* looked nothing like the riverboats that had carried them thus far. It was a steel-hulled, two-masted yacht fitted with a steam engine. At only fifty-four feet long, it had very limited carrying capacity.[93] Verhellen and Thornton, who had gone ahead, recognized that the lone ALC vessel on this body of water would take months to move all their loads. They thus contracted with the captains of Arab-style dhows to carry the excess.[94] Thus the expedition proceeded: dhows silently skimming across the inland sea of Tanganyika in advance of the smoke-belching *Good News*.

In fifteen years of service, the steam yacht had seen very hard use. Its hull was patched together with cement hauled in sacks over the Stevenson Road, and, according to Grogan, it had an engine tied together with "string and strips of sardine cans." The cabins were infested with gigantic cockroaches that dragged down the mosquito netting around the Europeans' beds with their weight.[95] In a familiar pattern, the captain was drunk and barely knowledgeable about his vessel. This was his first voyage. Dorsey described him as "a cockney Englishman and a riveter by trade." The African crew deftly took over, setting the sails and coaxing the engine to life.[96]

To add to the misery, high winds churned Lake Tanganyika, which is one of the largest freshwater bodies in the world. The passengers felt a sensation akin to being on a storm-tossed ship at sea. Grogan suffered from debilitating seasickness for the first two days. Five miles from their destination, a "tornado" struck the ship. Everyone huddled in the cabins, expecting to meet a watery end. But the vessel somehow remained afloat.[97]

It was early April. Almost eight months had passed since Dorsey's meeting with Leopold. It had been five months since expedition members had last seen the Indian Ocean at Chinde. Clearly, the supply line was going to be a challenge.

FACTS ON THE GROUND

The first view of M'Toa failed to inspire confidence. Hastily strung barbed wire festooned the State's stockade and choked the approaches. A banana orchard—vestige of the prosperous Arab town that gave the place its name—had been cut down to improve defensive sight lines. Dodging between the stumps, nervous soldiers patrolled the perimeter.[1] Situated on a steep hill overlooking the vast, blue expanse of Lake Tanganyika, the fort appeared little in need of these extreme measures. However, Captain Hecq, the Belgian commandant, was taking no chances. The situation inside only increased the new arrivals' unease. Four hundred restive Force Publique soldiers crowded the barracks, angry and anxious because for six months the African Lakes Company (ALC) had failed to deliver the cloth they'd been promised as payment.[2] A handful of Belgian officers, two terrified Scandinavian mercenaries, and a group of trading station managers also crowded inside, seeking protection.[3] It felt like a siege by an invisible enemy.

If the facts on the ground proved something of a shock, Dorsey and his fellow Europeans understood the larger causes. Eighteen months earlier and a thousand miles to the north, Leopold's bid for the southern Sudan had gone badly awry. Ignoring Van Eetvelde's advice ("gardez vos opinions," the king told him), Leopold charged two heroes of the Arab War, Francis Dhanis and Louis-Napoléon Chaltin, with hiring and training thousands of African soldiers. This army would be his tool for gaining control of the head of the Nile.[4] Ordered to converge on Khartoum with both stealth (since the whole exercise was in violation of a treaty) and all possible speed (since British and French forces were also headed there), the Belgian officers split their forces into two expeditionary groups.[5]

Chaltin and his army quickly fulfilled their initial mission. They dug in at a strategic area known as the Lado Enclave to which Leopold already had a plausible claim. Dhanis's much larger force, composed mostly of Batetela tribesmen, lagged behind. For reasons of secrecy, the king and his generals mapped a route that would take thousands of soldiers, porters, women, and children through the Ituri Forest on the northeast edge of the Congo Free State.[6] Everyone in charge should have known better. Many members of Stanley's Emin Pasha expedition starved while traversing the Ituri. Torrential rain turned the dense, equatorial forest into a literal quagmire. No one had enough food or water. Thirty days into the march, thousands of exhausted people seemed to be going in circles. Hired porters gradually melted into the forest, leaving their loads behind. For those remaining, the situation became a nightmare: men, women, and children dying of hunger, cold, and dehydration.[7]

By February of 1897, the hired soldiers had endured enough. They turned on their vastly outnumbered Belgian officers. Said Piani Kandolo, one of the Batetela leaders, "We revolted because we were treated like slaves."[8] Kandolo's statement was laden with powerful meanings, particularly because he aimed it at the man who had supposedly eliminated slavery in the Congo, Francis Dhanis. During the revolt, Dhanis hid in the forest with a small group of loyal soldiers. Nicolas Verhellen, who was also part of the expedition, survived because he was keeping the expedition's doctor company in a slow-moving rear guard.[9] Dhanis's brother, Louis, became one of the victims—dying a slow, miserable death from his infected wounds as the survivors retreated, carrying him on a stretcher.[10]

Once free of their Belgian officers, the rebels shouldered their Albini rifles and state-provided ammunition. They headed south—hopscotching down the string of former Arab settlements waging a guerrilla war against the Congo Free State and taking what they wanted from villages along the way. By the spring of 1899, their activities centered on the Maniema—the region through which Dorsey was supposed to build a telegraph line. The whole debacle apparently failed to lessen the king's faith in Francis Dhanis. The recently elevated baron successfully blamed his subordinates, most of whom were dead and thus unable to tell their side of the story. Dhanis publicly declared that the dead officers had behaved like cowards. "Send me Whites who are not afraid," he trumpeted to the press. "With the help of braver men, I would crush the rebellion."[11] Leopold and his advisors responded by ordering Dhanis to follow the rebels to the Tanganyika region and get the problem under control. At the moment that the telegraph expedition arrived at M'Toa, he was a long way from succeeding.[12]

If the situation terrified officials hiding in the fort, Thornton, who'd arrived weeks earlier and prided himself on being tougher than everyone else, took it in stride. The Australian engineer ordered his men to set up a camp a mile from the fort. To amuse himself, he supervised workers who strung a telephone line to the fort. Dorsey was too overwhelmed with recurring malaria to wrap his mind around the situation. He crawled into bed with a 104-degree fever, pausing only long enough to take in the view—a vast inland ocean—and in the distance, volcanic mountains with wisps of vapor drifting from their tops. In a rare fit of nostalgia, he commented that the landscape reminded him of Naples.[13]

Verhellen was less sanguine than Thornton about trying to build a telegraph line in the midst of a guerrilla war. He also worried about the unreliable ALC supply line. Having escaped by luck in Ituri, the situation rattled him. Alone in his tent, he drafted a letter home detailing why the expedition should have entered the Congo at Boma on the west coast and worked from Stanley Falls toward the lake rather than the other way around. Besides the supply line difficulties, he worried that one hundred Zanzibaris supplemented by the Karonga *askiri* would be inadequate to fend off the rebels.[14]

To make matters worse, officials in Brussels promised Dorsey that the commandant of the M'Toa garrison would supply him with workers to clear forest for the ten-foot wide "telegraph road," as well as to erect the line itself. However, Captain Hecq flat out refused. He probably feared sending unpaid Force Publique soldiers into villages to recruit, as they might be ambushed or recruited for the resistance. As a district commissioner, Dorsey was theoretically empowered to recruit on his own, but empty villages along the lakeshore and skittish locals did not bode well for doing so. To add to the sense of foreboding, hyenas prowled the edges of the telegraph camp at night. "Their continual wailing got on my nerves," Dorsey recalled.[15]

As weeks passed, the difficulties of constructing a telegraph line in a war zone became increasingly clear. Ammunition began to run low as Verhellen and his troops took aim at real and imagined enemies. Dorsey wrote letters to State officials begging for more—to no avail. He resorted to hiring a dhow to sail to Ujiji in the hope of purchasing guns and cartridges on the German side.[16] Finally, after two months and little progress, he decided to restart work farther down the planned path of the telegraph. Dhanis was headquartered at Sungula, around one hundred kilometers to the northeast. The Belgian officer might plausibly provide supplies and protection. Given their common history and comradery, Dhanis would have a harder time refusing Dorsey's requests than distant bureaucrats or the recalcitrant Commandant Hecq. Tents were packed, porters loaded, and once again the whole enterprise moved down the road.

This time the caravan did not include two familiar European members. After months of coming and going, mooching meals, socializing, and making use of Dr. Castellote's medical expertise, Grogan and Sharp crossed the lake to continue their journey toward Cairo. According to Dorsey, they did not even say thank you. "Goodbye, see you some of these days in England," they shouted through Dorsey's tent flap. Other European expedition members warranted "goodbye, you chaps."[17] Castellote, who had indulged his taste for trophy hunting with the Englishmen, was sorry to see them go. Everyone else swore not to take in any more stray gentlemen-adventurers.[18] Dorsey did not solicit the opinions of the Africans who'd cooked, cleaned, carried guns, and otherwise waited on the men for nearly seven months.

At first, all seemed as promised at Sungula. With plentiful workers available, construction proceeded at a rapid clip. Thornton took charge of one "brigade," which set about clearing a path from the town. Carey erected a camp farther along the route and put his crew to work. However, Dorsey now confronted a new problem—a food shortage. Hired laborers were expected to provide their own food, which was cooked on the spot by their womenfolk. Food acceptable to the Europeans and Zanzibaris proved more difficult to obtain. Since Dhanis seemed to have secured Sungula, he sent Verhellen and many of the *askiri* westward to Kabambarre where there was more to eat. However, he continued to be plagued by a sense of unease. Thus, he ordered the construction of a defensive *boma*—an enclosure made of thorny trees and brush around the main camp just outside of the village.[19]

Satisfied that he had taken proper precautions and that construction had settled into a routine, Dorsey decided to pass a steamy July morning with his friend, the baron, watching local people making mud bricks. In the distance, they heard gunfire. Dhanis remarked nonchalantly it was probably someone shooting at hippo down by the river. A few minutes later, a runner came shouting as he ran. The *wahuni*—the Swahili word for hooligans or thieves—were coming. The guerrilla forces had attacked the lookouts. Dorsey and Dhanis were the last to know. The wives of the workers had already begun to flee down the telegraph road, dragging their children behind them. Dhanis was blasé. "Oh well, let them go. They won't return before tomorrow, so their husbands won't get any dinner." The two men's amusement was interrupted by another volley of gunfire, this time closer. Dorsey decided it was time to return to the *boma*.[20]

Looking through his field glasses, he saw a surreal sight: thirty men from the expedition running for their lives. A huge group of soldiers followed in hot pursuit. The pursuers wore Force Publique uniforms. They proudly carried the State's familiar blue flag emblazoned with a large gold star. Their movements were coordinated using bugle calls learned from Dhanis's officers. The men carried Albini rifles, provided by the State, and fired bullets they'd managed to procure from various places, including those dumped (along with ivory) by nervous trading station managers.[21] The whole spectacle constituted vivid proof of Dhanis's previous missteps—not that he was inclined to take responsibility.

Eventually Dorsey and Dhanis's forces managed to fend off the attack. Dorsey patted himself on the back for having personally shot several attacking soldiers, including a scout perched in a tree. There were no European casualties. But as many as a hundred African soldiers had been killed or wounded. Injured *wahuni* were carried into the *boma* so that they could be nursed back to health, shipped down to Boma, and court-martialed for desertion (or so Dorsey reported).[22] After things settled down, Omari Muganda, one of Dorsey's favorite Zanzibaris, angrily told his boss that Muhammed, a Somali "table boy" who had a reputation as a braggart, had spent the battle hiding under Dorsey's bed. Dorsey gave Omari permission to inflict twenty lashes for cowardice.[23] Lust for punishment satisfied, everyone went back to work.

Throughout all of this, the telephone line strung between Sungula and Carey's camp continued to function. Carey used it to communicate that the rebels had left his workers and construction site alone. A few weeks later, he used it to convey a series of more urgent messages. Leopards had decided telegraph workers made easy prey and had so far killed six men. Clipperton was also very ill with what Carey described as smallpox. He requested that Dr. Castellote come as quickly as possible.

Dorsey followed a few days later, traveling along the telegraph clearing, by which time Clipperton had died. Burial could not wait in the intense tropical heat. Carey had ordered the *poseur* laid to rest under a large tree that was a local landmark. He carved Clipperton's name and death date into the bark and had ordered a makeshift cross of two iron crowbars lashed together with wire affixed to the tree. The leopard problem remained. The big cats stealthily leaped into the enclosure at night to grab penned up goats. They continued to find a way to their prey in defiance of fires, sentries, and Dorsey taking potshots with his Colt revolver.[24]

Kabambarre beckoned. Once a regional center for Omani Arab traders in ivory and slaves, more recently it had become a prize in the competition between Dhanis's forces and the rebels. In the fall of 1899, a decisive battle returned it to Belgian hands. Dhanis sent word requesting Dorsey hold the fort, wearing his title as a District Governor First Class, while Dhanis and Verhellen tried to suppress the rebels further. The town was also conveniently situated at a halfway point between M'Toa and Kasongo, toward which Thornton's part of the expedition was building.[25] Thus Dorsey and a company of Zanzibaris, including his personal servant, Mohammed, and his cook, Hamisi, as well as a group of soldiers and the usual porters set off.[26] Dorsey rode one of the muskat donkeys, whom he'd named Mokoloma—Pumpkin in

Swahili.[27] Everyone else traveled on foot—porters talking and singing, soldiers alternating between disciplined marching and joking and horseplay. Everyone was weary, worn down by hunger, fever, and the anxious knowledge that the *wahuni* traveled the same territory.

The countryside must have felt familiar to Dorsey. They were now in the heart of the Maniema—the former Arab stronghold and epicenter of the Arab War. He'd never been to Kabambarre, but it was not far from Riba Riba, where he and Chaltin had made their reputations and even closer to the point on the Lualaba where he'd reluctantly decided to end his explorations with the ailing Dr. Hinde. It was impossible not to notice that the once-densely populated countryside had emptied out. Along the road, villages lay in disrepair, people's homes abandoned, their palm roofs collapsing inward. In these places, only the burned-out shells of Arab traders' beautifully crafted houses remained—their neglected gardens and orchards returning to savanna. Everyone in Dorsey's entourage was hungry and had been living on canned sardines and rice for too long. Hence, the abandoned gardens full of orange, lime, and mango trees laden with still-unripe fruit imparted a sense of longing and melancholy. They gathered what they could and moved on.[28]

Dorsey found himself at a loss. How could he make coherent sense (and assign blame) for the ruin he was seeing and for which he held some responsibility? Empty villages and burned-out houses seemed wasteful to him. Having lived among Arabs in both the Congo and Zanzibar, he had some sense of what had been destroyed. But when he went to write up his account of the journey later, he felt obliged to remind his readers about the horrors of Arab slave trading. Caravans of slaves bound for the east coast had been driven by force along this route. The ruined wealth had been paid for by their suffering. People would be better off under State rule once the rebels were banished.

In a private letter to Roger Casement, Dorsey was more honest: "For the native I believe the change has been for the worse." Powerful Arabs made better rulers than the State's version of indirect rule, which put local headmen, "dirty Chiefs" in Dorsey's parlance, in charge. Moreover, the State's claim that slavery had been eradicated was a sham. "Slavery still exists and I can buy here to-day, or any day, as many women, men, and children as I might care for."[29] Dorsey's choice to put women first on the list was perhaps a minor slip. He knew better than to reveal his own involvement in slaving to the British consular officer. He also knew better than to knowingly buy male workers. But Dorsey had allowed his men to buy women from their previous owners. To give a semblance of justice to the transaction, he had the sellers sign a bill of sale written in Arabic, and then "married" the women to Zanzibaris who wanted them. This decision, he told Dhanis, seemed to satisfy everyone.[30]

In the public version of the story, Dorsey villainized the rebels by describing how they preyed on people, using their military skills and weapons to take what they wanted.[31] He seemed unable to wrap his mind around the key role of Dhanis in destabilizing the region. Not only had the Belgian commander made the decision to drive the Arabs out of the Maniema but also the Batetela mutiny set loose nearly a thousand trained and armed men whose actions had displaced waves of people southward. These migrations would have negative consequences for generations to come.[32]

The spread of disease was another consequence of State activity. Steamboats laden with European soldiers, traders, and adventurers as well as Force Publique soldiers brought new sicknesses far inland. Dorsey had already seen the results in the horrifying retreat from Riba Riba through a field full of smallpox victims. Infectious forms of dysentery, fevers, and eventually the scourge of Central Africa—sleeping sickness—were all moving upriver.[33] In Europe and America, the era of public health was dawning. But the Congo Free State had neither the means nor the mandate to implement any new methods for preventing the spread of infectious disease. Even smallpox inoculation, which Dorsey tried mostly without success, failed because the erratic supply line tended to ruin the vaccine. Dorsey's tidy box of medicines in packets and glass jars, carefully packed by Burroughs Wellcome and transported enormous distances, probably offered more psychological comfort than actual relief.[34]

Kabambarre proved a poor refuge. Inside the walls of the fort, death stalked Europeans. Castellote succumbed first, unable to save himself from an attack of dysentery. After three days of intense suffering, he succumbed. Expedition members all experienced repeated bouts of diarrhea and intestinal cramping from drinking untreated water. But conditions in Kabambarre increased the risk.[35] As in caravans (and European cities), the concentrated populations led to polluted wells, and lack of handwashing transferred disease to food. Dorsey's taste for champagne did have a practical side, but none of the Europeans could count on having enough bottled beverages to avoid drinking the water. It was discomfiting enough to be without an doctor now, but what Dorsey found in Castellote's possession increased his unease. As was customary, he went through the dead man's belongings to either sell them, distribute them to the living, or try to get them back to the doctor's family. To Dorsey's shock, Castellote's correspondence revealed he'd been telling State officials that Dorsey was incompetent.[36]

Within days, three Belgian officers assigned to the station had also died. Even without a doctor, Dorsey could easily ascertain the cause: blackwater fever. Named for symptomatic black urine, this severe form of malaria causes large numbers of red blood cells to explode in the circulatory system. The body's attempt to cleanse the blood overwhelms the kidneys and causes rapid (and agonizing) death. The Chef de Poste then succumbed to it. A carpenter hammered together coffins and Dorsey ordered the men buried in what passed for a cemetery. As the most senior European present, Dorsey conducted brief religious services. This was not a job he'd been trained to do or, indeed, wanted. The body of another Belgian officer was brought into the post; for a little variety, he'd been murdered. At least this death could be avenged. Dorsey sent out a party of Force Publique soldiers to round up someone they identified as the culprit. The next day Dorsey sent the man to Dhanis, who promptly had him court-martialed and hanged.[37]

Dorsey and a single Belgian officer, named Pertili, remained. "I had buried five Europeans in two weeks, and we two who were left felt rather blue," he wrote with characteristic understatement. A few days later, the American was overtaken with "agonizing" stomach cramps. "I thought my time had come." In the morning, he felt better. Psychic relief came in the form of a phone call from Thornton, who invited him to inspect a newly constructed section of telegraph line. Getting a phone call was still a novelty even in many parts of Europe and the United States, but Dorsey was matter of fact about the experience. He was less blasé about the opportunity it presented. "Never in my life have I been so thankful to get out of a place as Kabambarre."[38] He had no intention of going back.

Instead, he would set up headquarters for the expedition in Kasongo. This former Arab stronghold on the Lualaba River served boats coming and going to Stanley Falls. The decision may have been partially practical. The expedition was running out of cloth to pay workers. It was also running out of insulators, without which the copper wire could not be strung between the telegraph poles. Far from Lake Tanganyika, the supply line now depended on the State rather than the ALC. Dorsey had been churning out increasingly desperate letters begging State officials to send him what was needed. At Kasongo, his ability to secure supplies might be enhanced. Almost halfway through his three-year contract, the clock was ticking.

Fond memories of Kasongo also colored his decision. There, among the ruins of Arab houses, he had first met Dhanis five years earlier. Kasongo was where he'd taken a long, leisurely break after the Riba Riba expedition: sleeping on silk sheets, bathing in warm water, smoking European cigarettes, and generally enjoying himself. After his close call with death, he turned his back on privation.

Dorsey enjoyed a first taste of those luxuries while still on the road. In the company of his Zanzibari entourage, he stopped for the night at the home of an elderly Arab trader named Bwana Mussa. Somehow, the old man escaped the war and the ensuing turmoil with both his wealth and his life, cleverly figuring out how to coexist with both State officials and the rebels. Mussa lived in a large house, tended by servants. After a year of moldy tents, cockroach-infested boats, grimy garrisons, and fleabag port hotels, Dorsey was particularly impressed that the dwelling was "delightfully clean, inside and out."[39] The house's cool corridors, scented with incense and lined with finely woven palm mats, briefly transported him to other distant places.

After shaking off dust from the road, Dorsey met with Bwana Mussa on the *baraza* (a custom and a word he'd learned in Zanzibar). He found his host dressed to impress in a finely woven white tunic overlaid with an embroidered camel's hair burnoose. A green turban flecked with gold graced his head. The curved dagger in an elaborate sheath hanging from a heavy silver belt conveyed exotic manliness as well as wealth.

Mussa completed Dorsey's seduction by cradling the American's hand in his, turning it over, kissing it, while he professed how "grateful he was that God had been so good as to direct my course through his poor village."[40] Dorsey knew how to respond. He signaled one of the men in his entourage to bring gifts for his host, including a box of spectacles. He invited the old man to choose a pair that pleasingly corrected his vision and to help himself to a box of incense Dorsey had purchased in Zanzibar for such occasions. There were also gifts for the local chieftains who lined the porch.[41]

Never one to waste an opportunity, Dorsey eventually brought the conversation around to whether his host and the local "big men" might help him recruit workers. Clearing a path through dense jungle using machetes and shovels required hundreds of men accustomed to grindingly difficult physical labor, and the smallpox epidemic had killed four hundred of Thornton's workers. Whatever promises Mussa made (how could he say no?), Dorsey took his assurances seriously enough to pursue the matter with Dhanis.[42] He still didn't know how he would pay the men without cloth.[43]

Two months later, he was still wondering. Work on the line had ground to a halt. Dorsey expended his restless energy on supervising the construction of a house made of mud bricks, setting up a market, and once again hunting.[44] Finally, on Christmas morning, the supplies came in. He and Thornton had been sitting on the porch commiserating about the "blistering" heat and lack of supplies. They'd run out of everything, including coffee and tea, and were contemplating a dry holiday without even the possibility of palm wine when a line of porters came into view winding up the hill from the river with chop boxes strapped to their backs.[45]

Saved by the State! Dorsey ordered his house servants to wrap four bottles of Piper Heidsieck champagne in wet cloth and hang them in a breezeway to cool. Two bullocks were killed so that everyone could gorge themselves on meat. Hamisi, Dorsey's cook, selected the best cuts for the Europeans' table. The rest went to the Zanzibaris since "they are entitled to their Xmas"—by which Dorsey meant the day off and feast that was customary for European and American workers. Religion had nothing to do with it for either the nominally Christian expedition leaders or the Muslim Zanzibaris.[46] That night, Dorsey and Thornton dined on the beef as well as tinned asparagus, plum pudding and brandy sauce, brandy, and coffee. They topped off the evening with cigars that had been tucked into the boxes. Apparently a bureaucrat in Brussels had decided the menu and overseen the packing and shipping of these treats. In keeping with the customs of empire, the Zanzibaris provided entertainment on Boxing Day, competing for prizes and staging a nighttime "grand war dance" by the light of bonfires.[47]

The holidays over, everyone went back to work. Two large caravans set out with construction supplies and cloth to pay workers. One went to Thornton's camp. The other headed toward Sungula and what was now known as the Leopard's Camp. Carey was still trying to complete the eastern section of the line by building toward M'Toa. Dorsey dashed off an apology to Dhanis to whom he'd written a "rather rude letter" about the lack of supplies. It turned out that a State official at the Kilita station had heard a rumor that the telegraph expedition had been wiped out by the rebels and had decided to hold the supplies. Dorsey joked the *Blantyre Times* would soon publish news of their deaths. Two bottles of Mumm champagne, Dorsey's preferred brand, accompanied his letter. The ALC had finally delivered his order to M'Toa. The European expedition members now found themselves well-provisioned with libations.[48]

It was a new century, according to the European way of thinking about time. Here, in a place Joseph Conrad had just taught his readers to call the "heart of darkness," European fixations on measuring experience with calendars and watches was both meaningful and meaningless.[49] Dorsey, Dhanis, and the rest labored under the State's requirement of making regular reports using numerical terms: how many miles of line built, how many rebels killed. They were also acutely aware of the length of their employment contracts. But human bodies and the Congo's challenging environment did not respect the sanctity of contract or the logic of calendars. Thus, the new year heralded a series of departures both anticipated and not. Verhellen left for Brussels in the spring, "invalided out" with an inguinal hernia. Tickell, one of the remaining foremen, became too sick to continue. Louis Dhanis, Dorsey's secretary, was long gone, the first to "invalid out" in July 1899.[50] Louis's older brother, Francis, shared with Dorsey the news that he would return home when his contract ended in July. He was engaged to be married. "Don't play the goat and come out here again, as I have," Dorsey advised him, articulating his sense of being set up for failure by the State and regret at having left his family.[51]

Ten Europeans had set out from Chinde in the fall of 1898. Now there were three: Dorsey, Thornton, and one remaining *poseur*, A. J. Carey.[52] Thornton and Carey had been managing separate construction camps. Carey's, farther east, continued to be attacked by rebels. The decision was made that Carey would join Thornton. The latter presided over hundreds of laborers slowly hacking and digging their way through a tropical version of a malevolent enchanted forest. Ahead of them, densely tangled roots and branches blocked the sun. The shadows were so deep that the skin of the two white men developed a ghostly pallor.[53] Behind them, plants and animals waged a relentless campaign to reclaim what had already been cleared with so much effort. Seeds sprouted in the new, sunlit clearing, shooting toward the sky. The forest set about destroying the line almost as soon as they'd gotten it working. Termites put their mandibles to the task of felling the wooden telegraph poles. Like other animals and people, forest elephants took advantage of the new pathway, pausing to rub against the poles, occasionally knocking them over. The sun beat down on the vast green sea, generating intense thunderstorms. Frequent lightning strikes incinerated poles and shorted electrical equipment. It must have seemed like the whole environment conspired against threading a wire across it.[54]

Dorsey had indeed run out of patience with "playing the goat" but felt obliged to honor his contract, which didn't expire until August 1901, more than a year away. At least he had an excuse for not joining the other two men in the forest. He didn't fully trust the Zanzibaris guarding the expedition's limited supplies and expensive electrical equipment in his Kasongo house. By July he was also "desperately ill" with an ailment that rendered him virtually unable to move. He described it as "rheumatism," but he had no idea what was really wrong. By the end of September, he mustered enough energy to dictate a telegram to his family assuring them that he was still alive—barely. The symptoms would last up until his departure from Africa.[55] He was depressed, angry, and afraid all his efforts would come to naught. Far away, in the places he'd called home, his family enjoyed the pleasures of summer including ice cream, picnics, and trips to the seaside. In the forests of the Eastern Congo, however, many obstacles seen and unforeseen converged, bringing construction to a halt.

The previous spring, Thornton's crew had made slow, steady progress of two to four kilometers a week. Thornton diligently sent a progress report on Saturdays. In his clear, carefully written cursive script, it summarized how much distance had been cleared, how many holes dug, how many poles erected, how much wire strung.[56] Most of the hard work was being carried out by eighty Wachenzi tribesmen who'd been provided by Bwana Mussa. Dorsey's gracious green-turbaned Arab host had struck a bargain in which he garnered a cut of the men's lengths of cloth, or "doti," in return for acting as a labor contractor. Impatient and frustrated by the slow pace of work, Thornton also pressed into service some of the Karongo recruits. They were not happy about this. Like the Zanzibaris, these men had apparently been told that they would be *askiri*, like most of the Zanzibaris. Carrying a gun was a much higher status (and physically easier) work than digging holes, tending donkeys, or carrying water. They also found the demotion humiliating.[57]

To maintain discipline and compel "all hands" to dig and cut, Thornton resorted to corporal punishment so severe Dorsey felt compelled to chastise him. Humanitarian concerns may have played a minor role, but worries about protecting the State from accusations of labor abuses probably mattered more. Dorsey subscribed to the London *Times*, which somehow managed to reach him when nothing else did. In its pages, he could read all about the growing controversy over the treatment of rubber gatherers in nearby Kasai.[58] Leopold's instrumental compliment that Dorsey had been picked for the mission because he knew how to get along with the "natives" also shaped his efforts to avoid the harshest forms of coercion. Seasoned by many years of compelling Indigenous people in the far corners of the British empire to do his bidding while employers turned a blind eye, Thornton was irate about

Dorsey's correction. "You appear to think I am not capable of dealing with men in a just and correct manner," he fumed. "I am here to work. The men under me must work." Then he threatened to quit. "Release me if you don't think I can manage fairly."[59]

By early July, it became clear Thornton's motivational techniques weren't the only or even the worst problem hindering further progress. None of Thornton's workforce had been paid for two months. Handing out pay on Saturdays was one of the European customs Dorsey liked to maintain in Africa. That summer, Saturday after Saturday came and went without a disbursement of cloth. The consequences were dire. By convention, local men provided their own food. The Zanzibar and Karonga men received a rice ration but had to purchase everything else—meat, eggs, fruits, and vegetables. Without cloth, the workers had no means of purchasing food. Moreover, the path of the telegraph line was nearly twenty kilometers from the nearest Wachenzi villages where families might provide food. Thornton shared some of his own supply of rice with the Zanzibaris, but he kept all his canned food for himself.[60]

The State's unreliable supply line and lack of coordination lay at the center of the problem. Despite Dorsey's endless pleas, no cloth was forthcoming. In theory Thornton could pay the men in other trade goods. Dorsey was guarding a storehouse holding all kinds of items someone in Brussels thought Africans might like. These included one hundred forty-six Tyrolean hats, a Singer sewing machine, mirrors, brass wires, and lots of trade beads.[61] Dorsey didn't even try to pay workers with these supplies. He knew that most of what he had in storage would be viewed as luxuries. In contrast, cloth and beads functioned as currency. Thornton had tried paying the men in trade beads, but beads had been devalued in the food markets because, as Thornton told Dorsey, "The Baron has deluged the country with trade beads and the natives will take no more." He expected that the Wachenzi would walk off the job if no cloth appeared soon.[62]

Thornton recognized that his men were starving and that they were entitled to their pay. But this didn't stop him from beating one of the Karonga men who complained. The punishment was so brutal and humiliating that the man, Hamisi Mabrouki, fled the camp even though it would have been impossible for him to return home on his own.[63]

Thornton utterly failed to see a parallel with his own situation. Six weeks earlier he'd received a letter from his wife in Europe telling him the State had deducted £40 from his pay because he'd supposedly taken an advance. Without telling him, someone also decided that the State would retain half of his salary until he returned from Africa. Everyone, it seemed, was being cheated, though no one in the Thornton family was in imminent risk of starvation.[64]

Thornton was nothing if not persistent. He and Dorsey came up with a scheme for shifting the responsibility for recruiting and paying workers to maintain the eastern section of the line onto the State so they would have more cloth to pay construction workers. Three inexperienced Belgian officers had recently been sent out to take over the line's operation. "Another amateur," in Thornton's estimation, Lieutenant van den Broeck had already earned the Australian engineer's ire by "spoiling" a telephone at Sungula. He'd taken the apparatus apart, in the process breaking a delicate part. When the Belgians asked for help in compensating their workers, Thornton told them no. "They can make their own arrangements."[65] Both he and Dorsey harbored the suspicion that the State could provide cloth and other supplies but for mysterious reasons was holding out on them. They could not quite recognize that behind Leopold's impressive sales pitches lay an organization riddled with malevolent incompetence.[66]

Thornton also set about ridding the camp of nonessential and malingering workers. Most of the Karonga men departed without receiving their back pay. Instead, Dorsey sent the ALC agent a spreadsheet with the names of all the workers and the amounts still owed. He asked the agent to disburse pay to the men listed or to the survivors of those who had died. The ALC was then to contact State officials in Brussels for reimbursement. Thornton also made up his mind to quit. In his reasoning, the State failed to fulfill its side of the contract by providing men and materials he needed to get the job done. As he repeatedly told Dorsey and others, it was his professional opinion that using wooden telegraph poles constituted an enormous waste of money and effort because the poles had to be replaced so often. With a bit of prescience, he advised, a wireless system might better suit conditions in the Eastern Congo.[67]

Then, almost predictably, loads of cloth came through—just when it seemed expedition members must pack up and go home. This time, boxes and bales appeared without even an explanation for the delay. Thornton inventoried the supplies and found they'd still been shorted. He hypothesized someone had helped themselves. To supplement the cloth, Dorsey sent salt and other trade goods (though not the Tyrolean hats) with instructions that Thornton calculate their value using local valuations of "Americani" (units of cloth) as the standard. He also sent blankets because some of the workers said they were cold at night and therefore prefer them to bundles of cloth.[68]

Problems remained. The camp was a long way from sources of food. Inflation had driven up costs in the markets. Wachenzi workers continued to walk off the job. Mussa refused to find replacements. Dorsey sent a group of soldiers whom he'd "demoted" to workmen to fill in the gaps.[69] Somehow, the work continued.

Another year. Dorsey celebrated New Year's Day by writing Théodore Wahis, governor of the Congo Free State, giving notice. None of the three remaining European expedition members wished to renew their contracts.[70] Dorsey began planning his escape. His sense of honor and worries about future employment ensured that he would spend the remaining months finishing as much of the line as possible. He also intended to leave the completed portions in good working order, with maintenance workers in place. He planned to return to Europe by traveling east so that he could personally fulfill his promise to the Sultan that the surviving Zanzibaris would be returned home and receive their back wages.

And then there were two. At the beginning of March, Thornton rode down to Kasongo, which lay within easy traveling distance of the telegraph camp. Construction workers had finally hacked, dug, and burned their way out of the forest and were racing to erect poles across the savanna. Both men hoped the line between Kabambarre and Kasongo would be complete before they returned to Europe. As was their custom, they probably shared chilled champagne on Dorsey's front porch.

Then Thornton headed back to his camp. Several days later a worried messenger arrived with a request for a doctor. Thornton was very sick. "There wasn't a doctor within two hundred miles," Dorsey lamented. He planned to go himself the next morning. In the middle of the night, another messenger arrived: Thornton was dead. Carey accompanied the body to Kasongo. In death as in life, Thornton was probably slung in a hammock between two porters for the short trip. Dorsey ordered his rapidly decomposing body buried in a grove of mango trees.[71]

Dorsey went through Thornton's possessions. This dead man's correspondence offered no big surprises. Thornton had not been shy about making his grievances known. The shocker was his age. Although expedition members jokingly called him the "old man" because of his voluminous gray beard, they had no idea he was sixty years old—almost unthinkable in a place that routinely killed and disabled men in the prime of life. In the end, he outlived and outlasted a group of expedition members half his age. Dorsey inventoried Thornton's possessions and then sold them at public auction. The meager assemblage contained little of note except for sixteen books Thornton read and reread to pass the time.[72]

In his later account, Dorsey failed to mention Thornton's brutal motivational techniques and short temper. Instead, he spun Thornton's death into a fanciful illustration of African acceptance of European superiority. "The natives regarded him with veneration, and he was known throughout the whole country as 'Bwana Mse' (the old master)," he claimed. "Thousands of natives and Arabs came to the funeral" to pay their respects."[73] This seems unlikely.

Dorsey's depiction of Thornton as the old master does not explain how construction and maintenance continued apace with Carey and the three technologically incompetent Belgians nominally in charge. The answer is, of course, that Africans employed on the project were, at this point, perfectly capable of proceeding without any European supervision at all. That's exactly what they did. A closer look at the construction process gives some sense of why Thornton and Carey and then Carey alone, especially when they were sick or otherwise incapacitated, didn't really provide much guidance let alone control.

When there was enough cloth (or the promise of cloth) to pay a full workforce, and when Mussa and local headmen could cajole or coerce men to leave their fields and families, the number of local men working on the line numbered as many as eight hundred. Zanzibaris and Karonga men supplemented the mass of laborers by doing skilled work or, more often, providing security and probably working as what would have been called "drivers" on American plantations. Each morning, work groups set out from the main camp. One group carried tools for clearing the path of the telegraph—axes, saws, shovels, as well as blocks and tackle to pull out stumps and remove trees. Many of these tools had come all the way from Belgium. One of the Zanzibaris, Barata bin Juma, carried a compass, which he used to make sure the line was cleared in the correct direction. He also oversaw a crew using surveyor's chains to measure distances. In the forest, a second crew selected trees that could be used as telegraph poles. These were cut down and trimmed. Workers then fitted the poles with brackets and insulators before setting them upright in predug holes. A specially trained group of workers strung the wire. In a distinctive Belgian touch, it was painted black on the theory that local people would be less likely to cut it down and use it for their own purposes if it didn't sparkle in the sun.[74]

Other workers supported construction activities. "Donkey boys" and their animal helpers traveled between the main camp and work groups. On the way out, they brought drinking water to sustain men toiling in the intense tropical heat. Couriers also ferried supplies into the field and brought back broken or dulled tools. In camp, a blacksmith used a portable forge (also brought from Belgium), a grinding wheel, and files to perform maintenance. He also forged tools and fixtures as needed.

When the line reached the site chosen for a substation, a Zanzibari carpenter and another crew member put together a small wooden building with a table and seat for the operator.[75] The buildings also housed dry cell batteries, which provided power for the system. Thornton employed local workers to perform these tasks. By the time Dorsey left, he was confident they knew enough to keep the system operational and could be trusted to do it on their own. In a report to the governor, he wrote "These men are all natives, usually Bakusu and are thoroughly good at this work. They understand jointing, heading in, replacing insulation, and are excellent at soldering."[76] The substations were fitted with telegraph equipment. The major ones—notably Kabambarre, Sungula, and Kasongo—also had telephones that utilized the same duplex wire system as the telegraph. Because the expedition hadn't completed enough of the line to connect to either the Congo Free State system being built up the coast or Rhodes's line, which still hadn't made it past Ujiji, the strategic value of a telegraph did not justify paying specially trained operators. However, if the State had desired this, well-trained Africans would have been available because missionary schools offered courses in telegraphy.[77]

Brussels bureaucrats' lack of understanding about conditions in the Maniema meant there would be plenty of maintenance work for locals after Dorsey and Carey left, especially in replacing wooden poles. Dorsey estimated each pole would need to be reinstalled at least every four months, but a strong thunderstorm might render the entire system inoperable more quickly. Best practice in the English-speaking world of telegraph construction included the use of lightning protection especially on wooden poles and stations.[78] However, nothing of the sort was included on the packing list, perhaps because no one in Brussels quite grasped that the central Congo has one of the highest rates of lightning strikes in the world. Nor had they considered the devastating effect of lightning on electrical equipment. Consequently, lightning strikes repeatedly blasted big sections of the line. The Sungula station, for instance, was set on fire, ruining the electrical equipment.[79]

As Dorsey prepared to leave, far from Africa, controversy was growing over the treatment of African workers in the Congo Free State. The English-language press offered readers conflicting reports. In the summer of 1901, the *St. Louis Post-Dispatch*, for instance, published a full-page article suffused with pro-State, civilizing-mission rhetoric: "The Congo negroes, with few exceptions, adapt themselves easily to civilization, and make excellent workmen provided they are kindly treated."[80] Thanks to the wire services, other newspapers published versions of this story. Pro-State articles also typically claimed that State officials successfully quashed abuses by harshly punishing the whites responsible. Other newspapers (and sometimes the same papers) published increasingly sensationalized versions of accounts by former State employee describing atrocities. One widely circulated story described how State officials hired "cannibals" as Force Publique soldiers and allowed them to kill and eat uncooperative "natives."[81]

Neither of these ways of viewing the labor situation reflect reality as it was enacted by Africans and Europeans involved in the telegraph expeditions. Like many Europeans, Thornton genuinely believed violence or the threat of violence motivated workers he viewed as primitive and racially inferior. He also felt entitled to take out his own anger and frustration on those over whom he had power. Thornton believed he was capable of judging where the acceptable boundaries of this kind discipline lay. Like Dorsey, he'd learned by observing and talking to other experienced "hands" and had in turn modeled behavior for newer arrivals, including the four *poseurs*.[82]

Although they did not leave behind written evidence of their view of the expedition, the Africans were not the passive, unreasoning, or naive actors the press sometimes made them out to be. Significant numbers of Wachenzi workers cut their losses and walked off the job when cloth was not forthcoming. To do so, they risked not only the wrath of Europeans but also of their headmen and Bwana Mussa. However, they could and did go back to their homes and their fields if working for the expedition did not seem to be in their own self-interest. Some of them also embraced the work, particularly the more technical parts, as technically minded people in many cultures are inclined to do.

The situation of the Zanzibaris and Waronga men was complicated in different ways. They took a huge risk signing on to the expedition because they could not go home again without Dorsey's help. If Dorsey made a serious miscalculation (as Dhanis had in the Ituri Forest), they could die. These risks were balanced by rewards. Within the ranks of workers, they had special status. The soldiers among them had the power to inflict punishment on locals or even those within their own ranks who stepped out of line. Dorsey also allowed them special perks, including rations from expedition supplies and the endlessly troublesome expectation of temporary wives.

What aspects of this were exploitative? How could a realistic line be demarcated? How might the State (really Leopold and his cronies) continue to profit from the Congo's riches without violating the agreements, concrete and tacit, through which signatories to the Berlin Treaty and successive accords had agreed to allow Leopold to control the Congo and the lives of the millions of people within it? These were the questions Dorsey would face when he returned to Europe.

Meanwhile, it was time to go. Dorsey's scheduled departure date was June 15, 1901. True to form, his designated replacement failed to show up in time.[83] State officials in Brussels also came up with a few more requirements to inflict. A last-minute telegram ordered him to return to Europe via Boma on the west coast.[84] Dorsey had already arranged to follow the old caravan route going east, traveling to Ujiji on the lake and from there onward to Dar es Salaam and Zanzibar. He earnestly intended to fulfill his promise to the Sultan. Afraid that he might die before reaching Zanzibar, he'd even arranged with Justin Malfeyt to have a Belgian officer whose contract had expired travel with him.[85]

A series of potentially unpleasant conversations awaited him at the mouth of the Congo River. State officials in the justice department seemed fixated on how he'd handled the auctioning of Thornton's effects, even though he had followed written protocols.[86] The governor demanded written elaborations and clarifications regarding Dorsey's final report. Sitting thousands of miles away, Wahis could not understand why Dorsey hadn't built more of the line. That 284 kilometers had been built did not seem to satisfy him. He also made it known that Dorsey had complained too much about the supply line, forcing him to backpedal.[87]

Having temporarily placated his bosses, Dorsey sat down to write letters of reference for the Zanzibaris and Karonga men to whom he felt most indebted. Munie Ngomma, one of the soldiers he'd hired in Karongo, received a unique letter. It certified that the Snider rifle and thirty cartridges in Ngomma's possession had been legitimately obtained. The weapon was a reward for his "faithful service" as a "non-commissioned officer."[88] Dorsey wrote additional letters to the ALC and a trading company in Zanzibar requesting that they pay the balance of salary owed and bill the State. He also requested deck passage for the Zanzibaris, some of whom were now accompanied by wives and children. Four of the men came with him as he set off in one of the giant canoes he'd first come to know almost a decade before. It was his intention that they would return home via the Suez Canal.[89]

Later, he'd write in sentimental terms about the journey downstream, remembering the comradeship of the Arab War and lauding the progress toward civilization he claimed could be seen from the river and the railroad. This version of the facts was written when he'd already embarked on a new stage of his career: apologist for the State. By then, everyone he'd known from Africa—Casement, Parminter, Dhanis, even Grogan—had taken sides. That lay in the future. In the summer of 1901, he just wanted to go home. He was still very sick, eager to see his family, and worried about the future.

THE TRUTH ABOUT
THE CONGO

Wracked by fever and disillusionment, Dorsey returned to Brussels in the fall of 1901. Setting his misgivings aside, he proceeded to tie himself even more tightly to Leopold and the Congo Free State. For their part, State officials decided Dorsey's failure to complete the telegraph line could be forgiven. He still had his uses. He also knew too much to be summarily cut adrift. However, no seductive royal audience marked this return. Instead, a faceless bureaucrat issued an Étoile de service—one of the State's less prestigious medals. Pinned to Dorsey's court uniform, it announced his continued allegiance to his employer.[1]

He was initially reluctant to stay. It's easy to see why. By the time he returned to Brussels, he knew firsthand that most of Leopold's public claims were untrue. More importantly, the proprietor-king had ruthlessly breached the high-minded promises he'd made to the signatories of the Berlin Act. From Dorsey's first trip upriver almost a decade earlier, he'd recognized that opportunities for free trade had suffocated under the State's monopolistic policies. It took him longer to concede the State's failure to eradicate slave trading. His melancholy return visit to the burned-out villages of the Maniema offered overwhelming evidence that slavery persisted. By the time he'd tidied up the last stages of the telegraph expedition, he'd seen how State policies contributed to the immiseration of local people through political disruption, food shortages, and the spread of diseases.

And he'd been more than a witness. As a younger, less circumspect man, he'd bragged about burning villages. He'd even ordered severed hands displayed as a warning to thieves and mutineers. As leader of the telegraph expedition, he'd authorized brutal labor practices resulting in the starvation of hundreds of workers. If he hadn't wielded a *chicotte*—the hippo-hide whip—himself, he'd certainly authorized its use to punish Africans for perceived transgressions.[2] His time in the Congo made him acutely aware that greed, anxiety, and poor judgment shaped the behavior of many State officials and concessionaires. Men such as Dhanis and Chaltin might be honored as heroes when they returned home, but Dorsey was enough of a realist to recognize they'd risen into the upper tiers of State officials because service in the Congo was a job that few competent, not to mention scrupulous, people wanted.

By the early twentieth century, the widespread atrocities in Leopold's domains could no longer be kept secret, only explained away. Missionaries and travelers bore witness. Diplomats and politicians gathered information. Thanks to international wire services, journalistic accounts circulated to ordinary people on both sides of the Atlantic.[3] However, what the information meant and what to do with it raised difficult questions. Were the worst acts of violence just the work of rogue individuals, as Leopold claimed? Was a certain amount of violence necessary to the civilizing process, as widespread racist beliefs of the time would have it? Was the violence in the Congo Free State fundamentally different from the violence against what reformers of the time called "aboriginal people" in other parts of the world?

For almost two decades, Leopold had managed to stay one step ahead of his critics. He and his minions skillfully readied their defenses and versions of the facts. A shadowy public relations apparatus provided them to the print media. Aided by lawyers, lobbyists, sympathetic journalists, and consuls and other diplomatic representatives of both the State and Belgium, Leopold waged a relentless campaign of public relations and private influence on both sides of the Atlantic.[4] For six years after his return, Dorsey was a tool in Leopold's increasingly baroque efforts to spin what his public relations campaign titled "The Truth on the Congo."[5]

Elements of grand drama had always characterized the story of Leopold and the Congo Free State. Many characters, familiar and new, now crowded onto a global stage ready to play out the final act. They formed a noisy chorus as each voice strained to be heard amid the growing cacophony. In the limelight: two soon-to-be heroes: Roger Casement, appointed as British Consul to the Congo in 1900, and Edmund Morel, an obscure Liverpool shipping clerk turned crusading journalist. In the role of arch villain: Leopold II, now in his seventies and prepared to cling to every shred of power, influence, territory, and wealth he'd acquired over the course of his reign. The reformers aimed to unscramble what had been done in Berlin by forcing Leopold to turn the Congo over to the people of Belgium. It was a plan almost no one felt good about, but there seemed to be no viable alternative. In that moment, most humanitarian and equality-minded Europeans and Americans could not imagine enacting the obvious: giving the land back to the people who lived there so that they could determine their own destinies.

In this grand drama Leopold and his advisors sought to cast Dorsey in the role of the American professional adventurer, seemingly independent and unimpressed by a European monarch; the expert who had been "out" to Africa and could testify to its realities. Henry Morton Stanley had long starred in this role, playing to the galleries and, more importantly, newspaper and book buyers all over the world. But Stanley was an old man, in slow and bitter decline in London.[6] Dorsey proved himself an unconvincing understudy. After an initial awkward audition, he retreated to the edge of the action. For the first few years after his return, we mostly glimpse him there—a bit player. Eventually he reemerged, but not until he'd figured out how comfortably to rationalize his continued association with a king and an organization that had become the target of the first great humanitarian and anti-imperialist campaign of the twentieth century.

Let's pause to consider why Dorsey didn't sever his connection to the Congo Free State after returning to Europe. The answer has important implications. The history of the modern world is full of people like him, emissaries of "pity, science, and progress," as Joseph Conrad's narrator famously put it in *Heart of Darkness*. These men, and more rarely women, made it possible for villains like Leopold to carry out their agendas.[7] Dorsey never provided a straightforward answer in his own words. His personal archive contains only three pieces of paper from his years as an apologist.[8] They offer few clues. Instead, we must look to the patterns of his life, his values and self-image, as well as the circumstances in which he found himself.

Family loyalty—that is, loyalty to specific people—dominated Dorsey's value system. He enacted his beliefs primarily through being a steadfast breadwinner. As the eldest son of a widowed mother, he'd taken on this role at a formative age. From that point onward, others always depended on him for financial support, and no one would bail him out if he failed. The responsibility weighed heavily. Working for the Congo Free State provided a steady, middle-class income.

Being a servant of empire was a career he'd fallen into because it offered opportunities for someone of his background and talents: his organizational skills, ability to learn on the fly, steely resolve, and perhaps most importantly, his iron constitution. Unlike his most famous contemporaries, he'd never fallen in love with Africa and had only briefly flirted with the role of the explorer during his ill-fated trip with Sidney Hinde. Nor was he a true believer in imperialism or the civilizing mission. Loyalty to abstractions was not his style. Unlike Casement, his time in Africa also did not awaken any humanitarian impulses. Instead, the everyday racism of his Reconstruction-era youth hardened into a pragmatic view of "the natives" as the expendable means to his and his employers' ends.

This "pragmatism" became one of the ways he justified participating in the cruelty and human suffering inherent in the State's way of doing things. It helped to be surrounded by like-minded colleagues, friends, and family. In the end, he stayed because he couldn't find an acceptable way out.

Perhaps things would have been different if he'd settled into another kind of marriage. Or if he'd stayed single. As it was, he and Harriet settled on a conventional arrangement. She agreed to raise their children and make a home. He committed to supporting the whole enterprise financially. In adhering to an imperialist version of their "separate spheres," they both paid heavy personal prices. Nearly half their married life was spent apart, connected by letters, memories, and hopes about the future. Dorsey's loneliness during the telegraph expedition is palpable in his writings. During his absence, Harriet tried a conventional Victorian strategy to alleviate her isolation and lack of familial support. For a time, she lived in Washington, DC, with Dorsey's mother and unmarried and widowed sisters and aunts. His family was welcoming, but it must have been hard living with a house full of opinionated widows and maiden ladies. She also missed the life she'd made in Brussels. When Dorsey's telegram arrived announcing his return to Europe, she hurriedly booked passage for herself and little Rex on the *Livingston*. Dorsey's sister, Laura, volunteered to come along, although she didn't stay.[9] For the next few years, the little family would do what they could to have a life together.

And why didn't they go back to the United States? Probably because Dorsey's prospects were not assured. "Chef" of the telegraph expedition was the only job he'd ever secured for himself. Until he was thirty-five years old, his mother and grandmother used their connections to secure employment for him. By 1901 the family's supply of influential friends had dried up, and civil service reform barred easy passage back into the diplomatic corps. Amid the growing controversy around the Congo, how would letters of reference from Van Eetvelde or another of Leopold's ministers look to American employers? Moreover, life in Europe held significant attractions. The cost of living was lower in Brussels than in New York or Washington, DC.[10] Harriet's sister was still living in Paris—a short train ride away. Their children could be educated in prestigious Swiss or English boarding schools.[11]

If they'd returned to Washington or New York, Dorsey and Harriet would also have faced a very steep social climb to mingle with the kind of people they considered fitting. In Brussels, working for the State carried a great deal of prestige, depending on the circles in which one traveled. Dorsey and Harriet would not have chosen to associate with the socialists who were Leopold's most outspoken critics, but much of the bourgeoisie and the aristocracy admired the monarchy and everything associated with it. A wider swath of Belgians believed that Leopold's bold move to claim a giant piece of Africa benefited the entire nation.[12] In even the smallest details of everyday life, evidence abounded of Leopold's grip on the social life of Brussels. City directories (known as *almanachs*), for instance, included page after page of detailed biographical information about members of the royal family. The socially anxious or ambitious could also consult a key to the various medals and honors distributed by the King and government.[13] This special status led to opportunities for Dorsey and Harriet to mix with important people and to swirl into the *monde élégante*, as the Brussels newspapers sometimes called it, attending court functions including a *soirée dansant* the first winter they lived in Brussels. Elegant indeed.[14]

As a veteran State official, Dorsey could also share the company of men who'd had similar experiences in service to Leopold. He might be invited to join the Cercle Africain, a group that met monthly at the Hotel Ravenstein, Brussels's last remaining Burgundian townhouse. At dusk they trooped through an elaborate wrought iron gate into a building resembling a step-gabled Amsterdam canal house. There, in wood-paneled comfort, they listened to presentations that reinforced their sense of shared mission. Even within this group, members held to their own versions of what might or might not have happened in Africa. The day after Christmas, Commandant Hecq, whom Dorsey first met in a besieged fort on Lake Tanganyika, gave a presentation on "an episode in the Batetela revolt."[15] It's virtually certain that his version wouldn't have matched Grogan's or Dorsey's; both portrayed Hecq as uncooperative and cowering inside the fort. No matter. Grogan, the Englishman, would never have been invited. If Dorsey attended, he would have been wise to keep his mouth shut.[16]

Far from the equator, the days grew shorter as Dorsey and Harriet settled into their new life. Across the city, working men crowded the second-class commuter trains and hunched over beers, half-hidden from the street by steam-clouded café windows. Servants lit sitting room fires warding off the chill. Mothers bundled up their children. Under the streetlights, rain glistened on the cobblestone streets. Horses strained against their loads, their metal shoes slipping on the wet cobbles. Clutching their guidebooks, tourists took in the gilded seventeenth-century merchant's houses in the Grand Place, Brussels's central square, and Breughel's images of ice-skating peasants on view in the public art museum. Everywhere, coal smoke hung in the air—belched out by smokestacks and fireplaces. The city's woodlots had long ago gone up its many chimneys.

This place bore no resemblance to the mud-bricked, Arab stronghold of Kasongo—or any other African place Dorsey knew. By now, he'd accustomed himself to moving between two lives and the differing mindsets and personas they required. In the past, he'd used the distance to tell virtually unverifiable stories for his own ends. However, his new job required leveraging his experiences in defense of Leopold's continued control of the Congo. In an anonymous office building, the king's public relations men coached him in well-honed strategies: promote an image of the Congo Free State as an agent of humanitarianism and progress. Counter claims made by former State employees, missionaries, and reformers. Explain indisputable atrocities as the work of a few rogue individuals, not evidence of a systemic problem. Claim that the British behave just as badly. Do not mention your own accomplishments except in service to the State's goals.

Dorsey's public audition for the role of apologist came soon after receiving the Étoile. Still gaunt and weary from his travels, he met with a correspondent for the London *Times* who was probably on Leopold's payroll—given the State's practice of paying off journalists.[17] Together, they crafted an article rebutting accusations leveled by Edgar Canisius, an American who had recently worked for one of the rubber concessionaires, the Société Anversoise du Commerce au Congo. Canisius was grabbing headlines on both sides of the Atlantic with his account of leading a brutal campaign against members of the Budja tribe. He told journalists that agents of the Société Anversoise had forced the Budja to gather rubber "at the muzzle of a gun" and paid them so little that those who did not flee into the jungle starved to death. Canisius personally led a so-called punitive mission to retaliate for thirty of the company's hired soldiers being ambushed and killed. By the time he and the soldiers finished, at least three hundred local people were dead and multiple villages had been destroyed. He had come forward because he now felt remorse for his part in the atrocities.[18]

Having not spent time in the territories allotted to the rubber concessionaires, Dorsey could provide no plausible specifics to refute

Canisius's claims. Instead, he presented himself as an American who'd also worked for the State but had witnessed no atrocities of any significance (or that would embarrass him: *rougir* [blush] as he told a Brussels paper).[19] Even filtered through the journalist's pen, the interview comes across as a hodgepodge of talking points, opinions, and self-promotion. However, several aspects stand out as authentic and telling. Canisius, Dorsey said, must be "nursing a grievance" against the State. Fidelity to his employer was indisputably part of Dorsey's ethical code, second only to family loyalty. After all, he'd finished out his telegraph expedition contract even though he feared dying and privately thought the State had not held up its end of the bargain. He also told the reporter that he was quitting his job with the State to return to the United States. Although the article made it a point to underline that Dorsey spoke with "an unbiased mind," it's entirely possible that the decision to stay had not yet firmly been made.[20] Stay he did, but perhaps with the condition that he would not have to offer this kind of public testimony except when necessary.

By the new year, it is possible to glimpse him taking on additional assignments—a middle-aged man working diligently on yet another round of self-invention. Having failed to coach him into filling Stanley's flamboyant shoes, his shadowy masters in the State's propaganda apparatus seem to have decided to use him as a lower-key combination of speaker on Congo topics and occasional author of short articles that could be placed in English-language newspapers. In January he hosted a "conference" at the Grand Harmonie Hotel for an English-language audience. He again presented his talking points about disgruntled employees and the "great progress" being made in civilizing the Congo.[21] In the spring he accompanied more experienced State officials to a meeting of the British Aborigines Protection Association at the Mansion House in London. The Belgian contingent was there to take stock of the growing Congo reform movement, as it would come to be known; and to refute its claims, if possible. There, in a grand Georgian hall, they got an earful. E. D. Morel energized the sparse crowd with his no-holds-barred attack on the Congo Free State.[22]

Dorsey found it impossible to keep his mouth shut. As the press reported it, the American made the "naïve" claim that because he hadn't personally witnessed any atrocities, they weren't being committed. His remarks, "quite properly," said the reporter, were "received with laughter."[23] Ouch. A representative from the British Foreign Office at the meeting noted details about the American's claims to being an experienced Congo hand. They became part of a report sent to his superiors and to Roger Casement, who read it during a long voyage to his duties as British Consul in Congo.[24] It made Casement irate. Apparently, Dorsey's despairing letter about the persistence of slavery had left him with the impression that his friend had evolved into a critic of the State. "Mr. Mohun's testimony in favour of the Congo State is not that of an impartial witness, but of an interested advocate," he instructed Lord Landsdowne, the British Foreign Secretary. Casement also questioned the basis for Dorsey's authority: "Instead then of ten years spent in the Congo, Mr. Mohun has not been five years here," he fumed. "I have myself spent a longer period in the Congo State than Mr. Mohun, and I can assert that I have known of the commission of outrages and of gross cruelties . . . which have not been punished." His peevish tone signaled the end of their once-warm friendship. They'd irrevocably chosen different sides.[25]

Stuck swatting mosquitos in the dreary heat of Matadi, Casement found plenty of time to work himself into a state of intense frustration over the larger Congo situation. He'd accepted the consul's position with a sense of mission but had not been able to irrefutably document a widespread pattern of "outrages and of gross cruelties," as he put it. Like Morel, with whom he would soon form a close friendship, he believed punishing a few bad actors would not end the humanitarian crisis in the Congo Free State. Leopold's system of generating profits had to be reformed, particularly his use of concessions to push de facto governance off onto private entities.[26] If the accounts of missionaries and former State employees like Canisius were to be believed, evidence of the most horrifying atrocities would be found upstream in the strongholds of rubber concessionaires, particularly the Abir Congo Company.[27] However, for various reasons, including his own precarious health, he'd be unable to travel farther upstream than Kinshasa.[28]

Why did Leopold and his operatives put so much effort into gauging and trying to shape public opinion in Britain? And why would a report from a British consul carry more weight than the horror stories that had trickled out of the Congo for more than a decade? In a nutshell, Britain was the most powerful signatory of the Berlin agreement, which had given Leopold control over the Congo. In the imaginings of reformers, the British state might be able to reconvene the Congress and renegotiate the treaty because Leopold had violated both the free trade and antislavery provisions. Other reformers argued that the signatories had the right to discipline Leopold because the agreement designated them legal guardians of the Indigenous population.[29] The Crown's lawyers and professional diplomats thought otherwise. Even if such a move were legally possible, reopening the European partition of Africa was tantamount to cracking the lid on a Pandora's box of imperial rivalries and fragile alliances, including Britain's close dependence on Belgium as a bulwark against German aggression.[30] Hence, there was almost no possibility that the British government would lead an international effort to actively force Leopold to hand over his prized possession.

Leopold had a more nuanced understanding of the seriousness of the threat than many of his most outspoken critics. In private he declared, "a state cannot be maintained if the opinion of the world is against it."[31] At a personal level, maintaining control involved his ego and his global network of financial investments, some of which used the Congo as a form of collateral.[32] For all the autocratic trappings, he was also a constitutional monarch. His successive wills, beginning in 1889, made clear he intended to leave the Congo to the Belgian people. But he planned to do so in his own time and in his own way.

By the end of 1903 the foreign office, the British Parliament, and reform organizations had much more evidence of the State's brutalities.[33] Casement had finally managed to travel upriver to the rubber-gathering areas. He returned to Britain in early December and wrote up his findings in a one adrenaline-fueled, two-week push. The foreign office published a public version of the report in early 1904, adding to the pressure on Leopold. Led by Liberal members, the Parliament had already seriously considered a resolution calling for reconvening the great powers to "abate the evils" in the Congo.[34] The Belgian king was sufficiently rattled that he threatened to hand the Congo over to Germany if British "attacks" continued.[35]

The threat had little effect. Pressure continued to mount. Agitation that began taking shape with Morel's impassioned speech at the Mansion House gradually metamorphosed into a mass movement. By 1904 it had coalesced into the Congo Reform Association. Casement and Morel played central roles. Morel put his writing and lecturing schedule into high gear to deliver both facts and moral outrage, becoming the international spokesperson for the movement. Casement worked behind the scenes negotiating compromises between secular and religious reformers and plotting strategy with the movement's leadership. With his usual gift for forming intimate friendships, Casement bonded with Morel. He playfully addressed him as "Tiger" in his letters. Morel responded by christening Casement "Bulldog."[36] They were a formidable team, made even stronger by working with Protestant missionaries armed with cameras and determined to convince the public of the moral necessity of reforming the Congo.

Meanwhile, Dorsey kept a low profile. Family life resumed. Harriet was again pregnant. In March 1904 she gave birth to their second child, Cecil Peabody Mohun. Perhaps better still, Dorsey thought he'd found a way out of the increasing controversy that would allow him to continue to earn a living. Leopold offered him the position of Resident Director of the Pekin-Hankow Railroad. Dorsey would take up residence in the sizable Shanghai International Settlement in the Chinese treaty port. The family would join him later. It would realize his old dream of working in Asia, long ago thwarted by US State Department officials in retaliation for burning villages and accepting a medal from Leopold.

It was not to be. Dorsey managed to get only partway to Asia before being recalled to Brussels.[37] Leopold had been a little too high-handed with the Chinese government when he acquired the railroad from the American China Development Company. He'd also failed to outsmart his very smart investing partner, J. P. Morgan. In the end, the Chinese bought the railroad back from Morgan. Dorsey, with yet another mouth to feed, was obliged to go back to being an apologist for the State.[38]

He began working on some longer journalistic pieces. He wrote nearly two hundred pages about the telegraph expedition, perhaps hoping to claim a place in history while simultaneously doing his job as an apologist. This balancing act required fitting his story into the

Figure 15. Portrait of the Mohun family in Brussels, ca. 1904—Rex, Cecil, Dorsey, and Harriette (author's collection)

State's bigger narrative about bringing civilization to Central Africa—a dismal and daunting task. Even without this challenge, he didn't really know how to structure the kind of a book-length work that would put him in the company of Sydney Hinde and Ewalt Grogan. The resulting manuscript was never published.

The exercise did help him develop a more successful strategy for defending the State. It involved calling out representatives of British imperialism for being hypocrites. He knew many of the most important foreign office figures who were now lining up to investigate and criticize the State—most obviously Casement, but also Arthur Hardinge. He'd seen enough of British practices in East and Central Africa and had overheard enough conversations in the English Club in Zanzibar to recognize that at least some seemingly high-minded representatives of the British State had plenty to hide. He also seems to have found plausible Leopold's claim that the Congo reform movement was a conspiracy between Liverpool merchants who wanted the British government to take over Congo and Protestant missionaries who resented Catholic competition in saving souls and spreading civilization. Tasked with attacking the British in print, Dorsey could muster a tone of energy and authenticity that was decidedly lacking in his efforts to paint a picture of the State endowing Africans with the benefits of European civilization.

Thanks to his family's Catholic connections in the United States, he secured a print outlet for that outrage. The *Messenger* published a wide variety of articles related to the Catholic Church, including about the Church's overseas missions. Sitting down to dig some dirt on British colonial practices, Dorsey discovered the Aborigines Protection Society had done his research for him. In *The Aborigines' Friend*, he found plenty of damning material. He selected examples that spoke directly to accusations against the State. In Sierra Leone, the brutal methods of the "Frontier Police" tasked with gathering the hut tax had led to two major uprisings in the previous decade. In Bunyoro (now western Uganda), a British officer gave his troops a standing order to "shoot at sight" any Wunyoro carrying a gun, then watched as his sergeant shot a young man while his female companion gathered flowers, later justifying the practice as "necessary, and in the long run merciful." Then there was the judge in British Central Africa who excused the rape of a thirteen-year-old girl by members of the King's African Rifles on the grounds that "the loss of virginity is not prized in the least among unmarried native women." Given all this brutal behavior, Dorsey argued that "the British government might devote its time to reforming its own native troops and leave the reformation of the Congo forces to its own government."[39]

Further sharpening his pen, Dorsey invoked the imperialistic bluster of Cecil Rhodes and others by suggesting that the British government's real motive was to "annex" the Congo. "England might take her oath that she don't want the ivory, rubber, and minerals, and land of the Congo State," he declared, "but there is not a man, woman or child in Belgium who would believe her." The "people" (by which he meant Rhodes) who "took the Transvaal and the Orange Free State, would want nothing better than a philanthropic excuse to annex the Congo State. The map would then be all red from Cape to Cairo."[40]

A second article followed, detailing the steps Leopold had taken to investigate the claims of Casement's report and the reform movement. In September 1904 members of a Belgian Commission of Inquiry sailed from Antwerp to collect information in the rubber-gathering areas. Dhanis had also been pulled out of semiretirement to go upstream, this time as an investigator.[41] The Congo Free State "Government," Dorsey told his American audience, "fixes no limit upon the Commission, either as to the scope of its operations or the duration of its mandate." Witnesses would be protected. The truth would be reported. Problems would get fixed.[42]

Why was Dorsey publishing these carefully crafted articles in an American Catholic periodical? And why did he feel compelled to conclude the second one by opining that President Theodore Roosevelt had "no earthly reason" to involve the United States in the controversy?[43] Because the Congo Reform Association had opened a new front in its campaign to strip Leopold of his personal colony. In October 1904, E. D. Morel crossed the Atlantic to attend a peace conference in Boston. Many leading American progressives and anti-imperialists participated. Morel also delivered a petition to the White House asking for official intervention. The visit garnered many new donors and supporters, including Samuel Clemens, better known as Mark Twain.[44]

Lobbying and disseminating pro-Congo propaganda in the United States had long been part of Leopold's game plan. But although Leopold spent a great deal of money and effort cultivating the pope's support, it was only with the arrival of the Congo reform movement on American shores that he sought to inflame tensions between American Catholics and Protestants. Perhaps that tack had not been pursued because Leopold recognized that the American political elite was overwhelmingly Protestant or because of the constitutional separation of church and state. Confronted with graphic testimony from Protestant missionaries, he changed his mind. The power of the American Catholic Church to tell its congregations what to do and think as well as the anxieties of church fathers about anti-Catholicism at every level of American society offered special opportunities. As we'll see, the Catholic connection played out in an unexpected way for both Dorsey and Leopold. It did not, however provide Leopold with the edge he needed, because the reform movement had begun offering compelling visual proof of State misrule.

The propagandistic use of Congo photographs was not new. Leopold and his allies long recognized the medium's power in defining Africa in the minds of people who had never and would never visit it. In Belgium the appetite for "seeing" the Congo inspired commercial publishers to turn out postcards by the thousands. Actual travelers sent some home to friends and relations. Others seem to have circulated without leaving northern Europe. Belgium was also unique among European nations in having a magazine, *Le Congo illustré*, not created by the state, that used photographs and drawings to promote colonization.[45] A later era would find many of these images shockingly racist and sometimes brutal. But to many of Dorsey's white contemporaries, the imagery would have seemed both exotic and familiar—part of a genre that also included photographs of chain gangs and lynchings in the United States as well as family groupings and tableaux of mostly naked, brown-skinned workers laboring on colonial engineering projects.[46]

The photographs offered by the Congo reform movement stood out from the accepted posing of African bodies. Labeled by contemporaries as "atrocity photographs," the most compelling of these images featured children and adults exhibiting their mutilated limbs. Or, in a particularly moving image by the Protestant missionary Alice Harris, gazing at the severed and smoked hands and feet of loved ones laid out on a woven mat. The appendages had been hacked off by soldiers employed by the rubber companies, especially Abir, because their European supervisors required that they account for every bullet used by bringing in the hand of the person who'd been shot. The intent was to prevent soldiers from using ammunition for subsistence hunting but, like many ill-conceived motivational techniques employed in the Congo, it backfired.

The reform movement incorporated these and other images into hour-long meetings known as "lantern shows." Huge audiences came to view these pictures projected onto a screen.[47] Thousands of people left the lantern shows believing was something fundamentally worse about the way the Congo Free State governed Indigenous people than other colonial powers. Their outrage and sympathy further inflamed by impassioned speeches and hymns, participants rich and poor opened their purses to support the Congo reform movement and pestered their elected representatives to help force Leopold to hand over the Congo to the Belgian Parliament.

Historians have since confirmed what both Dorsey and Casement knew from experience: dismemberments were probably relatively rare. The worst suffering (and mounting death tolls) in the Congo Free State came from displacement, starvation, and disease.[48] However, for a British factory worker in a stuffy auditorium in Liverpool or a celebrated American such as Samuel Clemens attending a lantern show on the East Coast, the larger, population-wide suffering caused by State rule could seem like just one more problem in a troubled world. Besides, who should they believe? The genius of the lantern shows lay not just in the fact that seeing was believing but that the images of dismembered bodies allowed audiences to imagine how it *felt* to be the victim of a Force Publique soldier with a machete. This form of empathy was provoked without significantly transgressing Victorian standards of decency because there was nothing either sexual or scatological about the images.[49]

Leopold and his propagandists could not come up with an effective way to counter these visual messages. The best they could muster was a claim that the photos had been faked or misrepresented how limbs had come to be lost. Offering a crudely doctored image of Morel made Leopold look vindictive and unwilling to listen, undermining his claim that he was unaware of crimes committed in his name and would be willing to punish the perpetrators if the evidence seemed valid.

In November 1905, Leopold's Commission of Inquiry delivered its long-awaited report. Reformers had begun criticizing the committee even before it began working, but it had behaved honorably, diligently trying to verify the claims of Casement's report by interviewing foreign missionaries in areas controlled by the big rubber companies, particularly Abir. The report confirmed the reformers' descriptions of rubber company excesses. Concessionaires extensively used beatings, punitive raids, hostage taking, and other coercive methods to force local people to gather rubber for them. As a result, whole villages had emptied out as their inhabitants hid from their tormentors. The power exercised by the rubber concessionaires was excessive and unsustainable. The practice of rubber gathering needed to be reformed.[50]

A month later, a press release went out. Dateline Antwerp: "R. Dorsey Mohun, ex-American Consular Agent at Boma, Congo Independent State, has been appointed Director of the Abir Congo Company." Mohun had been offered the position "on King Leopold's recommendation for the purpose of furthering Congo reforms."[51] A gnomic, single-sentence paragraph followed: "The selection of an American for the position is considered significant." The wording had been carefully chosen. Like other Congo concessions, Abir gave the appearance of being a legally independent company—hence the "recommendation." The selection of an American was intended to signal that Dorsey was an independent actor. Few seasoned Congo observers were fooled. Bitter cynicism tinged Casement's reaction to the news. "The Abir 'reconstructed' will in no way differ from the old Abomination, as Mohun is simply a paid tool of Leopold," he wrote to Morel.[52]

Casement was correct. But Dorsey's inability to change the way Abir operated was not just because he indirectly worked for Leopold. He'd been handed the impossible task of ending labor abuses while generating profits. The problem lay not just in the malevolent incompetence of Abir's management but in the fundamental nature of the Congo rubber trade. In other parts of Africa, rubber was gathered through a free trade system. Local people gathered the sap of latex-bearing plants, which they sold. When they couldn't find any more of these plants close to their villages, they looked to other sources of income, and rubber-gathering stations moved to new locations. Abir and other Congo rubber concessionaires, by contrast, were contractually tied to specific stretches of forest. Moreover, Congo rubber came not from trees, which could regenerate sap after being tapped, but almost entirely from vines, which could not. By the time Dorsey took over Abir, most of the easily accessed vines had already been destroyed—hence the increasingly harsh methods employed by European station managers to coerce local people into finding rubber to meet the quotas set in Brussels.[53] The State's rubber production model was unsustainable in economic, ecological, and human terms.

Leopold seems to have been the last one to know that the rubber had run out. In September 1906, the State signed a secret agreement effectively taking over Abir. The king publicly declared the company would again be profitable within two years. Instead, the expedient of grinding the vine's bark to extract more rubber could not halt the company's inevitable collapse.[54] By then, Dorsey had again moved on. After a demoralizing seventeen months, he at last found a way to terminate his employment relationship with Leopold and the State. His exit strategy lay at a confluence of the Congo Free State, the American Catholic Church, and the last throes of Gilded Age politics. That confluence would begin to close the circle of his life's journey, returning him to the social worlds in which his family had long traveled.

THE CATHOLIC CONNECTION

James Gibbons was the most powerful Catholic in early twentieth-century America. Only the second American to be appointed a cardinal, he also presided over the Archdiocese of Baltimore—the epicenter of American Catholicism.[55] Costumed in his embroidered vestments, archbishop's miter, and ceremonial shepherd's crozier, he publicly celebrated mass in the Baltimore Cathedral—an airy neoclassical space designed by Benjamin Latrobe. From the more private spaces of his offices and residence, he shrewdly cultivated a large network of religious and secular connections. The Dorsey women considered Gibbons a friend.[56] "Our dear Cardinal Gibbons," Dorsey's Aunt Ella called him.[57] Gibbons might have described the relationship as closer to an acquaintance. He didn't, of course, because he needed the support of pious women. He gave most of his attention, however, to powerful men. These included secular friends of influence equivalent to his own. He even counted Theodore Roosevelt a friend, arguing with the president about whether the United States should withdraw from its newly acquired territory in the Philippines. Gibbons said yes. Roosevelt thought otherwise.[58]

Two of Gibbons's powerful connections came to play an important role in the final stages of the Congo controversy and in Dorsey's future. Nelson Aldrich was a probusiness Republican senator. Nicknamed the "general manager of the United States" by a muckraking journalist, he was one of the nation's most influential politicians.[59] Repeatedly returned to the Capitol by his constituents in Rhode Island, Aldrich suavely maneuvered his way into the powerful position of chairman of the Senate Finance Committee. He was also, not incidentally, a wealthy investor with a keen eye for opportunities. An interest in money ran in the family. His son E. B. Aldrich was an investor in his own right, and his daughter Abigail had married John D. Rockefeller Jr., principal heir to the enormous Standard Oil fortune. Gibbons's other pertinent connection was Thomas Fortune Ryan, a bona fide Gilded Age tycoon. Ryan had made a fortune in street railways, tobacco, and insurance. He and his wife were dedicated to the Catholic Church, making financial contributions so substantial that Pope Leo X named him to the papal nobility. To complete the triangle, Aldrich and Ryan founded the Continental Rubber Company in 1901 to exploit a new technique for extracting natural rubber out of a wide variety of plants.[60]

In late 1904 Gibbons entangled himself in the Congo controversy. The occasion was the International Peace Conference in Boston. E. D. Morel had publicly presented a "Memorial" or petition to President Roosevelt, asking for the United States to pressure Leopold. Gibbons sent off his own statement defending Leopold and the Congo Free State.[61] Gibbons seems to have sincerely believed the reform movement was a conspiracy among Protestant missionaries, Liverpool merchants, and the British government—all of whom hoped to benefit by stripping Leopold of control over the Congo. The movement, he wrote, was motivated "partly by religious jealousy and partly by commercial rivalry."[62] Like other members of the Church hierarchy, including the pope, he particularly feared that Catholic missionaries would be kicked out of the Congo or otherwise persecuted if reformers had their way.

Gibbons's decision to weigh in on the Congo controversy seems to have been taken without Leopold's knowledge, but the king's American operatives rushed to thank Gibbons and try to cement his commitment to the State. Gibbons probably already knew Gustavas Whiteley, the State's consul stationed in Baltimore. He may also have encountered Baron Moncheur, head of the Belgian legation in Washington. Henry Kowalsky, an American lawyer on retainer to Leopold, also penned a flattering letter.[63] A more surprising communication came from Samuel Philips Verner, a former Protestant missionary, who'd recently gained international fame by displaying a Congolese "Pygmy" named Ota Benga at the St. Louis World's Fair.[64]

Verner certainly seems to have been on Leopold's payroll; he claimed merely that because of the kindness he'd been shown by Catholics in Congo, he had made a promise to a Catholic missionary named Per van Kerkhoven that "on my return to America I should do anything I could to help dissipate the false accusations against the missionaries." Never one for subtlety, Verner laid the adjectives on thickly, claiming that even as a non-Catholic, he believed that the Catholic Church was "doing a grand, noble, magnificent work, worthy of all commendation." He'd also promised to "secure for them such rights as they richly deserve." Typical of Leopold's American defenders, he made a special point of saying he was not an "interested individual" but was only interested in the "cause of truth," wherever it might take him.[65]

Gibbons took the bait. Despite some public protestations to the contrary, he would remain on the hook for what remained of Leopold's life, exchanging cordial handwritten notes with the Belgian sovereign and, in 1908, accepting the Grand-Croix de l'Ordre de la Couronne for his stand on the Congo.[66] It was Gibbons who provided Leopold's agents with introductions to Aldrich and Ryan.[67]

Meanwhile, Leopold recognized the day was not far off when the Belgian Parliament would strip him of the Congo, with or without his cooperation. Growing awareness of his own mortality, too, set his calculating mind into overdrive. He spent the winter of 1905–6 at Cap Ferrat in the South of France. A new, young mistress who had just borne him a son kept him company at night. In the daytime, he sequestered himself on his yacht to better focus on putting as many assets as possible out of reach of the Belgian State.[68] Gibbons's American friends, with their deep pockets and loose financial morals, offered a particularly attractive solution. Besides, he'd always liked Americans.

As a result of this cogitating, and in consultation with his lawyers and Jean Jadot, his principal financial advisor, he created what were later known as the "trois Société's de 1906."[69] The three new businesses included a railroad company as well as two concessions to exploit the Congo's plant and mineral resources. The American Congo Company would focus on rubber. As its unwieldy name suggested the Société Internationale Forestière et Minière du Congo would have a concession to exploit both plants and minerals.

Leopold offered Thomas Fortune Ryan and a group of his business partners the opportunity to invest in both the American Congo Company and Forminière (as the Société Internationale Forestière et Minière du Congo was called). Leopold's offer was extraordinary: the company would have twelve years to prospect for mineral and forest products over an astonishing 347 *million* acres in the Kasai basin.[70] As a pro-State American journalist put it, the deal would paint a "streak of red, white, and blue" across the Congo.[71]

Every modern era has had its hot investments, whether tulips or tech stocks. In 1906 demand exceeded supply for copper, gold, diamonds, and other minerals that might be found in the Congo. As consumer demand for rubber-tired vehicles exploded, rubber seemed like a particularly lucrative investment despite the unsavory associations with slave labor. The "Bolivian Syndicate," which counted the Vanderbilt family and J. P. Morgan as major investors, already had a virtual lock on Amazonian rubber, which supplied much of the American market.[72] Leopold was offering the same kind of near monopoly. How could they say no?

The stockholders' investment illuminates a pattern that has gotten more attention in our own era than at the beginning of the twentieth century. Having been made at least partially accountable through regulation and bad publicity, American men who had made enormous fortunes in American railroads and streetcars, or banking and insurance, took their excess capital and invested it in infrastructure and resource extraction abroad. They were joined by entrepreneurs who'd already

212 · CHAPTER 10

been playing the game of global capitalism for a while—in this case, the Guggenheim brothers, heirs to a worldwide mining empire. While each Société had both Belgian and American boards of directors, on the American side at least many of the same names appeared on both boards. This structure would prove problematic for everyone involved and confusing to historians ever afterward.

In the last months of 1906, the wire services buzzed with articles about the Congo Free State. The usual positive press releases from the State's publicity apparatus were overshadowed by revelations about the extent of Leopold's efforts to cultivate political influence in the United States. The whistleblower was Henry J. Kowalsky, identified as a "fat and furious" New York and San Francisco lawyer.[73] Kowalsky was a genuinely disgruntled former state employee, albeit a particularly sleazy one. Sometime after sending his flattering letter to Gibbons, he'd been let go. The angry lawyer took his revenge by describing some of the ways he, Gustavas Whiteley (the State's consul general), and others had sought to influence various congressmen.

In at least some newspapers, articles about the American Congo Company appeared on the same page as the lobbying scandal.[74] The connection between Leopold's efforts to gain political support in the United States and the new company was no longer a secret. Senator Aldrich was too wily to be caught directly benefiting financially from an association with Leopold.[75] Instead, the names of his son E. B. Aldrich and son-in-law, John D. Rockefeller Jr., went on the list of major investors in the American Congo Company.[76] Whiteley also seems to have been cut in on the deal for his trouble.[77] Bernard Baruch, a financier and future advisor of presidents, was also a major investor.[78] After a wave of bad publicity, Rockefeller withdrew from the deal. Everyone else stayed in. There was far too much money to be made.

A few months later, another tiny, barely noticeable press release appeared in a few British and American newspapers. "Congo Authorities Want R. Dorsey Mohun as African Manager" of the new company, it announced.[79] Dorsey had finally found a way to sever his ties with the Congo Free State. The catch? It required his return to Africa.

MANIFEST DESTINY

For dinner guests gathered in Harriet and Dorsey's Brussels townhouse, the portly host and the elfin Chicagoan presented a study in contrasts. It wasn't just size or age that differentiated the two men.[1] They also represented a generational shift in the kind of Americans who'd found careers as imperialists for hire.[2] The age of the self-made, gentleman-adventurer was on the wane. Investors, particularly American investors, now wanted to minimize risk by hiring professionals to ensure their money was being well spent. Scientists and engineers had long been a part of resource exploitation, but the rapid expansion of programs and schools in American universities created a pool of highly trained men willing to go wherever they were needed.

Not yet thirty, Sydney Hobart Ball, Dorsey's guest, fit the new requirements to a T. The son of a prominent Chicago judge, Ball had already parlayed a University of Wisconsin degree in geology and mining engineering into a series of increasingly responsible and lucrative jobs. His résumé included stints with the US Geological Survey in Washington and in the American West. He'd also been employed by the Hudson Bay Company in Canada's far north, where he'd gotten a taste of the more unsavory aspects of corporate relations with Indigenous peoples.[3] Ball carried himself with the self-confidence of a man who believed he'd already found a successful path in life. No need to invent or reinvent himself.

Dorsey, pinching his champagne glass, sized up the younger man. Perhaps the encounter set off a touch of envy. Without a profession or formal training of any kind, he'd continually struggled to explain the nature of his expertise. By now, he had it down: former US consul, a decade spent in Africa, and a reputation as a "well-known explorer." He also touted an ability to earn the respect and cooperation of "the natives." At forty-three, he was relatively old—a malaria-plagued survivor, grown thick in the waist; a dinosaur that had somehow survived what was increasingly referred to as the "pioneering era."

Ball was intrigued but not impressed. Dorsey had yet again rewritten parts of his personal story. The long-ago lie to Chaltin about serving in the US Marine Corps remained firmly stuck to his official biography.[4] Sometime during his long stay in Brussels, he'd added another embellishment. He told Ball that he was a Virginian, with all the social and racial prestige that implied, rather than a child of Washington, DC, which might have given quite a different impression. Ball would have had no trouble seeing through the fabrication if he'd probed at all. Afterward, he wrote his mother that he liked the charming Mrs. Mohun better than her husband. Back in Chicago, his admiring parent copied the letter into a bound book.[5] Mothers and sons.

Soon thereafter, the two men learned they'd be working together as codirectors of what the press called the Ryan-Guggenheim Expedition. They'd been hired to ascertain where the most likely mineral resources lay in the Forminière concession. The task was mind-bogglingly difficult. They had two years to prospect a territory of approximately 370,000 square miles—larger than Texas and California put together. To accomplish this task, the company budgeted for the services of eleven Europeans—the two directors plus three geologists, three professional prospectors, a doctor, and two clerks.[6] Before the era of aerial surveys and without even good geological maps, they'd have to push their way on foot up the most likely watersheds, collecting samples and drawing topographical maps that could be analyzed later. Ball would oversee the scientific aspects of the mission. Dorsey agreed to manage the logistics, most importantly making sure the geologists and prospectors had porters.

Dorsey took the job reluctantly. He'd been angling for a more prestigious and less physically demanding position with the American Congo Company. Press releases (perhaps from his own pen) had already gone

Figure 16. The "charming" Mrs. Mohun as Sydney Ball might have
encountered her in 1908 (author's collection)

out announcing that the Belgian board of directors wanted him as the
African director overseeing their rubber operations in the Kasai region.[7]
But their American counterparts worried that Dorsey was too much
a creature of Leopold's Congo and might prove an embarrassment.
Eventually, they prevailed in their choice of a different American whose
reputation suggested he would be unlikely to tolerate the kind of atrocities burning up the headlines on both sides of the Atlantic.

Samuel P. Verner's efforts to promote himself as the foremost American expert on the Congo and a friend to Africans had finally paid off. A former Presbyterian missionary, Verner was best known for exhibiting the Pygmy man Ota Benga and other Africans as part of the 1904 St. Louis World's Fair. As noted, he was also unusual among Protestant missionaries in managing to stay in Leopold's good graces by cultivating Cardinal Gibbons and writing flattering pieces about the State. Yet by 1907 he'd had fallen on hard times. The offer of $10,000 a year in salary plus stock options proved irresistible.[8] No matter that he had no real business management experience. Verner promised that under his watchful eyes, a more humane labor system would be implemented in the company's rubber-gathering operations.[9] The Continental Rubber Company sent him off to Mexico to learn about their newest patented techniques for extracting rubber by grinding up plants. Then they sent him to Brussels for the obligatory meeting with Leopold.[10]

So, in the spring and summer of 1907, one of the many currents of American manifest destiny flowed up the Scheldt River and through the industrial canals to Brussels, carrying a boatload of international experts and adventurers as well as two middle-aged managers. This form of American expansionism lacked the flag-waving, jingoistic trappings of the recent Spanish-American War and its ugly aftermath in the Philippines.[11] Nor did it need the gunboats and soldiers sent to secure the United Fruit Company's hold on Central America. Leopold promised to take care of security for his investors. With quiet discretion, some of the richest and most powerful men in America slipped into private railroad cars waiting on a siding in Antwerp's new, cavernously grand rail station and cloistered themselves in fine hotels guarded by elaborately costumed doormen. They came in the company of lawyers, business managers, and technical experts to personally assess the people who had been entrusted to turn the proceeds of unfettered Gilded Age capitalism into even more money. They left convinced that this could be accomplished while simultaneously bringing about the "general improvement of the country and people" of the Congo. Africans could choose to work for wages without coercion. New, patented technologies and American scientific and technical expertise would make it possible to find and extract far more rubber, minerals, and other natural resources than had been possible with Leopold's more primitive methods. "The American invasion of the Congo," as Verner called it, promised to be both benign and profitable.[12]

Verner and Ball arrived on the same ship. Ball was impressed that Verner, "one of the company men," looked "mighty healthy" for someone who had spent so much time in Africa. "Talks well concerning the Congo Free State," he wrote his worried mother.[13] A later ship brought A. Chester Beatty, the titular president of the American Congo Company, and the American board of Forminière.[14] A Columbia University–trained mining engineer (and thus part of the new generation), Beatty had earned his many titles by being an extraordinarily hardworking advisor to the Guggenheims and by doing what needed to be done to ensure the smooth functioning the Continental Rubber Company's global operations. He'd hired Ball and had enough contact with Dorsey that Clare Mohun couldn't resist dropping into Beatty's New York office to put a good word in for her forty-three-year-old son.[15]

Enough was at stake that Samuel Guggenheim and Nelson Aldrich also appeared in Brussels. They made time to meet with Ball, who found them surprisingly unpretentious and easy to talk to. The young geologist displayed the reflexive anti-Semitism of his time and class in commenting that, although Guggenheim was a Jew, he seemed to have "considerable polish and education."[16] In turn, Aldrich and Guggenheim liked what they saw. They gave both Verner and the expedition the go-ahead before slipping back into their state rooms for the transatlantic crossing.

Just to make things more interesting and complicated, Clare had turned up in Brussels to visit her grandchildren and see her eldest son before he headed back to Africa. Ball went sightseeing with her. He was shocked and amused that this "old woman" was an enthusiastic tourist who impulsively jumped on and off streetcars if something or someone caught her attention. She volunteered to take a packet of Flemish lace handkerchiefs back to the United States, where she mailed them to Ball's mother with a chatty little note. It was the least she could do. Mothers of African adventurers had to stick together.[17]

✳

Many rituals needed to be performed before the expedition could get underway. These had become utterly familiar and perhaps banal for Dorsey, but they were new for Ball. First and foremost: the audience with Leopold. The aging king increasingly preferred to conduct business at Laeken, his château four miles outside of Brussels—no longer the quick jaunt around the corner to the Royal Palace.[18] Ball received additional, unwelcome instructions about court etiquette, scoffing at being required to wear a morning suit—a pinstriped costume with tails and a top hat—and balking at the incivility of a nine a.m. audience. Long accustomed to conforming, Dorsey donned his own suit without comment and picked up the geologist at his hotel. They rode out together in an electric cab—a modern conveyance replacing the carriages that had once been necessary for impressive arrivals.[19] So much about the world had changed since Dorsey's first meeting with the King fifteen years earlier.

Dorsey observed as Leopold worked his magic powers of seduction on the younger man. In beautiful English the sovereign-proprietor asked knowledgeable questions about a range of technical matters from methods of smelting ores to the use of electrically generated power in mines. As he had done so often to good effect, he beseeched the men to "treat the natives well" and relay any "real grievances" about mistreatment so that he could remedy them. He carefully explained to Ball that he should have some "forbearance" for English missionaries even though they were in cahoots with the British government. The latter, he confided, schemed to make the Congo part of the British Empire. In an added bit of theater, Dorsey and Ball had been told the interview would last ten minutes, but Leopold kept them for a full hour, giving the impression that he found everything they had to say important and fascinating. Ball was smitten. "He is a brilliant man of broad knowledge; a businessman of the highest power," he wrote his parents.[20]

Two weeks later, expedition members lined up against the railing of their ship as a photographer took an obligatory group portrait. Dorsey and Ball are in the back row, the older man towering over the younger. Dorsey wears a suit and tie, his white face swollen above his starched collar. Ball has chosen the uniform of the US Geological Survey, his previous employer. Smith and Shaler, his fellow American geologists, and Oliver, the British topographer, sport similar khaki, replete with knee-high gaiters. While Ball has chosen the kind of felt hat favored by Theodore Roosevelt, the other men wear pith helmets. Dr. L. H. Hollebecke, a Belgian doctor, carries a bound volume perhaps to signal his profession. The Reid brothers—two tough as nails Australian prospectors, hid their hands but not their disdain from the camera. Partly hidden in the back, the two Belgian clerks seem to wonder what they'd gotten themselves in for.[21]

"We are at last on our way South, all well and happy," Ball wrote home. The boat was far better appointed than the grubby steamer Dorsey and Casement and a group of unwashed Belgian officers had endured fifteen years earlier. The dining room was decorated with marble and onyx. The staterooms were spacious, the food good, the company genial.[22] The older man must have appreciated these comforts, but he might also have felt a sense of nostalgia and loss, perhaps even the presence of ghosts. He had been a different person when he helped wrap the body of a Belgian suicide in a tarp and spirit it off the boat at the beginning of his first voyage to Congo. He'd still been a romantic when he rhapsodized about Harriet's last-minute note to him. And perhaps even more so when he put down in writing how much he loved and admired Roger Casement—a friendship now irretrievably destroyed by the moral compromises he had made.

The voyage was routine, the arrival familiar. The State still hadn't built real wharves at either Banana or Boma. Passengers had to be offloaded in slings and transferred to motor launches. The absence of facilities sent an unmistakable message: Tourists, nosy journalists, and freelancing adventurers are not welcome here.[23] Matadi had grown but retained the flavor of a sunbaked, tropical entrepôt. Here, another familiar set of rituals was observed, including the farewell parties with endless toasts to those heading up-country. Hazards still awaited, but the specter of an early death had receded.

The State had also retained one of the most peculiar rituals of Congo hospitality: the assignment of a "boy" to each member of the expedition. Ball was tickled. He loved having a Black valet constantly available to dress him in the morning, wash and iron his clothes, and generally see to his every need.[24] Compared to Dorsey's relationship with the long dead Philip, Ball's attitude comes across as uncomplicated—the product of a different time and place in America's troubled history of race relations. The younger man's upbringing in Chicago, with its de facto practices of segregation and armies of southern migrants desperate for work, shaped his attitude toward darker-skinned people. He liked that his valet was compliant in a way that he would not have been able to compel at home. Because he did not take Henry Stanley as a model, Ball was not burdened by any sense that he would be a mentor to the young man; and because Congo itself had changed, he was also not as dependent on the knowledge of Africans for his own survival. A sunny sense of racial superiority also figured in Ball's attitude toward other Africans, at least at the beginning of the expedition. For instance, he took it for granted that when villagers crowded the riverbanks to waive, they were genuinely happy to see him and his fellow white passengers.[25] His experience, if not his overall worldview, was about to get more complicated.

No more two-hundred-mile marches around the cataracts with the bones of fallen porters and unlucky Europeans bleaching beside the narrow trail; they took the train to Kinshasa. As with the telegraph line, enterprising Africans had quickly learned how to operate the new technology. Engineers, firemen, brakemen, and conductors as well as station crews were almost all dark skinned. A European station manager told the Expedition members that he preferred it that way. As was the case among the steamboat operators Dorsey encountered in East Africa, whites drank too much. Many African crew members were adherents of Islam and thus avoided alcohol.[26] They also recognized an opportunity: a far better-paid and less dangerous way to earn cash wages than carrying loads for a caravan or working for the Force Publique.[27]

Beyond Kinshasa, the expedition members boarded a steamboat. They were headed up the Congo River and then one of its tributaries, the Kasai, where Ball had decided the best prospecting in Forminière's concession might be found. On a high, wooded bluff near a place known as Black River, they enjoyed an impromptu party in the company of Samuel Verner, who had established the headquarters of his rubber-gathering operations there. Verner ordered his cook to prepare a lavish supper, then serenaded his guests with a "gramophone concert." It was a few days before July 4, so to round out the night's festivities,

Verner lit bunches of firecrackers and tossed them into the midst of the Africans gathered around the fire. He assured his visitors that the men only looked scared, but in fact enjoyed the joke.[28] What was Verner thinking when deciding to commit this small act of cruelty? Sometimes even his closest friends weren't sure how to explain his behavior.[29]

Although Dorsey had spent some time in the Kasai during his travels as US Trade Consul, he had very limited experience in the southwestern part of the Congo Free State. Things had changed since his last visit too. The sobriquet *red rubber*, used by critics of Leopold's rule, originated with the type of rubber gathered in the region, which commanded particularly high prices. Hoping to extract more profit from the commodity, Leopold had forced out the fourteen trading companies in the region, consolidating their trade in the Compagnie du Kasai with the State as a 50 percent stockholder.[30]

In 1905 the State had also made a deal with a powerful local Kuba king to force the collection of rubber and taxes. The Catholic Church, the local representatives of the Compagnie, and the former Force Publique soldiers who worked for the king, routinely committed extortion, forced labor, and a variety of atrocities.[31] By the time the Ryan-Guggenheim Expedition showed up in the fall of 1907, the situation had reached a breaking point. In a bit of understatement, Ball later explained "when we got down in the Kasai country, we found it was not as peaceful as they had represented in Europe."[32] It would take a little while longer to find out this was not a good time to be wandering up and down riverbeds gathering mineral samples.

To look for possible mining sites, the geologists and prospectors had to reach the places Ball identified as worth prospecting. For travelers through the southern part of the Kasai, many caravan routes converged at a settlement called Luebo. Herman Wissmann, whom Dorsey had met on the ship to Zanzibar, was one of the first Europeans to pass through the region in the early 1880s, bestowing his name on a waterfall just upstream. A decade later, the location attracted not only European traders but also a unique group of missionaries who established the American Presbyterian Congo Mission there.[33] This is where Samuel Verner had done his two-year stint as a missionary before falling into an animal trap and severely wounding his leg, requiring a return home.[34]

It's almost certain that Verner told the expedition members about the mission. It's possible he also provided an introduction to its most famous missionary.

Dr. William Sheppard shared with Verner a southern background, but he was the descendant of slaves, not of enslavers. Ordained as a Presbyterian minister after training at Stillman College, he'd volunteered to go to Africa in partnership with a white missionary named Samuel Lapsley. Lapsley rapidly succumbed to malaria. Sheppard stayed on for seventeen years, forming a complex relationship with both State officials and the powerful Kuba tribal rulers.[35] He was also one of the first Europeans to call attention to the atrocities committed by the rubber trading companies.[36] Most people, African or European, found Sheppard's charisma, intelligence, and ability to connect with people irresistibly appealing. Ball was no exception. "In two minutes, we were exchanging tobacco and were the best of friends," he told his mother. He'd never met a "better host" than Sheppard and his wife. He loved everything about the civility and culture of Sheppard's house: the books, the "dainty" table linen, the cut flowers, and the conversation. "It was necessary for me to come to Africa to learn that a negro is sometimes better than a white man," he wrote home to Chicago.[37]

The sense of relief in entering this island of civility and kindness was compounded by the contrast with the "dirty Catholic mission" at Bena Makima, where they'd passed too much time trying to hire porters. The Scheutist fathers there had a special arrangement with Leopold. In conjunction with the Compagnie du Kasai, they ran a rubber plantation and also collected wild rubber. Both enterprises used forced labor. The "religious part of the show," as Ball put it, consisted of an occasional mass.[38]

At Luebo, the expedition split up. Dorsey went back to Luluabourg, where the State had a large post, to hire porters. Burned out even before Brussels and now increasingly short-tempered and impatient with scientists who didn't want to do any of the work of managing the expedition, he rubbed several people the wrong way. Ball delighted in the mean nickname the Swahili-speaking porters had bestowed on overweight Dorsey: Mafuta Mengi ("Much Grease").[39] More seriously, Dorsey had a near-fatal run-in with a drunk Belgian who'd forced a local woman back to his tent for some late-night singing and probably sex. When Dorsey told him to shut up, the Belgian grabbed his gun and threatened to kill him. The man was seized by an armed priest and locked up pending being sent back to Europe to his wife and children. It was time for everyone to take a break from one another.[40]

Ball decided to be constructive while waiting for enough porters. He and Dr. Hollebecke spent a day having a close-up look at the other problem that was devastating the Kasai: an epidemic of sleeping sickness. In Brussels Leopold and other State officials talked defensively about everything they were doing to counteract this terrible insect-borne disease, which fatally attacks the central nervous system. The State's efforts did little to prevent the disease's spread on riverboats and in caravans throughout the Congo watershed. Ball and Hollebecke talked with a physician named Kocher who ran a State-created hospital at Lusambo. Kocher had a reputation of being unusually compassionate as State-employed doctors went. He lamented being underfunded and overwhelmed. He'd resorted to paying patients' hospital expenses himself. The State did not provide any help at all in transporting patients to the hospital from other parts of the Kasai. Lusambo was a long walk from Luebo. Most of the sleeping sickness sufferers never made it there.

As with much else about the Congo Free State, press accounts provided poor preparation for the horrifying realities. At a local "sleeping sickness camp" Ball and Hollebecke wandered through a nightmare scene. The local Catholic mission doctor sent people here to die, largely uncared for. Ball was shaken by the sight of people in the last stages of the disease, eyes wide open, teeth chattering, lying side by side with corpses already being consumed by beetles and blowfly larvae. He was also rattled by the demographic implications of what the doctor told him. Infection rates ran as high as 60 percent in some regions. Within a decade, whole areas might be depopulated.[41] All the two men could think to do was give those still able to consume it spoonsful of salt— considered a luxury. "Good," one of the dying villagers told Ball in Swahili by way of thanks for this small comfort.[42]

Finally, aided by the liberal dispensation of bribes and probably some coercion by the Force Publique, Dorsey managed to secure the hundreds of porters needed. The geologists each teamed with a prospector and split up.

Several weeks later, Dorsey received a panicky and very worrying message: Ball's party had been in a shoot-out near a place called Kamsele. All of the European members of the party escaped without injury, but the porters had abandoned some of the supplies. Dorsey handed the courier a response: Ball was to bring all the remaining goods and personnel to a centrally located Catholic mission so that they could decide what to do. Spurred on by anxiety and adrenaline, the young geologist set the caravan on a forced march, covering the fifty kilometers to the mission in seven and a half hours.[43]

It's not clear whether Ball ever told Dorsey all the details of what had happened. As a lawyer's son, he probably understood the importance of having a plausible story and sticking with it. But he did confide the details to his diary in his tiny and barely legible handwriting. That account reveals a familiar pattern of malevolent incompetence and rookie mistakes resulting in more than one hundred African deaths. This time, a new generation was responsible and under the pressure of international outrage, the consequences potentially more serious for Ball and the expedition. In early October, Ball had left St. Joseph's mission in the southern Kasai as part of a caravan of nearly five hundred porters. He was traveling in the company of one of the Reid brothers, a State official named Imperator who was in charge of a small detachment of Force Publique soldiers and a Catholic priest named Pere Dalle, who may have been one of the rubber-factory-running Scheutist fathers, since he had his own soldiers with him. In addition to the expedition's supplies, the porters carried cloth and large containers of wine destined for another Catholic mission.

Hoping to travel in the coolest hours of the day, they set out very early. The caravan soon spread out with Ball and Reid taking up the rear, probably riding in hammocks strung between porters. Just outside of Kamsele, someone started shooting from the bushes with muskets, creating huge clouds of smoke. The Force Publique soldiers shot back while Ball and Reid lay on the ground hoping not to get hit by their own soldiers' bullets. Rather than turn back, Ball decided they should go on. A protracted battle resulted. Over the next seven hours they fought off the attackers, dodging from village to village. In another bit of bad judgment, they stopped for the night in what Ball described as a "not very friendly" village. Everything seemed to have calmed down until one of Pere Dalle's soldiers accidentally discharged a weapon, setting off another round of shooting. In the end, Ball estimated a total of 125 attackers had been killed.[44]

Safe in the company of Dorsey and a Belgian official named Le Grand, Ball left out some crucial details, including the possibility of turning back and the mistake that set off the second battle. He also failed to explain that this was not the first time that raiders attacked a caravan just after it left the mission. It was common knowledge among locals that such caravans carried cloth and wine.

Ball might have been able to adjust his story to cover for himself and Reid, but he could not protect Pere Dalle, who had made a further series of bad decisions. After the battle, the priest's hired soldiers decided it would please their employer if they rounded up a "traitor" who could be held responsible for alerting the attackers to the caravan's presence. Dalle took out his frustration by ordering them to hold the man while he fatally shot him in the stomach. Dalle also cut off the heads of several dead soldiers as a deterrent to desertion.[45]

Everyone decided the expedition had gotten off with a warning. But they needed to reconsider working in the Kasai. Dorsey and Ball decided to redirect prospecting to Lake Tanganyika and the Maniema region. The samples they'd been able to gather were hastily tucked away, chop boxes and other loads reorganized, and the whole expedition moved east.

Finally, the work of prospecting seemed to settle into a routine. Panning in the river bottoms and chipping at shoals of rock debris, the geologists began collecting tantalizing suggestions of mineral wealth: traces of gold, traces of copper, traces of other minerals. Frustratingly, they were not finding geological evidence of where the rocks emerged from the earth's crust before washing into streambeds. Ball thought part of the problem lay in the lack of African workers. If he had more porters, he could work faster and collect more samples. He blamed Dorsey and took umbrage at the latter's suggestion that he might try his hand at recruitment. Ball wrote the Forminière's directors in Brussels to complain. The return mail brought a carefully worded letter in French, cc'd to Dorsey. The board was disappointed, too—but mostly at Ball's failure to make any big finds.[46]

Everyone set aside their differences and went back to work. Dorsey again set up residence in Kasongo, his favorite spot in the Eastern Congo. Someone took a snapshot of him playing with a leopard cub on a leash, the walls and people of the old town blurry behind him.[47]

He'd also been back to Kabambarre—scene of a horrific series of deaths during the telegraph expedition. Like much of the rest of the Maniema, it had settled into a calmer stasis with the departure of the Batetela, though it was far from the ideal of "civilization" Leopold bragged about. The State seemed to function much as it had in Dorsey's many years there. A low hum of malevolent incompetence continued. Goods promised did not show up. Local officials ran their own tiny kingdoms, some poorly, some well. The endless paperwork did little to root out incompetence and corruption. Many officials ran scams or small businesses on the side. At one post visited by Ball, the commander expressed benevolence by taking in the unwanted children of his Belgian colleagues and their African mistresses.[48] People were still sold in the markets.

Traveling between these outposts in September of 1908, one might easily miss an enormous piece of news. Leopold had finally reached an agreement transferring control of the Congo Free State to the Belgian people. On September 9, the Chamber of Deputies voted yes to annexation. The Belgian Senate quickly followed suit. The deal had been a long time coming, but it went into effect on November 14 with little ceremony. On paper the changeover made no difference to the operation of Forminière and the American Congo Company, something Leopold had insisted on.[49] The Belgian government rebuffed British and American demands for a written document abolishing forced labor and opening the Congo to free trade. Moreover, no military officers or State officials would lose their jobs unless they'd been found guilty of "cruelty."[50]

Figure 17. 1908 snapshot of R. Dorsey Mohun with a leopard cub in
Kasonga (author's collection)

Someone, however, in the Kasai regional government decided this
would be a good time to legally prosecute Ball for the events at Kamsele,
more than a year earlier. The charges came as something of a shock.[51]
Dorsey himself as well as many of his contemporaries killed large numbers of Africans with far less justification. The expedition members had
worked themselves around to thinking of the whole event as a heroic act
of self-defense against savage forces. Arthur Smith, one of the American

geologists, even told his version of the story to the *New York Herald,* which published it under the exciting title "Explorers Rout Cannibals with Heavy Losses."[52]

The timing of the charges suggests why they might have been leveled. The British government was holding off on official recognition of the new colony until the Belgian government offered definitive proof that efforts were being made to put a stop to atrocities. The Americans must have seemed like an easy target—with the added benefit of making a point about Belgian sovereignty to the foreign representatives of the "American invasion." It's also possible the charges originated in the Compagnie du Kasai, which was in the process of suing the missionary William Sheppard for an article he'd published criticizing the Compagnie's labor practices.[53]

State officials instructed Dorsey to send Ball to Lusambo for trial. Reid was also called as a witness.[54] Dorsey wrote back asking for a clarification of the charges. Initially, he'd been given the impression the charge was "murder." This made little sense, even in the topsy-turvy world of the Congo State justice system. It turned out Ball was to be prosecuted for "inciting a war." Dorsey decided that Ball, whose grasp of French was shaky and whose naivete about State officials was seemingly boundless, needed an advocate. Rather than a lawyer, he sent Dr. Hollebecke as a go-between. He also instructed Ball to tell the truth to the Belgian official who would decide whether a trial was necessary. He confided to the other American expedition member, Millard Shaler, "I am certain Ball will be acquitted." Still, Dorsey worried that with the expedition's chief scientist taken out of the field with only a few months to go, the expedition would fail to make any significant finds. "It is disgusting to see our expedition smashed just at the finish," he complained.[55]

Ball did as he was told, climbing aboard a diminutive "handcar steamer" for the long trip downriver.[56] He put nothing in writing about the trial in either in letters or his diary. Instead, he passed some of the long hours in transit writing his mother a chatty letter about the sights. She was old enough to enjoy a familiar nineteenth-century American scene translated to an African context: His steamboat raced a train traveling along the riverbank. As crews cheered, the stokers threw "rotten

Congo wood" into both vehicles' boilers to generate more steam and therefore more speed. The only evidence of the political changeover, he told her, was the sound of the Force Publique military bands practicing the Belgian national anthem instead of the Congo Free State's tune.[57]

In the end the charges against Ball were dismissed, as Dorsey predicted. He also enjoyed a little schadenfreude at the expense of Verner, who had been fired after only a year. Verner had spent huge sums of money without consultation, problem solving by doing things like buying up entire rival trading posts for cash. He'd also sent a series of inflammatory, peevish letters to the American Congo Company's Belgian directors. They, in turn, complained to their American counterparts that "Mr. Verner does not appear to have any commercial spirit."[58] Eventually, the Brussels contingent exerted their right to replace Verner.

Sitting in a State-run guest house in Kinshasa waiting to go downstream, Dorsey wrote a long letter of reassurance to his own mother. No need to worry that the money he'd been sending to her would dry up. He felt confident his employers valued his work and would find him employment after the expedition ended. And, by-the-by, "I'm a strict teetotaler out here. Drink absolutely nothing but water. Will probably continue the same regime when I come home as I haven't had the slightest desire for a drink of any sort." He also wanted her to know he'd lost fifteen pounds.[59] Clare must have said something about both the champagne consumption and Dorsey's weight in Brussels a year and a half earlier. Her criticisms still burdened his mind.

By June most of the expedition members were gathered in Matadi, more than ready to head home. The Reid brothers, committed to a life of wandering and enticed by the mineral possibilities, stayed behind.[60] The geologists had also left all their scientific tools in Kinshasa to be used by future expeditions.[61] In Brussels, Leopold's man behind the scenes, Jean Jadot, debriefed both Dorsey and Ball, repeatedly summoning the latter until he felt all useful information had been extracted.[62] Despite the lack of big discoveries, the American board was happy with Ball's work, offering to set him up with an office in New York and a title.

A new, larger team was sent out to follow up on the Ryan-Guggenheim expedition's findings. When that expedition had retreated from the Kasai in 1907, they'd hastily stuffed their mineral samples into cases without properly labeling them. Concealed in one of the tubes was a small chip of crystal. A minerology professor at the University of Liège confirmed that it was a diamond. But where did it come from? And, more importantly, could more diamonds be found there? Eventually, someone asked Shaler, who was still working for the company, what he remembered. As it turned out, he recalled that the diamond had been found close to a place of extraordinary beauty that Shaler knew as the Pogge I waterfalls.[63] Near the town of Tshikapa, the site eventually became the epicenter of one of the largest industrial diamond mining operations in Africa.[64] Some of that would play out in a company town nicknamed Little America.[65]

That was in the distant future. For Dorsey, the present looked bleak. He hoped for future employment that would not require him to go back to Africa or to ask Harriet to leave Brussels, where she had created a life that suited her. Would the American board members of Forminière and the American Congo Company be interested in opening an office in Brussels? Beatty politely rejected the proposal.[66] Dorsey would need to find another job.

An era was ending. Dhanis had died a month earlier of septicemia.[67] Omari bo Amisi, Dorsey's "sergeant" and comrade in arms, had also passed away while en route to Kasongo to meet with Dorsey during the Ryan-Guggenheim expedition. Roger Casement was still among the living, but he'd left Africa permanently to take up a post as the British Consul General in Brazil. He was increasingly obsessed with a rubber regime every bit as brutal as the Leopoldian concessions but far larger in scale.[68]

Leopold's health was failing. Ball and Dorsey had caught a glimpse of the old man's decline in 1907 when the king had used his desk to keep himself upright.[69] But force of will had kept him going through the tough negotiations leading to the annexation of the Congo. As 1909 came to a close, it became increasingly apparent he would not last much longer. The press was told the problem was an "abdominal blockage." An operation was performed. The King emerged from the chloroform just long enough to trace his signature on one last bill. Then he was gone.[70]

Leopold died on December 17. The next day, his body was ceremonially transported from Laeken to St. Mary's Cathedral in Brussels for the state funeral. Huge crowds packed the sidewalks hoping to catch a glimpse of their king's last dramatic act in a reign that had been packed with drama. The slow passage of the horse-drawn hearse, the military honor guard, the windows along the route draped with crepe and brilliantly illuminated, did not disappoint.[71]

Behind the scenes, a different set of final acts were being performed. Worried loyalists and men who'd grown rich from Leopold's enterprises raced to keep the details of them from falling into the hands of his critics or the Belgian Parliament. Canny observers might have caught a change in the smoke pouring from the chimneys of certain state-owned buildings. For days, workers shoveled piles of paper into the furnaces. They could not, however, completely hide the international network of *sociétés anonymes* or the real estate and other valuables Leopold had bought with his ill-gotten gains.[72]

As Christmas approached, Dorsey might have consoled himself that he would not be sweating it out in the tropics, fending off loneliness by drinking with other Europeans, singing about goodwill toward men while compelling his employees to amuse the whites. For the first time since 1906, he could celebrate with his family in a place that understood the sentimental as well as religious meanings of the holiday. But he found little domestic solace. Christmas in the Mohun household was a "failure" in his blunt assessment. He'd been gone too long. Cecil, his younger son, now five years old, barely knew who he was.[73] Whatever happy family intimacy Dorsey had dreamed of wasn't happening.

Into the spring, Dorsey found himself still unemployed. Belgium had a new king. Albert I had visited the Congo months before his father's death, declaring his desire to usher in an era of reform. Under Albert's patronage, the Touring Club of Belgium produced a series of large-scale pictorial guides for would-be and armchair tourists curious about the country's new possession.[74] The day was not far off when the adventurous might drive an automobile along the routes once traversed by caravans. The Belgian Congo, as it was now called, slowly began to look and function like the other European colonies surrounding it.

In July the American investors in Forminière and the American Congo Company finally made good on their promise to take care of their expedition manager. The job offer came in the form of a handwritten note on the stationary of Villa Fasolt, an exclusive hotel in the German spa town of Karlsbad. The author was Paul Morton, yet another Gilded Age millionaire who'd made his money in railroads and street railways. "Have cables from America," Morton wrote to Dorsey. He'd checked the latter's references and found them acceptable. Morton had been drafted by Ryan to run the scandal-ridden Equitable Life Assurance Society. Perhaps in return, the American Congo investors gave Morton a seat on their board. Morton's attention was drawn to the challenge of developing rubber-gathering operations in regions of Africa that had not yet been fully explored or exploited. Thanks to his brief tenure as director of Abir, Dorsey could count natural rubber gathering and processing as one of his areas of expertise. Would he be willing to sign on to prospect in southern Africa on behalf of the blandly named and well-disguised Rubber Exploration Company?[75] Indeed he would.

Why the ten-month wait before offering Dorsey a job? Why had Beatty politely told him they didn't have anything for him? As it turned out, he was throwing a bit player off the scent of a big game playing out in New York board rooms and swank London hotels. Negotiations had been underway to combine two American rubber companies, Intercontinental Rubber and Continental Rubber, into a much bigger company that had access to J. P. Morgan's financial clout. As part of the deal, shares of the American Congo Company would be absorbed.[76] In other words, Beatty was telling the truth when he said there would be no need for a Brussels office for the company. He just didn't say why.

Paul Morton had been exploring possibilities in South Africa with representatives of the British South Africa Company, one of Cecil Rhodes's constructions, about a deal to purchase concessions in the Natal region.[77] Conventional wisdom suggested that Morton and his fellow investors were foolish to look for rubber in the relatively arid region below the equator. For more than half a century, American manufacturers had obtained most of their rubber supply from the Amazon. However, Continental Rubber and other rubber extraction companies were acutely aware that this source was not sustainable. Efforts to create rubber plantations in South America, Africa, and Asia had been plagued by devastating blight brought on by monocropping.[78] Morton's consortium concluded that the flow of raw rubber might be maintained by extracting usable latex out of a wider range of plants. Continental's guayule operation in Mexico used one such invention to extract latex-bearing sap out of a small gray desert shrub, providing what a later generation of investors would call "proof of concept."

The whole idea was a gamble justified by the investors' belief that all kinds of latex-bearing plants grew undiscovered in tropical regions around the world. Making money from these plants depended on several different kinds of people: botanists who could identify them; inventors, chemists, and engineers to figure out how to extract and purify rubber from them; and people like Dorsey to negotiate with those who controlled them. The Rubber Exploration Company's lawyers drew up a contract with Dorsey, who agreed to "make studies and reports and to make investigations and explorations." The investors also empowered him to negotiate possible concessions, although he was not to expend company money without express permission.[79]

As with the Ryan-Guggenheim Expedition, Dorsey was not to make any scientific judgments. He would be traveling in the company of a college-trained botanist named McPherson. He was to send plant samples to New York for analysis by experts.

Morton had a reputation for thoroughness and attention to detail verging on obsessiveness. It had helped him earn Ryan's trust, but it was also taking a toll on his health—his high blood pressure disqualified him from obtaining life insurance from his own company, which is perhaps why he was taking the waters at Karlsbad. Morton wanted Dorsey to meet him in Paris for further instructions. He also firmly insisted that his new hire meet with Julius Lay, the US consul who had done the initial legwork in South Africa. Lay would be stopping in London on the way to another posting in Brazil. Done and done.[80]

Once again, Dorsey headed south along the familiar route to East Africa, this time all the way to the city of Durban. His initial "investigations and explorations" would take place in the Natal region, best known as the home of the Zulu people. Through Lay, Morton had already been in negotiations with the British South Africa Company for the exclusive right to prospect for two years.[81] The scheme involved extracting rubber from several species of *Euphorbia*, which seemingly grew everywhere. The plants were certainly full of sticky, latex-bearing sap, but the analytical chemist was dubious about being able to purify it enough for industrial use.[82] Nevertheless, Dorsey and McPherson took a look. They were also dubious. Dorsey retreated to a hotel in Johannesburg to regroup.

The dense, equatorial jungle of Portuguese East Africa seemed like a better bet. *Landophilia* vines, which were the mainstay of the Congo rubber boom, grew there in abundance but had not been as thoroughly exploited. If that didn't work, they'd go to Madagascar, where other rubber companies were already scouring the landscape for latex-bearing plants. By late November, Dorsey and McPherson with a caravan of porters worked their way up and down the Maputo River looking for a combination of dense concentrations of *Landophilia* and ease of transportation to a port on the Delagoa Bay.[83] Then fever struck. A physician advised Dorsey to rush to Johannesburg for better medical care. A few days before Christmas, he underwent surgery—probably to remove kidney stones that were causing not only pain but also an internal infection as they scraped up Dorsey's urinary tract. He was, somewhat understandably, in a foul mood—firing off complaining letters to Edward Aldrich, Nelson's son and one of the officers of the Exploring Company. He'd apologize later.[84]

Dorsey didn't tell Harriet how sick he'd been, but he told her enough that she sent a cheerful Christmas telegram. "Hearts love. Congratulations. Cecil excited."[85] She still knew how to do the right thing, how to offer a few words that might partially make up for last year's "failure." "I am a very happy man in my wife and children," Dorsey wrote to his mother. "Every day of my life I return thanks to God for having made me take passage to Genoa in 1892."[86] It took until early January to gather enough strength to go back even just to his desk. He was, however, closing in on a deal with a Lisbon bank for a large concession.[87]

To make matters more complicated, Paul Morton dropped dead on January 19, 1911, age 53, from a cerebral hemorrhage brought on by high blood pressure. The rest of the investors intended to proceed as if nothing had happened. By late January, they were even ready to offer Dorsey a position as the manager of their new Portuguese East African concession. Dorsey demurred. His own recent brush with mortality had left him eager to finish up his current contract, which would expire in July.

One more stop with McPherson: Madagascar. Finding a concession on an island already overcrowded with British and French companies was unlikely. Dorsey concluded that much of the easily accessible latex-bearing foliage had already been destroyed by intensive rubber gathering.[88] However, he wanted to see some of the new patented Guiget rubber extraction machines in use—he'd seen detailed drawings in the London patent office. A manager of a small factory suspected his American visitor, who'd turned up in a sailboat, might be bent on industrial espionage. Dorsey couldn't resist providing a bit of dialogue in his report. "You can't see our machines. I can't let you see them without permission of London," the man blurted out before Dorsey had the chance to explain the purpose of his visit. "You may want to copy them." Not quite right. To Dorsey's amusement, the manager offered his two American visitors the opportunity to stay overnight in a room overlooking the shed sheltering the machine. From the window, they could easily view its operation. The manager had no objections to the men sitting nearby the next day and taking notes as workers fed lengths of a vine into its maw.[89]

In this final report, Dorsey's professionalism is striking. He worked hard to provide his employers with exactly what they'd asked for. He was still a quick study, easily wrapping his mind around the complexities of the rubber plants and rubber-processing machines. The characteristically dutiful eldest son, he had gotten up out of his sick bed and gone back for another round of heat and mosquitos and the endless, frustrating logistics that came with traveling in early twentieth-century Africa. Most of his pay went directly to Harriet. He still sent his mother and sister, Laura, smaller amounts.[90]

Did his wealthy employers appreciate his work? Perhaps in the polite way of their social class. But he would never be one of them, this descendant of "patriots and statesmen" as his grandmother Anna liked to say. In middle age, Dorsey knew this too. He just wanted a "better berth" than the ones he'd had before.[91]

Going back to the United States for a long visit had been the plan even before he accepted employment with the Rubber Exploration Company. Rex, his oldest son, was already in boarding school near Storm King north of New York City. He and Harriet agreed they were only visiting. "I am afraid we will never be able to live in America again, after having spent so many years of our life abroad," he told Clare. "Our means carry us so much further and the life is so much more tranquil." And then as a final rationalization: "environment has a lot to do with one's temperament, and ours is more continental than American."[92] In August, Dorsey, Harriet, and "Master Cecil," as the ship's manifest identified him, boarded the SS *Marquette*. They were going home.

AFTER AFRICA
AND CONCLUSION

In early December of 1911, Dorsey returned to the city of his birth. He and Harriet laid plans to enter Washington society in high, if somewhat antique, style. The Washington social columns announced they and their sons would spend Christmas and New Year's residing in a Lafayette Square townhouse.[1] No longer quite the height of fashion, this shady enclave of ambassadors and old money—with its view of the White House—still conveyed insider status. Perfect for people who now considered themselves "more continental, than American."

For the first time in years, most of the family would be together for the holidays. One can imagine the bustle of preparations at 2119 California Avenue, where Clare still lived with two of her sisters, Ella and Angie, as well as her daughter Laura. The most recent in a long line of all-female households, its residents also included a niece and sister-in-law as well as two Black servants. Little had changed. Laura still toiled in the patent office. Aunt Ella was employed there as well but also found the energy to follow in her mother Anna's footsteps as a popular Catholic writer.[2] The rest of Richard and Clare's children had long ago departed the city. Louis had been the first adult child to pass away, succumbing to dysentery as Dewey's ships shelled Manila Bay in the decisive naval battle of the Spanish-American War.[3] Philip had become a merchant captain, while baby sister Edith married a Navy man. Lee, now Mother Stephanie, remained at St. Mary's in Ohio. She directed her formidable intelligence and drive toward gradually earning the reputation as one of the foremost American Catholic nuns—eventually leading the order in founding two small colleges.[4]

As far as Dorsey and Harriet were concerned, their life also lay elsewhere. They planned to stay only a few months: long enough to enjoy the social season but not so long as to be caught in Washington's summer doldrums. In February they made the social pages again as attendees at the "Southern Ball," where they joined more than a thousand other guests, including President Taft and his wife. "World of Society Brilliantly Represented," the papers reported. Among the attractions: the spectacle of "lovely gowns and gems" as well as a group of young women in powdered wigs and facsimiles of eighteenth-century dresses dancing the minuet.[5] Nostalgia deepened into caricature—a usable past in support of Jim Crow and nativism.

Spring came and went with its usual riotous abundance of green. Around the tidal basin below the Lincoln memorial, new cherry trees—a gift from the city of Tokyo—bloomed. Dorsey and Harriet remained in residence. As Dorsey's health worsened, it became clear they would not be returning to Europe. He found himself in no condition to seek a desk job, let alone go out in the field again. He sought out a specialist at Johns Hopkins, one of the foremost teaching hospitals in the United States, in Baltimore. The visit provided more hope than cure. Malaria and other maladies had taken an irreparable toll on his body.

As the days grew warmer and the stay longer, the charms of the capital faded. Warrenton, Virginia—a historic town in the foothills of the Blue Ridge Mountains—offered a nearby refuge. Some Washingtonians spent the summer there, escaping the worst of the heat.[6] Surrounded by horse farms and white-pillared houses, not to mention the decaying remains of slave quarters, Warrenton still had the flavor of the antebellum South. By moving there, Dorsey and Harriet would now be the Virginians they'd once claimed to be.

As he began to recover, Dorsey found the determination to write his story for a broader public. His English-language contemporaries continued pouring out memoirs and explanations of events in Africa. During his years as an apologist for the state, he subverted his own impulse to claim a place in history. Later, he was too exhausted and overwhelmed with learning a new set of skills and figuring out the expectations of new employers to write anything but reports. Now, he had time on his hands.

What did he want to write about? His earliest adventurous years in the Congo, before everything became so complicated. He drafted a query to the editor of *The Century Illustrated Magazine*, where his most widely read article, "The Death of Emin Pasha," had appeared in 1895. The editor was intrigued enough to ask for samples. With his notes and diaries by his side, Dorsey wrote out two articles. Perhaps to counter the sting of how popular Sydney Hinde's memoir had become, he sketched his own account of their explorations on the upper reaches of the Congo River basin. Hinde and others had long known that any stories having to do with cannibalism would be popular, so Dorsey compiled his own take on what Europeans and Americans liked to think of as the bloodthirsty peoples of the Congo.[7]

Nothing came of his efforts. Perhaps the editor never responded because he was horrified by what he'd read. Too many years of working for the State and telling stories at wine-soaked dinner parties left Dorsey unable to gauge the sensibilities of his intended audience. The *Century* was a "high brow" periodical for intellectually curious people of refined sensibilities. Dorsey enlivened his account by graphically describing the pendulous breasts of the women from whom he had obtained milk for Hinde. Perhaps the former Congo officers in the Cercle Africain might have chuckled at the picture he painted, but his words would have deeply offended conventional American good taste. Without the purported moral argument that both sides in the Congo reform era had used to justify grisly tales of smoked human hands and other horrors, the cannibalism article comes across as blatantly sensational despite Dorsey's disclaimer that he wasn't making anything up. Another article he drafted suffered from a similar kind of blindness. His self-portrait as a man knowledgeable and sympathetic to Arab culture would have worked better if he hadn't also tried to claim that the Arabs were good overlords for the Africans.

In the same vein of bad judgment, he crafted a lecture titled "Exploring and Exploiting in Congo and South Africa," which he presented in several venues, including Catholic University in January of 1914.[8] His career as a lecturer did not take off.

Seven months later, Belgium was again in the headlines. This time, the news had nothing to do with the Congo. A chain of events, beginning with the assassination of the heir to the Austro-Hungarian Empire, Franz Ferdinand, and his pregnant wife, led with seemingly unstoppable momentum to the German invasion of Belgium on August 4, 1914. This was not supposed to happen. The treaty that had created Belgium in 1830 specified it would be perpetually neutral in European military affairs. Moreover, Albert, the new Belgian king, was a cousin of the German Kaiser, Wilhelm. What good was modern European royalty if cousins countenanced attacks on each other's countries?

Dorsey and Harriet's longtime Brussels friends and neighbors found themselves living in an occupied city watching pitiful clusters of refugees limp through bearing tales of the destruction wrought by massive Škoda mortars and trigger-happy German troops. European soldiers were again burning villages, but this time all continental Europe would soon be on fire.[9] Harriet was particularly distraught. She had put down deep roots in Brussels and still had a sister living in Paris. All she could do was contribute money to the Red Cross for Belgian humanitarian relief.[10]

Another spring. They'd decided even Warrenton was too hot in the summertime. A small newspaper ad published the day after Dorsey's fifty-first birthday suggested a solution. "Summer Home to Let," it announced. The property in question, "beautiful estate of the late Judge Hammond in Talbot County, eastern shore of Maryland," sounded suitably prestigious. The furnished house looked out over the water. It even included the use of a yacht.[11] The children would love it. Clare, Aunt Ella, and Laura could come to stay. The location not only offered the possibility of gracious living but also put the family close to its original settling place—Maryland being the first foothold of the "patriots and statesmen" whose names and stories the family so carefully preserved.

The idyll, far away from a world at war, did not last. On July 13, 1915, Dorsey suddenly passed away. The death certificate lists the cause as Bright's disease—a general term for chronic inflammation of the kidneys and associated with congestive heart failure. Both were probably the long-term consequences of malaria. Dorsey's body was rushed to Washington, where the family managed to arrange a funeral mass in the suitably grand Cathedral of St. Matthew the Apostle. Afterward, his kin laid him to rest in Oak Hill Cemetery in the plot his father had bought to bury his infant sister almost fifty years before.[12]

Unwilling to acknowledge the seriousness of his condition, he'd failed to update the will he'd made in 1898 before beginning the telegraph expedition. Perhaps he had not imagined dying so near to the place he was born rather than being buried under a tree in Africa with his name scratched in the bark.[13]

Obituaries soon appeared in the *New York Times* and Washington's *Evening Star*. It was in these yellowed clippings, cut out and preserved by an anonymous relative so long ago, that I first encountered my great-grandfather and his remarkable story. That *New York Times* obituary—the one that described him as a "soldier of fortune" and the "humane" governor of "natives"—also claimed he belonged to the fourth generation of his family to fight for the abolition of slavery. I'm almost certain that it was written by Dorsey's Aunt Ella. Still unmarried at the time of Dorsey's death, she'd inherited her mother Anna's role as a writer of "light Catholic literature." Perhaps not surprisingly, she'd carved out a niche writing moralizing adventure stories for boys. Ella had also embraced the task of not only preserving, but also burnishing the family's history and legacy—even going so far as to become an officer of the Daughters of the American Revolution.[14] The obituary needs to be read in light of her profession and political commitment to a nativist version of conservative Catholicism.

But it's really because of Cecil Peabody Mohun, Dorsey and Harriet's younger son, that I'm able to tell Dorsey's story. The little boy, who didn't recognize his own father when he came home for Christmas in 1909, grew up to be a successful New York stockbroker and a governor of the New York Stock Exchange.[15] Cecil appointed himself preserver and champion of his absent father's memory. "Uncle Peabo," as my father called him, collected Dorsey's papers and used his influence to have them microfilmed by the US National Archives. Then, in the summer of 1959, he contacted another orphaned son of empire, Léopold Dhanis, then the Belgian Ambassador in Washington, DC. Would Léopold ensure that the Royal Museum for Central Africa in Tervuren not only accepted the physical papers but created a display celebrating Dorsey's contributions to the Congo?[16]

Born a year apart, the two men may have known each other as children. Without doubt, they shared another bond: early on they'd lost the fathers they barely knew—orphans left to console themselves with heroic tales and other people's memories. They also benefited financially and socially from their fathers' careers. Léopold inherited the title of baron bestowed on his father by his namesake, the Belgian king. Dorsey's sacrifices paved the way for Cecil to wield real power from the inner sanctum of American capitalism.[17] Out of their exploitation of Africa, Dorsey and Dhanis had indeed created the foundation for the next generation's fortunes.

Léopold wrote the director, reminding him of Dorsey's connection to Francis Dhanis—still remembered as a hero in Belgium. The museum accepted the papers. But Cecil's timing was lousy. By the time the exhibit opened in 1961, the Belgian Parliament had voted to end colonial control.[18] The resulting Congo Crisis proved to be one of the most brutal and protracted episodes of African decolonization. Dorsey's papers were stored away for decades. They have now been recataloged and made available as part of a larger process in which the Belgian people are trying to come to terms with the nation's colonial legacy and culpability. My interest in telling Dorsey's story can also be viewed as a different kind of coming to terms, one that brings to light not only my family's involvement but also the culpability of Americans and American capital in the exploitation of Africa.

Dorsey's story also rebalances the emphasis in much recent historical writing about the Congo that casts kings, politicians, and reformers—most of whom never set foot in Africa—as heroes and villains. Dorsey was neither. Instead, he was a man not that dissimilar from his contemporaries in either ethics or worldview. However, he differed from so many other Gilded Age Americans in not only benefiting from European imperialism but also participating directly in it. In doing so, he confronted the kind of grave moral life-and-death choices most of them would never have to face except in the comfortable space of their imaginations. This book in no way aims to excuse what he did but only to explain it.

ACKNOWLEDGMENTS

Many people offered help and encouragement through the long journey of writing this book. In the beginning, University of Delaware students were my closest traveling companions. They listened patiently to my stories about Americans in the world and helped puzzle over why the topic was largely missing from their textbooks. As they pursued their own research projects, several generations of history majors taught me how rich, accessible, and relevant this area of research could be.

Dozens of librarians, archivists, and museum curators generously contributed their expertise to uncovering R. Dorsey Mohun's life. Nan Card from the Hayes Presidential Library opened the door to understanding the Mohun-Dorsey clan. The Dominican Sisters of Peace at St. Mary's gave me access to their private archive and graciously hosted an unforgettable research trip. Tom Morren, archivist at the Royal Museum for Central Africa, shared his knowledge of R. Dorsey Mohun's papers and pointed me toward the archives of relevant Congo Free State officials. Carrie Beauchamp took me behind the scenes in the Smithsonian's Museum Support Center to see objects collected in the Congo by Mohun and his contemporaries. Diane Wendt, also from the Smithsonian, went the extra mile in helping me understand Mohun's medicine trunk and obtaining a photograph for the book.

I owe a special debt of gratitude to my UD colleagues. Owen White volunteered to comment on early chapters, pointed out key scholarship to read, and generally helped me get a grip on how to write about the history of empire. Anne Boylan generously read the whole manuscript and gave me good advice about Catholics, US women's history, and Reconstruction-era Washington, DC. Rachael Beyer, Mike Forino, Greg Hargreaves, Kyle VanHemert, and Ben Wollet all took time away from their own research and writing to discuss chapters and listen to updates. Thank you, Elizabeth Higginbotham, for being a supportive friend and insightful reader.

Workshopping parts of this project for academic audiences was a crucial part of the writing process. Special thanks to my copanelists at annual meetings of the Society for the History of Technology, especially Laura, Ben Twagira, and Nina Lerman. Thanks also to Ruth Oldenziel for helping me hone my ideas and for inviting me to speak at Eindhoven University. Mary Yeager plucked my proposal for an early version of this story out of the single paper submissions pile for the Business History Conference and gifted me with an extraordinary commentator, Debora Silverman.

It takes a lot of talented and dedicated people to produce a book. Stacia Pelletier and Audra Wolfe provided timely advice on writing a publishable biography about a not-famous person. I owe many thanks to Rob Schultz for making the maps and helping with the images. It's been a pleasure to work with the production team at the University of Chicago Press. Special thanks to Tim Mennel, editor extraordinaire. Tim, I am fortunate indeed that you took on this project.

This book is dedicated to my father, Rick Mohun, who passed away midway through the process of writing. He did not know his grandfather or, indeed, much at all about the Mohun side of his family. He gave me the tiny cache of materials he'd inherited, which included most of the photographs in this book. He also encouraged my research even when it became clear that parts of the story did not reflect well on some of our ancestors. My father was a true adventurer—a sailor, mountaineer, traveler, and thinker. I'm grateful that he passed on those parts of the Mohun legacy. This book is also for my sister, Rowena Mohun, with love and admiration.

Erik Rau has been my daily companion through the long process of researching and writing. His skills as a historian and willingness to be a sounding board are reflected throughout these pages. His enthusiasm for both real and imagined travel makes every journey more meaningful and fun.

ABBREVIATIONS

Aldrich Papers	Nelson Aldrich Papers, Library of Congress
AUND	Archives of the University of Notre Dame
Ball Papers	Sydney Hobart Ball and Family Papers, Notre Dame University Special Collections
Boma Despatches	*Despatches from the United States Consuls in Boma, 1885–1895*, vol. 1, RG 59, National Archives and Records Administration
Cairo Despatches	*Despatches from US Consuls in Cairo, 1884–1886*, vol. 21, RG 84, National Archives and Records Administration.
Consular Regulations	United States Government, Department of State, *Regulations Prescribed for the Use of the Consular Service of the United States* (Washington, DC: Government Printing Office, 1896)
Final Report	R. Dorsey Mohun to Hon. Edwin F. Uhl, Assistant Secretary of State, Mohun Papers
Gibbons Papers	Cardinal Gibbons Papers, Archives of the Archdiocese of Baltimore
LWH Collection	Rutherford B. Hayes Presidential Library and Museums, Lucy Webb Hayes Collection (Hayes-2), Incoming Correspondence
Mohun Papers	Papers of R. Dorsey Mohun: microfilm in the National Archives and Records Administration; physical documents in Archives de Richard Dorsey Mohun, Royal Museum for Central Africa
NARA	National Archives and Records Administration
SMSA	St. Mary's of the Springs Archive, Columbus, Ohio

RBH Collection   Rutherford B. Hayes Presidential Library and Museums, Lucy Webb Hayes Collection (Hayes-2), Outgoing Correspondence

telegraph narrative   Untitled narrative about the 1898–1901 telegraph expedition, Item 22b, Mohun Papers (microfilm)

Zanzibar Despatches   *Despatches from U.S. Consuls in Zanzibar, British Africa, 1836–1906*, RG 59, National Archives and Records Administration

Zanzibar Gazette   *Gazette for Zanzibar and East Africa*

NOTES

Prologue

1. I have been unable to find any other traces of Nolo and or any of his descendants. On the challenges of finding the voices of African interpreters and other intermediaries, see Benjamin N. Lawrance, Emily Lynn Osborn, and Richard L. Roberts, introduction to *Intermediaries, Interpreters, and Clerks: African Employees in the Making of Colonial Africa*, ed. Benjamin N. Lawrance, Emily Lynn Osborn, and Richard L. Roberts (Madison: University of Wisconsin Press, 2006). Lawrance et al. note that "most of our information on intermediaries comes from official colonial records" (20). For a thoughtful analysis of the historiography on interpreters, see Tama Eadric M'bayo, "African Interpreters, Mediation, and the Production of Knowledge in Colonial Senegal" (PhD diss., Michigan State University, 2009). See also Frances E. Karttunen, ed., *Between Worlds: Interpreters, Guides, and Survivors* (New Brunswick, NJ: Rutgers University Press, 1994). For a broader analysis of the challenges of including African voices and African sources, see David M. Gordon, "Interpreting Documentary Sources on the Early History of the Congo Free State: The Case of Ngongo Luteta's Rise and Fall," *History in Africa* 41 (2014): 5–33.
2. John C. Billheimer to Edwin F. Uhl, June 6, 1898, vol. 10, Zanzibar Despatches.
3. "African Explorer Dead," *New York Times*, July 15, 1915.
4. Maya Jasanoff, *The Dawn Watch: Joseph Conrad in a Global World* (New York: Penguin Books, 2017), 6.
5. The best estimates of these numbers do not account for those who died abroad or decided not to return. Before 1908, the numbers were reconstructed from ship captains' records, further contributing to the undercount. By these methods, 50,269 US citizens were estimated to have arrived

back in the United States in 1880. Mohun returned to the US for the last time in 1912 in the company of 280,801 other Americans. US Department of Commerce, Bureau of Foreign Commerce, *Survey of International Travel* (Washington, DC: Government Printing Office, 1956), 44–45. See also Brandon DuPont, Alka Gandhi, and Thomas Weiss, "The Long-Term Rise in Overseas Travel by Americans, 1820–2000," *Economic History Review* 65, no. 1 (2012): 144–67; Joe Constanzo and Amanda Klekowski von Koppenfels, "Counting the Uncountable: Overseas Americans," *Migration Information Source*, May 17, 2013, Migration Policy Institute, https://www.migrationpolicy.org/article/counting-uncountable-overseas-americans.

6. For an overview of the global circulation of populations, see Jürgen Osterhammel, *The Transformation of the World: A Global History of the Nineteenth Century* (Princeton, NJ: Princeton University Press, 2014), 154–66.

7. For an influential synthesis focused on such places, see Daniel Immerwahr, *How to Hide an Empire: A History of the Greater United States* (New York: Farrar, Straus and Giroux, 2019). The historical and historiographical literature on US imperialism and empire is large and complex. For a comprehensive review, see Paul A. Kramer, "Power and Connection: Imperial Histories of the United States in the World," *American Historical Review* 116 (December 2011): 1348–91.

8. For a representative example, see Harvey Levenstein, *Seductive Journey: American Tourists in France from Jefferson to the Jazz Age* (Chicago: University of Chicago Press, 2000).

9. John P. Dunn, "Americans in the Nineteenth Century Egyptian Army: A Selected Bibliography," *Journal of Military History* 70, no. 1 (2006): 123–36; Jeremy Rich, *Missing Links: The African and American Worlds of R.L. Garner, Primate Collector* (Athens: University of Georgia Press, 2012); Tracey Jean Boisseau, *White Queen: May French-Sheldon and Imperialist Origins of American Feminist Identity* (Bloomington: Indiana University Press, 2004). See also Peter Duignan and L. H. Gann, *The United States and Africa: A History* (London: Cambridge University Press, 1984), in which Mohun is briefly described.

10. On Sheppard and other African Americans in Africa, see Ira Dworkin, *Congo Love Song: African American Culture and the Crisis of the Colonial State* (Chapel Hill: University of North Carolina Press, 2017), and Pagan Kennedy, *Black Livingstone: A True Tale of Adventure in Nineteenth-Century Congo* (New York: Viking, 2002). Stanley was British by birth but claimed the US as his country during the middle years of his life. His autobiographical writings provide a window on the period. See Henry M. Stanley and Nathaniel Cheairs Hughes, *Sir Henry Morton Stanley, Confederate* (Baton Rouge: Louisiana State University Press, 2000), and Henry M. Stanley, *My Travels*

and Adventures in America (Lincoln: University of Nebraska Press, 1982). Mohun is described briefly (and inaccurately) in Peter Duignan and Lewis H. Gann, *The United States and Africa: A History* (Cambridge: Cambridge University Press, 1984), 138–39. He also appears in Kathryn Barrett-Gaines, "Travel Writing, Experiences, and Silences: What Is Left Out of European Travelers' Accounts: The Case of Richard D. Mohun," *History in Africa* 24 (1997): 53–70.

11. Commodity histories contain some of the richest recent research and analysis on this topic. See, for example, Benjamin Mountford and Stephen Tuffnell, eds., *A Global History of Gold Rushes* (Berkeley: University of California Press, 2011), and John A. Tully, *Devil's Milk: A Social History of Rubber* (New York: Monthly Review Press, 2011). See also Michael Adas, *Dominance by Design: Technological Imperatives and America's Civilizing Mission* (Cambridge, MA: Belknap Press of Harvard University Press, 2006). There is also a growing literature on Americans employed by US financial and consumer corporations abroad. See, for instance, Nan Enstad, *Cigarettes, Inc.: An Intimate History of Corporate Imperialism* (Chicago: University of Chicago Press, 2018).

12. In 1900 the US State Department employed 1,228 domestic and overseas employees and maintained 41 overseas diplomatic posts. "Department History," Office of the Historian, US Department of State, https://history.state .gov/departmenthistory.

13. Larzer Ziff, *Return Passages: Great American Travel Writing, 1780–1910* (New Haven, CT: Yale University Press, 2000), 12–13.

14. Bruce A. Harvey, *American Geographies: U.S. National Narratives and the Representation of the Non-European World, 1830–1865* (Stanford, CA: Stanford University Press, 2001), 4–6; Andrew Daryl Witmer, "God's Interpreters: Protestant Missionaries, African Converts, and Conceptions of Race in the United States, 1830–1910" (PhD diss., University of Virginia, 2008).

15. Kathleen Bickford Berzock and Christa Clarke, *Representing Africa in American Art Museums: A Century of Collecting and Display* (Seattle: University of Washington Press, 2011). On the display of human beings, see Andrew Apter, "Africa, Empire, and Anthropology: A Philological Exploration of Anthropology's Heart of Darkness," *Annual Review of Anthropology* 28 (1999): 577–98; Pascal Blanchard, Gilles Boetsch, Nanette Jacomijn Snoep, and Musée du quai Branly, *Human Zoos: The Invention of the Savage* (Arles, France: Actes Sud, 2011); Pamela Newkirk, *Spectacle: The Astonishing Life of Ota Benga*, 1st ed. (New York: Amistad, 2015).

16. Mining engineer T. A. Rickard went so far as to claim that he and his fellow Americans were "the most important missionaries of civilization" among

the many nationalities represented in their profession. See Stephen Tuffnell, "Engineering Gold Rushes: Engineers and the Mechanics of Global Connectivity in Mountford and Tuffnell, *A Global History of Gold Rushes*, 243.

17. A. G. Hopkins has described this collection of traits and attitudes as "the culture of cosmopolitan nationalism." See A. G. Hopkins, *American Empire: A Global History* (Princeton, NJ: Princeton University Press, 2018), 316.

18. E. P. Thompson, *The Making of the English Working Class* (Harmondsworth: Penguin, 1968), 13.

19. Richard Dorsey Mohun is well-represented in both venues. See Wikipedia, s.v. "Richard Mohun," https://en.wikipedia.org/wiki/Richard_Mohun; "Mohun (Richard Dorsey Lorraine)," in *Biographie coloniale belge; Belgische koloniale biografie* (Brussels: Librairie Falk fils, 1951), 2:710–13.

20. Patricia Nelson Limerick, *Legacy of Conquest: The Unbroken Past of the American West* (New York: W. W. Norton, 1987), 36.

21. On masculinity and the pressures to be a breadwinner, see Margaret Marsh, "Suburban Men and Masculine Domesticity, 1870–1915," in *Meanings for Manhood: Constructions of Masculinity in Victorian America*, ed. Mark C. Carnes and Clyde Griffen (Chicago: University of Chicago Press, 1990), 119. On absent breadwinners, see P. B. Nutting, "Absent Husbands, Single Wives: Success, Domesticity, and Semi-nuclear Families in the Nineteenth-Century Great Lakes World," *Journal of Family History* 35 (Winter 2010): 329–45. On masculinity and family in the history of imperialism see Martin Francis, "The Domestication of the Male? Recent Research on Nineteenth-Century British Masculinity," *Historical Journal* 45 (September 2002): 640–41. Many of Dorsey's contemporaries in Africa married if they survived long enough to do so. Some, notoriously, had both African and European families. See Owen White, *Children of the French Empire: Miscegenation and Colonial Society in French West Africa, 1895–1960* (New York: Oxford University Press, 2010).

Chapter 1

1. Melanie A. Kavak and Mark D. Groover, "Blue Beads as Symbols of African-American Cultural Symbols," *Historical Archeology* 30 (Fall 1996): 49–75. The question of how much of African culture survived the Middle Passage and the process of slavery is the subject of extensive historiographical debate. For an overview, see France Ntloedibe, "A Question of Origins: The Social and Cultural Roots of African American Cultures," *Journal of African American History* 91, no. 4 (2006): 401–12, http://www.jstor.org/stable/20064123.

2. Chris Myers Asch and George Derek Musgove, *Chocolate City: A History of Race and Democracy in the Nation's Capital* (Chapel Hill: University of North Carolina Press, 2017), 85; Kate Masur, *An Example for All the Land: Emancipation and the Struggle over Equality in Washington, D.C.* (Chapel Hill: University of North Carolina Press, 2010), 113–14.

3. For an overview of late nineteenth- and early twentieth-century American ideas about Africa, see Jeannette Eileen Jones, *In Search of Brightest Africa: Reimagining the Dark Continent in American Culture, 1884–1936* (Athens: University of Georgia Press, 2010).

4. June Kinard, comp., *Early Immigrants to Virginia from the 1500s and 1600s,* Ancestry.com (online database). See also Joshua Dorsey Warfield, *The Founders of Anne Arundel and Howard Counties, Maryland: A Genealogical and Biographical Review from Wills, Deeds and Church Records* (Baltimore: Kohn & Pollock, 1905), 56. Hester Dorsey Richardson, *Side-Lights on Maryland History: With Sketches of Early Maryland Families* (Baltimore: Genealogical Publishing, 1967), 86.

5. Richardson, *Side-Lights on Maryland History,* which discusses Edward Dorsey at length, doesn't mention slavery in relation to any of the Maryland families discussed.

6. "Anna Hanson Dorsey, 1815–1896," unpublished biographical sketch, box 27, Mother Stephanie Papers, SMSA.

7. David M. Streifford, "The American Colonization Society: An Application of Antebellum Reform," *Journal of Southern History* 45 (May 1975): 201–20.

8. Penelope Campbell, *Maryland in Africa: The Maryland State Colonization Society, 1831–1857* (Urbana: University of Illinois Press, 1971), 43–45, 100–101. See also Tukufu Zuberi, *Swing Low, Sweet Chariot: The Mortality Cost of Colonizing Liberia in the Nineteenth Century,* Population and Development (Chicago: University of Chicago Press, 1995).

9. Zuberi, *Swing Low, Sweet Chariot,* 185.

10. Anna Hanson Dorsey to Lee Mohun, n.d., Mother Stephanie Papers, SMSA. Anna claimed he had gone to visit a Governor Roberts, who had been a hack driver in Petersborough, Virginia, when McKenney recruited him.

11. Anna Hanson Dorsey to Lee Mohun, n.d., Mother Stephanie Papers, SMSA.

12. "African Colonization," *New National Era,* February 13, 1873.

13. Daniel Kilbride, "What Did Africa Mean to Frederick Douglass?," *Slavery and Abolition* 36 (2015): 42.

14. Mansur, *Example for All the Land,* 13; Marie Tyler-McGraw, *An African Republic: Black & White Virginians in the Making of Liberia* (Chapel Hill:

University of North Carolina Press, 2007). Liberia was not the only place such immigrants considered. See, for example, Martin Robison Delany and Niger Valley Exploring Party, *The Condition, Elevation, Emigration, and Destiny of the Colored People of the United States: And, Official Report of the Niger Valley Exploring Party*, Classics in Black Studies (Amherst, NY: Humanity Books, 2004).

15. "Proscription by Liberia," *New National Era*, February 17, 1870; "Liberia. American Colonization Society," *National Republican*, January 22, 1873; "About Africa," *The Critic* June 9, 1883.

16. "American Colonization Society," *Evening Star*, January 16, 1878. For a thoughtful analysis of this kind of colonization justification, see Tyler-McGraw, *An African Republic*, 6–7.

17. A. G. Hopkins, *American Empire: A Global History* (Princeton, NJ: Princeton University Press, 2018), 292.

18. For more on this belief, see Hopkins, *American Empire*.

19. It's perhaps not surprising that Anna and her daughter Ella later became founding members of the Daughters of the American Revolution, which espoused this ideology.

20. There is no record of his immigration, but he was married in Washington in 1835 when he was twenty-six years old. Jordan Dodd, Liahona Research, comp. *Washington, D.C. Marriages, 1826–50* Ancestry.com (online database). He also appears in Michael Tepper, *New World Immigrants: A Consolidation of Ship Passenger Lists and Associated Data from Periodical Literature* (Baltimore: Genealogical Publishers, 1979), 2:383, as a sponsor of an Irish immigrant, John Fitzgerald, who came from Cork. This suggests the Mohuns may also have immigrated from Cork.

21. "Death of a Well-Known Citizen," *Evening Star*, June 21, 1879.

22. "Special Election," *Washington Union*, July 14, 1858.

23. Francis Mohun, Petition, June 17, 1862, Civil War Washington, http://civilwardc.org/texts/petitions/cww.00695.html.

24. "The End of the Rebellion," *Evening Star*, April 10, 1865.

25. Constance McLaughlin Green, *The Secret City: A History of Race Relations in the Nation's Capital* (Princeton, NJ: Princeton University Press, 1967); Asch and Musgrove, *Chocolate City*, 152–84.

26. Kenneth J. Winkle, "Emancipation in the District of Columbia," in *Civil War Washington: History, Place, and Digital Scholarship*, ed. Susan C. Lawrence (Lincoln: University of Nebraska Press: 2015), 60.

27. The 1860 Census counted 60,764 whites, 11,131 "Free Colored", and 3,185 "Slaves" living in the district. See "1860 Census, Population of the United

States, District of Columbia," table no. 2, 588. https://www2.census.gov
/library/publications/decennial/1860/population/1860a-45.pdf#.

28. Asch and Musgrove, *Chocolate City*, 136–37; Green, *The Secret City*, 76.

29. Asch and Musgrove, *Chocolate City*, 119–20.

30. For examples of the use of the term, see, for example, "Second Ward Republicans," *Evening Star*, May 14, 1868; "Is the Negro Dying Out," *New National Era*, June 30, 1870.

31. One of the Mohuns served as secretary at one of the first meetings. See "Board of Trade," *National Republican*, October 27, 1867. For Richard's involvement, see "Board of Trade," *Evening Star*, October 22, 1867.

32. "A Bill to Provide Railroad Facilities to the Capital of the United States," *National Republican*, December 15, 1868.

33. Masur, *Example for All the Land*, 1.

34. "War of the Races in Swampdoodle," *National Republican*, October 20, 1873.

35. Masur, *Example for All the Land*, 113.

36. Anna must have spent time there as a young woman because she memorialized the house in the long-winded title of one her early novels, *Woodreve Manor; Or Six Months in an American Town: A Tale of American Life* (Philadelphia: A. Hart, late Carey and Hart, 1852). The house is mentioned in family correspondence up through the 1890s, but no trace now remains except the name of a road.

37. "A Bill to Provide Railroad Facilities to the Capital of the United States," *National Republican*, December 15, 1868.

38. He owned property valued at $30,000 and had $28,000 in income. "Richard B. Mohun," 1870 United States Federal Census (manuscript), Ward 2, Washington, District of Columbia, 226.

39. 1870 United States Federal Census, Ward 2, Washington, District of Columbia, 226.

40. 1870 United States Federal Census, Ward 2, Washington, District of Columbia, 31.

41. For a few examples, see "My Life in Africa," *Evening Star*, January 19, 1876; "About Africa," *The Critic*, June 9, 1883.

42. On the Schufeldt Expedition, see "The Ticonderoga," *Evening Star*, January 15, 1879; also, Andrew C. A. Jampoler, *Congo: The Miserable Expeditions and Dreadful Death of Lt. Emory Taunt, USN* (Annapolis: Navy Institute Press, 2013), esp. chap. 2, "The U.S. Navy in West African Waters."

43. The formal name was the United States Exploring Expedition. The focus was on the Pacific rim, but the Smithsonian's collections still include objects acquired on the west coast of Africa.

44. Bayard Taylor, *The Lake Regions of Central Africa* (New York: Scribner, Armstrong, 1873). Other popular books about Africa from the time included Sir Richard Francis Burton, *Zanzibar: City, Island, and Coast* (London: Tinsley Brothers, 1872), and *Two Trips to Gorilla Land and the Cataracts of the Congo* (London: Marson, Low, and Searle, 1876).

45. Anna Hanson Dorsey to Hudson, June 20, 1885, Hudson Papers, AUND.

46. See, for example, "Dr. Livingston Not Found—Perhaps," *Evening Star*, July 30, 1872; "The Herald's African Explorer" and "Slavery in Africa," both from *Evening Star*, July 27, 1872.

47. "Lighting Up the Dark Continent," *Evening Star*, March 22, 1884.

48. The Rutherford B. Hayes Presidential Library holds an extensive collection of both Clare's newspaper articles and her correspondence with the Hayes family. Clare may have modeled her columns in part on the work of Cara Kasson, who wrote under the pen name "Miriam" for the *Des Moines Register*. Elden E. Billings, "Early Women Journalists of Washington," *Records of the Columbia Historical Society* 66 (1966): 94.

49. Anna Hanson Dorsey to Hudson, June 20, 1885, Hudson Papers, AUND. Most significantly, he had been one of the notetakers for the inquiry into the failed polar expedition of the *Jeanette*. Richard Wainwright to E. Chandler, recommendation for R. Dorsey Mohun, n.d., Applications and Recommendations for Public Office, RG 59, National Archives. Wainwright writes "I was Judge Advocate of the Jeanette Court of Inquiry. Mr. R. Dorsey Mohun was clerk to the court."

50. Robert G. Albion, "A Brief History of Civilian Personnel in the U.S. Navy," October 1943, https://www.history.navy.mil/content/history/nhhc /research/library/online-reading-room/title-list-alphabetically/b/brief -history-civilian-personnel-us-navy-department.html.

51. Three years previously there had been a congressional hearing after the rear admiral of the European Squadron had sent one hundred marines ashore from the *Quinnebaug* and another American ship to protect American property during a local uprising. He'd been reprimanded by Congress. Comanos to T. F. Bayard, June 10, 1885, Cairo Despatches; James A. Fields, *America and the Mediterranean World, 1776–1882* (Princeton, NJ: Princeton University Press, 1969), 374.

52. Anna Hanson Dorsey to Hudson, August 3, 1885, Hudson Papers, AUND.

53. *A Handbook for Travelers in Lower and Upper Egypt*, 7th ed. (London: John Murray, 1888), 115.

54. For an overview, see Cassandra Vivian, *Americans in Egypt, 1770–1915: Explorers, Consuls, Travelers, Soldiers, Missionaries, Writers and Scientists* (Jefferson, NC: McFarland, 2012). Some of the mercenaries wrote biographies; see

William Wing Loring, *A Confederate Soldier in Egypt* (New York: Dodd, Mead, 1884).

55. USS *Quinnebaug*, deck logs, vol. 21, June 4, 1885, RG 24, NARA.

56. D. Comanos to US Secretary of State, "Request to Appoint Rag Inspector," February 2, 1885, Despatches from US Consuls in Cairo Despatches.

57. John Cardwell to James D. Porter, "Trade with the East," June 22, 1886, Cairo Despatches.

58. Siba N. Grovugui, *Sovereigns, Quasi Sovereigns, and Africans: Race and Self Determination in International Law* (Minneapolis: University of Minnesota Press, 1996), 77 and passim.

59. Fields, *America and the Mediterranean World*, 378–79.

60. USS *Quinnebaug*, deck logs, vol. 25, January 6, 1887, RG 24, NARA.

61. 1892–93 diary, April 28, 1892, Papers of R. Dorsey Mohun, National Archives and Records Administration microcopy. Hereafter Mohun Papers. Only after I had done much of my research did I discover that Mohun's archive survives in its original, paper form in the collections of the Royal Museum for Central Africa in Tervuren, Belgium. The papers have been reorganized. The finding aid can be found here: https://www.africamuseum.be/sites /default/files/media/docs/research/collections/archives/richard-mohun .pdf.

62. USS *Quinnebaug* (II). See http://www.navsource.org/archives/09/86 /86114.htm.

63. For a detailed examination of these themes, see Scott Trafton, *Egypt Land: Race and Nineteenth-Century American Egyptomania* (Durham, NC: Duke University, 2004).

64. Marina Panagiotaki, M. S. Tite, and Y. Maniatis, "Egyptian Blue in Egypt and Beyond: The Aegean and the Near East," in *Proceedings of the Tenth International Congress of Egyptologists, University of the Aegean, Rhodes, 22–29 May 2008*, ed. P. Kousoulis and N. Lazaridis, Orientalia Lovaniensia Analecta 241 (Leuven: Peeters, 2015):1769–89, https://www.sciencenews.org /article/ancient-egyptian-blue-glass-beads-reached-scandinavia.

65. See, for example, "Egyptian Harems," *The Clarion Democrat*, November 26, 1885; "Down in Egypt Land," *The Waco Daily Examiner*, May 23, 1882.

66. Jay Sexton, "William H. Seward in the World." *Journal of the Civil War Era* 4, no. 3 (2014): 400. James A. Field, *America and the Mediterranean World, 1776–1882* (Princeton, NJ: Princeton University Press, 1969), 386.

67. Martin Waldo E. Jr. *Mind of Frederick Douglass* (Chapel Hill, University of North Carolina Press), 206–7. See also Frederick Douglass, "Missions in Egypt," [manuscript speech], Frederick Douglass Papers, Library of Congress, http://hdl.loc.gov/loc.mss/mfd.32015.

68. See, for instance, "Egypt's Khedive: How a Modern Pharoah Acts and Looks," *Boston Globe*, July 14, 1889.

69. "New Egypt," *New York Times*, April 25, 1875.

70. Field, *America and the Mediterranean World*, 424.

71. AHD to Lee Mohun, [1888], box 2C, Mother Stephanie Mohun Papers, SMSA.

72. Rachel Mairs and Maya Muratov, *Archeologist, Tourists, Interpreters: Exploring Egypt and the Near East in the Late 19th–Early 20th Centuries* (London: Bloomsbury Academic, 2015), 3.

73. "Consul Belfast R.D. Mohun, Record," April 1889, Applications for Civil Service, RG 59, NARA.

74. See Michael Adas, *Dominance by Design: Technological Imperatives and America's Civilizing Mission* (Cambridge, MA: Belknap Press of Harvard University Press, 2006).

75. R. D. Mohun to Daniel McCauley, Supt., Nicaragua Mail and Transport Co., Recommendations for Public Office, RG 59, NARA; AHD to Hudson, February 6, 1891, Hudson Papers, AUND.

76. Michael D. Olien, "After the Indian Slave Trade: Cross-Cultural Trade in the Western Caribbean Rimland, 1816–1820," *Journal of Anthropological Research* 44 (1988): 41–66.

77. ASCE Global Engineering Conference and Bernard G. Dennis, *Engineering the Panama Canal: A Centennial Retrospective: Proceedings of Sessions Honoring the 100th Anniversary of the Panama Canal at the ASCE Global Engineering Conference 2014*, Panama City, Panama, October 7–11, 2014 (Reston, VA: American Society of Civil Engineers, 2014), 72. The vision could be traced much further back to John Adam's presidency. See Mary W. M. Hargreaves, "Adams, John Quincy," *American National Biography*, https://doi.org/10.1093/anb/9780198606697.article.0300002.

78. On the United States' special relationship with Nicaragua, see David M. Pletcher, *The Diplomacy of Trade and Investment: American Economic Expansion in the Hemisphere, 1865–1900* (Columbia: University of Missouri Press, 1998).

79. "On the Scene of the Work," *New York Times*, April 30, 1891.

80. For visual images, see "The Nicaragua Canal," *Scientific American* 69 (January 31, 1891): 63. See also *Proceedings of the Nicaragua Canal Convention*, June 2–3, 1892, 31.

81. Anna Hanson Dorsey to Lee Dorsey, incorrectly dated 1889, Mother Stephanie Papers, SMSA.

82. Clare Mohun to Lucy Hayes, September 17, 1891; Clare to Hayes, [ca. 1891], LWH Collection. On the Emerys and the mahogany trade, see Karl Offen,

"The Geographical Imagination, Resource Economies, and Nicaraguan Incorporation of the Mosquitia, 1838–1909," in *Territories, Commodities and Knowledges: Latin American Environmental History in the Nineteenth and Twentieth Centuries*, ed. Christian Brannstrom and Stefania Gallini (London: Institute for the Study of the Americas, 2004), 173.

83. Offen, "Geographical Imagination," 74; Richard Dorsey Mohun to Rutherford B. Hayes, December 14, 1891, RBH Collection.

84. Clare Mohun to Rutherford B. Hayes, September 17, 1891, RBH Collection. No record survives of what he did with the land after he left Nicaragua. He seems to have abandoned or sold it.

85. Anna Hanson Dorsey to Hudson, February 6, 1891, Hudson Papers, AUND.

86. Anna Hanson Dorsey to Lee Dorsey, incorrectly dated 1889, Mother Stephanie Papers, SMSA.

87. "Nicaragua Canal: Message from the President of the United States," House of Representatives, 54th Congress, 2nd Session (Washington, DC: Government Printing Office, 1896), 90.

88. R. D. Mohun, New York, Arriving Passenger and Crew Lists, 1820–1957, Ancestry.com.

89. "All New York, U.S., Arriving Passenger and Crew Lists," Ancestry.com, https://www.ancestry.com/search/collections/7488/?arrival=1891&keyword=nicaragua+Greytown+American&fh=80&fsk=MDs3OTsyMA-61—61. Records for incoming passengers show steady traffic of Americans and Europeans from Greytown in the late 1880s and early 1890s, including a few women traveling alone who may have been family members.

90. Anna Hanson Dorsey to Hudson, February 10, 1892, Hudson Papers, AUND.

Chapter 2

1. 1892–93 diary, February 7, 1892, item 1, Mohun Papers; "Weather," *New York Times*, February 27, 1892.

2. Henry Morton Stanley, *How I Found Livingstone* (London: Sampson Low, 1887); *In Darkest Africa, or The Quest, Rescue and Retreat of Emin, Governor of Equatoria* (New York: Charles Scribner's Sons, 1890). Stanley was a prolific writer and the first effective publicist for the Congo Free State. See, for example Henry M. Stanley, *The Congo and the Founding of Its Free State: A Story of Work and Exploration* (New York: Harper & Brothers, 1885).

3. The historical literature on Leopold and the Congo is vast and contentious. For an excellent overview and analysis, see Aldwin Roes, "Towards a History of Mass Violence in the État Independent du Congo, 1885–1908," *South*

African Historical Journal 11, no. 62 (December 2010): 634–70. Best known and highly influential is journalist Adam Hochschild's *King Leopold's Ghost: A Story of Greed, Terror, and Heroism in Colonial Africa* (New York: Houghton Mifflin, 1998). Hochschild drew heavily on Jules Marchal's multivolume expose. The first volume is Jules Marchal and A. M. Delathuy, *L'État Libre du Congo: Paradis Perdu; L'Histoire du Congo 1876–1900* (Borgloon: Bellings, 1996). Ruth M. Slade, *King Leopold's Congo; Aspects of the Development of Race Relations in the Congo Independent State* (London: Oxford University Press, 1962), is a particularly clear and balanced analysis. I've also relied on Jean Stengers and Jan Vansina, "King Leopold's Congo, 1886–1908," in *The Cambridge History of Africa*, vol. 6, *From 1870 to 1905*, ed. R. Oliver and G. N. Sanderson (Cambridge: University of Cambridge, 1985), and Lewis H. Gann and Peter Duignan, *The Rulers of Belgian Africa, 1884–1914* (Princeton, NJ: Princeton University Press: 1979).

4. Louis Mohun, Military Pension Application, Department of Veterans Affairs, RG 15, NARA.

5. Clare Mohun to Rutherford B. Hayes, November 21, 1891, RBH Collection; Anna Hanson Dorsey to Father Hudson, February 10, 1892, Hudson Papers, AUND.

6. Mary Waggaman, "Anne Hanson Dorsey," *The Catholic Encyclopedia*, vol. 5 (New York: Robert Appleton Company, 1909), https://www.newadvent.org/cathen/05136a.htm. See also "Anna Hanson Dorsey Ill: A Talented Woman Known to All Readers of Catholic Literature," *Washington Post*, October 26, 1896.

7. Darcy Grimaldo Grigsby, *Colossal: Engineering the Suez Canal, Statue of Liberty, Eiffel Tower, and Panama Canal; Transcontinental Ambition in France and the United States during the Long Nineteenth Century* (Pittsburgh: Periscope, 2012), 47–49.

8. 1892–93 diary, February 27, 1892, Mohun Papers.

9. Jewett was a well-known writer, now best remembered for *The Country of the Pointed Firs* (1896).

10. 1892–93 diary, February 27, 1892, Mohun Papers.

11. 1892–93 diary, February 29, 1892, Mohun Papers.

12. 1892–93 diary, March 5, 1892, Mohun Papers.

13. 1892–93 diary, March 7, 1892, Mohun Papers.

14. 1892–93 diary, March 11, 1892, Mohun Papers.

15. Anna Hanson Dorsey to Lee Mohun, April 6, 1891 (incorrectly dated), Mother Stephanie Papers, SMSA.

16. 1892–93 diary, entries for March 13, 20, and 21, Mohun Papers. Four thousand French francs was worth about $768 in 1892.

17. Roosevelt was a distant cousin of Theodore Roosevelt.

18. 1892–93 diary, March 22, 1892, Mohun Papers.

19. For a more extensive analysis of this theme, see Vincent Viane, "King Leopold's Imperialism and the Origins of the Belgian Colonial Party," *Journal of Modern History* 80 (December 2008): 744, 756. Viane notes that there is a growing historiography on the relationship between colonies and metropoles.

20. *Bruxelles: Guide Illustré*, 8th ed. (Brussels: Libraire Européenne; C. Murquardt, 1890), 18, my translation. For du Pont's ownership, see front cover of the Hagley Library copy.

21. *Bruxelles: Guide Illustré*, 26.

22. It had previously been part of the Netherlands and before that, part of various European empires. Gann and Duignan, *Rulers of Belgian Africa*, 4.

23. "Report of the Commissioners of the United States to the International Exposition held at Brussels in 1897," Senate document #152, 55th Congress, 2nd Session (Washington, DC: Government Printing Office, 1896), 27. On the broader context of Leopold and his successors efforts to portray the Congo to the people of Belgium and the larger world, see Matthew G. Stanard, *Selling the Congo: The History of European Pro-Empire Propaganda and the Making of Belgian Imperialism* (Lincoln: University of Nebraska Press, 2011), 10; Vincent Van Reybrouck, David Van Reybrouck, and Bambi Ceuppens, eds., *Congo in België: Koloniale Cultuur in De Metropool* (Leuven: Leuven University Press, 2009).

24. 1892–93 diary, March 24, 1892, Mohun Papers.

25. E. J. Glave, "The Congo River of Today," *Century Illustrated Magazine* 39 (February 1890): 620; Séamas Ó Síocháin, *Roger Casement: Imperialist, Rebel, Revolutionary* (Dublin: Lilliput Press, 2008), 25. Ó Síocháin's biography of Casement is the most comprehensive and detailed of the many that have been written. It does not mention Dorsey, although there is plenty of evidence that they knew each other well.

26. The number 430 comes from Hochschild, *King Leopold's Ghost*, 90 (no source cited). Andrew C. A. Jampoler, *Congo: The Miserable Expeditions and Dreadful Death of Lt. Emory Taunt, USN* (Annapolis, MD: Naval Institute Press, 2013), 74.

27. Dorsey to William F. Wharton, Assistant Secretary of State, March 29, 1892, Boma Despatches. Taunt's story is documented in Jampoler, *Congo*.

28. The effort eventually succeeded. See 1892–93 diary, October 2, 1892, Mohun Papers.

29. Ó Síocháin, *Roger Casement*, 40.

30. 1892–93 diary, March 25, 1892, Mohun Papers. On Conrad see, Ó Síocháin, *Roger Casement*, 41.

31. Ó Síocháin, *Roger Casement*, 41.

32. Ó Síocháin, *Roger Casement*, 28.

33. Some of Casement's biographers have speculated about when Casement became sexually active with male partners. The first concrete evidence is from 1903 in Casement's so-called Black Diaries. The diaries suggest that he did not pursue sexual relationships with other middle-class men. Brian Lewis, "The Queer Life and Afterlife of Roger Casement," *Journal of the History of Sexuality* 14, no. 4 (2005): 368. See also Richard J. Ruppel, *Homosexuality in the Life and Work of Joseph Conrad: Love between the Lines* (New York: Routledge, 2008), 18. Ruppel thinks the room-sharing episode with Conrad in 1890 did not involve anything sexual. Dorsey left no evidence that he had sex with Casement or any other man. It's impossible to know whether he was just discreet or observed conventional societal boundaries. For more on intimate male friendships, see Donald Yacovone, "Abolitionists and the 'Language of Fraternal Love,'" in *Meanings for Manhood: Constructions of Masculinity in Victorian America*, ed. Mark C. Carnes and Clyde Griffen (Chicago: University of Chicago Press, 1990), 85–95.

34. 1892–93 diary, March 30, 1892, Mohun Papers.

35. The system of US trade consuls or "commercial agents" traced its roots to the earliest days of the republic and was still in his time remarkably unprofessionalized The system Dorsey knew was created by an act of Congress in 1792. Charles Kennedy, *The American Consul: A History of the United States Consular Service, 1776–1914* (New York: Greenwood Press, 1990), 22.

36. For an example, see A. W. Sollack to Dorsey, n.d., Zanzibar Despatches.

37. Hochschild, *King Leopold's Ghost*, 87. See also Neal Ascherson, *The King Incorporated: Leopold II in the Age of Trusts* (Garden City, NJ: Doubleday, 1964); Stengers and Vansina, "King Leopold's Congo, 1886–1908," 321 (see n. 3).

38. Philip Sheldon Foner, *Mark Twain Social Critic* (New York: International, 1972), 388.

39. William Appleman Williams, *The Roots of the Modern American Empire: A Study of the Growth and Shaping of Social Consciousness in a Marketplace Society* (New York: Random House, 1969), 207.

40. Gann and Duignan, *Rulers of Belgian Africa*, 35–6. Hochschild, *King Leopold's Ghost*, 78.

41. Williams, *Roots of the Modern American Empire*, 261; see also Hochschild, *King Leopold's Ghost*, 77–81.

42. Cleveland did not ultimately sign the Berlin Treaty. Many people, including his contemporaries, believed that he had, creating a great deal of confusion twenty years later when famous figures such as Mark Twain became involved in the Congo reform movement. See Hunt Hawkins, "Mark Twain's

Involvement with the Congo Reform Movement: 'A Fury of Generous In-dignation.'" *New England Quarterly* 51, no. 2 (1978): 165.

43. W. P. Tisdel, "My Trip to the Congo," *Century Illustrated Magazine* 39 (Feb-ruary 1890): 609–18, quote on 615.

44. John Hope Franklin, *George Washington Williams: A Biography* (Chicago: University of Chicago Press, 1985), 195.

45. Dorsey had already been approached by what his mother described as "a Syndicate of New York men" to purchase rubber for them. Clare Mohun to Rutherford B. Hayes, December 14th, 1891, RBH Collection.

46. George Washington Williams had, in fact, been hugely impressed when he met Leopold in 1884. Franklin, *George Washington Williams*, 181.

47. *Bruxelles: Guide Illustré*, 98 (see n. 20).

48. 1892–93 diary, March 26, 1892, Mohun Papers.

49. Operated by the British and African Steamer Navigation Company. Dorsey to Wharton, May 3, 1892, Boma Despatches.

50. 1892–93 diary, March 3, 1892, Mohun Papers.

51. E. J. Glave used it as an epigram for the first chapter of his memoir, *Six Years of Adventure in Congo-Land* (London: Sampson Low, Marston, 1893), 15. Glave was a close friend and confidant of Parminter and Casement.

52. 1892–93 diary, April 3 and 5, 1892, Mohun Papers.

53. 1892–93 diary, March 6, 1892, Mohun Papers. Casement was friends with a Reginald Heyn. See Ó Síocháin, *Roger Casement*, 40.

54. 1892–93 diary, March 6, 1892, Mohun Papers.

55. 1892–93 diary, April 8, 1892, Mohun Papers.

56. 1892–93 diary, April 12, 1892, Mohun Papers.

57. 1892–93 diary, April 15, 1892, Mohun Papers.

58. 1892–93 diary, April 19, 1892, Mohun Papers.

59. Jampoler, *Congo*, 5.

60. Richard Harding Davis, *The Congo and the Coasts of Africa* (New York: Charles Scribner's Sons, 1907), 43.

61. 1892–93 diary, April 28, 1892, Mohun Papers. Heyn was director of trans-portation for the SAB. Joseph Conrad had also known him during his time in the Congo. Joseph Conrad, *Last Essays*, ed. Harold Ray Stevens and J. H. Stape (Cambridge University Press, 2010), 458.

62. 1892–93 diary, April 28, 1892, Mohun Papers.

63. Hochschild, *King Leopold's Ghost*, 115.

64. Final Report.

65. Harding, *Coasts of Africa*, 47, 51.

66. David Van Reybrouck, *Congo: The Epic History of a People* (New York: Harper-Collins, 2010), 77.

Chapter 3

1. On Taunt, see Andrew C. A. Jampoler, *Congo: The Miserable Expeditions and Dreadful Death of Lt. Emory Taunt, USN* (Annapolis, MD: Naval Institute Press, 2013).

2. 1892–93 diary, March 25, 1892, Mohun Papers. In 1891 and 1892 Leopold imposed a new set of measures that severely restricted trade by outsiders. See Paul S. Reinsch, "Real Conditions in the Congo Free State," *North American Review* 178 (February 1904): 217. He was mandated by law to explore the Congo. "According to the previsions of law authorizing the sending of a Commercial Agent I visited the Upper and Lower valleys of the Kongo." Final Report.

3. On Conrad's journey, see Joseph Conrad, "The Congo Diary," in *The Works of Joseph Conrad: Last Essays*, ed. Owen Knowles and Harold Ray Stevens (Cambridge: Cambridge University Press, 2010). The "Explanatory Notes" by Knowles and Stevens in the same volume (pages 453–60) contain a great deal of detailed information about Conrad's journey and the people he met on it.

4. This was true for all Europeans in Africa. See Benjamin N. Lawrance, Emily Lynn Osborn, and Richard L. Roberts, "Introduction: African Intermediaries and the 'Bargain' of Collaboration," in *Intermediaries, Interpreters, and Clerks: African Employees in the Making of Colonial Africa* (Madison: University of Wisconsin Press, 2006), 9–10.

5. David Northrup, *Beyond the Bend in the River: African Labor in Eastern Zaire, 1865–1940* (Athens: Ohio University Center for African Studies, 1988), 33; Adam Hochschild, *King Leopold's Ghost: A Story of Greed, Terror, and Heroism in Colonial Africa* (Boston: Houghton Mifflin, 1998), 127.

6. It's not clear how Dorsey went about finding and hiring Philip, but there is evidence that the state provided other visitors with their own "boys" from a pool of available candidates. The state offered Dorsey's predecessor a Zanzibari "domestique" at 35 francs a month. État Independent du Congo to Emory Taunt, February 9, 1899, Boma Despatches. A Belgian doctor wrote in 1898 that after a welcome dinner at the Governor General's house in Boma, he was presented with his choice of boys who could "nous accompagner au poste et y remplir l'office de domestique de maison." Raymond Rihoux, *Congo 1898* (Tournai: Lithographie Tournaisienne, 1948), 67–68.

7. Photo dated June 1892, author's possession.

8. Dorsey later confirmed Phillip was in his late twenties when the picture was taken. 1894 diary, March 30, 1894, Mohun Papers.

9. "C'est le mode ici," Rihoux, *Congo 1898*, 77.

10. 1894 diary, March 30, 1894, Mohun Papers; Sidney Langford Hinde, *The Fall of the Congo Arabs* (New York: Thomas Whittaker, 1897), 252. E. J. Glave noted that the "public force" in Boma consisted mostly of Hausa (Houssa) soldiers. See E. J. Glave, "The Congo River of To-day," *Century Illustrated Magazine*, February 1890, 619.

11. Stanley had a boy Kalulu or Ndugu M'Hali, with whom he was photographed in a very similar pose sometime in the mid-1870s, but he also had an adult translator and go-between named Selim. James L. Newman, *Imperial Footprints: Henry Morton Stanley's African Journeys* (Washington, DC: Brassey's, 2004), 51, 57.

12. David Van Reybrouck, *Congo: The Epic History of a People* (New York: HarperCollins, 2010), 62; Jean Stengers and Jan Vansina, "King Leopold's Congo, 1886–1908," in *The Cambridge History of Africa*, vol. 6, *From 1870 to 1905*, ed. R. Oliver and G. N. Sanderson (Cambridge: University of Cambridge, 1985), 334.

13. E. J. Glave, *Six Years of Adventure in Congo-Land* (London: S. Low, Marston, 1893), 25.

14. Final Report, 21.

15. Dorsey to Wharton, June 30, 1892, Boma Despatches.

16. The flow of the river is 1.5 million cubic feet per second. Jampoler, *Congo*, 5.

17. For a global view of the importance of steamboats in imperialism, see Daniel Headrick, *The Tools of Empire: Technology and European Imperialism* (Oxford: Oxford University Press, 1988).

18. Six thousand miles is from Jampoler, *Congo*, 6. Stanley Falls, upstream from Kinshasa, was the other barrier.

19. Final Report, 8.

20. W. P. Tisdel, "My Trip to the Congo," *Century Illustrated Magazine* 39 (February 1890): 619. Europeans already knew that draft animals that would have been used in other parts of the world for this task did not survive very long in the Congo.

21. Final Report, 9.

22. For an overview of the porterage system, see Stephen J. Rockel, *Carriers of Culture: Labor on the Road in Nineteenth-Century East Africa* (Portsmouth, NH: Heinemann, 2006). Historians disagree about the degree of coercion involved in recruiting and retaining porters. Rockel views them as independent agents seeking economic opportunities. Hochschild (*King Leopold's Ghost*, 125) describes the Congo porters as virtual slaves. It is clear that contract laborers in the Congo had fewer protections than they did in East Africa. See S. J. S. Cookey, "West African Immigrants in the Congo, 1885–1896," *Journal of the Historical Society of Nigeria* 3 (December 1965):

261–70; Ruth Rempel, " 'No Better than a Slave or Outcast': Skill, Identity, and Power among the Porters of the Emin Pasha Relief Expedition, 1887–1890," *International Journal of African Historical Studies* 43 (2010): 279–318.

23. Final Report, 14–15; David Van Reybrouck, *Congo: The Epic History of a People* (New York: HarperCollins, 2010), 84. For more detail about the railroad, including estimates on death rates, see Stengers and Vansina, "King Leopold's Congo," 341.

24. 1892–93 diary, entries for August 23, 24, 27, 28, 1892, Mohun Papers.

25. Final Report, 18, 22.

26. "White" because of the color of their robes.

27. 1892–93 diary, August 28, 1892, Mohun Papers.

28. Final Report, 22.

29. Rockel, *Carriers of Culture*, 131–35.

30. 1892–93 diary, September 2, 1892, Mohun Papers.

31. Hinde, *Fall*, 35; Glave, "Realm of the Congo," 619.

32. Rockel, *Carriers of Culture*, 99.

33. 1892–93 diary, September 12, 13, 1892, Mohun Papers.

34. Rockel, *Carriers of Culture*, 11, 171–73.

35. Rockel, 4–6, 67, 132.

36. Conrad, "Congo Diary," 126, 131.

37. Commissioner, "Realm of the Congo," 619; Final Report, 22–23. Rockel (*Carriers of Culture*, 139–40) also describes this problem in more general terms.

38. For more on European colonial understandings of nakedness, see Philippa Levine, "States of Undress: Nakedness and the Colonial Imagination," *Victorian Studies* 50, no. 2 (2008): 189–219. Levine describes clothing as one of the three "Cs," along with Christianity and civilization (191).

39. 1892–93 diary, September 8, 1892, Mohun Papers.

40. 1892–93 diary, September 16, 1892, Mohun Papers.

41. 1892–93 diary, September 15, 1892, Mohun Papers. On the events leading up to the war, see Ruth Slade, *King Leopold's Congo: Aspects of the Development of Race Relations in the Congo Independent State* (London: Oxford University Press, 1962), 109.

42. 1892–93 diary, September 15, 1892, Mohun Papers.

43. Final Report, 26.

44. Conrad had reported to Delcommune when he arrived in Kinshasa but received a somewhat different reception. Delcommune chided him for arriving two days late and set him to work packing ivory. Stevens et. al., "Explanatory Notes," 461 (see n. 3).

45. 1892–93 diary, September 26, 1892, Mohun Papers.

46. 1892–93 diary, October 5, 1892, Mohun Papers. More than $6 million in today's money.

47. 1892–93 diary, October 2, 1892. He ended up paying $195 a month in exchange for food and "passage for myself and three servants." Final Report, 27.

48. 1892–93 diary, October 17, 1892, Mohun Papers.

49. For a thoughtful analysis of the social nature of the Congo's culture of violence, See Aldwin Roes, "Towards a History of Mass Violence in the État Independent du Congo, 1885–1908," *South African Historical Journal* 62 (December 2010): 634–70.

50. Joseph Conrad, *Heart of Darkness: A Case Study in Contemporary Criticism*, ed. Ross C. Murfin (New York: St. Martin's Press, 1989), 23, 40.

51. Conrad, *Heart of Darkness*, 37. I have used *Heart of Darkness* here as a historical source with the awareness of Chinua Achebe's influential critique of the novella as racist and really about Africa or Africans because it does reflect Conrad's encounter with many of the same people and places that Dorsey encountered less than two years later.

52. Robert W. Harms, *River of Wealth, River of Sorrow: The Central Zaire Basin in the Era of the Slave and Ivory Trade, 1500–1891* (New Haven, CT: Yale University Press, 1981), 29, 39, 40.

53. Harms, *River of Wealth*, 5, 41.

54. Slade, *King Leopold's Congo*, 84–94.

55. 1891–92 is often given as the turning point. See Stengers and Vansina, "King Leopold's Congo," 337.

56. Herman J. Viola, *Thomas L. McKenney, Architect of America's Early Indian Policy, 1816–1830* (Chicago: Swallow Press, 1974).

57. Dorsey was even more erratic, spelling the river's name multiple different ways in his diary and official reports.

58. Final Report, 27.

59. Final Report, 32.

60. 1892–93 diary, October 19, 1892, Mohun Papers.

61. Final Report, 27, identifies him as Fernand. Dorsey's diary calls him Stephen, 1892–93 diary, October 19, 1892. He is also identified in some sources as Fernand Alexandre Robert De Meuse. For a biographical sketch, see *Biographie coloniale belge; Belgische koloniale biografie* (Brussels: Librairie Falk fils, 1952), 5:230–31. For Demeuse's photographic career, see Christaud M. Geary, *In and Out of Focus: Images from Central Africa, 1885–1960* (Washington, DC: Smithsonian Institution, 2002), 32. Identified as Captain, Final Report, 31–32.

62. 1892–93 diary, October 20, 1892, Mohun Papers; Final Report, 32.

63. 1892–93 diary, October 20, 1892, Mohun Papers.

64. 1892–93 diary, November 21, 1892, Mohun Papers.

65. R. D. Mohun, "Trade in the Kongo Free State," *Monthly Consular and Trade Reports* (Washington, DC: United States Bureau of Manufactures, 1892), 40:444.

66. Dorsey would have known them as "pygmies."

67. Harms, *River of Wealth*, 41.

68. Dorsey described these canoes as "small" (1892–93 diary, October 25, 1892). The largest dugouts might be sixty feet long and crewed by as many as sixty paddlers. See also, Harms, *River of Wealth*, 93–94.

69. For a list of trade goods, see Final Report, 18.

70. Final Report, 53.

71. 1892–93 diary, October 30, 1892, Mohun Papers.

72. Final Report, 36; Claire Polakoff, "The Art of Tie and Dye in Africa," *African Arts* 4, no. 3 (1971): 28–80.

73. 1892–93 diary, October 31, 1892, Mohun Papers.

74. 1892–93 diary, November 2, 1892, Mohun Papers; Final Report, 41.

75. Harms, *River of Wealth*, 81–83, 235.

76. 1892–93 diary, November 2, 1892, Mohun Papers.

77. Final Report, 32.

78. 1892–93 diary, November 6, 1892, Mohun Papers.

79. 1892–93 diary, November 13, 1892, Mohun Papers. His final report to the State Department played up the drama of the event. Final Report, 47–50.

80. 1892–93 diary, December 2, 1892, Mohun Papers.

81. 1892–93 diary, December 31, 1892, Mohun Papers.

Chapter 4

1. Some scholars have used the word *Swahili* as an ethnonym for the people described in this and successive chapters. I've used *Arab* because, in this era, they described themselves as Arab or Omani. See David M. Gordon, "Interpreting Documentary Sources on the Early History of the Congo Free State: The Case of Ngongo Luteta's Rise and Fall," *History in Africa* 41 (2014): 6. Gordon describes Swahili as "an evolving coastal identity" in this era.

2. 1892–93 diary, September 30, 1892, Mohun Papers.

3. Final Report, 59. See also mention of Dumbele, 1892–93 diary, January 16, 1893, Mohun Papers.

4. Final Report 60; 1892–93 diary, January 21, 1893, Mohun Papers.

5. 1892–93 diary, February 7, 1893, Mohun Papers.

6. 1982–83 diary, February 9, 1893, Mohun Papers.

7. The forces were likely a mix of Zanzibaris, Soudanese, and regional conscripts and mercenaries—neither Dorsey nor Chaltin explains.

8. Dorsey to Assistant Secretary of State, April 17, 1893, Boma Despatches.

9. 1892–93 diary, March 6, 1893, Mohun Papers.

10. For a particularly thoughtful analysis of Tip's place in the Congo, see David Northrup, *Beyond the Bend in the River: African Labor in Eastern Zaire, 1865–1940* (Athens: Ohio University, 1988), 23–9. See also Ruth Slade, *King Leopold's Congo: Aspects of the Development of Race Relations in the Congo Independent State* (London: Oxford University Press, 1962), 94. Slade also provides a particularly useful map insert.

11. Heinrich Brode, *Tipoo Tib: The Story of His Career in Central Africa* (Chicago: Afro-Am Press, 1969), vii.

12. Dorsey used the term *Kiswahili*.

13. Slade, *King Leopold's Congo*, 99; Northrup, *Bend in the River*, 44.

14. Slade, *King Leopold's Congo*, 101–2.

15. Slade, 95, 99.

16. Slade, 98–99.

17. 1892–93 diary, March 8, 1893, Mohun Papers.

18. 1892–93 diary, March 8, 1893, Mohun Papers.

19. *Biographie coloniale belge; Belgische koloniale biografie* (Brussels: Librairie Falk fils, 1948), 2:915.

20. 1892–93 diary, March 14, 1893, Mohun Papers.

21. 1892–93 diary, March 10, 1893, Mohun Papers.

22. Final Report, 65.

23. 1892–93 diary, March 13, 1893, Mohun Papers.

24. 1892–93 diary, March 26, 1893, Mohun Papers.

25. Dorsey to Assistant Secretary of State, June 21, 1893, Boma Despatches, 6.

26. 1892–93 diary, March 31, 1893, Mohun Papers.

27. June 21, 1893, Boma Despatches, 7.

28. 1892–93 diary, March 31, 1893, Mohun Papers.

29. 1892–93 diary, April 12, 1893, Mohun Papers.

30. Robert Edgerton, *The Troubled Heart of Africa: A History of the Congo* (New York: St. Martin's Press, 2002), 99; Edgerton cites R. P. P. Ceulmans, *La question Arabe et le Congo, 1883–1892* (Brussels: MARSC, 1959), 339.

31. "Hodister (Arthur)," in *Biographie coloniale belge*, 2:516.

32. Hodister thus had many of the characteristics of colonial figures sometimes described as *décivilisé*. See Owen White, "The Decivilizing Mission: Auguste Dupuis-Yakouba and French Timbuktu," *French Historical Studies* 27 (Summer 2004): 541–66.

33. 1892–93 diary, April 11, 1893, Mohun Papers; Dorsey to Assistant Secretary of State, June 21, 1893, Boma Despatches.

34. Dorsey to Assistant Secretary of State, October 1893 Report, 10, Boma Despatches.

35. Dorsey to Assistant Secretary of State, April 17, 1893, Boma Despatches.

36. Alexis-Marie Gochet, *Soldats et missionnaires au Congo de 1891 à 1894* (Brussels: Desclée, de Brouwer, 1897) 46. Dorsey never bothered to correct this misrepresentation of his nonexistent military career. Identification as an "ancien Officier de la marine militaire" continued to be included in Belgian biographical sources even after the principles were dead and gone. See *Biographie coloniale belge*, 2:710.

37. George M. Fredrickson, *The Inner Civil War: Northern Intellectuals and the Crisis of the Union* (New York: Harper & Row, 1965).

38. 1892–93 diary, April 8, 1893, Mohun Papers.

39. 1892–93 diary, April 18, 1893, Mohun Papers.

40. Gochet, *Soldats et missionnaires*, 42, 46.

41. June 21, 1893, Boma Despatches, 14.

42. Gochet, *Soldats and missionnaires*, 47.

43. Final Report, 71.

44. Final Report, 72.

45. Final Report, 74.

46. Gochet, *Soldats et missionnaires*, 54.

47. June 21, 1893, Boma Despatches, 22. Dorsey was most probably vaccinated in childhood. Washington officials had required vaccination in response to an 1872 epidemic in the city. See "Rules and Regulations in Regard to Small-Pox," *Evening Star*, October 19, 1872.

48. June 21, 1893, Boma Despatches, 25–27.

49. June 21, 1893, Boma Despatches, 28.

50. Some of which eventually ended up in the Royal Army and Military History Museum in Brussels in a display case about the Arab War celebrating their achievements. It was still in place when I visited in 2017.

51. Final Report, 79.

52. For more on the controversies surrounding claims by European travelers about cannibalism in Africa and elsewhere, see Laurence Goldman, *The Anthropology of Cannibalism* (Westport, CT: Bergin & Garvey, 1999), and William Arens, *The Man-Eating Myth: Anthropology and Anthropophagy* (New York: Oxford University Press, 1979). Dorsey's travelling companion Sidney Langford Hinde made a significant reputation and sold numerous copies of his memoir by making claims about cannibalism in the Congo.

Dorsey may have been influenced by those successes to include his own story, which may or may not have been fabricated.

53. Final Report, 80–81.
54. Final Report, 37.
55. See Andrew C. A. Jampoler, *Congo: The Miserable Expeditions and Dreadful Death of Lt. Emory Taunt, USN* (Annapolis, MD: Naval Institute Press, 2013), 110–13, for a lengthy discussion about the *Florida*.
56. 1892–93 diary, September 9, 1893, Mohun Papers.
57. 1892–93 diary, September 11, 1893, Mohun Papers.
58. Final Report, 95.
59. Final Report, 117.
60. Final Report, 118.
61. 1892–93 diary, October 4, 1893, Mohun Papers.
62. Final Report, 119.
63. Final Report, 121.
64. Final Report, 123.
65. Final Report, 125.

Chapter 5

1. Ruth Slade, *King Leopold's Congo: Aspects of the Development of Race Relations in the Congo Independent State* (London: Oxford University Press, 1962), 110, 114. There is no recent scholarly biography of Dhanis despite his importance. Marie-Louise Comeliau, *Dhanis* (Brussels: Etudes Colonial, 1943), is hagiographic but provides a starting place. Dhanis's papers await a biographer at the Royal Museum of Central Africa in Tervuren.
2. There is a growing literature on the construction of heroism and empire. See John M. MacKenzie, "Heroic Myth of Empire," in *Popular Imperialism and the Military*, ed. John M. MacKenzie (Manchester: University of Manchester Press, 1992): 109–38; Berny Sèbe, *Heroic Imperialists in Africa: The Promotion of British and French Colonial Heroes, 1870–1939* (Manchester: Manchester University Press, 2013); Edward Berenson, *Heroes of Empire: Five Charismatic Men and the Conquest of Africa* (Berkeley: University of California Press, 2011); Michael Dawson, *Soldier Heroes: British Adventure, Empire, and the Imagining of Masculinities* (London: Routledge, 1994).
3. Michael Lieven, "Heroics and the Making of Heroes: The Anglo-Zulu War of 1879," *Albion: A Quarterly Journal Concerned with British Studies* 30 (Autumn 1998): 419.
4. "Warm Welcome to Baron Dhanis," *New York Times*, October 13, 1894.

5. Many of these narratives fit neatly into the archetypal pattern described by Joseph Campbell in *The Hero with a Thousand Faces*. They involved the hero's journey to a mysterious place, testing by encounters with dark forces, and eventual triumphant emergence. Conrad's *Heart of Darkness* turns that archetypal narrative inside out.

6. Sèbe, *Heroic Imperialists*, 2, 54.

7. Final Report, 129.

8. Final Report, 128.

9. Final Report, 141.

10. Final Report, 141.

11. Final Report, 143.

12. Final Report, 147.

13. Hinde later wrote his own account of the Arab campaign and its aftermath, including his interactions with Dorsey. It remains one of the most widely cited English-language sources for the history of the Congo Free State in this era. Sidney Langford Hinde, *Fall of the Congo Arabs* (New York: Thomas Whitaker, 1897). See also S. L. Hinde, "Three Years' Travel in the Congo Free State," *Geographical Journal* 5, no. 5 (1895): 426–42.

14. Final Report, 148. Dorsey arrived December 20, 1893. There is no mention of these events in his 1892–93 diary.

15. Final Report, 148; Slade, *King Leopold's Congo*, 114.

16. Comeliau, *Dhanis*, 15.

17. Ruth Slade, *King Leopold's Congo*, 110, 114.

18. Slade, *King Leopold's Congo*, 114; Hinde, *Fall of the Congo Arabs*, 31, 127, 137. Sèbe (*Heroic Imperialists*, 176–77) points out that this list of characteristics was typical of the way imperial heroes were described, but in Dhanis's case at least, they contain a grain of truth.

19. Final Report, 160.

20. Final Report, 148.

21. Nancy Rose Hunt provides a very evocative and useful description of this pervasive feeling. See Nancy Rose Hunt, *A Nervous State: Violence, Remedies, and Reverie in Colonial Congo* (Durham, NC: Duke University Press, 2016), 5.

22. Final Report, 150.

23. Hinde, *Fall of the Congo Arabs*, 184–85.

24. R. Dorsey Mohun, "The Death of Emin Pasha," *Century Illustrated Magazine* 49 (February 1895): 592.

25. Final Report, 150.

26. Jack P. Maddex, *The Virginia Conservatives, 1867–1879: A Study in Reconstruction Politics* (Chapel Hill: University of North Carolina Press, 1970).

27. *Biographie coloniale belge; Belgische koloniale biografie* (Brussels: Librairie Falk fils, 1948), 1:510–11; Hinde, *Fall of the Congo Arabs*, 28.

28. Hinde included more than a dozen references to cannibalism in *The Fall of the Congo Arabs*; see pages 65–9, 118–19, 283–5. Cultural historians have pointed out that cannibalism is a common theme in colonial literature of the time. Intriguingly, they suggest that it may express psychological anxiety about being consumed by a non-European other. See Dawson, *Soldier Heroes*, 89.

29. See, for example, 1894 diary, January 1, 1894, Mohun Papers.

30. Final Report, 153.

31. Final Report, 152.

32. Final Report, 155.

33. Final Report, 154.

34. See Hinde, *Fall of the Congo Arabs*, for a map and very detailed description (page 236 and facing).

35. Final Report, 157.

36. Final Report 159.

37. Final Report, 160.

38. Final Report, 160.

39. The *New York Times*, for example contains numerous articles beginning in the late 1880s. See, for example "Emin Pasha's Resolve," October 3, 1887; "Emin Pasha," May 6, 1888; "The White Pasha," August 4, 1888.

40. Daniel Liebowitz and Charlie Pearson, *The Last Expedition: Stanley's Mad Journey through the Congo* (New York: W. W. Norton, 2005), 6–9.

41. Berenson, *Heroes of Empire* (n. 2), chap. 3.

42. See, for example, the series of articles on the Arab Campaign in the *Times* beginning with "The Congo State," March 19, 1894.

43. Liebowitz and Pearson, *The Last Expedition*, 310.

44. 1894 diary, March 14, 1894, Mohun Papers. The entry gives a list and description of the expedition participants. They also included an African chief named Piani Gongi. Gongi was going back to his home territory after having helped the Europeans in the Arab Campaign.

45. 1894 diary, January 3, 1894, Mohun Papers. So great was public interest in Emin Pasha that the journals along with other documents related to his life were translated into English and published in 1897. See Emin Pasha, and Georg Schweitzer, *Emin Pasha, His Life and Work* (1897; New York: Negro Universities Press, 1969).

46. Sometime during this period, he had a photograph taken of himself and his "colorbearers," one of whom was most likely Omari. Mohun, "Death of Emin Pasha."

47. Final Report, 178.
48. Final Report, 178.
49. Final Report, 180.
50. 1894 diary, March 4, 1894, Mohun Papers.
51. Most directly, Rudyard Kipling's 1888 novella *The Man Who Would Be King*, but also, of course, Kurtz in *Heart of Darkness*.
52. 1894 diary, March 13, 1894, Mohun Papers.
53. 1894 diary, March 3, 1894, Mohun Papers.
54. 1894 diary, March 15, 1894, Mohun Papers.
55. Hinde, *Fall of the Congo Arabs*, 251.
56. Hinde, 248–49.
57. Francis Dhanis to Richard Dorsey Mohun, March 24, 1894, File 34, R. Dorsey Mohun Papers, Royal Museum for Central Africa.
58. 1894 diary, March 16, 1894, Mohun Papers.
59. Final Report, 187. Hinde spelled the name Waginia. Hinde, *Fall of the Congo Arabs*, 252. They seem to have frequently changed crews by striking bargains for help in riverside villages.
60. See photograph of similar vessels, one with a shelter in Touring Club de Belgique, *Panorama du Congo* (Brussels: Imprimerie scientifique Charles Bulens, 1912), "Fascicule IV—Des Falls à Bukama, " (no page numbers).
61. Hinde, *Fall of the Congo Arabs*, 252.
62. Final Report, 190.
63. Final Report 195.
64. 1894 diary, March 30, 1894, Mohun Papers.
65. 1894 diary, March 30, 1894, Mohun Papers.
66. Final Report, 200.
67. Final Report, 207; 1894 Diary, April 10, 1894, Mohun Papers.
68. Hinde, *Fall of the Congo Arabs*, 273.
69. 1894 diary, April 11, 1894, Mohun Papers; Final Report, 209.
70. Final Report, 211.
71. Final Report, 212, 214; 1894 diary May 4, 1894, Mohun Papers.
72. Slade, *King Leopold's Congo*, 113; Comeliau, *Dhanis*, 134–5.
73. 1894 diary, May 8, 1894, Mohun Papers.
74. Dorsey to Josiah Quincy, November, 3, 1893, Boma Despatches.
75. Mohun, "Death of Emin Pasha,"594.
76. Mohun, "Death of Emin Pasha," 591.
77. Mohun, "Death of Emin Pasha," 591–98. A somewhat longer version, but with nearly the same wording, including dialogue, was also included in his final report to the State Department. See Final Report, 219–31.
78. 1894 diary, May 10, Mohun Papers.

79. Mohun, "Death of Emin Pasha," 594–95.
80. Final Report, 233.
81. Final Report, 231. Dhanis himself wrote to the *Times* (of London) announcing that he was returning to Europe and describing the capture, trial, and hanging of Emin Pasha and Hodister's alleged murderers. "Capture of Emin Pasha's Murderers," *Times* (London), July 27, 1894.
82. 1894 diary, May 10, 1894, Mohun Papers.
83. Dorsey repeatedly crossed paths with Senga during his time in Congo. I can't find him anywhere in the secondary literature, but he seems to have been an important figure. Dorsey's diary entries suggest that he was an African chief, not Arab, and that his home territory was somewhere on the Lualaba. He was supposed to go on the expedition with Dhanis and Hinde but seems not to have ended up going with them. Bosco Muchukiwa, *Territoires ethniques et territoires étatiques: Pouvoirs locaux et conflits interethniques au Sud-Kivu (R.D. Congo)* (Paris: Harmattan, 2006), 54, suggests Piana Senga was Ngongo Lutete's son.
84. Slade, *King Leopold's Congo*, 113; Comeliau, *Dhanis*, 134–35; Barbara A. Yates, "Educating Congolese Abroad: An Historical Note on African Elites," *International Journal of African Historical Studies* 14, no. 1 (1981): 39. Yates found evidence that two children, one Congo Lutete's eldest son, were placed at the Josephite's Collège de la St. Trinité, where "they remained in Belgium about six years at the expense of the Colonial Administration." She misidentifies Congo Lutete as leader of the anti-European forces and the children as "hostages." It is more likely that Dhanis felt responsible for his ally Lutete's death and perhaps also for the welfare of the children.
85. Group photo, "La Conquête du Manyema par Le Commandant Dhanis," *Congo Illustré* 3 (October 1894): 153, 157.

Chapter 6

1. "Weddings Past and to Come," *New York Tribune*, November 23, 1894, 7. Her sister is identified as Mrs. Theodore King. Dorsey sent a telegram from Paris to the State Department on October 3, 1894, asking for confirmation of a month's leave. See Mohun to Secretary of State, October 3, 1894, Boma Despatches.
2. Except for the photograph of Dorsey and Philip taken at the very beginning of his journey, those documents have disappeared.
3. Historians have given most of their attention to women who accompanied their husbands as missionaries or colonial officials' wives. See, for instance, Mary A. Procida, *Married to the Empire: Gender, Politics and Imperialism in*

India, 1883–1947 (Manchester: Manchester University Press, 2002). I've been unable to find any literature on the enclaves of women who waited for their husbands in the metropoles of Europe.

4. Joseph Conrad, *Heart of Darkness: A Case Study in Contemporary Criticism,* ed. Ross C. Murfin (New York: St. Martin's Press, 1989), 93. Literary critics have understood Kurtz's nameless fiancée as an allegorical symbol of Europeans' unwillingness to confront what was going on in their colonies. See Jeremy Hawthorn, *Joseph Conrad: Narrative Technique and Ideological Commitment* (London: Edward Arnold, 1990), 183–89; Peter Hyland, "The Little Women in the Heart of Darkness," *Conradiana* 20, no. 1 (1988): 4. For a feminist reading, see Nina Pelikan Straus, "The Exclusion of the Intended from Secret Sharing in Conrad's 'Heart of Darkness,'" *Novel: A Forum on Fiction* 20, no. 2 (1987): 123–37.

5. For the inventory of objects still in the Smithsonian's collections, see http://collections.si.edu/search/results.htm?q=Mohun+Richard+Dorsey&start=0%7D.

6. AHD to Lee Mohun, November 8 [1894], Mother Stephanie Papers, SMSA. Anna claimed that Leopold had offered Dorsey a job as an inspector at the salary of $12,000 a year.

7. Dorsey to Assistant Secretary of State, September 30, 1894, Boma Despatches. In an 1898 will, he left "all my orders and decorations, medals, guns, Turkish seal ring and watch and chain" to his infant son Reginald. R. Dorsey Mohun will, April 15, 1898, Probate Division, Office of the Register of Wills, Washington, DC.

8. "L'Arrivée du Comassie," *Indépendence Belge* (September 20, 1894); [no title], *Indépendence Belge*, September 21, 1894. Dorsey eventually "presented" the female cub to the Smithsonian's National Zoological Park. See George Brown Good, ed. *The Smithsonian Institution, 1846–1946: The History of Its First Half Century* (Washington, DC: Smithsonian Institution, 1946), 457.

9. AHD to Lee Mohun, November 8, [1894], Mother Stephanie Papers, SMSA.

10. AHD to Father Hudson, n.d., X-4-a, CHUD, UNDA.

11. AHD to Father Hudson, n.d., X-4-a, CHUD, UNDA.

12. 1896 Census. Boyd's Directory puts Anna at 2119 California St. NW in 1896; 1900 Census shows Ella owned the house and Laura, Clare, Edith, and her kids as well as a group of people with the shared surname Bennett, who were cousins, were also living there. The occupations of neighbors suggests respectability but not wealth (lots of civil servants).

13. Sister Mercia M. Rice, O. P., *A Treasured Legacy: Mother Stephanie Mohun, O.P., Her Life and Legacy* (Columbus, OH: St. Mary of the Springs, 1988), 14.

14. Allan Nevins, *Grover Cleveland: A Study in Courage* (New York: Dodd, Mead, 1933), 515, 530, 549.
15. 26 Congressional Record–House, 53rd Congress, 2nd Session, 4138–39 (April 26, 1894).
16. AHD to Lee, dated September 25, 1893 [incorrectly dated by Anna]: "he [Dorsey] does not yet know of the Cleveland Election and the removal of his best-friends in the State Department." Mother Stephanie Papers, SMSA.
17. R. D. Mohun, 'Trade in the Kongo Free State," *Reports from the Consuls of the United States* 40 (September–December 1892): 443–46.
18. Kristin L. Hoganson, *Consumers' Imperium: The Global Production of American Domesticity, 1865–1920* (Chapel Hill: University of North Carolina Press, 2007).
19. "At the Hotels," *New York Times*, November 18, 1894.
20. [No title], *New York Herald*, November 13, 1894; "Matrimony Notices," *New York Tribune*, November 23, 1894.
21. "Mohun-Barry," *New York Herald*, November 23, 1894; Robert Bruce Mullin, "St. George's Episcopal Church," in *The Encyclopedia of New York City*, ed. Kenneth T. Jackson (New Haven, CT: Yale University Press, 1995), 1034.
22. Anna Hanson Dorsey to Daniel Hudson, February 1884, Hudson Papers, AUND. Anne C. Rose, *Beloved Strangers: Interfaith Families in Nineteenth-Century America* (Cambridge, MA: Harvard University Press, 2001), 84–85. Hudson was the product of a mixed marriage. See John W. Cavanaugh, *Daniel Hudson, CSC: Priest, Editor, Pioneer* (Notre Dame, IN: Ave Maria Press, 1960), 6.
23. "Matrimony Notice," *New York Tribune*, November 23, 1894.
24. Mohun to Gresham, January 14, 1895, Applications and Recommendations for Public Office, General Records of Cleveland Administration, 1893–97, box 84, RG 59, NARA.
25. See, for instance: [no title], *The Dial* 18 (207): 93; *Current Literature* 3 (March 1895): 281; "Century for February" *Boston Journal*, February 1, 1895.
26. White House invitation, February 21, 1895, item 20a, Mohun Papers.
27. A. A. Adee to Consular Bureau, January 24, 1895, , item 10, Mohun Papers. Remarkably, all of this negative correspondence eventually ended up in Dorsey's personal papers and was preserved by his family.
28. Unknown to Adee, n.d., item 10, Mohun Papers.
29. Adee to Uhl, February 7, 1895, Mohun Papers.
30. In 1898 he willed it to his young son. See R. Dorsey Mohun, Will, April 15, 1898, District of Columbia Probate Division.
31. February 21, 1895, Applications for Public Office, box 84, RG 59, NARA.
32. Mary Jo Arnoldi, "From Diorama to the Dialogic: A Century of Exhibiting Africa at the Smithsonian's Museum of Natural History," *Cahiers d'études*

africaines 39 (1999): 703. "Mohun, Dorsey, Collection Notes," box 76, Gordon Gibson Papers, National Museum of Natural History Archives. See also catalog cards that give the date (March 1895) and mode of acquisition (purchase), http://collections.si.edu/search/results.htm?q=Mohun+Richard+Dorsey&start=0%7D.

33. *Annual Report of the Board of Regents of the Smithsonian Institution for 1895, Including the Report of the United States National Museum* (Washington, DC, 1896), 30.

34. https://www.si.edu/museums/arts-and-industries-building.

35. *Annual Report,* 8.

36. *Annual Report* , 7.

37. Otis T. Mason, annual report (typescript) (1895), 2, "Curator's Reports," box 3, Smithsonian Institution Archives.

38. "Inventory of Objects," R. Dorsey Mohun Collection, accession 29024, National Museum of Natural History, Museum Support Facility, Suitland, Maryland.

39. "Inventory of Objects."

40. Object number E175019–0, R. Dorsey Mohun Collection, National Museum of Natural History, Museum Support Facility, Suitland, Maryland.

41. Otis T. Mason to G. Browne Good (February 1895), box 3, "Curator's Reports," Record Unit 158, Smithsonian Institution Archives.

42. Nathan Cardon, *A Dream of the Future: Constructing a New South Empire* (Oxford: Oxford University Press, 2018), 102.

43. Clare Mohun to Henry T. Thurber, April 24, 1895, Grover Cleveland Papers, ser. 2.

Chapter 7

1. Norman R. Bennett, *A History of the Arab State of Zanzibar* (London: Methuen, 1978), 1. For examples of traveler's descriptions, see Dr. W. S. W. Ruschenberger's 1833 account quoted in Cyrus Townsend Brady Jr., *Commerce and Conquest in East Africa: With Particular Reference to the Salem Trade with Zanzibar* (Salem, MA: Essex Institute, 1950), 93, and Major F. B. Pearce, *Zanzibar: The Island Metropolis of Eastern Africa* (New York: E. P. Dutton, 1920), 143–44.

2. *Consular Regulations* (1896), 189.

3. "Consul at Zanzibar Now in London," *New York Times,* June 18, 1895. Dorsey's successor claimed Dorsey had "purchased furniture in London" and had it shipped to Zanzibar at US government expense but could find only one desk remaining. Billheimer to Department of State, May 12, 1898, Zanzibar Despatches.

4. For a detailed analysis from the European perspective, see Kenneth Ingham, *A History of East Africa*, 2nd ed. (London: Longman, Green, 1963).

5. "Local News," *Gazette for Zanzibar and East Africa*, July 24, 1895.

6. Wissmann was one of many notable explorers and soldiers who received administrative appointments as rewards for their service. Dane Kennedy, *The Last Blank Spaces: Exploring Africa and Australia* (Cambridge, MA: Harvard University Press, 2013), 83.

7. On Wissmann, see Norman Robert Bennett, *Arab versus European: Diplomacy and War in Nineteenth-Century East Central Africa* (New York: African Publishing Company, 1986), 12.

8. Michelle R. Moyd, *Violent Intermediaries: African Soldiers, Conquest, and Everyday Colonialism in German East Africa* (Athens: Ohio University Press, 2014), 6. Wissmann had also been peripherally involved with Emin Pasha. Moyd, *Violent Intermediaries*, 83. The word *askiri* means "warrior" in Swahili.

9. Bennett, *Arab versus European*, 165–74, 177; Bennett, *History of the Arab State of Zanzibar*, 162–63.

10. "Local News," *Zanzibar Gazette*, July 24, 1895.

11. Robert Nunez Lyne, *An Apostle of Empire: Being the Life of Sir Lloyd William Mathews, K.C.M.G., Lieutenant, Royal Navy; First Minister of the Zanzibar Government* (London: G. Allen & Unwin, 1936), 177. Arthur Hardinge, the British consul general during Dorsey's time in Zanzibar had been installed as the British governor with the "primary aim of the gradual elimination of slavery." Bennett, *History of the Arab State of Zanzibar*, 176.

12. Abdul Sheriff describes this arrangement as a "hybrid state." See Abdul Sheriff and Ed Ferguson, *Zanzibar under Colonial Rule* (London: J. Currey, 1991), 16. Bissell writes "The cultural impetus to cultivate allies and clients started at the top of the social order and ran through political and social affairs. . . . The Sultan's power was anything but unlimited. . . . He had to consult, convince, or co-opt others." William Cunningham Bissell, *Urban Design. Chaos, and Colonial Power in Zanzibar* (Bloomington: Indiana University Press, 2011), 39.

13. Norman R. Bennett and George E. Brooks, *New England Merchants in Africa: A History through Documents, 1802 to 1865* (Brookline, MA: Boston University Press, 1965); Frank J. Klingberg and Cyrus T. Brady, "Commerce and Conquest in East Africa: With Particular Reference to the Salem Trade with Zanzibar," *Journal of Southern History*17 (Winter 1951): 556.

14. Fahad Ahmad Bishara, *A Sea of Debt: Law and Economic Life in the Western Indian Ocean, 1780–1950* (Cambridge: Cambridge University Press, 2017), 105–6; John C. Wilkinson, *The Arabs and the Scramble for Africa* (Sheffield: Equinox, 2015).

15. *Zanzibar Gazette* "Local News," July 24, 1895.

16. Dorsey to Uhl, October 7, 1895, vol. 9, Zanzibar Despatches.

17. Bissell, *Urban Design*, 22.

18. Bishara, *A Sea of Debt*, 45.

19. Kennedy, *The Last Blank Spaces*, 120, 123.

20. Image of Sailor's Rest, "Zanzibar 17," 1890's–1900's, CO 1069/183, Photography: The World through the Lens, British Colonial Office: Photographic Collection, , National Archives, Kew, United Kingdom, Gale Primary Sources, Nineteenth Century Collections Online, http://tinyurl.galegroup .com/tinyurl/5vXN83.

21. R. Dorsey Mohun, "Bombardment of Zanzibar," *Cosmopolitan* 25 (June 1898): 157.

22. F. B. Pearce, *Zanzibar: The Island Metropolis of Eastern Africa* (New York: E. P. Dutton, 1920), 208. For photographs, see the Smithsonian online exhibit *Sailors and Daughters: Early Photography and the Indian Ocean*, http://indian -ocean.africa.si.edu/zanzibar-cosmorama/#slide-10.

23. See, for instance, Frederick Russell Burnham and Mary Nixon Everett. *Scouting on Two Continents* (Garden City, NY: Doubleday, Page, 1926), 94. Burnham had dinner with both Dorsey and Tippu Tip (though not together) during his 1896 visit to Zanzibar. In Zanzibar, Tip was also known by his legal, given name: Hamed bin Mohammed Al Marjebi. Bishara, *A Sea of Debt*, 37.

24. "Local News," *Zanzibar Gazette*, July 24, 1896.

25. Pearce, *Zanzibar*, 208.

26. Mrinalini Sinha, "Britishness, Clubbability, and the Colonial Public Sphere: The Genealogy of an Imperial Institution in Colonial India," *Journal of British Studies* 40, no. 4 (October 2001): 489–90.

27. Final Report, 60; 1892–93 diary, January 21, 1893. See chapter 5 for the original account.

28. John M. Mackenzie, *The Empire of Nature: Hunting, Conservation, and British Imperialism* (Manchester: Manchester University Press, 1988), ix, 34–35.

29. "Sport on the Kongo: Dumbele and the Rogue Elephant," *Zanzibar Gazette*, August 28, 1895.

30. Dorsey's immediate successor made an inventory of the consulate's contents. See Seth A. Prad to Department of State, "Taking over the Consulate," January 15, 1898, Zanzibar Despatches.

31. *Consular Regulations* (1896). The library also contained the 1888 version that Dorsey must have brought with him. He would also have been familiar with the US Department of State, *The United States Consul's Manual: A Practical Guide for Consular Officers*, 2nd ed. (Washington, DC: Hudson and Taylor,

1863). The volume had clearly been compiled (and added to) to professionalize the consular service and to create a written set of criteria against which consular employees could be held accountable.

32. Charles Kennedy, *The American Consul: A History of the United States Consular Service, 1776–1914* (New York: Greenwood Press, 1990), 209.

33. US Department of State, *Consul's Manual*, 131.

34. Mohun to Uhl, July 23, 1895, Zanzibar Despatches.

35. Mohun to Uhl, August 12, 1895, Zanzibar Despatches.

36. Billheimer to Uhl, June 6, 1898, Zanzibar Despatches.

37. US Department of State, *Consul's Manual*, 133.

38. *Consular Regulations* (1896), 43.

39. Kennedy, *The American Consul*, 147.

40. Cleveland Twist Drill letter, August 22, 1896; *Street Railway Journal*, November 13, 1896; Savage Repeating Arms Company, November 10, 1896; Miscellaneous Letters Received for the year 1896, Consular Posts, Zanzibar, Records of Foreign Service Posts, vol. 045, RG 84, NARA.

41. *Consular Regulations* (1896), 22.

42. Billheimer to Uhl, June 6, 1898, vol. 10, Zanzibar Despatches. Billheimer was Dorsey's successor as Consul. He summoned Omari because he suspected the translator might have been a fiction on Dorsey's part and that his predecessor had pocketed the $200 a year the translator was paid. Omari presented himself and showed Billheimer receipts.

43. A *barazza*, also spelled *baraza*, was also the name of the porches or outdoor meeting places in Omani Arab-style houses.

44. "Local News," *Zanzibar Gazette*, August 4, 1897.

45. "Mr. S.L. Hinde: Explorer and Colonial Official," *Times* (London), October 21, 193. Hinde later became commissioner of the East Africa protectorate.

46. "Cannibals and Their Customs," *Zanzibar Gazette*, December 11, 1895. The editor also included a review of the lecture in the *African Review*, which quoted missionaries who claimed that Christianizing Africans was the cure for cannibalism.

47. Bissell, *Urban Design*, 39.

48. "Local News," *Zanzibar Gazette*, December 25, 1895.

49. Robert N. Lyne, *Zanzibar in Contemporary Times: A Short History of the Southern East in the Nineteenth Century* (New York: Negro Universities Press, 1969), 206.

50. Bennett, *History of the Arab State of Zanzibar*, 177. In today's money, this sum would equal at least $25 million. See https://www.measuringworth.com/calculators/ukcompare/relativevalue.php.

51. Lyne, *An Apostle of Empire*, 178.

52. Lyne, *Zanzibar in Contemporary Times*, 177–78; "Christmas at Chwaka and Dunga," *Zanzibar Gazette*, December 25, 1895.
53. "Christmas at Chwaka and Dunga," *Zanzibar Gazette*, December 25, 1895.
54. "Notice," *Zanzibar Gazette*, January 1, 1896.
55. "Local News," *Zanzibar Gazette*, January 29, 1896.
56. "Local News," Zanzibar Gazette, February 5, 1896.
57. "Local News," *Zanzibar Gazette*, February 12, 1896.
58. Mohun to Underhill, April 9, 1896, Zanzibar Despatches. In the Despatches, Dorsey called the event the Ubaruki Rebellion after what he must have heard in club gossip as the leader's name: Ubarak. The memoirs of the British consul, Hardinge, name the leader as Mubarak of Gazi (Sheikh Mubarak bin Rashid) and the rebels as Mazrui tribesmen. Arthur Henry Hardinge, *A Diplomatist in the East* (London: J. Cape, 1928), 181–83.
59. Hardinge, *Diplomatist in the East*, 182–83.
60. "Local News," *Zanzibar Gazette*, April 22, 1896.
61. Illustrated fable by Roger Casement for his godson Reginald D. Mohun, September 24, 1896, MS 41,654, National Library of Ireland. Casement inscribed the book "To Reginald Dorsey Mohun from an admiring Godfather R.C. September 24th 1896." The author's father remembers the book being shared among his siblings when they were children. My cousin, Abby, sold the book to the library in 2006. Casement also turns up in a notice in the *Zanzibar Gazette* when he left Mozambique for West Africa. See "Local News," *Zanzibar Gazette*, October 26, 1898.
62. Photos, Mother Stephanie Mohun Papers, SMSA.
63. Cheryl Lynn Krasnick Warsh and Veronica Jane Strong-Boag, *Children's Health Issues in Historical Perspective* (Waterloo, ON: Wilfrid Laurier University Press, 2005).
64. Mohun to Rockhill, July 16, 1896; E. D. Vialle and Janmahmed Hunsraj to Messrs. Arnold Cheney and Co. Zanzibar, July 23, 1896 (copy), Zanzibar Despatches.
65. Lloyd's agent on behalf of National Board of Marine Underwriters, name illegible to Mohun, March 1, 1897, Miscellaneous Letters, Zanzibar Consular Records; Mohun to Rockhill, August 11, 1896, Zanzibar Despatches.
66. Mohun to Underhill, June 21, 1896, Zanzibar Despatches. In his memoirs, Arthur Hardinge, who authorized the arrest and deportation, described the execution of Hilal's departure as being more respectful than Dorsey's account would suggest. Hardinge, *Diplomatist in the East*, 189–90.
67. Ingham, *A History of East Africa*, 174.
68. R. Dorsey Mohun, "The Bombardment of Zanzibar," *Cosmopolitan* 25 (June 1998): 158.

69. Hardinge, *Diplomatist in the East*, 190, 191.

70. Khalid bin Barghash to Mohun, August 26, 1896, Zanzibar Consular Records.

71. Basil Cave to Mohun, August 26, 1896, Zanzibar Consular Records.

72. Mohun, "The Bombardment of Zanzibar," 160.

73. Mohun, 160–61.

74. Mohun, 160–61.

75. Mohun, 162.

76. Hardinge, *Diplomatist in the East*, 191.

77. Hardinge, 191.

78. Hardinge, *Diplomatist in the East*, 192. For a vivid account (from a European perspective) of the young man's return to Zanzibar, see Estella Cave, Viscountess, *Three Journeys* (London: T. Butterworth, 1928).

79. "Local News," *Zanzibar Gazette*, September 30, 1896.

80. Photo in the author's collection.

81. Bennett, *History of the Arab State of Zanzibar*, 180–81.

82. "Local News," *Zanzibar Gazette*, November 10, 1897.

83. Dorsey had his doctor send a note explaining the situation. He also sent a scrawled message saying that he had a fever of 103 degrees. Daniel M. Stimson, MD, to State Department, January 15, 1898, Zanzibar Despatches.

84. Laura Mohun to Lee Mohun (Mother Stephanie), October 26, 1896, Mother Stephanie Papers, SMSA.

Chapter 8

1. Wills and Probate Records for R. Dorsey Mohun, Washington, DC, Wills and Probate Records, box 0527 (accessed through Ancestry.com).

2. Matthew G. Stanard, *Selling the Congo: A History of Pro-empire Propaganda and the Making of Belgian Imperialism* (Lincoln: University of Nebraska Press, 2011), 37–38. "The Human Zoo of Tervuren," Royal Museum for Central Africa, Tervuren Belgium. https://www.africamuseum.be/en/discover/history_articles/the_human_zoo_of_tervuren_1897#:~:text=AfricaMuseum%20traces%20its%20origins%20to,the%20colonial%20project%20in%20Congo.

3. Stanard, *Selling the Congo*, 38. The museum exhibits have been completely redone, however. See Royal Museum for Central Africa, Tervuren Belgium, http://www.africamuseum.be/en/home.

4. They had died of influenza the previous summer. David Van Reybrouck, *Congo: The Epic History of a People* (New York: HarperCollins, 2010), 65.

5. This chapter and the next have been influenced by James Scott's observation that modernity is characterized by a disconnect between the abstract

ways states view their subjects (and nature) and the way the same people understand their worlds and how to live in them. The Congo Free State could be understood as a protoversion of what Scott calls "high modernism." See James C. Scott, *Seeing Like a State: How Certain Schemes to Improve the Human Condition Have Failed* (New Haven, CT: Yale University Press, 1998).

6. For a concise description of the structure of the State's administration, see Ruth Slade, *King Leopold's Congo: Aspects of the Development of Race Relations in the Congo Independent State* (London: Oxford University Press, 1962), 171–72. For Dorsey's description of Van Eetvelde, see his telegraph narrative

7. "Eetvelde (Van)(Edomond)," *Biographie coloniale belge; Belgische koloniale biographie* (Brussels: Librairie Falk fils, 1951), 2:329, 343–44.

8. For the initial negotiations between Mohun and Eetvelde, see Van Eetvelde to Mohun, February 23, 1898, item 18, Mohun Papers. The situation in the Sudan reached a state of crisis in a standoff between the British and French in Fashoda at the head of the Nile, July of 1898. For more on Leopold's involvement with the Sudan, see Martin Weans, *European Atrocity, African Catastrophe: Leopold II, the Congo Free State, and Its Aftermath* (London: Routledge Curzon, 2002), 148–50.

9. Telegraph narrative, 1–2.

10. R. Cherer Smith, "The Africa Trans-Continental Telegraph Line," *Rhodesiana* 33 (September 1975): 16. Robert I. Rotberg, *The Founder: Cecil Rhodes and the Pursuit of Power* (New York: Oxford University Press, 1988), 509–11, 592.

11. Telegraph narrative, 2.

12. Simone M. Müller, *Wiring the World: The Social and Cultural Creation of Global Telegraph Networks* (New York: Columbia University Press, 2015), 234.

13. Dorsey's narrative and Verhellen's diary do not agree about the third lineman's name, which was either Tisdell or Teakill. He had worked for the Indian Telegraph Service. The fourth member was named Long. The telegraph narrative says that he was hired in Chinde to help Dhanis. For a list of the members, see telegraph narrative, 3. "Journal de route de la mission du Commissaire de district Richard Mohun," file 02, H.01.004, Archives de Nicolas Verhellen, RMCA.

14. Castellote's first name does not appear in any of the surviving records. Telegraph narrative, 3; "Journal de route," Archives de Verhellen.

15. Telegraph narrative, 3. The first page of Verhellen's brief, handwritten diary provides the most accurate list of participants. "Journal de route," Archives de Verhellen; "Verhellen (Nicolas)," *Biographie coloniale belge*, 2:949;

"Dhanis (Antoine)," *Biographie coloniale belge; Belgische koloniale biographie* (Brussels: Librairie Falk fils, 1958), 5:255.

16. Collections record for R. Dorsey Mohun medicine chest, https://www .si.edu/es/object/nmah_1003982?width=85%25&height=85%25&iframe =true&back_link=1&destination=spotlight/health-medicine.

17. Telegraph narrative, 3–4.

18. Francis A. De Caro and Rosan A. Jordan. "The Wrong Topi: Personal Narratives, Ritual, and the Sun Helmet as a Symbol," *Western Folklore* 43, no. 4 (1984): 233–48.

19. Ryan Johnson, "European Cloth and 'Tropical' Skin: Clothing Material and British Ideas of Health and Hygiene in Tropical Climates," *Bulletin of the History of Medicine* 83 (2009): 554, 557.

20. Le Secrétaire Général, Département de l'Intérieur to Mohun, August 17, 1898, item 10, Mohun Papers.

21. Some sources also spell M'Toa as Mtoa or Toa. It has largely disappeared. The nearest extent town is Kalemie. M'Toa is also where Stanley first entered the Congo in 1877 at the beginning of the trip that would make him the first white man to cross the continent and travel the length of the Congo River. For a recent description, see Tim Butcher, *Blood River: The Terrifying Journey through the World's Most Dangerous Country* (New York: Grove Press, 2008), 109.

22. See, for example, "The Hiring of Slaves by British Officials," *Anti-Slavery Reporter* (January/February 1892):12–14: "Slave Porters in British East Africa," *Anti-Slavery Reporter* (January/February 1896): 47–48.

23. These numbers are from the narrative he later drafted. Telegraph narrative, 4. Before leaving Brussels, he calculated the amount as 2,093 loads. See handwritten notes on the last page of "Liste des Instruments et Matériaux," item 18, Mohun Papers.

24. The British had been tightening down on labor recruitment in their East African protectorates by private expeditions and other European government entities. Although these restrictions carried the gloss of humanitarianism and paternalism, part of the motive was pragmatic. As Dorsey's acquaintance Arthur Hardinge, governor of British East Africa, reported to Parliament, British government activities in the region required a vast army of local workers, particularly porters. Private expeditions drained the available labor force, literally removing them from entrepôts such as Zanzibar City, where her Majesty's servants could easily gather them up. See Arthur Hardinge, "Report for the Year 1897 on the Trade and General Conditions of the British Central Africa Protectorate," command paper 8683 (London: Her Majesty's Stationery Office, 1899), 54–56.

25. In 1898 the ALC's legal name was the African Lakes Trading Company for reasons explained below. However, no one, including Dorsey, called it that.

26. J. B. Wolf, "Commerce, Christianity, and the Creation of the Stevenson Road," *African Historical Studies* 4 (1971): 363–71.

27. John McCracken, *A History of Malawi, 1859–1966* (Woodbridge: Boydell & Brewer, 2012), 48.

28. Telegraph narrative, 5.

29. Verhellen's diary doesn't include Dhanis on the list of people who sailed on the *General*, but Dhanis's entry in the *Biographie coloniale belge* explicitly places him on the ship.

30. Letterbook copies of telegrams from Castellote and Mohun, dated September 6, 1898, item 7, Mohun Papers; "Central African Protectorate," *Zanzibar Gazette* (October 26, 1898). The *Zanzibar Gazette* stated "Some of the officers of Mr. R.D. Mohun's Central African expedition are now in Bombay awaiting orders to cross to Zanzibar or Mombasa.

31. Telegraph narrative, 5.

32. Norman R. Bennett, *A History of the Arab State of Zanzibar* (London: Methuen, 1978), 168.

33. "Local News," *Zanzibar Gazette*, September 7, 1898.

34. "Regulations to be observed by caravan leaders and others in the engagement and treatment of Porters," File 66, Mohun papers.

35. Telegraph narrative, 6.

36. Copybook letters of reference from Mohun, May 5, 1901 (Ngomma letter, item 133; the rest of the letters, items 147–50, 158–62), File 3, Mohun Papers; Telegraph narrative 5.

37. Telegraph narrative 6.

38. The editor of the *Zanzibar Gazette* noted Dorsey's presence at the club. In the same item, he also noted that Roger Casement had left his position as British consul at Delagoa Bay in Portuguese East Africa to take up a new role as consul to Gabon and the Congo Free State. This move led to Casement's eventual central role as a critic of the Congo Free State. "Local News," *Zanzibar Gazette*, October 26, 1898.

39. Edward Paice, *Last Lion of Empire: The Life of "Cape-to-Cairo" Grogan* (London: Harper Collins, 2001), 33–37.

40. Paice, *Last Lion of Empire*, 49.

41. The lady was Gertrude Watt. Paice, *Last Lion of Empire*, 49–50.

42. Leda Farrant, *The Legendary Grogan: The Only Man to Trek from Cape to Cairo, Kenya's Controversial Pioneer* (London: H. Hamilton, 1981), 22.

43. Telegraph narrative, 7.

44. Telegraph narrative, 7.

45. M. Newit, *A History of Mozambique* (London: Hurst, 1995), 11; McCracken, *History of Malawi*, 51, 55–56.

46. The ubiquitous Cecil Rhodes had paid £10,000 a year for the "opening up and pacifying Nyasa country" as part of his deal with the British government to charter the British South Africa Company. R. C. F. Maugham, *Africa as I Have Known It: Nyasaland—East Africa—Liberia—Senegal* (London: John Murray, 1929), 11.

47. Takashi Oishi, "Indian Muslim Merchants in Mozambique and South Africa: Intra-Regional Networks in Strategic Association with State Institutions, 1870s–1930s," *Journal of the Economic and Social History of the Orient* 50, no. 2/3 (2007): 287–324.

48. Maugham, *Africa as I Have Known It*, 25.

49. McCracken, *History of Malawi*, 75. The rainy season brought other problems as torrential rains caused flooding and washed-out portage roads.

50. Telegraph narrative, 9.

51. Telegraph narrative, 9; Ewart S. Grogan and Arthur H. Sharp, *From Cape to Cairo* (Fairford, Gloucestershire: Echo Library, 2014), 24.

52. Chinde camp photographs, item 23, Mohun Papers.

53. Mohun to African Lakes Corporation, Ltd., Chinde, November 10, 1898, item 7, Mohun Papers. As far as I can tell, no Indian soldiers ever joined the expedition. It may be that the British did not want private expeditions passing through with their own Indian mercenaries.

54. Telegraph narrative, 9–10.

55. The description of the landscape is from Maugham, *Africa as I Have Known It*, 35–36.

56. Daniel R. Headrick, *The Tools of Empire Technology and European Imperialism in the Nineteenth Century* (New York: Oxford University Press, 1981), 74; Carina E. Ray and Jeremy Rich, eds., *Navigating African Maritime History* (Liverpool: Liverpool University Press, 2009), 122.

57. Telegraph narrative, 10.

58. Telegraph narrative, 10.

59. The town was also called Katunga. It no longer exists. See Mike Bamford, "The Search for Katunga: 'Blantyre's Port,'" *Society of Malawi Journal* 62 (2009): 37–51.

60. Telegraph narrative, 13.

61. In 1898 representatives of the British government estimated that the mortality rate in the lake area was 9 percent for Europeans overall and 20 percent for government officials. "Annual Report on the British Central African Protectorate, 1897–8," *Parliamentary Papers*, command paper 9048, 29.

62. Telegraph narrative, 14–15.

63. In 1907 it was renamed Nyasaland.

64. Andrew Ross, *David Livingstone: Mission and Empire* (London: Hambledon Continuum, 2002), 168. Many missionary groups, including both Catholic and Protestant missions in the Congo Free State, operated what were commonly called "industrial schools," which bear a strong resemblance to both settlement houses in the anglophone world and polytechnic schools such as the Tuskegee Institute. The ideologies of uplift and self-sufficiency ("industrial redemption") are also similar. See, for example, Paul Allen Williams, "The Disciples of Christ Congo Mission (DCCM), 1897–1932: A Missionary Community in Colonial Central Africa" (PhD diss., University of Chicago School of Divinity, 2000), 336–38; and William Scott, "Central African Experiences," *Society of Malawi Journal* 38 (1985): 62, on Presbyterian "industrial missions." See also "Annual Report on the British Central African Protectorate, 1897–8," *Parliamentary Papers*, command paper 9048, 9, which notes that most of the offices of the African Transcontinental Telegraph had a "native assistant" trained in telegraphy.

65. McCracken, *History of Malawi*, 38–39, 44, 53; Piers Brendon, *The Decline and Fall of the British Empire: 1781–1997* (London: Jonathan Cape, 2007), 199; John S. Galbraith, *Crown and Charter: The Early Years of the British South Africa Company* (Berkeley: University of California Press, 1974), 205.

66. McCracken, *History of Malawi*, 53–54.

67. McCracken, *History of Malawi*, 62. Piers Brendon described Johnston as a "freelance agent of imperial expansion" with "a whiff of charlatanism." See Brendon, *Decline and Fall*, 200.

68. On the Rifles, see McCracken, *History of Malawi*, 66.

69. *Parliamentary Papers*, command paper 2327, 34, 37; For an uncritical view of the system, see Colin Baker, "Tax Collection in Malawi: An Administrative History," *International Journal of African Historical Studies* 8 (1975): 40–62. For Dorsey's understanding of the system, see telegraph narrative, 37–38.

70. Telegraph narrative, 15.

71. "Annual Report on the British Central African Protectorate, 1897–8," *Parliamentary Papers*, command paper 9048.

72. McCracken, *History of Malawi*, 79.

73. Telegraph narrative, 16.

74. McCracken, *History of Malawi*, 46.

75. Telegraph narrative, 17.

76. For a detailed explanation of the negotiations around Rhodes's involvement with the company, see Galbraith, *Crown and Charter*, 225–27, 231. See also Hugh W. Macmillan, the Origins and Development of the African Lakes Company, 1978–1908" (PhD thesis, Edinburgh University, 1970).

77. Telegraph narrative, 16.

78. Telegraph narrative, 16.

79. Both Dorsey and Grogan repeated this story in their accounts. Grogan got it second hand from Sharp, who was still tagging along with the expedition.

80. Telegraph narrative, 26.

81. Telegraph narrative, 25–26.

82. Telegraph narrative, 24.

83. Telegraph narrative, 31. Dorsey took exception to Grogan's later description of the two telegraph camps, which made a blatantly nationalistic comparison of strutting Belgians and quiet Englishmen "rotten with fever" getting the job done. Dorsey pointed out that there were in fact no English nationals in Fox's team at Karonga and only two Belgians in Dorsey's expedition. Grogan and Sharp, *Cape to Cairo*, 45–46; Telegraph narrative, 31.

84. Telegraph narrative, 29.

85. Grogan and Sharp, *Cape to Cairo*, 41.

86. Telegraph narrative, 29; Grogan and Sharp, *Cape to Cairo*, 42.

87. Telegraph narrative, 33.

88. There is no mention of the Karonga men in Mohun's telegraph narrative or Grogan's account, but they are listed in Dorsey's copybook for 1900 when he sent them back with a request that the ALC agent pay them and seek reimbursement from the Congo Free State. See list of Karonga employees with amounts due, item 7; Mohun to "Sir" (ALC agent at Karonga), May 15, 1900, item 7, Mohun Papers.

89. Telegraph narrative, 34, 37.

90. Telegraph narrative, 35.

91. Telegraph narrative, 36.

92. Telegraph narrative, 36–37.

93. Edward C. Hore, *Tanganyika: Eleven Years in Central Africa* (London: Stanford, 1892), 272, and Alfred J. Swann, *Fighting the Slave-Hunters in Central Africa: A Record of Twenty-Six Years of Travel & Adventure Round the Great Lakes and of the Overthrow of Tip-Pu-Tib, Rumaliza, and Other Great Slave-Traders* (Philadelphia: J. B. Lippincott, 1910), 90–91 on portaging in the parts and building, 190 for image of the newly launched boat. Image also available at "Building the SS Good News," Pat in the World (blog), October 29, 2017, https://patintheworld.com/2017/10/29/building-of-the-ss-good-news/.

94. Telegraph narrative, 39.

95. Grogan and Sharp, *Cape to Cairo*, 55.

96. Telegraph narrative, 39.

97. Telegraph narrative, 40; Grogan and Sharp, *Cape to Cairo*, 55.

Chapter 9

1. Ewart S. Grogan and Arthur H. Sharp, *From Cape to Cairo* (Fairford, Gloucestershire: Echo Library, 2014), 86.

2. Telegraph narrative, 70.

3. Grogan claimed that the Scandinavians asked for poison so that they could kill themselves if they fell into the hands of the Batetela mutineers. Grogan and Sharp, *From Cape to Cairo*, 86.

4. Estimates of how many soldiers were involved in the actual revolt vary wildly even in the accounts of participants such as Dhanis. Dhanis's biographer, Marie-Louise Comeliau, put the number at six thousand, with two thousand armed with Albini rifles. See Marie-Louise Comeliau, *Dhanis* (Brussels: Collection Études Colonials, 1943), 159. A later study described it as "the largest expedition assembled in Africa during the course of the 19th century." See Pierre Salmon, *La révolte des Batetela de l'Expédition du Haut-Ituri, 1897: Témoignages inédits* (Brussels: Académie Royale des Sciences d'Outre-mer, 1977), 7.

5. Martin Ewans, *European Atrocity, African Catastrophe: Leopold II, the Congo Free State and Its Aftermath.* (London: Routledge Curzon, 2002), 149. See also Robert O. Collins, *King Leopold, England, and the Upper Nile, 1899–1909* (New Haven, CT: Yale University Press, 1968); and George Neville Sanderson, *England, Europe & the Upper Nile, 1882–1899; A Study in the Partition of Africa* (Edinburgh: University Press, 1965).

6. Dhanis likely took the more circuitous route because, while the Congo Free State had some claim to the Lado Enclave, Dhanis was headed to Khartoum, which Leopold had explicitly promised not to pursue. See Ewans, *European Atrocity*, 149.

7. Comeliau, *Dhanis*, 215–16. According to Comeliau, Verhellen provided particularly explicit testimony about the harsh conditions (218).

8. Salmon, *La révolte des Batetela*, 60.

9. "Verhellen (Nicholas)," *Biographie coloniale belge; Belgische koloniale biographie* (Brussels: Librairie Falk fils, 1951), 2:950.

10. Ewans, *European Atrocity*, 150.

11. Salmon, *La révolte des Batetela*, 59–60. Since most of the officers had been killed by their troops, they were unable to defend themselves. However, Henri Bodart later wrote a scathing account that includes descriptions of Dhanis's paralysis and mood swings in the aftermath—a pattern Mohun also described in his diary account of the Arab War. For Bodart's account, see Salmon, 16.

12. "Dhanis (Francis)," *Biographie coloniale belge; Belgische koloniale biografie* (Brussels: Librairie Falk fils, 1948), 1:322.

13. Telegraph narrative, 70.

14. "Journal de route de la mission du Commissaire de district Richard Mohun, de 20 août 1898 à 26 décembre 1898, responsable pour le placement de la ligne télégraphique de N'Towa-Nyangwe à Stanley-Falls. 1898–1899," H.07.004, Archives Nicolas Verhellen, HA.01.0004, RMCA.

15. Telegraph narrative, 72.

16. Mohun to Secrétaire Générale, June 14,1899, item 7, Mohun Papers.

17. Telegraph narrative, 71.

18. Telegraph narrative, 72.

19. Telegraph narrative, 73–74.

20. Telegraph narrative, 74.

21. Grogan and Sharp, *Cape to Cairo*, 56.

22. Telegraph narrative, 80. The entry for Francis Dhanis in the *Biographie Coloniale* (1:318) treats this battle as a turning point in the State's efforts to control the rebels. This is contradicted by the fact that Dhanis's successor, Justin Malfeyt, is also credited with getting the problem under control two years after Dhanis's departure from the Congo. See "Malfeyt (Justin)," *Biographie coloniale belge; Belgische koloniale biografie* (Bruxelles: Librairie Falk fils, 1952), 3:590.

23. Telegraph narrative, 80–81.

24. Telegraph narrative, 83.

25. On Mohun's request for a replacement for Verhellen, see Mohun to Dhanis, August 28, 1899, File 287, Archives de Dhanis, RMCA. Verhellen was never officially replaced with another European. One of the Kasonga men, Munie Ngomma, may have been put in overall charge. See Ngomma discharge letter, May 5, 1901, item 3, Mohun papers.

26. In the telegraph narrative, Dorsey gives the impression he traveled alone, but he wrote Dhanis about issues involving the Zanzibaris at Kabambarre. Mohun to Dhanis, December 10, 1899, File 287, Archives de Dhanis, RMCA.

27. Telegraph narrative, 109. He also sometimes traveled in what he called a "hammock," although he never mentions it in the telegraph narrative, probably because he didn't want to portray himself as a participant in decadent and unmanly imperial activities. Mohun to [illegible], item 8, Mohun Papers.

28. Telegraph narrative, 84.

29. In 1902 Casement quoted from the letter without Dorsey's knowledge as part of his efforts to build a case against Leopold and the State. Roger Casement to the Marquess of Lansdowne, June 18, 1902, "The Congo Free State, 1863–1906," document 161, volume 23, in *British Documents on Foreign Affairs: Reports and Papers from the Foreign Office Confidential Print* (Bethesda, MD: University Publications of America, 1997), 212.

30. Mohun to Dhanis, December 10, 1899, File 287, Archives de Dhanis, RMCA.
31. Telegraph narrative, 86.
32. Dorsey's observations, experience, and confusion bear a startling semblance to the observations of the journalist Tim Butcher, who traveled the same route in 2004 and tried to make sense of the ruined Belgian towns and infrastructure and the predations of the Mai rebellion, which had a similar impact on local people to the Batetela rebellion. See Tim Butcher, *Blood River: The Terrifying Journey through the World's Most Dangerous Country* (New York: Grove Press, 2008). Anthropologist and historian Jan Vansina offers a particularly astute analysis of the way generations of displacement have created instability in the Congo. See Jan Vansina, *Being Colonized: The Kuba Experience in the Rural Congo, 1880–1960* (Madison: University of Wisconsin Press, 2010), 28.
33. Vansina, *Being Colonized*, 138, 140–41, 145.
34. Many of the vials of medicine remain full today. Those containing opiates were removed in the 1970s by US Federal Drug Enforcement agents. Personal communication with Diane Wendt, Division Head, History of Medicine, National Museum of American History.
35. Telegraph narrative, 84.
36. Mohun to "Excellency," November 4, 1899, item 7, Mohun Papers. Dorsey wrote the letter to control the damage. "Excellency" is probably the governor of the Congo Free State.
37. Telegraph narrative, 87.
38. Telegraph narrative, 87.
39. Telegraph narrative, 89.
40. Telegraph narrative, 89.
41. Telegraph narrative, 89–90.
42. Mohun to "Excellency," November 4, 1899, item 7, Mohun Papers.
43. Dhanis did eventually arrange with Bwana Mussa to provide workers for the line. Thornton to Chef de Poste, June 13, 1900; Thornton to Dhanis, May 20, 1900; Thornton to Dhanis, July 18, 1900, item 5, Mohun Papers.
44. Telegraph narrative, 98–100, 109–12.
45. Telegraph narrative, 112–13.
46. Telegraph narrative, 113.
47. Telegraph narrative, 113.
48. Mohun to Dhanis, December 29, 1899, File 287, Archives de Dhanis, RMCA.
49. Conrad's novella, *The Heart of Darkness*, had been serialized in *Blackwood's Edinburgh Magazine*, February, March, and April, 1899. See Philip V. Allingham, "The Initial Publication Context of Joseph Conrad's *Heart of Darkness* in *Blackwood's Edinburgh Magazine* ('Maga'): February, March, and April,

1899," *Victorian Web: Literature, History, and Culture in the Age of Victoria*, http://www.victorianweb.org/authors/conrad/pva46.html.

50. Louis Dhanis's official biography is silent about where he went, although it suggests that he remained in the Congo until 1902. See "Dhanis (Antoine)", *Biographie coloniale belge*, 5:256. Mohun's addendum to his final report to Governor General Wahis puts the departure date as July 1899. See Mohun to governor general, October 7, 1901, item 5, Mohun Papers. A man named Long, whom Dorsey had hired in Chinde to help Dhanis, also headed back toward the lakes. He is a somewhat mysterious figure about whom Mohun wrote very little. He appears in expedition photographs as a tall, dour-faced young man in a large hat.

51. Mohun to Dhanis, December 29, 1899, File 287, Archives de Dhanis, RMCA. In another letter he described feeling "sick and tired of being made a fool of." Mohun to Dhanis, May 5, 1900, file 287, Archives de Dhanis, RMCA. Francis Dhanis handed over his commission to Justin Malfeyt on July 4, 1900. Dorsey and Dhanis both knew Malfeyt from the Arab War. Comeliau, *Dhanis*, 237; "Malfeyt (Justin)", *Biographie coloniale belge*, 3:589.

52. Four poseurs: Carter, Carey, Tickell, Clipperton; Thornton, Castellote, Dhanis, Verhellen, Long, and Mohun.

53. Telegraph narrative, 65–66.

54. As in many infrastructural projects of the era, nature was an important actor in shaping the challenges of the telegraph expedition. For an in-depth analysis, see Ashley Carse, *Beyond the Big Ditch: Politics, Ecology, and Infrastructure at the Panama Canal* (Cambridge, MA: MIT Press, 2014), 5–9.

55. Mohun, handwritten draft telegram addressed to California Ave., Washington, DC, September 30, 1900, item 7, Mohun Papers. It is unclear who the intended recipient was. It is possible that Harriet had traveled to the United States to stay with the Mohun clan.

56. For multiple examples, see Thornton copy book, item 5, Mohun Papers.

57. Thornton to Mohun, June 25, 1900, item 5, Mohun Papers.

58. The newspapers were also passed around between Thornton, Mohun, and Dhanis. See Thornton to Mohun, July 1, 1900, item 5, Mohun Papers. *Times* coverage in 1899 and early 1900 included articles by discontented former employees, see "An Englishman's Account of Congo State Methods," May 26, 1899, and coverage of the debates in the Belgian Parliament about what to do about alleged abuses in the rubber concessions. See "The Congo Free State," *Times* (London), April 24, 1900; and "Belgium and the Congo," *Times* (London), April 26, 1900. See also Mohun's request to Dhanis that he share his copies of "Times and any other English papers." Mohun to Dhanis, May 5, 1900, file 287, Dhanis Papers.

59. Thornton to Mohun, June 23, 1900, item 5, Mohun Papers.

60. Thornton to Mohun, July 8, 1900, item 5, Mohun Papers.

61. List of trade goods, n.d., item 7, Mohun Papers.

62. Thornton to Mohun, July 1, 1900, item 5, Mohun Papers.

63. Thornton to Mohun, May 20, 1900, item 5, Mohun Papers.

64. Thornton to Mohun, May 20, 1900, item 5, Mohun Papers.

65. Thornton to Mohun, July 1, 1900, item 5, Mohun Papers.

66. An early historian of the Congo described the hierarchical nature of the Congo Free State's administration and its requirements for reporting as "an arrangement ideally contrived to multiply correspondence and to paralyze effective action." See Keith Berriedale, *The Belgian Congo and the Berlin Act* (Oxford: Clarendon Press, 1919), 118, quoted in Ruth Slade, *King Leopold's Congo: Aspects of the Development of Race Relations in the Congo Independent State* (London: Oxford University Press, 1962), 172.

67. Thornton to Dhanis, June 17, 1900; July 18, 1900, item 5, Mohun Papers.

68. Thornton to Mohun, July 26, 1900, item 5, Mohun Papers.

69. Thornton to Mohun, August 27, 1900, item 5; "Road Pass," August 27, 1900, item 8, Mohun Papers.

70. Mohun to "Excellency," January 1, 1901, item 7, Mohun Papers.

71. Telegraph narrative, 90–91.

72. Mohun to governor general, Boma, March 14, 1901, item 8; Mohun to Director of Justice, Boma, March 14, 1901, item 8, Mohun Papers.

73. Telegraph narrative, 91. Mohun even changed the date of Thornton's death in the narrative, moving it closer to his own departure, to elide the question of who was supervising the camp while he and Carey were burying Thornton. See Mohun to "Excellency," March 6, 1901, item 7, Mohun Papers.

74. "The Telegraph across the Congo State," *Liverpool Mercury*, June 20, 1899.

75. Names and skills of Zanzibaris are taken from letters of reference, n.d., item 3; tools are from "Liste des Instruments et Matériaux," item 5, Mohun Papers. The technical press of the time noted that "the personnel is nearly all native" on the Congo telegraph projects. See "Telegraph Construction in the African Wilds," *Telegraph Age* 20 (1903): 143.

76. Mohun to Governor General Wahis, Congo Free State (August 29, 1901), item 8, Mohun Papers.

77. Many missionary groups, including both Catholic and Protestant missions in the Congo Free State operated what were commonly called "industrial schools," which bear a strong resemblance to both settlement houses in the Anglophone world and polytechnic schools such as the Tuskegee Institute. The ideologies of uplift and self-sufficiency ("industrial redemption") are also similar. See, for example, Paul Allen Williams, "The Disciples of Christ

Congo Mission (DCCM), 1897–1932: A Missionary Community in Colonial Central Africa" (PhD diss., University of Chicago School of Divinity,
2000), 336–38; and William Scott, "Central African Experiences," *Society
of Malawi Journal* 38 (1985): 62 on Presbyterian "industrial missions." See
also, "Annual Report on the British Central African Protectorate, 1897–8,"
Parliamentary Papers, command paper 9048, 9, which notes that most of the
offices of the African Transcontinental Telegraph had a "native assistant"
trained in telegraphy.

78. Willis H. Jones, *Pocket Edition of Diagrams and Complete Information for Telegraph Engineers and Students* (New York: Telegraph Age, 1902), 250.

79. Mohun to governor general, Congo Free State (August 29, 1901), item 5,
Mohun Papers.

80. "Belgium to Annex Congo Free State," *St. Louis Post-Dispatch*, July 7, 1901.

81. See, for example, "Cannibals Eat Natives," *Republican and Herald* (Pottsville,
PA), January 3, 1902; and "A Disgrace to Civilization," *Ottawa Daily Republic*,
January 4, 1902.

82. Jan Vansina particularly eloquently observed that the "colonial relationship"
was profoundly unequal. "It was regulated by the requirements, orders, and
moods of the dominant party." Vansina, *Being Colonized*, 54.

83. Mohun to Malfeyt, May 12, 1901; governor general, June 19, 1901, item 5,
Mohun Papers.

84. Mohun to governor general, May 12, 1901, item 5, Mohun Papers.

85. Malfeyt to governor general, April 21, 1901; "Mohun, Richard," Personnel
d'Afrique—Fonds Colonie, portefeuille 2098, dossier 11.006, dépôt Joseph
Cuvelier, Archives d'État Belge.

86. Mohun to director of justice, October 8, 1901, item 5, Mohun Papers.

87. Mohun to governor general, October 8, 1901, item 5, Mohun Papers. Wahis
and his successor Emile Wangermée both disliked Dorsey. Wahis repeatedly
inserted an evaluation into Dorsey's confidential personal file describing
him as very intelligent but not "serious" enough. Wahis did not consider
him a good candidate for continued employment as an official in the Congo.
See Notes du 2 semestre 1900, "Mohun, Richard," Personnel d'Afrique—
Fonds Colonie, portefeuille 2098, dossier 11.006, dépôt Joseph Cuvelier,
Archives d'État Belge.

88. Mohun, May 5, 1901, Ngomma letter, item, 133, the rest of the letters, items
147–150, 158–162, File 3, Mohun Papers. item 147 includes a note about two
men who claimed skills they didn't have: cooking and carpentry.

89. They made it as far as Boma with him. See Mohun to Governor General
Wahis, October 7, 1901, item 5, Mohun Papers. At least fifty of the Zanzibaris made it back to Zanzibar. In December 1901 the British Foreign

Office received a request from the British Consul in Zanzibar to ask Mohun whether the men had been "repatriated" and if they were dead, how much was owed to their survivors. Roger Casement was also involved as British Consul to Congo. See Farnall to Underwood, December 31, 1901, PRO FO 2/491/21, National Archives of Great Britain. The four men who went to Boma with him are named in a letter he sent the governor general, which implies that the men left the Congo in October on the *Albertville* and transited through Europe. See Mohun to governor general, October 7, 1901, "Mohun, Richard," Personnel d'Afrique—Fonds Colonie, portefeuille 2098, dossier 11.006, dépôt Joseph Cuvelier, Archives d'État Belge.

Chapter 10

1. Decree awarding medal, November 11, 1901, item 10e, Mohun Papers.
2. Beginning with his first caravan travel, see chapter 4; On the use of the chicotte, see also telegraph narrative, 30, in which he explains that this practice was used all over Africa.
3. For a succinct list of what was known in the 1890s, see Ruth M. Slade, *King Leopold's Congo; Aspects of the Development of Race Relations in the Congo Independent State* (London: Oxford University Press, 1962), 180–81. The literature on efforts to expose atrocities in the Congo Free State and impose reform is extensive. A useful analysis and overview can be found in Aldwin Roes, "Towards a History of Mass Violence in the État Independent du Congo, 1885–1908," *South African Historical Journal* 62 (December 2010): 634–70.
4. Neal Ascherson, *The King Incorporated: Leopold II in the Age of Trusts* (Garden City, NJ: Doubleday, 1964), 255.
5. The phrase was utilized in a variety of contexts. Most influentially, the State began publishing *La verité sur le Congo* [The truth on the Congo] in 1903. It was a magazine with articles in three languages that was distributed on European passenger trains. See also Frederick Starr, *The Truth about the Congo* (London: T. W. Laurie, 1907), a collection of essays originally written for the *Chicago Tribune* by an American journalist.
6. Adam Hochschild, *King Leopold's Ghost: A Story of Greed, Terror, and Heroism in Colonial Africa* (Boston: Houghton Mifflin, 1998), 235–36. Stanley died on May 10, 1904.
7. Joseph Conrad, *Heart of Darkness: A Case Study in Contemporary Criticism*, ed. Ross C. Murfin (New York: St. Martin's Press, 1989), 25.
8. It's possible that his younger son, Cecil Peabody Mohun, removed documents that he thought reflected badly on his father before making the

archive available to the National Archives for microfilming in the 1950s. The manuscript of the telegraph narrative was microfilmed in full, but someone removed the apologist second half before or after it was deposited in the Royal Museum for Central Africa in Tervuren.

9. "Mrs. R. Dorsey Mohun, Miss Laura and Master Reginald Mohun sailed yesterday from New York for Antwerp on the Kensington," *Washington Times*, August 15, 1901.

10. Richard Dorsey Mohun to Clare Mohun, November 26, 1910, author's collection.

11. Reginald Mohun eventually attended school at the Institut Grünau in Berne. Institut Grünau photobook, n.d., author's collection.

12. For more on the range of political positions within Belgium regarding annexations, see S. J. S. Cokey, *Britain and the Congo Question, 1885–1913* (New York: Humanities Press, 1968), 227. Ascherson, *The King Incorporated*, 261.

13. See, for instance, *Almanach Poche: Bruxelles et ses Faubourgs pour 1900* (Brussels: A. Manceaux, 1899), 253–57.

14. "L'Hiver Dansant," *Le Meuse*, February 20, 1901. The invitation was one of the three documents they kept. See Invitation for February 8, 1902, item 20b, Mohun Papers.

15. Belgian newspapers regularly noted the *Cercle*'s meeting but gave few details. On Hecq's presentation, see [no title], *Indépendence Belge*, December 26, 1901. Dhanis first turns up in reports about these meetings in 1904 when Leopold coaxed him out of retirement. See [no title], *Indépendence Belge*, January 6, 1904. For more about these meetings, see "Au Cercle Africain," *Le soir*, January 28, 1904; "Au Cercle African," *Le soir*, July 12, 1904.

16. I could not find Dorsey's name in any newspaper articles about the meetings until 1905. See "À travers la ville," *Petit bleu de matin*, February 2, 1905. The occasion was a lecture by a female British explorer. See "Miss French Sheldon," *Journal de Bruxelles*, February 10, 1905. It's unclear whether that's because he wasn't important enough to garner special mention or because he didn't attend. I suspect it's the former. Francis Dhanis was important enough to attend, but he'd quit the service of the State and married a Baroness named Estelle de Bonhomme. He'd retreated with her to her family's chateau at Hogue. "Le marriage du Baron Dhanis," *Le Petit Bleu du matin*, January 17, 1901. He doesn't show up in accounts of the Cercle Africain meetings until 1904 when he reentered the service of the State for the purposes of going on a fact-finding mission prompted by growing accusations about abuses. [No title—account of Cercle meeting], *Indépendence belge*, January 6, 1904.

17. Ascherson, *The King Incorporated*, 255; Hochschild, *King Leopold's Ghost*, 239.

18. Hochschild, *King Leopold's Ghost*, 192–93. Editors who took the original account off the wire services added their own sensationalist titles and sometimes exaggerated the details. See, for example, "Natives Killed Like Dogs in the Congo Free State," *Brooklyn Daily Eagle*, November 7, 1901.

19. "La situation au Congo," *Journal de Bruxelles*, January 13, 1902.

20. "The Congo State," *Times* (London), November 11, 1901.

21. "La situation au Congo," *Journal de Bruxelles*, January 13, 1902.

22. Ruth Slade, "English Missionaries and the Beginnings of the Anti-Congolese Campaign in England," *Revue belge de philologie et d'histoire* 33 (1955): 45.

23. "Mansion House Meeting of Protest against the Congo State," *West Africa*, May 24, 1902, clipping in Roger Casement Atrocities, FO 629/9, National Archives of the United Kingdom. See also "The Congo Free State: Demand for an International Inquiry," *Manchester Guardian*, May 16, 1902, for a list of the major participants.

24. The timing is unclear. Casement left for Congo on March 28, 1902, but he doesn't seem to have known about Dorsey's attendance at the meeting until later. See Séamas Ó Síocháin, *Roger Casement: Imperialist, Rebel, Revolutionary* (Dublin, Ireland: Lilliput, 2008), 136–37.

25. Roger Casement to the Marquess of Landsdowne, June 18, 1902, document 161, *British Documents on Foreign Affairs*, pt. 1, ser. G, vol. 23 (Bethesda, MD: University Publications of America, 1997), 212. In his handwritten draft, Casement included the information that he had sailed with Dorsey to Congo and used a pen to indicate that he did not want the information included in the print version. See Casement to Lord Lansdowne, June 18, 1902, FO 629/9.

26. William Roger Louis, "Roger Casement and the Congo," *Journal of African History* 5, no, 1 (1964): 107.

27. The name is confusing. The Company was originally created by a group of British and Belgian investors who named it the Anglo Belgian India Rubber Company. After 1898 the company was renamed the Abir Congo Company. Those familiar with the Congo simply called it Abir.

28. About Abir, see Ó Síocháin, *Roger Casement*, 131. Casement had returned to England in the Winter of 1901–2 and returned to Boma on May 6, 1902 (Ó Síocháin, 138).

29. Stanley Shaloff, *Reform in Leopold's Congo* (Richmond, VA: John Knox Press, 1970), 92.

30. Lawyers advising the crown thought the British government did not have the right to reopen the conference, and no one wanted to open the question of how Africa had been partitioned to further discussion. See Louis, "Roger

Casement and the Congo," 100. In 1901 it also mattered to Leopold that the Belgian Parliament had just debated whether or not to annex the Congo (Louis, 100). Many Congo reform advocates believed that the question could and should be reopened. For a more detailed study of the diplomatic landscape, see John B. Osborne, "Wilfred G. Thesinger, Sir Edward Grey, and the British Campaign to Reform the Congo, 1905–9," *Journal of Imperial and Commonwealth History* 27 (1999): 59–80.

31. My translation. Draft of a letter from Leopold II to Félix Fuchs, 10 XI 03, Archives of the Académie Royale des Sciences Coloniales, Correspondance Leopold II–Van Eetvelde, cited in Ruth Slade, "King Leopold II and the Attitude of English and American Catholics towards the Anti-Congolese Campaign," *Zaire* 11 (June 1957): 593.

32. Ascherson, *The King Incorporated*, 237. For a revealing, astute analysis from the time, see G. S. H. Pearson, "Memorandum Respecting the Relations between Belgium and the Independent State of the Congo," February 21, 1906, *British Documents on Foreign Affairs*, document 199. See also a less detailed analysis from 1903, "Memorandum on the Relations between Belgium and the Independent Congo State," April 1, 1903, document 186.

33. Until Casement began gathering information, the foreign secretary knew little more than informed readers of the newspapers. The foreign office employed a Congo expert named Harry Farnall, but he relied mostly on clipped newspaper articles, which were pasted into enormous volumes for consultation by civil servants and politicians. Louis, "Roger Casement and the Congo," 101.

34. Shaloff, *Reform in Leopold's Congo*, 87.

35. Louis, "Roger Casement and the Congo," 108.

36. Louis, 104.

37. [no title], *San Francisco Chronicle*, March 8, 1904.

38. Ascherson, *The King Incorporated*, 235–36.

39. R. D. L. Mohun "The Congo Free State: Why Should England Arraign the Belgian Administration There?," *Messenger* 42 (1904): 525–26.

40. Mohun, 528.

41. He was not exactly an objective observer, having been on Abir's payroll as a "Conseiller technique" since 1902. See "Dhanis (Antoine)," *Biographie coloniale belge; Belgische koloniale biographie* (Brussels: Librairie Falk fils, 1958), 5:324. He kept a journal of the trip. See Baron Francis Dhanis, large Abir journal, April 21–September 11, 1904, Archives de Dhanis, RMCA.

42. R. D. L. Mohun, "The British Government v. The Congo Free State," *Messenger* 23 (1905): 69.

43. Mohun, 69, 72.

44. Hunt Hawkins, "Mark Twain's Involvement with the Congo Reform Movement: 'A Fury of Generous Indignation,'" *New England Quarterly* 51, no. 2 (1978): 147–75.

45. Under the editorship of Alphonse-Jules Wauters, *Le Congo illustré* promoted the State's civilizing efforts for a popular audience. Folded into *Le Mouvement géographique* in 1896, it continued to promote "colonization" into the 1920s. See Henri Nicolai, "Le Mouvement géographique, un journal et un géographe au service de la colonisation du Congo," *Civilisations* 41 (1993): 257–77. According to Nicolai, Wauters was not an agent of Leopold and did not always follow the State's messaging.

46. See Dora Apel and Shawn Michelle Smith, *Lynching Photographs* (Berkeley: University of California Press, 2007).

47. For a particularly thoughtful analysis of these photographs in their historical context, see Kevin Grant, "The Limits of Exposure: Photographs in the Congo Reform Campaign," in *Humanitarian Photography: A History* ed. Heide Fehrenbach and Davide Rodogno (Cambridge: Cambridge University Press, 2015), 64–88.

48. Jan Vansina, *Being Colonized: The Kuba Experience in Rural Congo, 1880–1960* (Madison: University of Wisconsin Press, 2010), 129–35, 145. For an overview of the debate on the number of victims of State rule, see Roes, "Towards a History of Mass Violence," 11–16 (n. 3). Whatever other brutalities European nations sanctioned in other parts of Africa, dismemberment seems to have been unique to the Congo. Both sides repeatedly used accusations and evocations of cannibalism, but no one offered photographic evidence. For a thoughtful analysis of the sensationalism around violence in the Congo Free State, see Jean-Luc Vellut, "Réflexions sur la question de la violence dans l'histoire de l'État indépendant du Congo," in *La nouvelle histoire du Congo*, ed. Pamphile Mabiala Mantuba-Ngoma (Paris: Harmattan, 2004), 269–88.

49. Grant, "The Limits of Exposure," 66.

50. Commission chargée de faire une enquête dans les territoires l'État du Congo, *Evidence Laid before the Congo Commission of Inquiry at Bwembu, Bolobo, Lulanga, Baringa, Bongandanga, Ikau, Bonginda, and Monsembe. Together with a Summary of Events (and Documents Connected Therewith) on the A.B.I.R. Concession Since the Commission Visited That Territory* (Liverpool: J. Richardson, 1905), 20, http://archive.org/details/evidencelaidbefo00congrich.

51. "Congo Post for American," *New York Times*, December 9, 1905.

52. Casement to E. D. Morel, LSE Morel F8/25–583, Morel Papers, London School of Economics.

53. Robert Harms, "The End of Red Rubber: A Reassessment," *Journal of African History* 16 (January 1975): 75, 77.

54. Harms, 87–88.

55. John Tracy Ellis, *The Life of Cardinal Gibbons: Archbishop of Baltimore 1834–1921* (Milwaukee: Bruce, 1952).

56. Notably, Dorsey's grandmother, Anna Hanson Dorsey, who corresponded with Gibbons in the 1880s. See Dorsey to Gibbons, December 12, 1879, item 74 U4; Dorsey to Gibbons, October 5, 1880, item 75 K5; Dorsey to Gibbons, December 30, 1897, item 74 V2, Gibbons Papers.

57. Ella Dorsey seems to have provided the main connection between Leopold's agents in the United States, the Catholic Church, and Dorsey. See James Gustavas Whitely to Ella Dorsey (March 21, 1906), Ella Dorsey correspondence, SMSA.

58. Gibbons to Theodore Roosevelt, April 27, 1904, item 101 G12, Gibbons Papers.

59. Jerome L. Serenstein, "King Leopold II, Senator Nelson Aldrich, and the Strange Beginnings of American Economic Penetration of the Congo," *African Historical Studies* 2 (Spring 1969): 189.

60. Serenstein, 194. Aldrich also had streetcars in common with Ryan. Both had made their first big fortunes in what were then called "traction companies." Streetcars and railroads were a common denominator among American investors in African rubber. See Matthew Josephson, *The Robber Barons: The Great American Capitalists, 1861–1901* (New York: Harcourt, 1934), 385–87; "Rubber Committee, June 1, 1910," Aldrich Papers.

61. Morel himself said that it was "greatly to my astonishment" that Gibbons publicly opposed him, which may have been disingenuous since Leopold had already been cultivating Catholic bishops in England. E. D. [Edmund Dene] Morel, *Red Rubber: The Story of the Rubber Slave Trade Flourishing on the Congo in the Year of Grace 1906* (London: T. Fisher Unwin, 1906), 7.

62. Carbon copy of memo by Gibbons, December 15, 1906, item 104 M2, Gibbons Papers.

63. Henry Kowalsky to Gibbons, October 21, 1904, item 101 Q1, Gibbons Papers.

64. See Pamela Newkirk, *Spectacle: The Astonishing Life of Ota Benga* (New York: Amistad, 2015).

65. Samuel Phillips Verner to Gibbons, October 26, 1904, item 104 F7, Gibbons Papers.

66. Secrétaire d'état département des affaires étrangères to Gibbons, January 14, 1908,105, A7, Gibbons Papers; handwritten note from Leopold II to Gibbons, January 8, 1907, 105 A6, Gibbons Papers.

67. Serenstein, "King Leopold II," 196. Ryan later visited Leopold in Brussels and conveyed his regards in a letter to Gibbons. See Thomas F. Ryan to John Cardinal Gibbons, November 2, 1906, 104 G7, Gibbons Papers.
68. Ascherson, *The King Incorporated*, 263.
69. Translation: the three societies of 1906. *Forminière, 1906–1956* (Brussels: L. Cuypers, 1956), 77.
70. Ascherson, *The King Incorporated*, 266–67.
71. "Wack on Congo Affairs," *New York Tribune*, December 14, 1906.
72. Richard P. Tucker, *Insatiable Appetite: The United States and the Ecological Degradation of the Tropical World* (Berkeley: University of California Press), 230.
73. "Lobbyist for a King," *Soldier Clipper*, January 2, 1907.
74. See, for instance, the *New York Tribune* for December 14, 1906, which printed four articles about the Congo on page 3: "Congo Details Out: Official Bulletin Gives Exact Terms of Ryan Concession," "Wack on Congo Affairs," "Britain, America, and the Congo," and "Ameliorating Congo Conditions."
75. Serenstein, "King Leopold II," 193–94.
76. "Rubber Lands Concession," *Evening Star*, December 12, 1906.
77. Ascherson, *The King Incorporated*, 267.
78. Serenstein, "King Leopold II," 189.
79. "American Congo Company," *New York Times*, March 5, 1907.

Chapter 11

1. Sydney Hobart Ball to Elizabeth Hall Ball, March 22, 1907, outgoing correspondence, MSN/MN 0513–1 [box 1], , Ball Papers.
2. Mining engineers were in demand. See Carroll Pursell, *The Machine in America: A Social History of Technology* (Baltimore: Johns Hopkins University Press, 1995), 166–67.
3. Sydney Ball to Elizabeth Ball, March 31, 1907, box 1; Sydney Hobart Ball Diary, January 1908, MSN/MN0513–272, box 272, Ball Papers.
4. His Congo Free State personnel file went so far as to list him as lieutenant. See "Mohun, Richard," Details Biographiques, Personnel d'Afrique—Fonds Colonie, portefeuille 2098, dossier 11.006, dépôt Joseph Cuvelier, Archives d'État Belge.
5. Sydney Ball to Elizabeth Ball, March 22, 1907, box 1, Ball Papers.
6. Sydney Ball to Thomas Ryan, March 8, 1911, Aldrich Papers. This document is the closest thing to a final report that survives.
7. "American Congo Company: Congo Authorities Want R. Dorsey Mohun as African Manager," *New York Times*, March 5, 1907.

8. Verner also had a personal connection to Bernard Baruch who, early in his career, worked for the American Congo Company financiers. See Phillips Verner Bradford and Harvey Bloom, *Ota: The Pygmy in the Zoo* (New York: St. Martin's Press, 1999), 198–99.

9. S. P. Verner, "The American Invasion of the Congo," *Harper's Weekly*, May 4, 1907, 656. Internal company correspondence shows the American board of directors genuinely intended to ameliorate the labor situation. See "Instructions for the Chief of the Station at Black River," October 7, 1907, Aldrich Papers.

10. Bradford and Bloom, *Ota Benga*, 197–99.

11. This pattern is often described by historians as an "informal empire." Regarding rubber, see Richard P. Tucker, *Insatiable Appetite: The United States and the Ecological Degradation of the Tropical World* (Berkeley: University of California Press, 2000), x.

12. Verner, "American Invasion of the Congo," 644, 656.

13. Sydney Ball to Elizabeth Ball, March 5, 1907, box 1, Ball Papers.

14. To get a sense of the complex, interlocking structure of the American Congo Company, Forminière, and the Continental Rubber Company, as well as Beatty's central place in all three, see documents titled "Rubber Committee" and "Rubber Data," June 1, 1910, Aldrich Papers. Beatty also earned the nickname "the copper king" as well as a substantial fortune working for the Guggenheims in the Guggenheim Exploration Company.

15. A. Chester Beatty to R. Dorsey Mohun, May 10, 1907, item 16, Mohun Papers.

16. Sydney Ball to Elizabeth Ball, May 31, 1907, box 1, Ball Papers.

17. Sydney Ball to Elizabeth Ball, May 26, 1907; Clare Mohun to Elizabeth Ball, June 25, 1907, box 1, Ball Papers. Ball's devoted mother copied this letter along with all his letters to her into composition books.

18. Invitation addressed to R. Dorsey Mohun, May 14, 1907, item 16, Mohun Papers.

19. Sydney Ball to Elizabeth Ball, May 15, 1907, outgoing correspondence, box 1, Ball Papers.

20. Sydney Ball to Elizabeth Ball, May 15, 1907, outgoing correspondence, box 1, Ball Papers.

21. Société Internationale Forestière et Minière du Congo, *Forminière: 1906–1956* (Brussels: Éditions L. Cuypers, 1956), 76.

22. Sydney Ball to Elizabeth Ball, May 31, 1907, box 1, Ball Papers.

23. Richard Harding Davis, an American muckraking journalist who visited a year earlier, had a similar impression. See Richard Harding Davis, *The Congo and the Coasts of Africa* (New York: Charles Scribner's Sons, 1907), 43–44.

The British Consul framed the lack of facilities in a slightly different way. He observed that the taxes collected by the State and the successor Belgian Government were not being put into port facilities. See W. G. Thesinger to Sir Edward Grey, February 18, 1909, document 36, British Documents of Foreign Affairs, pt. 1, ser. G Africa, vol. 24, 344.

24. Sydney Ball to Elizabeth Ball, June 27 and June 30, 1907, box 1, Ball Papers. Ball's correspondence does not include the name of his servant.

25. Sydney Ball to Elizabeth Ball, June 27, 1907, box 1, Ball Papers.

26. Sydney Ball to Elizabeth Ball, June 30, 1907, box 1, Ball Papers.

27. Thesinger's research suggested that working for the railroad was one of the few employments for Africans in the Congo that allowed workers to pay the required head tax and still have money to live on. See Thesinger to Gray, February 18, 1909, *British Documents on Foreign Affairs*, pt. 1, ser. G, vol. 23 (Bethesda, MD: University Publications of America, 1997), 343–44.

28. Sydney Ball to Elizabeth Ball, July 2, 1907, box 1, Ball Papers.

29. Roger Casement, who had also known the former missionary, described him as "cracked." His biographers suggest mental illness ran in his family and was exacerbated by bouts of malaria. Bradford and Blume, *Ota Benga*, 116.

30. Jan Vansina, *Being Colonized: The Kuba Experience in the Rural Congo, 1880–1960* (Madison: University of Wisconsin Press, 2010), 87.

31. Vansina, *Being Colonized*, 86–88.

32. Sydney Ball to Elizabeth Ball, October 12, 1907, box 1, Ball Papers.

33. Bradford and Bloom, *Ota Benga*, 39–40.

34. Bradford and Bloom, *Ota Benga*, 86. Verner's version of the story is told in Samuel Phillips Verner, *Pioneering in Central Africa* (Richmond, VA: Presbyterian Committee, 1903).

35. Vansina, *Being Colonized*, 66.

36. In 1908, Sheppard was sued for libel by the Compagnie du Kasai. They lost the case. See William E. Phipps, *William Sheppard: Congo's African American Livingstone* (Louisville, KY: Geneva Press, 2002), 166–72.

37. Sydney Ball to Elizabeth Ball, August 11, 1907, box 1, Ball Papers. Dorsey was also part of the group staying with Sheppard, but I have been unable to locate a diary or many letters from this expedition in Mohun's papers.

38. Sydney Ball to Elizabeth Ball, July 31, 1907, box 1, Ball Papers; Vansina, *Being Colonized*, 91.

39. Sydney Ball to Elizabeth Ball, October 1, 1908, box 1, Ball Papers.

40. Sydney Ball diary, September 17, 1907, box 272, Ball Papers.

41. The direst predictions turned out to be incorrect because sleeping sickness epidemics are periodic. See G. Hide, "History of Sleeping Sickness in East Africa," *Clinical Microbiology Reviews* 12, no. 1 (1999): 112–25.

42. Sydney Ball to Elizabeth Ball, September 3, 1907, box 1, Ball Papers.

43. Identified as St. Joseph's but probably the one at Bena Makima, not the one outside of which Ball had been ambushed.

44. Sydney Ball diary, October 3, 4, and 5, 1907, box 272, Ball Papers.

45. Sydney Ball diary, October 5, 1907, box 272, Ball Papers.

46. Le Secrétaire du Forminière to Ball, unsigned typescript copy cc'd to Mohun, October 14, 1908, item 16, Mohun Papers.

47. Author's collection.

48. Sydney Ball to Elizabeth Ball, November 9, 1908, box 1, Ball Papers.

49. *Encyclopedia Britannica* (1911), s.v. "Congo Free State."

50. Sylvanus John Sodienye Cookey, *Britain and the Congo Question, 1885–1913* (New York: Humanities Press, 1969), 208, 297. Great Britain did not officially recognize the Belgian Congo until 1913 (271).

51. The impulse may have originated with the Compagnie du Kasai.

52. "Explorers Rout Cannibals with Heavy Losses," *New York Herald*, January 5, 1908. The account somehow managed to put both Verner and Beatty on the scene. Other accounts made it sound like the conflict was over rubber. See, for example, "Mow Down 125 Natives in Fight for Congo Gum," *Fort Worth Star Telegram* [Hearst Syndicate], January 5, 1908.

53. Phipps, *William Sheppard*, 165–66.

54. Mohun to Shaler, December 5, 1908, item 6, Mohun Papers.

55. Mohun to Shaler, December 5, 1908, item 6, Mohun Papers.

56. Sydney Ball to Elizabeth Ball, February 1, 1909, box 1, Ball Papers.

57. Sydney Ball to Elizabeth Ball, January 9, 1909, box 1, Ball Papers.

58. A. Rouffant to [American] Board of Directors, American Congo Company, November 4, 1907, Aldrich Papers.

59. Dorsey Mohun to Clare Mohun, March 18, 1909, author's collection.

60. Société Internationale Forestière et Minière du Congo, *Forminière*, 84.

61. "General Instructions," December 31, 1908, item 6, Mohun Papers.

62. Sydney Ball to Elizabeth Ball, July 12, 1909, box 1, Ball Papers.

63. Société Internationale Forestière et Minière du Congo, *Forminière*, 90–91. Ball reported the diamond to the American investors in 1911. See Sydney Ball to Thomas F. Ryan, March 8, 1911, Aldrich Papers.

64. By 1939 Forminière's mining operations in the Congo basin accounted for 67 percent of global diamond production. Société Internationale Forestière et Minière du Congo, *Forminière*, 111.

65. Harvey O'Connor, *The Guggenheims: The Making of an American Dynasty* (New York: Covici Fiede, 1937), 181–82. The mining operation now belongs to a Chinese firm.

66. A. Chester Beatty to R. D. L. Mohun, December 7, 1909, item 16, Mohun Papers.

67. "Dhanis (Antoine)," *Biographie coloniale belge; Belgische koloniale biographie* (Brussels: Librairie Falk fils, 1958), 1:325.

68. Séamas Ó Síocháin, *Roger Casement: Imperialist, Rebel, Revolutionary* (Dublin, Ireland: Lilliput, 2008), 259; John A. Tully, *The Devil's Milk: A Social History of Rubber* (New York: Monthly Review Press, 2011), 95–99.

69. Sydney Ball to Elizabeth Ball, May 15, 1907, Ball Papers.

70. Neil Ascherson, *The King Incorporated: Leopold II in the Age of Trusts* (Garden City, NY: Doubleday, 1964), 288–89.

71. "Une impressionnante cérémonie," *Le Petit Bleu du matin*, December 19, 1909.

72. Ascherson, *The King Incorporated*, 299. There has been a lot of speculation on the part of historians as to what exactly was burned. Account books and other financial records seems like the most likely items. See Aldwin Roes, "Towards a History of Mass Violence in the État Indépendant du Congo, 1885–1908," *South African History Journal* 62 (2010): 32–33.

73. Dorsey Mohun to Clare Mohun, November 26, 1910, author's collection.

74. Touring Club de Belgique, *Panorama du Congo* (Brussels: Charles Bulens, 1912).

75. Paul Morton to Mohun, July 1, 1910, item 15, Mohun Papers.

76. "Rubber Interests Merge," *New York Times*, November 5, 1909.

77. Paul Morton to Mohun, July 1, 1909, item 15, Mohun Papers.

78. They miscalculated. By 1913, the amount of plantation rubber using Brazilian trees grown in Asia exceeded Amazonian wild rubber in the American market and was growing steadily less expensive as growers refined their techniques. Tully, *The Devil's Milk*, 72. On similar efforts to find new sources of wild rubber by British investors, see J. Forbes Munro, "British Rubber Companies in East Africa before the First World War," *Journal of African History* 24 (1983): 369–79.

79. "Rubber Exploration Company and R.D.L. Mohun Agreement," copy without signatures, File 15, Mohun Papers.

80. Morton to Mohun, August 8, 1909, item 15, Mohun Papers.

81. Paul Morton to Julius Lay, March 15, 1910, item 15, Mohun Papers.

82. R. Marloth to Lay, April 5, 1910, item 17, Mohun Papers.

83. Mohun to Clare Mohun, November 26, 1910, author's collection. Delagoa Bay was also known as Lorenço Marques. Casement was British consul there when Dorsey and Harriet lived in Zanzibar.

84. Mohun to E. B. Aldrich, January 8, 1911, item 15, Mohun Papers.

85. Harriet Mohun to Dorsey Mohun, December 23, 1910, item 15, Mohun Papers.

86. Dorsey Mohun to Clare Mohun, November 26, 1910, author's collection.

87. Mohun to Harold van der Linde, January 8, 1911, item 15, Mohun Papers.

88. Mohun to E. B. Aldrich, April 28, 1911, item 15, Mohun Papers. Recent scholarship has confirmed his impression. P. Danthu, H. Razakamanarivo, L. Razafy Fara, P. Montagne, B. Deville-Danthu, and E. Penot, *When Madagascar Produced Natural Rubber: A Brief, Forgotten, yet Informative History*, Archive ouverte, Hal-Cirad, n.d., http://hal.cirad.fr/cirad-00771066.

89. Mohun to E. B. Aldrich, April 28, 1911, item 15, Mohun Papers.

90. Dorsey Mohun to Clare Mohun, March 18, 1909, author's collection; pay receipt, November 24, 1911, item 15, Mohun Papers.

91. Dorsey Mohun to Clare Mohun, March 18, 1909, author's collection.

92. Dorsey Mohun to Clare Mohun, November 26, 1910, author's collection.

After Africa and Conclusion

1. [no title], *Evening Star*, December 12, 1911. The address was 4 Jackson Place.

2. *Thirteenth Census of the United States 1910-Population, Washington, D.C., 10th Ward*, Records of the Bureau of the Census, Record Group 29, National Archives, Washington, DC. "Ella Loraine Dorsey," in *A Woman of the Century: Fourteen Hundred-Seventy Biographical Sketches Accompanied by Portraits of Leading American Women in All Walks of Life*, ed. Frances Elizabeth Willard and Mary Ashton Rice (Buffalo, NY: C. W. Moulton, 1893), 254.

3. Characteristically, Clare pursued Louis's government pension after his death. See Louis Mohun Pension File, RG 15, NARA.

4. Sister M. Mercia Rice, *Treasured Legacy: Mother M. Stephanie Mohun, O.P. Her Life and Letters* (Columbus, OH: St. Mary of the Springs, 1988).

5. "The Southern Ball," *Evening Star*, February 6, 1912.

6. Their movements can be traced through small announcements in the Washington newspapers. See, for example, [no title], *Washington Herald*, October 23, 1914.

7. Dear Sir, July 5, 1913; "Cannibalism," item 4, Mohun Papers.

8. [no title], *Washington Times*, January 30, 1914.

9. For an overview, see Edward J. Klekowski and Libby Klekowski, *Americans in Occupied Belgium, 1914/1918: Accounts of the War from Journalists, Tourists, Troops and Medical Staff* (Jefferson, NC: McFarland, 2014).

10. "7,000,000 Belgians Facing Starvation: Collecting Pennies for Relief of Belgians," *Evening Star*, November 22, 1914, lists Harriet as one of the contributors.

11. "Summer Homes to Let," *Pittsburgh Press*, April 13, 1915.

12. "Richard Dorsey Mohun Dies at Royal Oak, Maryland," *Evening Star*, July 14, 1915; District of Columbia Burial Permit 13001, July 15, 1915, Oak Hill Cemetery Records, Oak Hill Cemetery, District of Columbia.

13. Family lore claimed that he also bequeathed stock in gold and other minerals to his sons. It's possible that he set up a trust in emulation of the American millionaires who were his last employers, but I've been unable to find any proof.

14. "Dorsey, Miss Ella Loraine," in Willard and Rice, *Woman of the Century*, 254–55.

15. "C. Peabody Mohun, Ex-Governor of the Stock Exchange, 76, Is Dead," *New York Times*, March 23, 1981.

16. C. Peabody Mohun to Director, Museum of Ter Fueren [*sic*], March 17, 1960, "Mohun, Peabody," 1959.58, RMCA.

17. My own grandfather, Reginald "Rex" Mohun, had a less illustrious career as a civil servant—the traditional Dorsey family business. Family lore suggests that his inheritance allowed him to live very well on a bureaucrat's salary.

18. C. Peabody Mohun to L. Cahen, May 26, 1961, "Mohun, Peabody," 1959.58, RMCA.

INDEX

Page numbers in italics refer to figures. "RDM" refers to Richard Dorsey Mohun.

thoughts of, from Congo Free State, 67, 69, 103; in Washington, DC, 141, 195, 237–38; and World War I, 240; in Zanzibar, 119, 122–39

Mohun, Laura, 27, 31–34, 38, 43, 140, 195, 235, 237

Mohun, Lee (Sister, later Mother, Stephanie), 11, 17, 24, 107–8, 134, 237–38

Mohun, Louis, 25, 28–29, 31, 46, 107, 140, 237

Mohun, Philip, 237

Mohun, Reginald Dorsey "Rex," 133–34, 136, 138–41, *139*, *142*, 145, 150, 195, 202, 236

Mohun, Richard Dorsey: appearance of, 2, 20, 107, 229; in Belgium, 33–44, 141–42, 145, 150, 195–97, 201, 213–14, 217, 231; birth of, 8, 9; childhood knowledge of Africa, 10, 11, 17; children of, 133–34, 194–95, 201; courtship and marriage, 33–34, 105, 111–12, 194–95, 236; death of, 3, 240–41; in Egypt, 19–24; entertainments sought by, 33, 34, 125, 129–30, 152–53, 164, 196, 238; family background of, 10–16; family stories about, 3, 306n13; finances of, 3, 27–29; friendship with Casement, 37–38, 43–44, 133–34, 174, 199, 207, 219; health of, 2, 25, 27, 46, 70, 180–81, 190, 234, 238; honors and awards, 103, 106–7, 110, 141, 191; loyalty as value of, 7, 94, 194, 198; in Nicaragua, 25–29; photographs of, 50, *51*, *95*, 125, *126*, *163*, 202, 226, 227; racial attitudes of, 16, 57, 73, 155, 194; and religion, 33, 112; violence against Africans used or sponsored by, 1, 16, 59–60, 87, 173, 181–82, 191–92; voyage to Congo

Free State, 44–46; Washington, DC, homecomings, 107–18, 139–40, 237–38; will of, 141, 241, 274n7. *See also* career (RDM); diary entries (RDM); reports to US State Department (RDM); travels (RDM); writings and lectures (RDM)

Mohun, Richard (father of RDM), 10, 14–16, 18

Moncheur, Ludovic, 210

Morel, E. D., 38, 193, 198–99, 201, 204, 209

Morgan, J. P., 112, 201, 211, 232

Morton, Paul, 232–35

Moskit people, 25

mosquitos, 48, 54, 55, 89, 130, 154, 166, 199, 235

Moussanghela (Arab architect), 90

Mozambique, 133, 152–54

M'Toa, Congo Free State, 147–48, 168, 170, 283n21

Mubarak bin Rashid, 133, 280n58

Muganda, Omari, 173

Muni-Mohare (Arab leader), 102

Mussa, Bwana, 177–78, 181, 184, 185, 188

Natal region, Belgian Congo, 234

Native Americans, 42, 62

New York (ocean liner), 107

New York Herald (newspaper), 69, 86, 228

New York Times (newspaper), 3, 26, 241

Ngomma, Munie, 165, 189, 289n22

Nicaragua, 4, 25–29, 46, 83

Nicaragua Mail and Transport Company, 25

Nicaraguan Canal Construction Company, 26

Nserera (Arab leader), 75

Nyangwe, Congo Free State, 71